Praise for *The Right To A Healthy Environment*

"David Boyd helped Vancouver develop our bold plan for becoming the greenest city in the world, and with this authoritative and inspiring book he identifies a prerequisite for making Canada the greenest country. We owe it to ourselves, our children, and future generations to include the right to a healthy environment in the Canadian constitution."

– Gregor Robertson, Mayor of Vancouver, co-founder of Happy Planet

"David Boyd doesn't just talk about a paradigm shift, he shows us a path to get there. This book will be important to environmentalists, legal scholars, and policy makers, and to everyone who cares about moving from rhetoric to action on climate and the environment. It is also inspiring and a very good read."

– Dr. Alex Himelfarb, Director of the Glendon School of Public and International Affairs, York University, and former Clerk of the Privy Council (2002-06)

"Boyd's scholarship in environmental human rights is unmatched by any other scholar working in the field worldwide ... This book makes a profoundly important contribution to the fields of environmental law, human rights law, and constitutional law in Canada. The subject touches a matter of universally acknowledged importance to Canadians and the world at large."

– Lynda Collins, Common Law Section, University of Ottawa

"This book highlights that Canada, despite being a wealthy and developed country, lags significantly behind the rest of the world on environmental performance. There is a critical need for Canada to do more, especially from the point of view of protecting human health and well-being. This book explains why environmental rights for Canadians would provide the much-needed impetus for Canada to do more."

– Nickie Vlavianos, Faculty of Law, University of Calgary

The Right to a Healthy Environment

Law and Society Series

W. Wesley Pue, General Editor

The Law and Society Series explores law as a socially embedded phenomenon. It is premised on the understanding that the conventional division of law from society creates false dichotomies in thinking, scholarship, educational practice, and social life. Books in the series treat law and society as mutually constitutive and seek to bridge scholarship emerging from interdisciplinary engagement of law with disciplines such as politics, social theory, history, political economy, and gender studies.

A list of titles in the series appears at the end of the book.

The Right to a Healthy Environment

Revitalizing Canada's Constitution

David R. Boyd

UBCPress · Vancouver · Toronto

21 20 19 18 17 16 15 14 5 4 3

Printed in Canada on FSC-certified ancient-forest-free paper (100% post-consumer recycled) that is processed chlorine- and acid-free.

Library and Archives Canada Cataloguing in Publication

Boyd, David R. (David Richard), 1964-
The right to a healthy environment : revitalizing Canada's constitution / David R. Boyd.

(Law and society, ISSN 1496-4953)
Includes bibliographical references and index.
Issued also in electronic formats.
ISBN 978-0-7748-2412-5 (bound); ISBN 978-0-7748-2413-2 (pbk.)

1. Environmental law – Canada. 2. Constitutional law – Canada. 3. Human rights – Canada. 4. Environmental ethics – Canada. I. Title. II. Series: Law and society series Vancouver, B.C.)

KE5110.B69 2012 344.7104'6 C2012-903438-X
KF3775.ZA2B69 2012

Canadä

UBC Press gratefully acknowledges the financial support for our publishing program of the Government of Canada (through the Canada Book Fund), the Canada Council for the Arts, and the British Columbia Arts Council.

This book has been published with the help of a grant from the Canadian Federation for the Humanities and Social Sciences, through the Award to Scholarly Publications Program, using funds provided by the Social Sciences and Humanities Research Council of Canada.

UBC Press
The University of British Columbia
2029 West Mall
Vancouver, BC V6T 1Z2
www.ubcpress.ca

This book is dedicated to Canadian citizens, activists, and political leaders who

- recognize that protection of the environment is a fundamental Canadian value

- understand that a healthy environment is essential to human well-being

- and take the actions necessary to achieve constitutional recognition of the right to live in a healthy and ecologically balanced environment.

The environment is humanity's first right.

– Ken Saro-Wiwa, 1995

We in Canada are fortunate that we can afford to have a civilization of the better rather than a civilization of the more.

– Pierre Elliott Trudeau, 1970

The Constitution is the expression of the sovereignty of the people of Canada. It lies within the power of the people of Canada, acting through their various governments duly elected and recognized under the Constitution, to effect whatever constitutional arrangements are desired within Canadian territory.

– Supreme Court of Canada, 1998

If we unbalance Nature, humankind will suffer. Furthermore, as people alive today, we must consider future generations: a clean environment is a human right like any other. It is therefore part of our responsibility towards others to ensure that the world we pass on is as healthy, if not healthier, than when we found it.

– His Holiness, the Dalai Lama, 1990

Contents

Figures and Tables

FIGURES

TABLES

Preface

This book is a sequel to *The Environmental Rights Revolution: A Global Study of Constitutions, Human Rights, and the Environment* (UBC Press, 2012). *The Environmental Rights Revolution* represents five years of exhaustive research about the effects of including environmental protection provisions in national constitutions. In recent decades, the majority of the world's nations have incorporated environmental protection requirements into their highest laws, declared the right to live in a healthy environment a fundamental human right, and thus created legal road maps for a sustainable future. Canada, sadly, is not yet among these nations. Our constitution remains silent on the subject of environmental protection. Nevertheless, I encourage readers to consult *The Environmental Rights Revolution* for the full (and inspiring!) details regarding the three-quarters of the world's nations whose constitutions include environmental rights and/or responsibilities.

Some readers may be cynical about the prospects of amending the Canadian constitution to recognize environmental rights and responsibilities. Canada's constitution is notoriously difficult to amend, as the debacles of Meech Lake and the Charlottetown Accord demonstrated. To potential cynics I offer the following plea: Think about the Canada you are passing on to your children. Can we not emulate Sweden and Norway, similar northern nations striving to pass on to the next generation countries in which the most serious environmental problems have been solved? Think about the courageous individuals in Latin America who stood up to military dictatorships and then created bold new constitutions including environmental rights and responsibilities. Think about the brave people of Eastern Europe, who defied the Soviet empire and then rewrote their constitutions to include the right to a healthy environment. Think of the citizens of Africa, who cast aside the shackles of colonialism to gain independence and wrote constitutions that aspire to achieve the right to a healthy environment. Think of people in Egypt,

Libya, Morocco, and Tunisia, where the recent Arab Spring led to the downfall of dictators and their replacement with constitutional democracies that have enshrined the right to a healthy environment or are considering doing so. Think of the citizens of Iceland, who endured a complete economic collapse and rewrote their constitution as part of their response, incorporating the right to a healthy environment and rights of Nature. If the citizens of more than 140 nations – in every region of the world – can summon the foresight, courage, and intelligence to create constitutions recognizing our dependence upon safe water, clean air, fertile soil, and healthy ecosystems, then so too can Canadians. By converting our highest ideals into constitutional rights and responsibilities, we can build the Canada we want. It may be difficult, even daunting, but surely so is almost everything that is worth doing. As Nelson Mandela wrote, "It always seems impossible, until it's done."

Acknowledgments

Countless individuals made valuable contributions to this book. I am particularly indebted to three outstanding Canadians, each of whom has extensive expertise in the fields of constitutional law and environmental protection. Dale Gibson wrote a white paper on Canada's constitution and the environment in 1970 as well as several pioneering articles on the constitutional right to a healthy environment in the 1980s. Jim MacNeill worked in the Privy Council Office in the early 1970s under Prime Minister Trudeau, publishing a comprehensive study on environmental management and its constitutional implications before going on to write the Brundtland Commission's landmark report on sustainable development, which emphasized the need to extend constitutional status to the right to a healthy environment. Barry Strayer was Pierre Trudeau's constitutional advisor for fifteen years and is a retired Federal Court judge.

I also benefited from enlightening conversations with environmental law experts who have written about the right to a healthy environment, including Will Amos, William Andrews, Lynda Collins, Stewart Elgie, Paul Muldoon, John Swaigen, Margot Venton, and Toby Vigod. I would like to thank some of the protagonists directly involved in the development and repatriation of Canada's *Constitution Act, 1982*, for sharing their reflections and insights, including Lloyd Axworthy, Tom Axworthy, Jean Chrétien, Marc Lalonde, Svend Robinson, and Roy Romanow. My research also benefited from the assistance of P.G. Forest, Ron Graham, Leah Harms, Toby Heaps, and Sarah Miller. I genuinely appreciate the support provided by Jim Boothroyd, Lisa Gue, Tony Maas, Tim Morris, Carol Newell, Devon Page, Peter Robinson, and Terre Satterfield. To David Ohnona, Ken Rempel, Paul Richardson, and Ethan Smith, thanks for listening.

I would also like to thank three anonymous peer reviewers who provided helpful suggestions and encouragement. Thanks again to the hard-working folks at UBC Press, with whom I have a long-standing and wonderful relationship, including Randy Schmidt, Peter Milroy, Ann Macklem, Emily Rielly, Kerry Kilmartin, Laraine Coates, and Harmony Johnson. Finally, the book benefited from the expertise of a talented group of freelancers, including Deborah Kerr, Cheryl Lemmens, Jenna Newman, Irma Rodriguez, and Martyn Schmoll.

Abbreviations

CELA	Canadian Environmental Law Association
CEPA	*Canadian Environmental Protection Act*
EBR	*Environmental Bill of Rights, 1993* (Ontario)
EC	European Community
ECHR	European Court of Human Rights
ENGO	environmental non-governmental organization
EU	European Union
GHGs	greenhouse gases
IACHR	Inter-American Commission on Human Rights
ICCPR	*International Covenant on Civil and Political Rights*
ICESCR	*International Covenant on Economic, Social and Cultural Rights*
IUCN	International Union for the Conservation of Nature
MP	Member of Parliament
NDP	New Democratic Party
NGO	non-governmental organization
NOx	nitrogen oxides
OECD	Organisation for Economic Co-operation and Development
PCBs	polychlorinated biphenyls
SARA	*Species at Risk Act*
UK	United Kingdom
UN	United Nations
UNECE	United Nations Economic Commission for Europe

The Right to a Healthy Environment

1 Canada Needs Constitutional Environmental Rights

> All human beings have the fundamental right to an environment adequate for their health and well-being.
>
> – World Commission on Environment and Development, *Our Common Future*

Among the myriad responses to the mounting environmental challenges of the twentieth century and in particular their damaging effects on people's health and well-being was the emergence of a new human right. The right to a healthy environment is intended to ensure that everyone has access to clean air, safe water, fertile soil, and nutritious food, as well as the conservation of biological diversity and ecosystem functions. Rachel Carson, author of *Silent Spring,* first suggested the concept in the early 1960s. Carson testified before President John F. Kennedy's Scientific Advisory Committee, urging it to consider "a much neglected problem, that of the right of the citizen to be secure in his own home against the intrusion of poisons applied by other persons. I speak not as a lawyer but as a biologist and as a human being, but I strongly feel that this is or ought to be one of the basic human rights."[1]

The first formal articulation of the right to a healthy environment came in the 1972 *Stockholm Declaration,* which emerged from the inaugural global environmental conference in Sweden: "Principle 1: Man has the fundamental right to freedom, equality and adequate conditions of life, in an environment of a quality that permits a life of dignity and well-being, and he bears a solemn responsibility to protect and improve the environment for present and future generations."

Human rights are intended to recognize our most cherished values and express our moral identity as a people.[2] A human right must possess three defining characteristics, in that it must be universal (held by all persons); moral (existing whether or not a particular nation, government, or legal system recognizes it); and essential (ensuring the dignity and quality of life of all human beings).[3] The right to a healthy environment meets these three requirements. As a biological species, all humans depend on healthy ecosystems for life, health, and well-being. Tim Hayward, author of *Constitutional Environmental Rights,* asserts that "as a moral proposition, the claim that all human beings have the fundamental right to an environment adequate for their health and well-being is ... unimpeachable."[4] Henry Shue writes that "unpolluted air, unpolluted water, [and] adequate food" are among the basic human rights.[5] According to Birnie and Boyle, constitutional acknowledgment of the right to a healthy environment "would recognize the vital character of the environment as a basic condition of life, indispensable to the promotion of human dignity and welfare, and to the fulfillment of other rights."[6] Only a few scholars question the legitimacy of this right. Miller claims that "clean air, like other welfare aspirations, is best understood as a goal" rather than a right.[7] Similarly, Robertson and Merrills argue that "if one wishes to see some objective achieved – a clean and healthy environment, for example – it is tempting to say that this is a right to which we are all entitled. But it is not a good idea to take wishes for reality."[8]

The philosophical question of whether or not the right to a healthy environment is a legitimate human right appears to have been conclusively put to rest by the widespread recognition, implementation, and enforcement of the right.[9] Since the dawn of the modern environmental era in the 1960s, recognition of the essential connection between human rights and a healthy environment has steadily increased. As of 2012, at least 92 percent of the world's countries (177 out of 193) recognize the right to a healthy environment, through their constitutions, laws, court decisions, or international treaties and declarations (see Chapter 6).

In practice, the right to a healthy environment includes both a substantive right to environmental quality and a suite of procedural safeguards to ensure that it is fulfilled, including the rights to information, to participate in decision making, and to seek remedies for past, present, or anticipated violations. The right establishes a corresponding obligation on governments to respect, protect, and fulfill it. Respecting the right means that governments cannot take actions that violate the right. Protecting the right requires governments to take steps to prevent third parties from violating it. Fulfilling the right involves taking positive steps to ensure that it is fulfilled, such as ensuring the provision of safe drinking water. Like all human rights, the right to a healthy environment needs to be enforceable to be effective. Also like all human rights, it is not absolute but must be balanced with competing rights. Finally, the right to a healthy environment confounds traditional categories of human rights. It is both a negative (liberty) right, used to protect individuals from unwarranted government interference, and a positive (welfare) right, which requires the state to take action and expend resources. It is both an individual and a collective right, a substantive and a procedural right. These multiple aspects have led to some scholarly confusion about its meaning and scope, but as this book will demonstrate, citizens, legislatures, and courts in many countries have had little trouble in defining, applying, and enforcing it.

Why is it important for the right to a healthy environment to be entrenched in the constitution? A constitution is the supreme or highest law of a nation, meaning all other laws must be consistent with it. It establishes the rules that guide and constrain government powers, defines the relationships between institutions, and protects individual rights. A constitution also reflects and reinforces a society's deepest and most cherished values, acting as a mirror of a country's soul.[10] The logical argument for according constitutional status to the right to a healthy environment is straightforward.[11] Fundamental human rights should enjoy the strongest legal protection available in today's society – constitutional protection – to ensure that they are respected and fulfilled. The right to live in a healthy environment meets the test for recognition as a fundamental human right (significant moral importance, universal, practicable). Therefore, it should be protected by Canada's constitution. Even more importantly, there is now empirical evidence, based on the experiences of more than a hundred nations, indicating that constitutional entrenchment of environmental rights and responsibilities contributes to stronger laws, increased enforcement, an enhanced role for citizens, and improved environmental performance.

Do Canadians have a constitutional right to live in a healthy environment? The answer, if you asked Canadians, would probably be yes. If you asked lawyers, they would probably hedge their bets, responding that though the right is not explicitly mentioned in the constitution, it may be implicit in another right, such as the right to life. What about the Canadian government's position? In 2006, a petition was filed with the federal commissioner of the environment and sustainable development, asking, "Does the Government of Canada recognize that Canadians have a right to clean water, clean air, and a healthy environment?"[12] The response, although long, evasive, and convoluted, can be summarized in a single word: No.[13] One can search the text of Canada's constitution, including the *Charter of Rights and Freedoms,* in vain for any reference whatsoever to the environment. In a country where Nature is an integral element of our national identity, and in an era where scientific evidence establishes our basic dependence on a healthy environment, it is striking that our constitution makes no reference to it.

Does this constitutional lacuna matter? Absolutely. This book will argue that the omission of environmental rights and responsibilities from Canada's constitution is more than a mere oversight; it is a fundamental defect that must be rectified. There are five compelling reasons why constitutional recognition of the right to a healthy environment is imperative for Canada's future well-being:

- Environmental protection has evolved into a fundamental value held by the overwhelming majority of Canadians.
- There is an urgent need to improve Canada's poor environmental performance and preserve this country's magnificent landscapes, natural wealth, and biodiversity.
- It is vital to protect Canadians' health from environmental hazards such as air pollution, contaminated food and water, and toxic chemicals.
- Uncertainty regarding the responsibility of all levels of governments for environmental protection has undermined efforts to make Canada more sustainable and therefore needs to be clarified.
- Environmental rights and responsibilities are fundamental elements of Indigenous law, and acknowledging them would mark an important step toward reconciliation with Aboriginal people.

Each of these reasons is discussed in detail in this chapter.

Respecting the Environmental Values of Canadians

> All Canadians love the land.
>
> – Citizens' Forum on Canada's Future, *Report to the People and Government of Canada*

Canada is blessed with an extraordinary abundance of natural wealth – vast forests, untamed wilderness, thousands of rivers and lakes, a wonderful network of parks and protected areas, and unique landscapes. As the second-largest nation on Earth, Canada is home to 20 percent of the world's fresh water, 20 percent of the remaining wilderness, 25 percent of the world's wetlands, and the longest coastline.[14] Canadian woodlands represent one-tenth of the world's forested area, one-quarter of its temperate rainforests, and more than one-third of its boreal (northern, conifer-dominated) forests.[15] There are more than seventy-two thousand identified species in Canada, and scientists expect that it is home to thousands of as-yet unidentified species.[16] Canada is also one of the world's last strongholds for a range of iconic wildlife including grizzly bears, whooping cranes, mountain goats, caribou, and wild salmon. Bounded by the Pacific, Arctic, and Atlantic Oceans, Canada is also a maritime nation, with a marine area even larger than our huge land mass.

Our vast, beautiful, and diverse landscapes are at the heart of who we are as a people and are a source of tremendous national pride. As the Molson Canadian beer commercial says, "This land is unlike any other. We have more square feet of awesomeness per person than any other nation on Earth. It's why we flock towards lakes, mountains, forests, rivers, and streams. We know we have the best backyard in the world. And we get out there every chance we get." From polar bears, loons, and caribou on coins to the Vancouver Canucks and Toronto Maple Leafs, Canada's currency, flags, and hockey jerseys are emblazoned with images drawn from our natural heritage. Even as the country's population has grown increasingly diverse, Nature has remained constant as a unifying value, along with multiculturalism and universal health care.[17] As the Supreme Court of Canada has repeatedly observed in decisions spanning the past fifteen years, environmental protection is a fundamental value for Canadians.[18]

According to public opinion polls, nine out of ten Canadians worry about the impacts of environmental degradation on their health and the health of their children and grandchildren.[19] Nine out of ten are concerned or seriously concerned about climate change, the loss of biodiversity, and pollution. Nine out of ten believe that sustainability should be a national priority, and eight out of ten agree that we need stricter laws and regulations to protect the environment. Among the fifty-seven nations for whom recent data are available from the World Values Survey, Canadians rank behind only the citizens of Andorra, Norway, Argentina, and Switzerland in terms of favouring environmental protection over economic growth and job creation.[20]

More than 95 percent of Canadians agree that access to clean water is a basic human right, and it seems likely that a similar proportion would endorse the right to live in a healthy environment.[21] Canadians overwhelmingly say that our most valuable natural resource is water, more precious than oil and gas, forests, or minerals.[22] Additional statistics show that

- 98 percent of Canadians view nature as essential to human survival
- 90 percent of Canadians consider time spent in natural areas as children to be very important
- 85 percent of Canadians participate regularly in nature-related activities
- 82 percent of Canadians say that Nature has very important spiritual qualities for them personally.[23]

Thus it is anomalous that Canada's constitution, the highest expression of peoples' fundamental values, is silent on the environment. Canada's constitutional vacuum stands in stark contrast to 147 nations worldwide, where the constitution either entrenches everyone's right to live in a healthy environment (94 nations) or explicitly describes government's fundamental responsibility to protect the environment (142 nations). Constitutional recognition of environmental rights and responsibilities would both reflect and reinforce an essential Canadian value, just as the *Charter of Rights and Freedoms* reflects and reinforces our commitment to equality.

Improving Canada's Environmental Record

Contrary to the myth of a pristine green country providing environmental leadership to the world, a huge pile of studies proves beyond a reasonable doubt that Canada lags behind other nations in terms of environmental performance. According to researchers at Simon Fraser University, Canada's environmental performance ranks twenty-fourth out of the twenty-five wealthiest nations in the Organisation for Economic Co-operation and Development (OECD).[24] The OECD has published blistering criticisms of Canada's weak laws and policies, perverse subsidies for unsustainable industries, and poor environmental performance.[25] The conservative Conference Board of Canada ranked Canada fifteenth out of seventeen large, wealthy industrialized nations on environmental performance.[26] Sweden, Finland, and Norway top the rankings. According to the Conference Board, these Scandinavian nations also outstrip Canada in terms of economic competitiveness and innovation, debunking the myth that there is a trade-off between strong environmental protection and economic prosperity. A collaborative research project involving Yale University, Columbia University, and the World Economic Forum ranked forty-five nations ahead of Canada in environmental performance.[27] Nine of the countries ranked in the World Economic Forum's top fifteen for environmental performance are also in the top fifteen for global competitiveness, again undermining the notion of economy-environment trade-offs.

Published in 2009, a comprehensive comparison of nations with federal governance systems concluded that "Canadian environmental quality and environmental policy are worse than one might expect in a relatively wealthy country."[28] A 2010 survey of over five thousand experts – from government, academia, business, non-governmental organizations, and other institutions – found that

- 60 percent rated Canada's performance in protecting Canadians from the health impacts of pollution as poor or very poor
- 65 percent rated Canada's performance in protecting fresh water as poor or very poor
- and 85 percent rated Canada's efforts to address climate change as poor or very poor.[29]

Another measure of environmental performance is the ecological footprint. Canadians have, on an individual basis, the seventh-largest per capita ecological footprint in the world.[30] If all 7 billion people on Earth consumed resources and produced waste at the prodigious rate of Canadians, we would require three additional planets.

Once internationally renowned as an environmental leader, Canada "is now a laggard in both policy innovation and environmental performance, known for inaction and obstruction."[31] Canada had built a strong reputation over decades by demonstrating leadership on issues such as acid rain, ozone depletion, protection of the Arctic, and rules governing the world's oceans. As recently as the early 1990s, it was the first industrialized nation to ratify the *UN Convention on Biological Diversity* and the *UN Framework Convention on Climate Change*. Yet today Canada is a notorious saboteur at international environmental forums. For years we have garnered countless "fossil of the day" and Colossal Fossil awards for blocking progress at international climate change negotiations. Under Prime Minister Stephen Harper, Canada became the only country in the world to turn its back on legal obligations under the *Kyoto Protocol*. Canada, along with Russia and the USA, fought against the extension of the global regime for reducing greenhouse gas emissions. In 2010, Canada earned the Dodo Award for obstructing international biodiversity negotiations.

Canada is the only industrialized nation that exports asbestos and promotes its use, despite the World Health Organization's call for the end of all uses of asbestos.[32] Along with countries such as Kazakhstan, Kyrgyzstan, and Zimbabwe, Canada has repeatedly blocked proposals to add asbestos to the

Rotterdam Convention, an international agreement that limits trade in hazardous substances. In 2006, Canada rejected a UN agreement to limit the destructive fishing practice of bottom trawling. In 2010, it sided with Japan to block the protection of Atlantic bluefin tuna under the *Convention on International Trade in Endangered Species,* despite population declines of more than 80 percent.

Global leaders, including Ban Ki-moon (UN secretary-general), José Manuel Barroso (president of the European Commission), and Rajendra Pachauri (head of the Intergovernmental Panel on Climate Change), have been unusually frank in criticizing Canada's failure to live up to expectations in protecting the environment.[33] In 2012, one of the world's leading scientific journals, *Nature,* published an unprecedented critique of the federal government's policy of muzzling environmental scientists, stating that "Canada's generally positive foreign reputation as a progressive, scientific nation masks some startlingly poor behaviour."[34]

In the past, many Canadians subscribed to the illusion that "Canada's environmental record is among the best in the world."[35] Today even Canada's political leaders, who usually defend the country come hell or high water, admit that it is an environmental laggard. During a year-end interview in 2006, Prime Minister Harper acknowledged that "Canada's environmental performance is, by most measures, the worst in the developed world. We've got big problems."[36]

Constitutional recognition of the right to a healthy environment can have a positive effect on environmental performance and people's quality of life, as nations with environmental provisions in their constitutions

- have smaller per capita ecological footprints
- rank higher on comprehensive indices of environmental performance
- are more likely to have ratified international environmental agreements
- have been more successful in reducing greenhouse gas emissions
- and have achieved deeper cuts in emissions of nitrogen oxides and sulphur dioxide.[37]

Gus Speth, former dean of the Yale School of Forestry, stated "I am very excited about the move to rights-based environmentalism. Lord knows we need some stronger approaches."[38] In light of the experiences of other countries, it is highly likely that amending Canada's constitution to recognize environmental rights and responsibilities would spur significant improvements in Canada's environmental performance.

Protecting Canadians' Health from Environmental Hazards

Canada has surprisingly weak rules governing air pollution, drinking water safety, contaminants in our food, and toxic substances used in and produced by our economy.[39] Despite well-established evidence of deaths and illnesses caused by air pollution, Canada has no legally binding national air quality standards – unlike the USA, Australia, and Europe.[40] On a per capita basis, we pump out more air pollution – volatile organic compounds, nitrogen oxides, sulphur dioxide, and carbon monoxide – than any other nation in the OECD.[41] Contradicting the perception that air quality is improving, Environment Canada reports that average levels of smog are up 13 percent since 1990.[42] Canadian industries in the heavily populated Great Lakes region discharge twice as much cancer-causing pollution per facility as their American competitors.[43]

Unlike the USA and Europe, Canada has no national standards for ensuring the safety of drinking water, choosing instead to rely on unenforceable guidelines that are enshrined in law by some provinces but not others.[44] The national patchwork of drinking water laws and regulations puts people's health in jeopardy, particularly in smaller communities, rural areas, and reserves.[45] Thousands of Aboriginal people living on reserves in Alberta, Manitoba, Ontario, and Quebec lack access to running water, resulting in elevated levels of waterborne illnesses.[46]

Canada also lags behind other wealthy nations in rules governing food safety. Hundreds of pesticides sold in Canada – formulated with active ingredients including atrazine, carbaryl, paraquat, and trifluralin – are banned in other nations because of concerns about their impact on human health and ecosystems.[47] Permissible levels of pesticide residues on food in Canada are, in some cases, hundreds of times higher than in comparable European rules.[48] As well, Canada allows the use of antibiotics and hormones to make livestock grow faster, practices that are banned in Europe because of adverse effects on human health and the environment.

Canada's weak rules and poor environmental performance have substantial negative effects on human health. According to the World Health Organization, exposure to environmental hazards (such as air pollution, contaminants in water and food, and toxic substances in consumer products) contributes to thirty-six thousand premature deaths in Canada annually and approximately 13 percent of all illnesses and injuries.[49] Another study estimated that for just four categories of illness – cardiovascular disease, respiratory illness, cancer, and congenital afflictions (birth defects) – environmental hazards contributed to as many as twenty-five thousand deaths and 1.5 million days in hospital annually.[50] The Conference Board of Canada, a respected think-tank not known for alarmist prognostications, warns that life expectancy for today's Canadian children will be shorter than for their parents.[51] Unlike Australia, the USA, and all nations in the European Union, Canada has no national environmental health strategy to systematically address these problems.[52]

The potential health benefits of strong environmental laws and policies are best illustrated by Sweden, whose constitution mandates the government to pursue a healthy environment for the benefit of present and future generations. Renowned as a global leader in environmental protection, Sweden has experienced the slowest rise in health care costs among industrialized nations, a pattern attributed, in part, to its pioneering efforts to reduce pollution and prevent people from being exposed to toxic substances.[53]

Clarifying the Responsibility of All Governments to Protect the Environment

Canada's constitution divides jurisdiction over various matters between the federal government and the provinces. Because the environment is not mentioned in the constitution, there is extensive uncertainty about the allocation of responsibility in this field. This uncertainty sabotages both federal and provincial governments' willingness and ability to enact and enforce environmental laws and regulations. Constitutional ambiguity also results in a lack of transparency and accountability.[54]

Ottawa justifies its environmental laws, policies, and programs based on its constitutional authority related to criminal law, trade and commerce, fisheries, navigation and shipping, agriculture, federal lands, interprovincial works, the peace, order, and good government of Canada, works or undertakings for the general advantage of Canada, taxation and spending, and the negotiation and signing of treaties. Provincial governments defend their environmental policies based on ownership of natural resources, property and civil rights, civil law, agriculture, and matters of local concern. The constitutional changes made in 1982 clarified that provinces are primarily responsible for managing forests, electricity generation, and non-renewable resources.

For at least a hundred years, it has been understood that Canada's constitutional arrangement is inadequate for tackling environmental problems.[55] In 1912, a paper on water pollution published by Prime Minister Laurier's Commission of Conservation identified the problems associated with jurisdictional uncertainty.[56] In 1961, a workshop attended by Canada's leading constitutional lawyers, civil servants, and academics held as part of the Resources for Tomorrow conference warned that jurisdictional problems were likely to become more critical in the future.[57] In 1969, Prime Minister Pierre Trudeau said, "This challenge of pollution of our rivers and lakes, of our farmlands and forests, and of the very air we breathe, cannot be met effectively in our federal state without some constitutional reforms or clarification."[58] In 1970, Dale Gibson, one of Canada's leading constitutional law experts, concluded that amendments were required to dispel doubts about the environmental powers of both levels of government and to provide for improved environmental management.[59]

Passing the buck for environmental responsibility between federal and provincial governments was decried as early as 1971. A witness testifying before the Special Joint Committee of the Senate and the House of Commons on the Constitution of Canada observed, "Everyone says 'Oh dear it is a pity. But perhaps some other level will look after it.' Meanwhile things get grubbier and grubbier."[60] In 1978, the Canadian Environmental Law Association concluded that the constitution's silence "led to jurisdictional buck-passing between the federal and provincial governments, failure to pass needed laws, erratic and haphazard enforcement of existing legislation, and pollution havens."[61] In 1984, J.P.S. MacLaren argued that "the spectre of constitutional challenge" prevented Ottawa from effectively implementing or enforcing environmental laws.[62] In 1991, lawyer Paul Muldoon asserted that the federal government's constitutional powers were inadequate to support a strong role in environmental protection.[63] In 1992, the Supreme Court ruled that the environment "is a constitutionally abstruse matter which does not comfortably fit within the existing division of powers without considerable overlap and uncertainty."[64] In 1996, Kathryn Harrison criticized Ottawa's tendency to defer to the provinces on environmental policy.[65] In 2007, Stewart Elgie concluded that the ongoing uncertainty about the scope of jurisdiction sabotaged the federal government's ability to address modern environmental challenges, such as climate change.[66]

Another major problem caused by constitutional uncertainty is that corporations often challenge Canadian environmental laws – both provincial and federal – as being beyond the jurisdiction of the government that passed them. For example, the Supreme Court of Canada struck down a Manitoba law that imposed liability upon industrial polluters whose mercury discharges harmed fisheries.[67] Provisions of the federal *Fisheries Act* have been struck down in cases involving environmental damage inflicted by logging companies.[68] The federal *Clean Air Act* was challenged by the Canadian Metal

Company in 1982 but upheld by a Manitoba court.[69] The *Ocean Dumping Control Act* was attacked by logging company Crown Zellerbach and narrowly upheld by the Supreme Court in 1988.[70] In a case involving the Oldman Dam, the constitutionality of the federal environmental assessment process was challenged by the Government of Alberta but upheld by the Supreme Court.[71] The ability of municipal governments to protect the environment was also the subject of a constitutional challenge. When the town of Hudson (Quebec) banned the use of pesticides for cosmetic or non-essential purposes, lawn-care companies sued, arguing that municipalities had no jurisdiction to regulate pesticides. The Supreme Court ruled that all levels of government have a part to play in environmental protection, although it did not clarify the boundaries between those roles.[72]

In the 1990s, Ottawa came within a hair's breadth of losing its ability to regulate toxic pollution because of a constitutional challenge. The case arose when Hydro-Québec was charged with dumping PCBs into the St. Maurice River, in violation of the *Canadian Environmental Protection Act (CEPA)*. *CEPA* is Canada's primary pollution law, regulating industrial air pollution, vehicle emissions, and the manufacture, import, sale, use, and release of thousands of toxic chemicals.

Hydro-Québec's defence to the charge of dumping PCBs was that *CEPA* was unconstitutional – that the federal government lacked the requisite authority to regulate toxic substances. According to Hydro-Québec, pollution was a local matter falling within the provincial government's exclusive jurisdiction. Although most Canadians would reject such a defence as nonsense, Hydro-Québec was successful before the Quebec trial court, which struck down the impugned sections of *CEPA*. Ottawa appealed to the Quebec Superior Court and the Quebec Court of Appeal but lost both appeals. All three Quebec courts sided with the polluter, striking down key provisions of the *Canadian Environmental Protection Act*. The last hope for *CEPA*'s salvation lay with Canada's highest court, the Supreme Court.

Faced with the absence of a clear constitutional mandate for federal environmental law, lawyers defending *CEPA* were left to do the best they could with a handful of sub-optimal options:

- the trade and commerce power of the federal government
- its criminal law power
- and Parliament's residual jurisdiction under the vague "peace, order, and good government" power to legislate respecting matters of national

concern, as provided for in the introductory paragraph of section 91 of the *Constitution Act, 1867.*

By the narrowest possible margin (five to four), the Supreme Court upheld the constitutionality of Canada's most important environmental law. The four dissenting judges, led by the chief justice, agreed with Hydro-Québec and the Quebec courts that *CEPA*'s provisions prohibiting the release of toxic substances into the environment were unconstitutional. According to these judges, a substance that affected groundhogs but that had no impact on people could be labelled "toxic" and made subject to wholesale federal regulation, thus undermining the constitution's carefully balanced division of powers.[73] Had one more judge joined their opinion, it would have blown an immense hole in Canadian environmental law.

Fortunately, five Supreme Court judges upheld *CEPA*'s constitutionality. To do so, however, required some judicial creativity, as they relied on the federal government's criminal law power. Because of the constitution's silence regarding environmental protection, the courts and Ottawa are forced to perform jurisdictional gymnastics to validate its role in protecting the environment. The notion that, today, in the twenty-first century, Canada's Parliament must justify environmental legislation on the basis of its power to enact criminal laws or its residual peace, order, and good government power is, frankly, absurd. In an article called "Polluting the Law to Protect the Environment," David Beatty described the Supreme Court's *Hydro-Québec* judgment as "the jurisprudential equivalent of a serious spill of toxic waste" because its logic deviated so widely from previous court decisions.[74]

Canada's constitutional gap is also used to delay, block, or water down proposed environmental legislation and regulations. A classic example is federal endangered species legislation. The USA passed a strong *Endangered Species Act* in the early 1970s, yet three decades of prolonged effort from environmentalists and scientists were required in Canada before the weak *Species at Risk Act (SARA)* was passed in 2002. Whereas the American law applies to endangered species wherever they may live, Canada's law is limited to protecting species on federal lands and waters, thus excluding huge swaths of provincial and private land. Experts describe *SARA* as "subsidized voluntary stewardship," in contrast to the stronger regulatory model relied upon in the USA.[75] In part by playing the constitutional card, provinces and industries opposed to *SARA* delayed the law and eventually secured "federal legislation that would help to cement a more decentralized vision of Canadian environmental responsibilities."[76] Another example was the Nuclear Control and Administration Act, introduced in 1977 to replace a badly outdated law governing the use of nuclear energy. Provinces objected that the proposed legislation invaded their jurisdiction and delayed its passage for twenty years.[77] In 2012, it became clear that the Conservative government led by Prime Minister Stephen Harper was exploiting a very narrow perspective of constitutional jurisdiction in order to emasculate the federal role in protecting Canada's environment.

The USA, once regarded as an environmental leader, is similarly hampered by constitutional silence on this issue. As Oliver Houck points out, the USA "still clings to the constitutional notion that environmental laws are justified as protecting interstate commerce, causing considerable confusion when the objects, such as endangered species or isolated wetlands, are not in commerce at all."[78] The studies cited earlier to demonstrate Canada's poor environmental record also prove that the USA is a laggard.[79]

The European Union (formerly known as the European Community) was originally in a similar position, as its founding document, the quasi-constitutional Treaty of Rome *(Treaty Establishing the European Economic Community)*, was enacted in 1957 without any mention of the environment.[80] Most early EC environmental laws were weak directives that set goals but left states to develop programs and monitor progress (similar to today's Canadian air and water quality guidelines). EC laws required the unanimous consent of national governments, meaning that any recalcitrant country held a veto. Environmental laws were justified on the basis of preventing economic disparities (by harmonizing national environmental rules). In other words, European Community environmental laws were ostensibly based on achieving economic, rather than ecological, objectives.

In order to overcome the uncertainty caused by the EC's inability to pass legislation with environmental objectives, the Europeans "did a straightforward thing" and "dropped the fiction."[81] The *Single European Act* passed in 1987 is a quasi-constitutional law that explicitly authorizes legislation to protect the environment.[82] No more games, no linguistic gymnastics requiring legislatures and courts to tie themselves in knots to create convoluted rationales for environmental laws. And the outcome for Europe? Ascendance to global environmental leadership, both in words, and more importantly, in actions. Europe has dramatically reduced air and water pollution, eliminated the use of dozens of pesticides and other hazardous chemicals, made progress in shifting to clean energy and reducing greenhouse gas emissions, and slashed both water and electricity use through aggressive conservation measures and full-cost pricing.[83]

Canada's constitution, rather than requiring governments to protect the environment by imposing a responsibility upon them, constrains their action. Constitutional recognition of the right to a healthy environment would clarify the situation by imposing a duty upon all levels of government to respect, protect, and fulfill this right.

Recognizing Indigenous Law

Indigenous, English, and French legal systems existed for centuries in Canada prior to the passage of the *Constitution Act, 1867,* and continue to operate today.[84] Indigenous law can be defined as "those procedures and substantive values, principles, practices, and teachings that reflect, create, respect, enhance, and protect the world and our relationships within it."[85] Although great strides have been made in integrating common law and civil law, far less progress has been made in terms of finding an appropriate place for Indigenous law, leaving Canada's legal system incomplete.[86] And yet, as the Supreme Court has acknowledged, the ongoing project of reconciliation with the Aboriginal peoples of Canada requires the integration of Indigenous legal concepts into Canadian law. For example, the court wrote that "aboriginal interests and customary laws were presumed to survive the assertion of sovereignty, and were absorbed into the common law as rights."[87] As well, the *UN Declaration on the Rights of Indigenous Peoples,* which Canada endorsed in 2010, refers repeatedly to the importance of recognizing and respecting Indigenous laws and legal institutions.[88]

One of the bedrock elements of Indigenous law common to many Aboriginal societies is the idea of a living Earth, with a set of rights and responsibilities governing the relationships between humans and the natural world. As John Borrows has written, "The land's sentience is a fundamental principle of Anishinabek law," and it contributes to "a multiplicity of citizenship rights and responsibilities for Anishinabek people and the Earth."[89] Similarly, Mi'kmaq law is rooted in ecological relationships, extending legal personality to animals, plants, insects, and rocks, and imposing legal obligations on Mi'kmaq persons.[90]

Borrows concludes that "only through a pluralistic, multi-juridical framework can we fully respect the place of Indigenous legal thinking" in the shaping of Canadian legal traditions.[91] Because of their central importance in First Nations' culture and law, incorporating environmental rights and responsibilities into Canada's constitution would mark a significant step toward the integration of Indigenous and Canadian law. This could "expand and improve Canada's legal system and benefit Aboriginal peoples along with our society as a whole."[92]

Overview of the Book

Chapter 2 explores, from a Canadian perspective, the arguments for and against entrenching the right to a healthy environment in the constitution. Chapter 3 reviews the history of proposals, dating back to 1969, to include environmental rights and responsibilities in Canada's constitution. It also examines legislative environmental bills of rights, which have been passed by a handful of provinces and territories and debated but not enacted at the federal level. Ultimately, the validity of the arguments made by proponents and opponents of constitutional environmental rights should be evaluated by assessing the practical effects of recognizing these rights. Therefore, Chapters 4 and 5 identify the countries that have incorporated environmental rights and responsibilities into their constitutions and examine the extent to which these provisions have influenced environmental laws, court decisions, and most importantly, environmental performance. Chapter 6 traces the evolution of the right to a healthy environment in international law and identifies the implications for Canada. Extrapolating from the experiences of other nations, Chapter 7 describes the specific types of tangible impacts that constitutional recognition of environmental rights and responsibilities would have in Canada. Chapter 8 explores the political and legal avenues for achieving constitutional recognition of the right to a healthy environment, including the daunting process of direct amendment and the alternatives involving judicial interpretation of existing constitutional provisions. Chapter 9 offers a draft Canadian Charter of Environmental Rights and Responsibilities and assesses the prospects for incorporating such a document into Canada's constitutional framework.

Conclusion

We live in an era of unprecedented environmental damage at the hands of human beings. As medical doctors Eric Chivian and Aaron Bernstein concluded in their book *Sustaining Life: How Human Health Depends on Biodiversity*, "Our behavior is the result of a basic failure to recognize that human beings are an inseparable part of Nature and that we cannot damage it severely without severely damaging ourselves."[93] Canadians love this country's beauty, immense landscapes, and diverse wildlife. We express deep concerns about environmental problems and their effect on human health and ecological integrity. Yet our environmental performance, compared to other wealthy industrialized nations, is an international embarrassment. Our dismal record contradicts our fundamental values, jeopardizing our health, our magnificent natural heritage, and our legacy for future generations.

A similar gap used to exist with respect to social values. Prior to 1982, Canadians thought of themselves as tolerant, compassionate, and egalitarian. To some extent this was true, but the perception outstripped reality. Since 1982, the new constitution and the *Canadian Charter of Rights and Freedoms* have contributed to significant advances in women's, gay, and Aboriginal rights, and have enhanced the protection of civil and political rights for all Canadians. As Matthew Mendelsohn wrote, "The values in the *Charter* may not have reflected who we were as a country then, but it is those values which have created who we are as a country today."[94] Today, the *Charter* is cherished by an overwhelming majority (88 percent) of Canadians.[95] Yet Canada's constitution fails to reflect the strong environmental values held by most Canadians. We live in the twenty-first century with a constitution that is built for the twentieth century. Greening Canada's constitution could force us to live up to our ideals.

2
The Pros and Cons of the Right to a Healthy Environment

> Any state which is constitutionally committed to the implementation and protection of human rights ought to constitutionalize a right to an adequate environment.
>
> – Tim Hayward, *Constitutional Environmental Rights*

The potential advantages and disadvantages of constitutionalizing the right to live in a healthy environment have been passionately debated around the world since human rights and environmental concerns began converging in the late 1960s. This chapter will summarize these predominantly philosophical debates from a Canadian perspective. However, Hayward cautions "against supposing that the issue of effectiveness of a constitutional environmental right can be settled one way or the other by means of purely theoretical argument."[1] Therefore, Chapter 5 provides a comprehensive examination of the extent to which the theoretical advantages and disadvantages are being borne out in the ninety-four nations whose constitutions already incorporate the right to a healthy environment.

Advantages of Constitutional Environmental Rights

Proponents argue that constitutional recognition of environmental rights will clarify governments' responsibility to protect the environment, close the gap between words and actions, and ultimately contribute to improved environmental performance through a broad range of legal and extra-legal outcomes

- providing a stimulus for stronger environmental laws
- bolstering the implementation and enforcement of existing environmental laws, regulations, and policies
- offering a safety net to fill gaps in environmental legislation

- protecting environmental laws and regulations from rollbacks under future governments
- promoting democracy through greater citizen participation in decisions and actions to protect the environment, in part via procedural rights (access to information, participation in decision making, and access to justice)
- increasing accountability
- ensuring a level playing field with social and economic rights in decision making
- fostering environmental justice by protecting the environmental rights of all Canadians, particularly vulnerable populations
- and playing an educational role, reflecting and reinforcing the environmental values expressed by Canadians.

Impetus for Stronger Environmental Laws

Constitutional protection of a right offers the strongest possible form of legal protection because a constitution is the "fundamental and paramount law of the nation."[2] A basic principle of constitutional law is that all laws, regulations, and government policies must be consistent with the constitution or risk being struck down by the judiciary. Canada's *Constitution Act, 1982*, states, "Any law that is inconsistent with the provisions of the Constitution is, to the extent of the inconsistency, of no force or effect."[3] Lawmakers and government decision-makers must always consider the implications of their actions on constitutionally protected rights.[4]

Entrenchment of a constitutional right to a healthy environment generally requires the enactment of stronger environmental laws in order to respect, protect, and fulfill the right. This would certainly be the case in Canada, as international comparisons of environmental laws and standards demonstrate that Canada lags behind other industrialized nations.[5] Stevenson suggested that constitutional recognition of the right to a healthy environment in Canada would cause environmental laws to improve "to a state in which they no longer flatter to deceive but justify the high hopes and claims of the draftsmen and legislators."[6] Knowing that environmental laws have a constitutional backstop may encourage governments to enact stronger versions of them with the confidence that they will withstand legal challenges.

Improve Enforcement of Environmental Laws

A constitutional right is accompanied by an obligation upon governments to respect, protect, and in some circumstances, take proactive steps to fulfill the right.[7] In theory, constitutional recognition of the right to a healthy environment should ensure that governments establish and adequately resource systems for implementing, monitoring compliance with, and enforcing environmental laws and regulations. Canada has a long history of lackadaisical enforcement of environmental laws.[8] Constitutionalizing the right to a healthy environment could "act as a powerful catalyst stimulating the more effective enforcement of existing environmental protection laws."[9] As de Sadeleer writes, a constitutional environmental provision "imposes on the law-maker and subordinate authorities an obligation that they may not evade. Equivocation is no longer an option."[10] The procedural rights available to citizens can provide both a stimulus for enhanced enforcement by the state and a supplementary means of enforcing environmental laws.

Provide a Safety Net

Where environmental laws are weak, uneven, unenforced, or non-existent, constitutional provisions can offer a safety net for resolving environmental problems that existing legal and regulatory frameworks do not address.[11] The constitutional right to a healthy environment could help address Canada's gaps in environmental legislation, regulations, policies, and implementation. Such gaps may occur because of delays in addressing particular issues or because new threats arise. Delays may be caused by constitutional uncertainty, a lack of legal and/or technical resources, or a failure to assign priority to particular environmental problems. For example, no Canadian government has developed new health or environmental regulations for nanotechnology, despite extensive scientific concerns.[12] The existence of a constitutional right to a healthy environment gives concerned citizens and communities a set of tools that may be effective in addressing problems despite the absence of legislation.[13] Rights provide a flexibility and open-endedness that no law or regulation could ever furnish.[14]

Prevent Environmental Rollbacks

Constitutions are harder to amend than ordinary laws. As Hayward states, "The point of constitutionalizing rights is to set them above the vicissitudes of everyday politics, and this is also effectively to raise them above the possibility of routine democratic revision."[15] Constitutional entrenchment of the right to a healthy environment may prevent governments from taking actions that weaken current environmental laws and standards. In effect, the right could ensure that today's environmental laws establish a floor below which future rules for environmental protection cannot descend.

Another benefit of constitutionalizing the right to a healthy environment is that all prospective laws and regulations would be screened to determine whether they were consistent with the right (to avoid controversy, litigation, and potential embarrassment). In Canada, the Department of Justice is responsible for ensuring that all new laws and regulations are consistent with the *Charter* and would perform a similar task for the constitutional right to a healthy environment.[16] Provincial governments employ comparable processes to pre-screen laws for *Charter* compliance.[17]

Strengthen Democracy

People in differing regions of Canada "do not have an equal ability to access information about, and participate in, environmental decision-making," because mechanisms are lacking or are too expensive, time consuming, or ineffective.[18] Worse yet, Canada finished last in a 2010 study comparing the effectiveness of freedom of information laws in parliamentary democracies.[19] Constitutional environmental provisions can substantially increase the public's role in all aspects of environmental governance, through strengthening procedural rights such as access to information, participation in decision making, standing in judicial review, and the ability to enforce environmental laws. As Chiappinelli states, constitutional environmental rights could address the "institutional disenfranchisement" of individual citizens at the hands of powerful corporations and faceless bureaucracies.[20]

Foster Accountability

In the absence of a constitutional right to a healthy environment, it can be difficult to hold governments accountable for failing to protect human health and the environment. There may be a lack of publicly available information, an absence of opportunities to participate in decisions that have significant environmental consequences, and a lack of access to tribunals or courts when a person or community suffers harm because of environmental destruction or pollution. Both the substantive and procedural aspects of the constitutional right to a healthy environment can contribute to overcoming these problems, ensuring the availability of processes and forums that enable citizens and groups to hold governments accountable. As M.C. Mehta, the prominent Indian lawyer, wrote, "Ordinarily it is very difficult for a citizen to go to court for environmental relief under the existing laws. It is only under the constitutional provisions that it became possible ... to move the courts for judicial relief."[21]

Constitutionalizing the right to a healthy environment would enhance the role of courts in ensuring accountability by facilitating citizen access to judicial remedies. The nature and scope of human rights are often defined and refined through litigation. Stephens argues that courts are ideally suited for this role: "The institution of adjudication (in its independence), the process of argumentation (according to criteria of rationality), and the decision-making process (according to law) means that courts, international and national, are uniquely placed to speak beyond the confines of the dispute at hand and confront the major environmental challenges of our time."[22] Citizens could use the constitutional right to a healthy environment in seeking remedies for violations of the right and also in a preventive manner, to avoid prospective environmental damage. In theory, the impartiality of courts should enable them to balance competing economic, social, and environmental interests, individual and collective interests, and public and private interests. As Du Bois observes, courts "can make a unique contribution by insulating environmental protection measures – typically accompanied by high short-term costs and resultant political disfavor – from political horse-trading."[23] Constitutional protection of the right to a healthy environment could also contribute to increasing the effectiveness of environmental law by ameliorating problems such as establishing causation, meeting the burden of proof, and assigning liability.[24]

Level the Playing Field

Canada's poor environmental record demonstrates that economic and social considerations often override environmental concerns. The purpose of a constitutional right to a healthy environment is to seek a better balancing of competing interests, not to unilaterally trump economic and social priorities.[25] As Brandl and Bungert wrote, "Declaring an environmental right in a constitution challenges the privileged position accorded economic freedoms."[26] Every day, government policy-makers, administrative agencies, and courts make countless decisions with environmental consequences. Constitutional protection of the right to a healthy environment could tip the balance in many regulatory, administrative, corporate, and judicial decisions, increasing the likelihood that future development will in fact be sustainable.[27]

Another advantage of constitutionalizing the right to a healthy environment is the prospect of a level playing field with competing rights. Canadian legal and political systems have historically favoured private property over the public interest or the common good. Property rights, though deliberately excluded from the *Charter*, enjoy strong and extensive protection in Canada, both in legislation and the common law. Environmental legislation often constrains the exercise of property rights, recognizing that there are circumstances in which the public interest trumps private interests. Constitutional recognition of environmental rights and responsibilities validates such legislation and protects it from attack.

Environmental Justice

"Environmental justice" refers to an equitable distribution of environmental risks and benefits. Yet both in Canada and internationally, a disproportionate burden of harm from environmental degradation – toxic pollution, habitat destruction, etc. – is borne by Aboriginal people, the poor, ethnic minorities, or other disadvantaged groups.[28] At the heart of constitutional law is "the idea of protecting minorities from majoritarian actions," or protecting the weak from the strong.[29] Thus the constitutional right to a healthy environment should, in theory, alleviate environmental injustices by providing a minimum standard of environmental quality for all members of society. It could increase the probability of effective protection, provide vulnerable individuals, affected communities, and civil society with a powerful tool for holding governments accountable, and offer remedies to people whose rights are being violated. According to Fredman, "Human rights also constitute a focus for political and grassroots campaigning, giving a specific and authoritative legitimacy to demands for their fulfillment."[30] Similarly, lawsuits asserting the right to a healthy environment "can be used as mobilizing tools to gather community support and momentum on issues of environmental justice."[31]

Education and Public Values

A country's constitution is intended to express, enshrine, and protect the most fundamental and cherished values of its people. According to Brandl and Bungert, "Constitutional provisions provide a model character for the citizenry to follow, and they influence and guide public discourse and behaviour."[32] As Kiss writes, "Every constitution has educational value. Constitutionalization of fundamental rights and freedoms has undoubtedly contributed to securing for them general acceptance and observance."[33] The public tends to be more familiar with constitutional principles than the dull details of laws and regulations.[34] According to Swaigen and Woods, "Rights have a subtle, positive moral force whose effect is greater than that of specific rules or standards. The introduction of rights contributes to an evolutionary process of attitudinal and linguistic changes supportive of eventual improvements in environmental quality."[35]

Constitutional recognition of the right to a healthy environment would both reflect and reinforce the Canadian public's growing concerns about the severity of today's environmental problems, underscoring the fact that a healthy environment is a fundamental element of human well-being and a prerequisite to the full enjoyment of other human rights.[36]

Critiques of Constitutional Environmental Rights

Not everyone is convinced that constitutionalizing the right to a healthy environment is a good idea.[37] Opponents argue that the right is philosophically unsound or would result in greater costs than benefits. The most common criticisms allege that the right is

- too vague to be meaningful
- a threat to industrial activity in Canada, particularly in the natural resource sectors
- redundant because of existing human rights protections and environmental laws
- undemocratic, in that it transfers power from elected legislators to unelected judges
- not justiciable, meaning not appropriate for adjudication by courts
- unduly focused on individuals
- likely to open the floodgates to litigation
- capable of diverting attention from other more important human rights
- anthropocentric, because it fails to recognize the rights of Nature
- and likely to be ineffective.

Many of these arguments could be applied to all human rights. Each of these potential drawbacks will be examined in detail below, along with rebuttals from proponents of rights.

VAGUENESS

A common criticism of constitutionalizing the right to a healthy environment is that there is too much uncertainty about what level of environmental quality will be protected.[38] In the words of prominent Canadian environmental lawyer Dianne Saxe, "The mere assertion of a right fails to give sufficient guidance in making the hard choices of pollution control."[39] This concern is exacerbated by the fact that many different adjectives are used to describe the environmental right in constitutions and legislation, including healthy, adequate, clean, safe, and ecologically balanced. There is also uncertainty about the beneficiaries of the right and who bears the corresponding duties. Are future generations included among prospective beneficiaries? Do the duties imposed by the right extend to private actors as well as government? As a result of these uncertainties, it is speculated, the right will be difficult to implement, meaningless, and ineffective.[40]

The rebuttal to this critique is that constitutional provisions are by necessity brief and inherently vague. The right to a healthy environment is no more vague or uncertain than any other right protected by Canada's *Charter of Rights and Freedoms,* from freedom of expression to protection from cruel and unusual punishment. The precise meaning of these words and phrases emerges over time, shaped by legislatures, courts, culture, and history. As well, it is the nature of human rights that they are dynamic rather than static, evolving with human values.

In the case of the right to a healthy environment, quantitative standards will change over time in response to the development of scientific knowledge and technological progress. As Kiss and Shelton write, "The variability of implementation demands imposed by the right to environment in response to different threats over time and place does not undermine the concept of the right, but merely takes into consideration its dynamic character."[41] For example, the so-called safe level of exposure to toxic substances such as benzene and lead has fallen repeatedly in recent decades.[42] Ambiguity can be an advantage because it provides flexibility in filling gaps in legislation, dealing with emerging issues, and responding to new knowledge in the fields of science, health, and ecology.[43]

A Threat to the Economy

Critics warn that constitutionalizing the right to a healthy environment could act as a trump card, enabling activists to block or delay many types of industrial activity, particularly in a country such as Canada, where resource extraction is a vital part of the economy. For example, in 2010, Conservative MP Mark Warawa described a proposed federal law recognizing the right to a healthy environment (which would be weaker than a constitutional right) as a "kill the Alberta oil sands bill" and a "shut down Hydro-Québec bill."[44] Tom Huffaker, vice-president of the Canadian Association of Petroleum Producers, claimed that the same draft legislation would "significantly increase the risks and costs of doing business in Canada, in our view. The result will be a loss of competitiveness for Canada, with reduced investment in economic opportunities and fewer jobs."[45]

These arguments appear to lack merit, in that rights are rarely absolute and are almost always balanced against other rights. In its first section, Canada's *Charter* contains a uniquely Canadian balancing approach that weighs the rights of individuals against the public interest or collective good. Government actions may in certain circumstances be justified despite violating the fundamental rights and freedoms set forth in the *Charter*. For instance, free speech is governed by laws prohibiting or restricting pornography, hate literature, false advertising, excessive noise, and other forms of communication. In the *Keegstra* case, which dealt with a teacher who made extensive anti-Semitic remarks, the Supreme Court of Canada upheld the *Criminal Code* provisions banning the promotion of hatred against an identifiable group as a reasonable limitation on freedom of expression.[46] As well, the *Charter* is equipped with a notwithstanding clause, allowing Parliament or provincial legislatures to override some of its provisions. The aim of environmental rights is not to eliminate the balancing of competing constitutional rights, but rather to produce greater weight for environmental considerations vis-à-vis rights such as property and freedom of commerce.

Just as the right to free speech is not a right to say anything at any time or place, the constitutional right to a healthy environment would not be the right to pollution-free air, pure water, and pristine ecosystems. As Beatty observes with respect to constitutional rights, "Even when the language of the text is strong and categorical, it is never understood to provide an absolute, ironclad guarantee."[47] Rather than trumping economic activity, the right to a healthy environment would compel, or at least increase the likelihood of, sustainable development. For example, Norway, where the right enjoys constitutional status, continues to be one of the world's major oil and gas exporters. Unlike Canada, however, Norway pioneered innovative ways to reduce air pollution and greenhouse gas emissions from the oil and gas industry.[48] Norway also charges substantially higher royalties on these publicly owned natural resources, enabling the country to build up a publicly owned sovereign wealth fund with a value of more than $600 billion as of 2012.[49]

REDUNDANT

The argument that the constitutional right to a healthy environment is redundant has two aspects. The first is based on the proposition that human rights already recognized in Canada, such as the right to life, can be given a green interpretation in cases involving environmental harm. The second is based on the notion that existing Canadian environmental laws are adequate and that tort law (which deals with nuisance and negligence) already offers the same remedies for environmental harm that a right to a healthy environment could provide.

Among the established rights that could potentially be used to address environmental degradation and adverse health effects are the rights to life, liberty, and security of the person, and equality rights. For instance, it is often argued that the right to a healthy environment is an extension of the right to life because humans are dependent upon clean air, potable water, and healthy ecosystems that furnish a vast range of irreplaceable services (from pollination to water filtration). Advantages of greening current human rights include widespread acceptance of the binding legal nature of these rights and the presence of established courts, commissions, and other bodies for seeking redress.[50]

On the other hand, the scope for pressing existing human rights into the service of environmental ends is circumscribed. Some situations, such as those calling for preventive or precautionary measures or where Nature rather than human health is threatened, cannot be comfortably shoehorned into existing human rights boxes. There are limits to judicial creativity, and there are legitimate concerns about relying on judicial activism. Extensive judicial activism (expanding other rights to address environmental harms in the absence of express recognition of the right to a healthy environment) could bolster a key argument against constitutional environmental rights – that shifting environmental decision making from legislatures to courts is undemocratic.

At the end of the day, greening other constitutional rights and recognizing the right to a healthy environment need not be considered mutually exclusive. Given the extent of Canada's environmental problems, it would seem that both greening existing human rights and expanding the family of rights to include the right to a healthy environment are potentially useful approaches.[51]

As to the second part of the redundancy argument, it is true that environmental laws and policies have proliferated during the past four decades in Canada, both federally and provincially. However, though progress has been made on some issues, environmental laws and policies have failed to solve many of the problems they were intended to address, as demonstrated by Canada's dismal environmental record. International comparisons of laws governing air quality, drinking water, food safety, toxic substances, and conservation of biological diversity reveal that Canadian rules are often far weaker than their counterparts in other industrialized nations.[52] In this context, the right to a healthy environment can scarcely be described as redundant.

Undermines Democracy

Opponents of constitutional recognition of human rights argue that transferring decision-making power from elected legislators to unelected judges is undemocratic.[53] The basic argument is that in a democracy, important decisions ought to be made by elected individuals who, at least in theory, represent the viewpoints of their constituents. This perspective views the legislature's role as determining *what* should be done and the courts' role as limited to reviewing *how* things are done.[54] In other words, courts ought to focus on process, not substance, and should avoid disturbing the decisions of elected governments about the distribution of risks, costs, and benefits within society. With specific reference to the environmental context, Sax warned that courts "should not be authorized to function as an environmental czar against the clear wishes of the public and its elected representatives."[55] Brandl and Bungert describe the potential for costly uncertainty due to the "destabilizing juridification of environmental politics."[56] The excessive focus on legal matters leads to a disproportionately large role for lawyers, to the exclusion of the broader public. Furthermore, these critics argue, courts lack the institutional capacity, technical expertise, and resources required to address complex environmental issues and are the wrong place for resolving polycentric issues involving conflicting values and diverse interests.[57] Some judges share these concerns. Canada's Federal Court has repeatedly stated that it is not an "academy of science" and is thus not equipped to second-guess experts employed by government.[58] In dismissing a recent lawsuit against chemical giant E.I. DuPont, an American judge wrote, "The potential effects of these chemicals on human health are of great public concern. Issues of institutional competence, however, caution against judicial involvement in regulatory affairs. Courts are designed to remediate, not regulate."[59]

A small but vocal minority of Canadians believes that courts and judges have too much power.[60] These concerns have increased in recent decades largely due to the expansion of the judiciary's role in public policy resulting from the *Charter of Rights and Freedoms.* Courts are accused of lacking accountability because judges are appointed, rather than elected. Litigation by so-called special interest groups is perceived as an elite means of circumventing or undermining the more democratic forums offered by electoral politics. Thus, in attacking the proposed *Canadian Environmental Bill of Rights* that was before Parliament in 2011, the Canadian Association of Petroleum Producers warned that "the delicate art of politics on which the respect for federal and provincial powers now depends will become subject to rulings by federal courts [in lawsuits] brought by environmental activists."[61] Governments, critics suggest, have learned that the *Charter* can be used to avoid responsibility for controversial decisions by shifting them into courts, as was the case in the same-sex marriage debate.[62] Some critics argue that the process of pre-screening laws for *Charter* compliance provides further evidence of the growing and inappropriate power of the judiciary.[63]

On the other hand, courts have a legitimate supervisory role in constitutional democracies such as Canada. Key elements of that role involve defending the rule of law, ensuring that government laws, policies, and actions are within their constitutionally defined jurisdiction, and adjudicating claims that constitutional rights have been violated. Courts also have extensive experience and expertise in defining and refining the parameters of human rights. In the words of Alan Dershowitz, "Rights serve as a check on democracy, and democracy serves as a check on rights."[64] A careful balancing of power is reflected in Canada's political system, which has many built-in safeguards, including the balancing test in section 1 of the *Charter* and the notwithstanding clause. Although it is used infrequently by governments to override court decisions, the Supreme Court of Canada described the notwithstanding clause in section 33 of the *Charter* as "the ultimate parliamentary safeguard."[65] Courts rarely have the final say in disputes about human rights because dialogues with legislatures are more likely.[66] Kent Roach concludes that "when the Court has the last word, it is because the legislature and the people have let it have the last word."[67] The judicial role may constrain the legislature but does not disable it, so that courts play an important but secondary role in the development of public policy.[68] Peter Russell wrote that "fear-mongering about a Canadian juristocracy borders on the hysterical."[69]

In response to concerns about technical expertise, it should be acknowledged that courts are adept at filtering complex facts in a broad range of contexts, from DNA evidence in criminal cases to Byzantine corporate structures in commercial litigation. Elected representatives are no more likely than judges to have the technical, medical, or scientific expertise required to resolve complicated environmental challenges. The bottom line is that constitutional protection for human rights in Canada enhances, rather than undermines, democracy and accountability.

Non-Justiciable

Some scholars make a related argument, claiming that issues raised by the right to a healthy environment are not justiciable, meaning not appropriate or suitable for adjudication by a court.[70] For many years, the prevailing opinion was that social, economic, and cultural rights (and by extension the right to a healthy environment) ought not to be justiciable.[71] The main arguments were the subversion of democracy (allowing judges to substitute their opinion for elected legislators), the judicial system's lack of capacity for resolving complex polycentric disputes, and the vagueness of social, economic, and environmental rights.[72] According to critics, it is the exclusive purview of the legislature to determine how a government's budget is allocated, and courts have no jurisdiction or competence in this field. The concern is that these rights may represent open-ended claims on societal resources and that judicial decisions allocating those resources could be made without consideration of other societal priorities.[73] Leading constitutional scholar Cass Sunstein once claimed that courts are incapable of properly enforcing social, economic, and environmental rights because they cannot create government programs and lack the resources to oversee implementation of their orders. He argued that it would be a "large mistake, possibly a disaster" to incorporate positive rights, including the right to a healthy environment, in the new constitutions of Eastern European nations.[74] Similarly, writing about South Africa's new constitution, Davis warned that justiciable social and economic rights would act as a Trojan horse for politics to enter the courtroom, placing an undue amount of power in the hands of unelected judges.[75]

Today, however, a growing number of scholars – including Sunstein and Davis – believe that economic, social, and environmental rights ought to be considered justiciable.[76] Courts apply the principles of proportionality and reasonableness in cases that call for a careful balance between the economic and social rights of individuals and the public interest (recognizing societal priorities and limited government resources).[77] The acclaimed decision of South Africa's Constitutional Court in *Grootboom*, a case about the right to housing, demonstrated that "the legal enforcement of social and economic rights isn't so different from the protection that is provided by the more traditional political and civil guarantees."[78] *Grootboom* involved a group of homeless people asserting their constitutional right to housing. South Africa's Constitutional Court did not require the government to address the needs of the specific individuals who brought the lawsuit but ruled that the government's existing efforts to address homelessness were inadequate. The court ordered the government to develop and implement a comprehensive and effective strategy to fulfill the right of access to housing. Innovative and successful judicial interpretation and application of social and economic rights in a number of countries appears to be answering many, if not all, of the objections that were raised against their implementation and enforcement. In light of these judicial developments, Sunstein and Davis reversed their opposition and now endorse the justiciability of social and economic rights.[79] Ramcharan concludes, "There is no doubt that the era of justiciability of economic, social, and cultural rights has arrived."[80] There is a growing trend toward the justiciability of social and economic rights in Canada, although the results have yet to live up to the expectations of would-be right-holders.[81]

In addition, Schwartz points out that constitutions are not merely legal documents but are also political, social, and moral instruments that reflect a nation's hopes and aspirations for its future.[82] From this perspective, even if concerns about enforceability and justiciability are legitimate, there are other compelling reasons for including the right to a healthy environment in Canada's constitution.

Excessive Focus on Individuals

Human rights have been criticized for focusing excessively on individuals at the expense of the broader public interest.[83] The focus on rights is accompanied by a lack of attention to responsibility, leading to erosion of community.[84] In the environmental context, Handl suggests that a focus on individual rights is inappropriate because the environment is a public good.[85] Weiss argues that the obligation to protect the planet deserves equal billing with the right to a healthy environment.[86] Similarly, Swaigen, Woods, and others suggest that environmental duties and responsibilities (such as the duty to conserve natural resources) could be more effective than rights alone.[87]

The rebuttal to these criticisms is that environmental damage and degradation harm both individuals and the public interest. According to Raz, "At least some constitutional rights are primarily means of formal or informal institutional protection of collective goods."[88] As well, in law, there can be no right without a corresponding responsibility.[89]

Opens the Floodgates to Litigation

Some opponents of constitutionalizing the right to a healthy environment warn that it would open the floodgates to litigation, choking off investment and impeding economic development.[90] Tom Huffaker, vice-president of the Canadian Association of Petroleum Producers, claimed that if proposed federal legislation recognizing the right to a healthy environment were enacted, "The carefully balanced policies of government and the wise counsel of public servants will be held hostage to the court actions of single-interest groups."[91] Warren Everson, senior vice-president of the Canadian Chamber of Commerce, warned that the same draft legislation would result in "an endless litigation process brought by private parties."[92]

Hayward responds that "professed worries about opening the floodgates to litigious busybodies who threaten to undermine the legitimate activities of hard-pressed businesspersons or to overload the courts ring very hollow in view of the prodigious expense involved in engaging in such a pastime."[93] Other significant constraints on litigation include restrictions on access to courts (standing), long delays, and the risk of losing. It is important to recognize that though much of the literature on the right to a healthy environment focuses on judicial enforcement of the right, litigation is merely a means to an end. The aim of constitutionalizing the right to a healthy environment is to ensure the enjoyment and protection of the right, not to foster litigation.

WATERS DOWN EXISTING RIGHTS

Another argument states that recognizing the right to a healthy environment would diminish, devalue, or water down the importance of other, more basic human rights.[94] As Miller states, "A plethora of rights might lead to a depreciation of those which we value most."[95] This is one of the arguments relied upon by the Government of Canada in its refusal to recognize the right to water.[96]

Conversely, some scholars believe that recognizing new rights, such as the right to a healthy environment, will complement, enrich, and enhance pre-existing rights.[97] Proponents of the right to a healthy environment point out that human rights evolve over time, as demonstrated by the abolition of slavery, the evolution of Aboriginal rights, the recognition of women as persons, the demise of state-sanctioned racial segregation, and the growing recognition of same-sex marriage. The UN General Assembly has articulated guidelines for new human rights, concluding that such rights should be consistent with existing international human rights law, be fundamental and based on the inherent dignity of the human person, be sufficiently precise to create clear rights and obligations, provide effective implementation machinery, and attract broad international support.[98] Given that the right to a healthy environment meets all the criteria for being a human right, it seems odd that Canada would exclude it from constitutional recognition because of an unwritten limit on the number of human rights that can be effectively protected.

Anthropocentric

The right to a healthy environment is sometimes criticized because of its allegedly anthropocentric approach, focusing on the environment solely as an instrument for providing human health and well-being.[99] Some philosophers and activists argue that because the environment has intrinsic value, ecosystems rather than merely humans should be protected. In other words, Nature itself ought to be protected, and human rights approaches are inherently flawed.

The notion that Nature should have legal rights dates back many centuries.[100] The idea gained widespread notoriety in 1972 when Christopher Stone wrote a seminal article called "Should Trees Have Standing?" in which he argued that there was no legal barrier to granting rights to Nature given that other non-human entities such as ships and corporations had legal rights conferred upon them.[101] The idea attracted additional attention when endorsed by Justice Douglas of the US Supreme Court in his dissenting opinion in a pioneering environmental lawsuit.[102] Nash asserts that the extension of legal rights to Nature represents the logical evolution of rights.[103] Sunstein argues that animals already enjoy some legal rights, at least in some nations.[104]

However, profound questions remain.[105] Should rights be limited to sentient creatures, or held by all living organisms, including plankton and bacteria? Should rights be extended to non-living elements of Nature, such as stones, rivers, or mountains? How would these rights be exercised – by specially appointed guardians or by ordinary citizens acting on behalf of Nature?

Until recently, these debates could be considered largely philosophical. However, the new constitutions of Ecuador and Bolivia include pioneering provisions recognizing the rights of Nature, transforming abstract concepts into legally binding rights. Bolivia has enacted a *Law on the Rights of Mother Earth* and led a debate at the UN General Assembly on a proposed Universal Declaration of the Rights of Mother Earth.[106] In 2011, an Ecuadorean court enforced the rights of Nature in a case involving damage to a river.[107] Shelton asserts that "by developing a holistic, rights-based approach to environmental quality, long-term soundness of environmental conditions and concern for biological diversity can be brought into relationship with human rights ... reflecting the reality of human connectedness with all natural systems."[108] Canada should closely monitor the experiences of other countries to ascertain whether the constitutional protection of a human right to a healthy environment has a "fortuitous spill-over effect to non-humans" or whether extending constitutional recognition to the rights of Nature is also warranted.[109]

Likely to Be Ineffective

Critics claim that constitutional environmental rights would be ineffective.[110] There can be major gaps between laws on paper and laws in action, even constitutional laws.[111] Ruhl writes that "in itself, a constitutional amendment would not save a single wetland or forest; it would remove no cement plants or automobile exhausts; and it would clean no streams."[112] Lazarus suggests that creating competing moral claims (such as the right to a healthy environment versus the right to property) could produce a polarized atmosphere where "compromise and deliberative discussion are difficult."[113] A strong argument can be made that problems related to political economy – capitalism's focus on limitless growth, the relentless and sometimes reckless pursuit of new technologies, harmful forms of production, and pervasive wealth inequity – are the root causes of society's environmental crisis and are not addressed by a constitutional right.[114] The legal system is generally conservative and tends to favour those with education, money, and power, rather than the poor and marginalized communities who bear the disproportionate burden of environmental harm.[115] The opponents of stronger environmental regulation are powerful and organized, whereas the prospective beneficiaries are weak and diffuse. Scheingold argued that misperceptions about the power of rights have led social movements to focus on legal tactics instead of potentially more effective political strategies and warned that the law cannot be expected to transcend the political system in which it is embedded.[116] Some academics assert that the influence of courts in bringing about social transformation has been exaggerated.[117] Andrew Petter believes that the *Charter* has been misused by the Canadian government in reporting to the UN Committee on Economic, Social and Cultural Rights. According to Petter, Canadian delegations "invoke legal interpretations of abstract constitutional rights as a substitute for real evidence of substantive social progress and as a smokescreen for political failings."[118]

Another argument used to suggest the ineffectiveness of constitutional rights to a healthy environment is that the most pressing environmental problems facing humanity today are global in scope. Therefore, critics suggest, individual rights are of limited utility in addressing issues such as climate change or the loss of biodiversity. Finally, Dianne Saxe warns that constitutional rights focus on constraining or compelling government actions, when in fact the activities of private parties, both individual and corporate, cause the lion's share of environmental harm.[119] Even proponents of recognizing the right to a healthy environment have reservations about its effectiveness, "because property rights, government powers, and judicial conservatism are woven so deeply into the fabric of society, it is not certain that the right would tip the balance in any particular dispute in the foreseeable future."[120]

In response to these arguments, it must be acknowledged that constitutional rights and responsibilities are not silver bullets for today's environmental problems. As Epp concluded, "Rights are not magical solutions to any or all problems."[121] Despite constitutional rights to equality, forms of discrimination such as racism and sexism continue to adversely affect many individuals in contemporary Canadian society. Yet surely it is incontrovertible that rights have contributed to some amelioration of the wrongs they are intended to address.[122] There are experts who believe that a rights-based approach to environmental protection is the only effective alternative to today's market-based approach, which is failing to adequately protect the environment.[123] Cullet argues that economic globalization needs to be counterbalanced by the globalization of the right to a healthy environment.[124] The right is not anti-government but rather pro-government, requiring a larger role for the state in protecting and restoring environmental quality and biological diversity. Although private actors do cause the majority of environmental damage in Canada, these businesses and individuals almost always require government permits or authorization for their activities. Ultimately, the effectiveness of constitutional environmental rights should not be judged on the basis of theoretical arguments but on practical experience and empirical evidence.

Conclusion

On paper, constitutional recognition of the right to a healthy environment offers a host of potential benefits for human and ecological well-being as well as democracy. Many of the arguments marshalled against the right to a healthy environment have been levelled at other human rights and found wanting. All human rights are phrased in brief, general terms whose meaning develops over time. Rights are almost always balanced against competing rights. Courts have a legitimate role to play in protecting human rights and holding governments accountable for fulfilling constitutional responsibilities. Whether and to what extent the potential benefits and drawbacks of constitutionalizing the right to a healthy environment will be borne out is best answered with empirical evidence. On-the-ground experience with the right to a healthy environment in ninety-four nations (see Chapter 5) will shine new light on the arguments discussed in this chapter.

Canada's experience with constitutional rights began in 1982, with the advent of the *Canadian Charter of Rights and Freedoms.* Although it has been suggested that focusing on constitutional issues divides Canadians, polls indicate that 88 percent of Canadians believe that the *Charter* "has been a good thing" for Canada, and 75 percent of Canadians believe that it contributes to national unity.[125] Adding the right to a healthy environment to Canada's constitution should be unifying in that both the *Charter* and environmental protection represent widely held and fundamental Canadian values.

3
The History of Environmental Rights in Canada

> Our present Constitution provides specific protection for the use of the French and English languages, but if we succeed in destroying our environment it will matter very little whether the last 'I told you so' is spoken in either French or English.
>
> – Jim Egan, "Testimony before the Special Joint Committee of the Senate and the House of Commons on the Constitution of Canada"

The omission of environmental provisions from Canada's original constitution, the *British North America Act, 1867,* should come as no surprise, since ecological concerns were far less pressing in the nineteenth century. The world's earliest constitutional references to the environment (made by Italy in 1948 and Madagascar in 1959) involved protecting natural landscapes and beauty. Specific references to the right to a healthy environment first appeared in the constitutions of Eastern European communist nations during the 1960s. However, these constitutions were paper tigers, used to disseminate propaganda rather than protect human rights. It was not until the 1970s that environmental concerns began finding their way into national constitutions in democratic nations where the provisions could have real impact. Pioneers in enacting constitutions with extensive environmental provisions included Switzerland (1971), Portugal (1976), and Spain (1978).

This chapter sets forth the history of efforts, dating back to 1969, to include the right to a healthy environment and other environmental provisions in Canada's constitution. To provide a comprehensive perspective, it also describes the history of legislative environmental bills of rights at the federal, provincial, and territorial levels, while distinguishing the effects of these laws from constitutional provisions.

The Trudeau Era

> Can there be a Canadian whose outlook has not been deeply marked by the stretches of seemingly infinite space – the high seas of our maritime regions, the boundless horizons of our prairies, the endless unfolding of the St. Lawrence Valley, the limitless reaches of our Great Lakes? We all feel the call of the north, a window which opens out on the infinite, on the potential, on the future.
>
> – Pierre Elliott Trudeau, *A Time for Action*

It was Prime Minister Pierre Trudeau, the great lightning rod for Canadian pride, affection, anger, and resentment, who ignited and oversaw the process of constitutional reform that stretched from 1968 to 1982. Trudeau is remembered for many accomplishments (and missteps), but none larger than the repatriation of Canada's constitution and the enactment of the *Canadian Charter of Rights and Freedoms.*

Trudeau understood that foreign control of the constitution was a long-standing burr in Canada's side. In 1926, the British government's Balfour Declaration offered full political autonomy to the self-governing dominions of its empire. In hindsight, former prime minister Jean Chrétien observed that no one at that time would have expected Canada to be among the last British colonies to achieve complete legal independence.[1] Modest steps toward independent nationhood were taken from time to time. For example, in 1931, the *Statute of Westminster* removed the British Parliament's legislative authority over Canada (and other dominions including Australia and New Zealand). The sole remaining exception to Canada's ability to write its own laws after 1931 involved the constitution, which could be amended only by the body that enacted it, the Parliament of the United Kingdom. In another step toward complete independence, the ability to appeal decisions from the Supreme Court of Canada to the UK's Judicial Committee of the Privy Council ended in 1949.

Many prime ministers attempted to repatriate the constitution and end Canada's quasi-colonial status. King (1927), Bennett (1931), St. Laurent (1950), Diefenbaker (1960), and Pearson (1964) all convened federal-provincial conferences in pursuit of constitutional reform. All failed. A major stumbling block was the inability of federal and provincial governments to agree on a formula for future constitutional amendments.

Trudeau's ambitious goal, which he first articulated in the late 1960s, was not only to repatriate the *British North America Act, 1867* (to free the constitution from British control and achieve full legal independence), but also to establish constitutional recognition of fundamental human rights and freedoms. The latter goal represented a departure from British tradition, in that the UK had never created a written bill of rights or given courts the authority to judicially review government decisions that allegedly violated human rights.

Before entering politics, Trudeau advocated the urgent need to protect a broad suite of human rights. In an article titled "Economic Rights," which he wrote as a law professor at the Université de Montréal in 1962, he argued that "civil rights were only one aspect of human rights" and that society could ill afford to neglect other rights. He concluded, "If this society does not evolve an entirely new set of values ... it is vain to hope that Canada will ever reach freedom from fear and freedom from want. Under such circumstances, any claim by lawyers that they have done their bit by upholding civil liberties will be dismissed as a hollow mockery."[2]

Once Trudeau became the minister of justice in 1967, his views on rights apparently began to shift. He suggested that though a constitutional guarantee of economic rights was desirable and "should be an ultimate objective of Canada," it "might take considerable time to reach agreement on the rights to be guaranteed."[3] Trudeau also argued that "economic rights could not be constitutionally secured because they could not be judicially enforced."[4] The alleged lack of enforceability was one of the main rationales advanced by Trudeau's constitutional advisor, Barry Strayer, for excluding social and economic rights from the constitution.[5] On this basis, Trudeau concluded that it was "advisable not to attempt to include economic rights in the constitutional bill of rights at this time."[6]

In 1968, the Liberal government, under Prime Minister Lester B. Pearson, released a discussion paper proposing a new charter of rights, which was limited to civil and political rights. The timing appeared to be propitious, as the UN declared 1968 as International Human Rights Year. In 1969, Ottawa released a report that stated, "If we can indeed agree on those rights and freedoms we deem essential to all Canadians, we should be prepared to give them special legal protection. Expressed in a constitutional document they would be both a statement of common purpose for, and a limitation on, all governments within Canada."[7]

Seven first ministers' meetings on constitutional change were held between 1968 and 1971. Environmental concerns were a key agenda item at several of these meetings, although the concept of a right to a healthy environment does not appear to have been discussed.[8] The main environmental topic involved jurisdiction, and not surprisingly there were differences of opinion. The federal government argued that it should have the jurisdiction to address international and inter-provincial pollution in situations where the provinces had failed to solve the problem.[9] Some provincial premiers were supportive of Ottawa's proposal, whereas others suggested that more time was required to gain experience in dealing with pollution, and others recommended an exclusive division of powers between federal and provincial governments. In the short term, conflicting opinions and other priorities meant that the environment was not included in the consensus package of constitutional reforms called the Victoria Charter (which ultimately failed). In the longer term, disagreements about jurisdiction contributed to an ongoing reluctance to address environmental concerns in future constitutional talks.

Although it is conventional wisdom that all provinces formed a united front opposing federal involvement in environmental protection, this is a misconception. Six provinces – Saskatchewan, Manitoba, New Brunswick, Nova Scotia, Prince Edward Island, and Newfoundland – supported a significant federal role.[10] In 1970, Saskatchewan's attorney general, D.V. Heald, proposed constitutional amendments that would have strengthened Ottawa's environmental jurisdiction.[11] The four larger provinces were resistant, yet all provinces agreed on the need for minimum national standards, fearing unfair competition from provinces or regions that might otherwise lower the bar. Jim MacNeill, who worked on constitutional issues and environmental management in the Privy Council Office at the time, was surprised by the level of agreement.[12] At a first ministers' meeting in September 1970, Prime Minister Trudeau gave a compelling speech about the importance of clarifying the federal government's constitutional responsibility to protect the Canadian environment.[13]

Trudeau and the Environment

Pierre Trudeau's interest in environmental policy also predated his political career. In 1961, he attended the watershed Resources for Tomorrow conference in Montreal, along with hundreds of experts in all aspects of resource management. The growing problem of pollution was a prominent theme at the conference, and as a participant on a panel discussing jurisdictional challenges, Trudeau spoke of the need for all governments to contribute to solutions.[14] Yet throughout the 1960s, Ottawa consistently denied that environmental protection was its responsibility. After becoming prime minister,

Trudeau pointed at the constitution as a major obstacle blocking progress in addressing pollution.[15] The Progressive Conservatives and New Democrats, in opposition, argued that either the federal government had jurisdiction to protect the environment or it should seek constitutional amendments giving it such jurisdiction.[16] For example, NDP MP Randolph Harding asserted that "it is the duty of this government, which has hidden behind the gimmick of constitutional issues in order not to accept responsibility for pollution control, to iron out constitutional problems in this field."[17]

As public concern about the environment surged, the Government of Canada was forced to respond. In the Throne Speeches of 1969 and 1970, Trudeau warned of "the threat to our well-being and the well-being of future generations" posed by issues such as resource depletion and the "many-headed hydra" of pollution. Speaking in Australia in 1970, Trudeau said, "If part of our heritage is our wilderness, and if the measure of Canada is the quality of life available to Canadians, then we must act should there be any threat to either. We must act to protect the freshness of our air and the purity of our water, we must act to conserve our living resources. If necessary, we must offer leadership to the world in these respects and withstand the cries of complaining vested interests."[18]

Despite these eloquent words, Trudeau initially opposed the creation of a federal environment department, based on his perception that Ottawa lacked jurisdiction.[19] However, in response to rapidly mounting public concerns about pollution, he changed his mind and presided over the creation of Environment Canada in 1971. He later boasted, inaccurately, that the new agency was "the first ministry of the environment ever set up in Canada, and probably anywhere."[20]

Trudeau oversaw the introduction of a raft of new laws and policies including the *Arctic Waters Pollution Prevention Act, Clean Air Act, Canada Water Act, Environmental Contaminants Act,* and the *Environmental Assessment and Review Process Guidelines Order*. These initiatives "staked out new and untested federal jurisdiction."[21] Trudeau was prime minister when Nahanni National Park was created, and he approved the first comprehensive plan calling for national parks in all thirty-nine of Canada's natural regions.

Trudeau had a genuine and deep-rooted affinity for Canadian nature. He paddled many great Canadian rivers including the Ottawa, Coppermine, and Thelon. Following the Liberals' 1979 election loss to Joe Clark and the Progressive Conservatives, Trudeau took a train to the Rocky Mountains for a holiday with his three sons and also paddled a canoe down the Nahanni River in the Northwest Territories. He described canoeing as a way of finding his bearings, of going "as far away as possible from everyday life, from its complications and from the artificial wants created by civilization."[22] He also went scuba diving in the Atlantic, Pacific, and Arctic Oceans with famed oceanographer Joseph MacInnis. Trudeau was the first Canadian prime minister to tour the Arctic, a journey that "strengthened the image of his intimacy with nature and the Canadian frontier."[23] He spoke passionately about the need for environmental protection and recognized the unique place of the Arctic in Canadian mythology and national identity: "Canada regards herself as responsible to all mankind for the peculiar ecological balance that now exists so precariously in the water, ice and land areas of the Arctic archipelago. We do not doubt for a moment that the rest of the world would find us at fault, and hold us liable, should we fail to ensure adequate protection of that environment from pollution or artificial deterioration."[24]

And yet despite his passion for nature, Trudeau apparently never mentioned the idea of including the right to a healthy environment in the new Canadian constitution. Conversations with several of his advisors and confidantes from that era indicate that the subject "simply never came up" and was "not on our radar screen."[25] It is inaccurate to suggest that the subject never arose, as the next section of this chapter illustrates, but the idea of a constitutional right to a healthy environment never captured Trudeau's imagination. James Raffan, author of *Fire in the Bones*, the best-selling biography of Canadian paddling legend Bill Mason, wrote, "At a policy level, it is difficult to make direct connections between Trudeau's love of canoes and wilderness and his governmental decisions."[26]

Early Proposals for Constitutional Environmental Rights

Trudeau's proposals sparked a tremendous degree of public interest in constitutional reform during the late 1960s and early 1970s. The first proposal calling for inclusion of the right to a clean or healthy environment in Canada's constitution was made in 1969. At a conference hosted by the Science Council of Canada, Noel Lyon of McGill University's Faculty of Law wrote, "I am disturbed by the obsessive interest of those constitutional lawyers who dominate current public discussion with traditional legal and political rights and their apparent unawareness of the need for protection of what I will call the fundamental environmental rights of man."[27] A Special Joint Committee of the Senate and the House of Commons on the Constitution of Canada (the Molgat-MacGuigan Committee) held hearings across Canada. In Vancouver, during the first week of January 1971, the committee turned hundreds of people away from a public meeting.[28] Lyon testified before the committee and recommended that a new constitution recognize environmental rights: "The critical condition of many parts of our environment, and the growing pressures on it resulting from rapid growth of population and technology indicate a need for early recognition in our fundamental law of environmental rights ... We must somehow ensure that we establish a priority for [environmental] rights that is equal to that of the political and legal rights set out in the proposed *Charter of Human Rights*. Otherwise the environment will simply lose by default."[29]

Similar submissions to the Molgat-MacGuigan Committee were made by numerous individuals, including

- Jim Egan, vice-president of the Cowichan-Malahat branch of the Society for Pollution and Environmental Control
- Derrick Mallard, executive director of the Vancouver branch of the Society for Pollution and Environmental Control
- Mary Balf, Thompson Basin Pollution Probe (Kamloops, BC)
- Omar Paquette, speaking for another BC-based environmental group
- and Claire L. McLaughlin, policy chair, Toronto and District Liberal Association.

Egan made an eloquent plea for constitutional recognition of the right to a healthy environment:

> No priority could be more deserving or more urgent than immediate constitutional guarantees of full protection for every aspect of our environment as an irreducible primary right without which all other rights become meaningless – the right of the individual to clean air, uncontaminated water, wholesome nutritious food free of chemical residues and harmful or unproven additives. In addition we feel that if these essential rights be violated, immediate redress through the courts should be available and, further, that all levels of government be held liable in the event that they either contribute to the impairment of air or the environment, or through dereliction of duty, knowingly allow the environment to suffer deterioration.[30]

Balf testified that "a constitutional law which will give to all Canadians freedom from the pollution of their environment is absolutely essential and urgent."[31] Paquette urged "protection of the constitution for the rights of our fellow citizens to conserve our air, our water, and land," stating that "the right to live in a healthy climate is fundamental and requires priority over all others."[32] McLaughlin suggested that a constitutionally protected "Environmental Bill of Rights would guarantee our right to clean air, clean water, a tolerable noise level and recreational opportunities ... Such a Bill of Rights would give individual citizens and conservation groups recourse to stop the destruction of our ecology."[33]

In addition, many experts and citizens advocated before the Molgat-MacGuigan Committee that extensive federal powers to protect the environment ought to be incorporated in the new constitution. The problems of pollution and environmental degradation were discussed by the committee on more than fifty occasions. In its *Final Report*, the committee acknowledged "widespread agreement that jurisdiction over pollution is at present complicated at best and confusing at worst," resulting in annoyed voters and befuddled politicians.[34] Thus, the committee recommended that constitutional amendments provide "an increase in Federal jurisdiction over air and water pollution."[35] Specifically, it urged that control over these forms of pollution be a matter of concurrent jurisdiction between the provinces and Parliament, with Ottawa possessing paramount powers. The committee concluded, "Because pollution control is so urgently needed, we feel that any confusion which exists in constitutional powers should be ended as quickly as possible."[36]

Throughout the 1970s, environmental lawyers in Canada repeatedly called for constitutional changes to recognize that "every person has the right to a healthy and attractive environment."[37] Workshops held at the University of Manitoba in 1971 and 1972 suggested that "some forms of pollution may violate the right to life, liberty, and security of the person in the Canadian Bill of Rights" and concluded that "we need an environmental right which is just as essential to society as freedom of speech, freedom of religion, and freedom of education."[38] In 1974, Franson and Burns wrote that governments had failed to recognize and protect the right to a healthy environment, "probably because the safest course, politically, is usually not to raise controversial issues, but to let them lie dormant."[39] The Canadian Environmental Law Association (CELA) played a leading role in advocating constitutional recognition of environmental rights and responsibilities. A book published by CELA's research arm in 1978 argued that, "like freedom of speech, freedom of religion, and other basic rights, environmental quality should be recognized by law as an inalienable right, for without an environment capable of supporting the human race, all other rights are useless."[40]

Despite the groundswell of public support expressed in testimony before the Molgat-MacGuigan Committee and advocacy by public interest environmental lawyers, the idea of constitutionally entrenching environmental protection never reached critical mass in the same way as Aboriginal rights or women's rights, which after extensive and contentious debates were eventually included in the constitution. As noted earlier, Trudeau and his advisors argued that economic and social rights (and by extension the right to a healthy environment) would not be enforceable and therefore ought not to enjoy constitutional recognition. According to Williams, however, "Many laymen appearing before the Molgat-MacGuigan Committee viewed this approach as excessively legalistic."[41]

Bill C-60, introduced in 1978, was the forerunner of the *Constitution Act, 1982*. An early version of the bill contained a section setting forth the aims of the Canadian federation, which identified "the commitment of all Canadians to the balanced development of the land of their common inheritance and to the preservation of its richness and beauty in trust for themselves and generations to come."[42] This so-called Canada clause reflected deep-seated Canadian values but was deleted due to a lack of consensus among provincial governments.[43]

The Canadian Environmental Law Association made a submission on Bill C-60 to the Special Joint Senate/House of Commons Committee on the Constitution of Canada, recommending a variety of environmental provisions including both procedural and substantive rights to environmental quality. According to CELA, "The new Constitution is the ideal place to firmly entrench a commitment to the individual's right to a clean environment."[44] Other recommendations advanced by CELA included establishing a constitutional duty on governments to protect environmental quality, prevent pollution havens, conduct environmental impact assessments, and provide the public with various procedural rights, including access to government information and the right to participate in decision making. Unfortunately, the report of the 1978 special joint committee (co-chaired by Lamontagne and MacGuigan) contained no references to environmental protection.

Despite CELA's efforts, there was little public discussion of the idea of environmental rights. In one of the few articles written on the topic during the constitutional debates of the late 1970s and early 1980s, Geoff Mains observed that "the constitutional debate that has embroiled Canadians over the past few years has been largely ignored by environmentalists."[45] Mains argued persuasively that from an ecological perspective Bill C-60 "contains little more than dishwater" and called for recognition of the right to a clean environment, plus associated procedural rights.[46]

There was a last-minute attempt to include environmental protection in the new constitution. In 1981, Diana Davidson, president of Vancouver People's Law School Society, urged the Special Joint Committee of the Senate and the House of Commons on the Constitution of Canada (the Hays-Joyal Committee) to recognize environmental rights, stating that "no issue more fundamentally underlies the nature of a national compact."[47] Later that year, while carrying out its clause-by-clause review, the committee considered including an explicit reference to a healthy environment under clause 31 of the proposed Constitution Act, 1980 (which became section 36 of the *Constitution Act, 1982*). NDP MP Svend Robinson moved that section 31 be amended to include "fully implementing the *International Covenant on Economic, Social and Cultural Rights* and the goals of a clean and healthy environment and safe and healthy working conditions."[48] Robinson argued, "Surely in these days of acid rain and threats to our environment in a number of different sectors, we should reaffirm our commitment to the concept of a clean and healthy environment."[49] Unfortunately, Jean Chrétien, the minister of justice at the time, described Robinson's proposed amendment as "high-sounding rhetoric" and added, "I am waiting soon for an amendment to inscribe in the constitution the apple pie and the recipe of my Aunt Berthe, and I do think that we cannot put everything [in] there."[50] Only two MPs voted in favour of the motion (Robinson and his NDP colleague Lorne Nystrom), whereas all twenty-two Liberal and Conservative MPs and senators opposed it.[51]

In parliamentary debates about the final version of the new constitution in 1981, NDP MP Derek Blackburn expressed disappointment that it "did not guarantee to all Canadians the right to live and work in a safe and healthy environment. This challenge still lies ahead. Those of us in this chamber who have worked hard to fight against pollution and polluters, to make our lakes and rivers clean and productive, to make the air we breathe clean and pure, the workplace safe and healthy, will continue our struggle until we win. And win we will."[52]

Ultimately, despite Trudeau's affinity for nature, despite the efforts of a small but dedicated band of environmentalists, and despite innovative provisions in the new constitutions of other nations, Canada's political leaders ignored the idea of a right to a healthy environment. Indeed, the environment was completely left out of the *Constitution Act, 1982,* including the *Charter.* John Swaigen, one of Canada's leading environmental lawyers since the early 1970s, co-authored CELA's constitutional submission and, in the midst of the *Charter* debates, edited a book called *Environmental Rights in Canada.* Looking back at this era, Swaigen concluded that the concept of a right to a healthy environment was simply "too far out" to gain traction with the political leaders of the day.[53] Roy Romanow, former Saskatchewan premier and one of the architects of the constitutional agreement hammered out in 1981, explained that the oversight occurred because politicians were struggling to pare down an unworkable range of issues to the bare essentials, provinces were concerned about maintaining control over natural resources, and no political insiders were championing the environmental cause.[54]

Jim MacNeill explained that Trudeau's interest in clarifying environmental responsibilities in the constitution, so clearly articulated in his speech to first ministers in September 1970, was overshadowed by the ensuing October Crisis in Quebec. Thus, the Victoria Charter (1971), Trudeau's first attempt at repatriating the constitution, did not address environmental matters. It was rejected by Quebec. By the time constitutional negotiations returned to the front burner in the late 1970s and early 1980s, economic and political circumstances had changed dramatically. The 1973 and 1979 oil crises had caused economic havoc and contributed to a downturn in public concern about environmental problems. The opposition of provincial governments to federal intervention in environmental management had increased significantly, led by both Quebec and the Western provinces. These changes meant that the stars were not aligned for incorporating environmental rights and responsibilities in the new constitution.

Quebec refused to formally recognize the new constitution, although its position does not affect the legal applicability of the constitution or the *Charter.* More importantly, Quebec's dissatisfaction led to two controversial and unsuccessful attempts to make substantial changes to the constitution, efforts that ultimately backfired, adding fuel to the fire of Quebec nationalists and casting a chill over future efforts to achieve constitutional reform.

Environmental Rights in the Aftermath of the New Constitution

Ironically, after the repatriation of the constitution and the enactment of the *Charter,* interest surged in constitutional recognition for environmental rights. In 1983, NDP MP Jim Fulton argued in the House of Commons that Canada needed constitutional changes to enable stronger environmental protection.[55] That same year, Dale Gibson, one of Canada's leading constitutional law scholars, advocated the "creation of a constitutional guarantee of environmental quality."[56] According to Gibson, the most likely form of entrenchment relating to the environment that could realistically be expected "would be a vague and sweeping statement akin to constitutional declarations of freedom of speech or rights of privacy: that every citizen has the right to enjoy a reasonable standard of purity in the natural environment."[57] In 1985, the Law Reform Commission of Canada published a comprehensive report called *Crimes against the Environment* in which it proposed adding a new offence to the *Criminal Code* to deter "conduct which seriously compromises a fundamental societal value, that of a safe environment or the right to a reasonable level of environmental quality."[58] This recommendation was never acted upon, although the Supreme Court of Canada later cited the report in endorsing the concept of the right to a healthy environment.[59]

In 1988, in the most detailed analysis of the prospective entrenchment of environmental rights in the Canadian constitution published to date, Gibson proposed inserting three sections into the *Charter*.[60] The first section would establish basic rights to a healthy environment, to its use, and to its preservation; define the term "environment"; and list the purposes intended to be served by protecting the environment. The second section would impose an obligation on governments to make and enforce laws implementing these rights. The third section would clarify that citizens could go to court when governments failed to fulfill their environmental responsibilities. Gibson's proposals were published in the midst of the next era of constitutional debates in Canada, presided over by Prime Minister Mulroney.

Gibson's proposed amendments to the *Charter* were as follows:

> 15.1(1) Right to Beneficial Environment
> Everyone has the right to a beneficial environment, and to enjoy its use for recreational, aesthetic, historical, cultural, scientific and economic purposes, to the extent reasonably consistent with:
>
> (a) the equivalent rights of others;
> (b) the health and safety of others; and
> (c) the preservation of a beneficial environment in accordance with subsection (2).
>
> (2) Everyone has a right to the preservation of a beneficial environment, so as to ensure its future enjoyment for the uses set out in subsection (1).

(3) For the purposes of this section, "environment" includes land, water, air and space, and the living things that inhabit them, as well as artificial structures and spaces that are beneficial to humans or to other components of the environment.

15.2(1) Duty to Make and Enforce Environmental Laws
The Parliament and Government of Canada, and the Legislatures and Governments of the Provinces have the duty, within their respective areas of jurisdiction, to make and enforce laws and programs for the implementation of the rights set out in section 15.1.

(2) Content of Laws
The laws and programs referred to in subsection (1) shall include, without restricting the generality thereof:

(a) the creation and maintenance of an environmental protection agency for each jurisdiction, responsible for determining minimum standards of environmental quality and preservation appropriate for each aspect of the environment, in each area of the jurisdiction, and to vary such standards, partially or wholly, temporarily or permanently, where the agency deems such variation to be advisable;
(b) the creation of effective measures to enforce such minimum standards within the jurisdiction;
(c) the right of everyone resident within the jurisdiction to be informed by the environmental protection agency, by means of appropriate public notice, of all pending determinations or variation of such minimum standards and allowing a reasonable time before each determination or variation is decided upon by the agency; and
(d) the right of everyone resident within the jurisdiction to make representations of fact, law, or policy to the environmental protection agency about any determination or variation of such minimum standards.

15.3 Judicial Review
After this section and sections 15.1 and 15.2 have been in force for more than one year, everyone has the right to apply under subsection 24(1) to a court of competent jurisdiction for a declaration that the Parliament or the Government of Canada, or the Legislature or

Government of a province, has failed to fulfill some or all of the duties imposed by section 15.2.

The Mulroney Era

Because Quebec refused to endorse the new constitution, constitutional debates were still percolating in 1984 when Brian Mulroney became prime minister. At the same time, the environmental concerns of the Canadian public were increasing rapidly. Although not regarded as a nature-lover or outdoorsman in the same way as Trudeau, Mulroney did build a relatively strong record on the environmental file, leading to his surprising selection as Canada's Greenest Prime Minister by a panel of environmental experts in 2003. He oversaw the creation of six new national parks, the passage of Canada's first comprehensive pollution law (the *Canadian Environmental Protection Act*), and the creation of an ambitious multi-billion-dollar Green Plan that the head of the UN Environment Programme called a model for the world. Under Mulroney, Canada not only took a number of important steps to clean up its own act, but became an outspoken advocate for environmental protection at the international level. Mulroney used his charm to coax the recalcitrant American government to act on acid rain, presided over the first international conference on climate change, and hosted the negotiations that led to the successful *Montreal Protocol on Substances That Deplete the Ozone Layer*. Under his leadership, Canada was the first industrialized nation to ratify the *UN Convention on Biological Diversity* and the *UN Framework Convention on Climate Change* in 1992. Despite his green bona fides, when he turned his attention to revising the constitution, Mulroney made no effort to include environmental rights or responsibilities.

The Meech Lake Accord

In 1987, in an effort to "bring Quebec back into the constitutional family," all ten premiers and Prime Minister Mulroney reached agreement on a package of reforms including recognition of Quebec as a distinct society. The Meech Lake Accord proposed shifting extensive powers from Ottawa to provincial governments. Some lawyers expressed their belief that a constitutional amendment recognizing environmental rights was a realistic possibility.[61] The year 1987 also marked the publication of the landmark report of the World Commission on Environment and Development (Brundtland Commission) called *Our Common Future*, which popularized the concept of sustainable development. The Brundtland Commission urged all countries to revise their legal systems to meet environmental challenges and highlighted the need for constitutional recognition of the right to a healthy environment and the reciprocal responsibility of government.[62] Canada enthusiastically endorsed the commission's report, yet there was no mention of the environment in the Meech Lake Accord.[63]

In 1988, environmental lawyer William Andrews bemoaned the fact that "despite the Brundtland Commission's endorsement of environmental rights, there has been [no] noticeable pressure to amend the *Charter* to incorporate environmental rights."[64] In 1989, NDP MP Jim Fulton repeated his earlier call for constitutional changes to protect Canada's environment.[65] In 1990, when the provinces of Manitoba and Newfoundland did not approve the Meech Lake Accord within the required period of three years, the proposed constitutional amendments died.

The Charlottetown Accord

Following the failure of Meech Lake, Mulroney doggedly initiated a second round of constitutional negotiations intended to secure Quebec's approval of the *Constitution Act, 1982*. Again efforts were made to put the environment on the agenda. In 1990, the Canadian Bar Association recommended that "the Government of Canada should adopt a long-term strategy to entrench the right to a healthy environment in the Canadian Constitution. In the interim it should enact a statute enunciating the right of every Canadian to a healthy environment. No statute should be enacted that is inconsistent with that right."[66]

In part, the Canadian Bar Association's recommendation was based on the "growing acceptance in international law of environmental quality as a fundamental human right."[67] In Parliament, NDP MP Jim Fulton called on the government to include an "environmental Charter of rights" as part of its Green Plan.[68] Fulton's call was repeated by NDP leader Audrey McLaughlin.[69] In 1991, Len Taylor, an NDP MP from Saskatchewan, brought a motion that "the government should establish a Bill of Environmental Rights to empower Canadians to fight polluters and guarantee all Canadians the right to live in a healthy environment."[70] Taylor urged the Mulroney government to include environmental rights in the proposed package of constitutional amendments. His speech was followed by congratulations from Liberal MP and future prime minister Paul Martin, who expressed full support for an environmental bill of rights (although it is unclear whether Martin was referring to a constitutional or legislative bill of rights).[71] The response from Progressive

Conservative MP Lise Bourgault, on behalf of the Mulroney government, was that an environmental bill of rights was unnecessary and could "prevent the implementation of an industrial project designed to provide employment for fear that a bee will not be gathering nectar."[72] The Canadian Environmental Law Association and Pollution Probe continued to urge that the *Charter of Rights and Freedoms* be amended to include a right to a healthful environment.[73] Also in 1991, Ontario's Ministry of the Attorney General undertook a study that looked at constitutions in other countries, found twenty-five that enshrined the right to a healthy environment, and concluded that the entrenchment of such a provision could no longer be considered a novel idea.[74]

In 1991, Ottawa's tepid response to growing calls for constitutional entrenchment of environmental rights and responsibilities was to suggest enshrining recognition of Canadians' environmental values in a proposed Canada clause: "The Government of Canada proposes ... a Canada clause that acknowledges ... a commitment to the objective of sustainable development in recognition of the importance of the land, the air and the water and our responsibility to preserve and protect the environment for future generations."[75] The clause was intended to offer symbolic and educational value but to have little or no legal effect. Further public consultation took place through the Citizens' Forum on Canada's Future (known as the Spicer Commission), another Special Joint Committee of the House of Commons and the Senate on a Renewed Canada (the Beaudoin-Dobbie Committee), and discussions with Aboriginal peoples. The report of the Citizens' Forum, which noted that "the importance of the environment is a core value in all regions of Canada and an essential element of Canadian society," concluded that "Canada's unspoiled natural beauty is a matter of great importance [and] is threatened by inadequate attention to protecting our environment."[76] The Canadian Environmental Law Association and Pollution Probe put forward a comprehensive proposal for incorporating the environment into the constitution through recognition of clearly articulated individual rights and government responsibilities.[77] The West Coast Environmental Law Association published a similar proposal.[78] Civil society created a draft social charter that included the right to a healthy environment.[79]

The Beaudoin-Dobbie Committee recommended a different Canada clause, including the phrase "we pledge to honourably discharge our responsibility to our children, so that they may do the same for their own, of ensuring their prosperity and the integrity of their environment," or alternatively "Canada is committed to the responsible stewardship of its land, water, resources, and environment."[80] Beaudoin-Dobbie also recommended a new social covenant including commitments to universal health care, adequate social services, high-quality education, labour rights, and the integrity of the environment, although these general pledges were framed as unenforceable goals rather than enforceable rights. The reference to the environment was phrased as a commitment to "protecting and preserving the integrity of the environment in an economically sustainable manner."[81] The modest environmental provisions recommended by the Beaudoin-Dobbie Committee were panned by environmental lawyers as inadequate.[82] Elaine Hughes wrote that "an examination of the federal constitutional proposals reveals little by way of environmental protection and much that is environmentally dangerous," such as giving the provinces exclusive jurisdiction over tourism, mining, forestry, recreation, housing, and municipal affairs, as well as imposing limits on the federal spending power.[83] Hughes concluded that the "Canada clause has all the substance of Santa Claus."[84]

The ensuing Charlottetown Accord recommended that a section be added to the constitution outlining the commitment of the governments, Parliament, and the legislatures to the preservation and development of Canada's social and economic union. This new provision would contain a series of policy objectives related to the social union, including "protecting, preserving and sustaining the integrity of the environment for present and future generations." With respect to the economic union, one of the policy objectives was "ensuring sustainable and equitable development."[85] These objectives were intended to be non-justiciable, meaning that citizens would be unable to hold governments accountable for perceived violations through recourse to the courts. Another new section of the constitution, delineating fundamental Canadian values, made no reference to the environment. Overall, the environmental provisions in the Charlottetown Accord were very weak and fell far short of the recommendations advanced by the Canadian Bar Association and Canadian Environmental Law Association.[86] As environmental lawyers Barbara Rutherford and Paul Muldoon concluded, "Such inattention to the environment is inexcusable in a modern constitution. It represents not only a failure to respect the evident concerns of Canadian citizens and the expressed commitments of Canadian governments, but also a failure to recognize the interdependence of economy and environment."[87]

In referendums held in October 1992 (one national and one in Quebec), the Charlottetown Accord was rejected. Quebec nationalists portrayed the results as a slap in the face to Quebec, spurring the 1995 referendum in which

Quebecers narrowly rejected a proposal to separate from Canada. Since that time, the notion of comprehensive constitutional reform has been widely considered anathema by both the public and politicians.

In an interesting twist, though both the Meech Lake and Charlottetown Accords failed to include recognition of the right to a healthy environment, Prime Minister Mulroney was advocating for the adoption of this right at the international level. With Mulroney at the helm, Canada signed the 1989 *Hague Declaration on the Environment* following an international environmental conference. The *Hague Declaration* recognized "the right to live in dignity in a viable global environment, and the consequent duty of the community of nations vis-à-vis present and future generations to do all that can be done to preserve the quality of the environment."[88] However, it was not legally binding and was signed by only twenty-three other nations.[89] Mulroney continued to seek a legally binding global agreement that included an enforceable right to live in a healthy environment. During preparations for the 1992 Earth Summit in Rio de Janeiro, Canada lobbied unsuccessfully for the incorporation of the following environmental rights provision in the draft text that later became the *Rio Declaration:* "All persons have the right to live in an environment capable of assuring his [sic] health and well-being."[90]

Mulroney said in a speech at Rio, "What remains is for governments to provide the leadership the world so desperately needs. Let us find that will and marshal that leadership to the task at hand on behalf of the five billion people we represent. Our children, the Rio generation, will be our judges and our beneficiaries."[91] Despite Mulroney's efforts, nations agreed only to the weakly worded, non-binding *Rio Declaration,* which laid out twenty-seven principles, not including the explicit right to a healthy environment proposed by Canada. Mulroney continued to urge the international community to adopt a true Earth Charter of environmental rights and responsibilities with 1995, the fiftieth anniversary of the founding of the United Nations, as the target completion date.[92] Those international efforts were also unsuccessful.

Legislating the Right to a Healthy Environment

> What the Canadian people want is an environmental bill of rights, a bill of rights which will recognize the right of Canadians to a clean and safe environment, and one which will have sufficient teeth.
>
> – Jim Manly, *House of Commons Debates*

Following the failures of the Meech Lake and Charlottetown Accords, advocates, scholars, and politicians shifted their attention to legislated environmental rights.[93] Environmental lawyer Paul Muldoon observed that because chances of a constitutional amendment were slim and courts not yet inclined to read the right to a healthy environment into existing *Charter* provisions (as implicit in the right to life, liberty, and security of the person), the "next best solution" would be the enactment of legislated environmental bills of rights by both federal and provincial governments.[94]

There have been modest successes in securing legislative recognition of the right to a healthy environment at the provincial and territorial level. Although the difference may not be immediately apparent, constitutional and legislated environmental rights are like Siberian tigers and Siamese cats – related, but with dramatically different degrees of strength. A constitution is the supreme law of a nation, meaning that all other laws and regulations must be consistent with it or face being struck down. Ordinary legislation, in contrast, does not override other laws. As well, constitutions are better known to citizens, as they express a society's most cherished values and represent a road map toward a desired future. In contrast, the dreary details of legislation are unknown to the majority of people. Thus, a constitutional right to a healthy environment is likely to have far greater legal, symbolic, and practical importance than a legislated right. Nevertheless, some experts contend that a legislated bill of environmental rights could "promote the fulfillment of environmental obligations, and to help maintain and strengthen our regime of environmental protection in Canada."[95] Legislated environmental rights and responsibilities could serve as stepping-stones to future constitutional change and could also flesh out the details of the constitutional right.

As early as the 1970s, academics and activists advanced proposals for federal and provincial legislation granting environmental rights to citizens. For example, proposals for legislative recognition of the right to a healthy environment were included in the first two editions of the book *Environment on Trial*. Considered a pioneer in the field of Canadian environmental law, the book outlined the essential components of an environmental bill of rights, including the right to a healthy environment and a host of other procedural and administrative features such as access to information, public participation in standard-setting, the right to bring a class action, the right to judicially review administrative decisions, and the appointment of an environmental ombudsman.[96] It is interesting that many of the procedural proposals set forth in *Environment on Trial* have been incorporated into

Canadian law in one way or another. The substantive right to a healthy environment remains the critical missing link. Similarly, in a 1974 law review article, Franson and Burns recommended that "legislation should be enacted, by the provincial and federal governments, recognizing the right of Canadians to a clean, healthful, and aesthetically pleasing environment."[97]

In 1981, Liberal MP Charles Caccia brought a private member's motion for a federal environmental bill of rights.[98] Members of all parties expressed support for the motion, including then environment minister John Roberts (Liberal) and future environment minister Tom McMillan (Progressive Conservative). Nevertheless, Caccia's motion went nowhere, like most efforts advanced by backbenchers in Canada's parliamentary system. McMillan voiced regrets that the Liberal government did not include environmental rights in its constitutional reform package.[99] The next day, he introduced a motion calling on Environment Minister Roberts to "explain fully to the House why the government's bill of rights [the *Charter*], while addressing almost every other subject under the sun, contains not a single reference to environmental rights."[100]

Despite subsequently serving as Canada's environment minister (1983-84), Charles Caccia failed to introduce the environmental bill of rights that he had called for as a backbencher, although he did commission a study on the subject from the Canadian Environmental Law Research Foundation.[101] In 1985, as an opposition MP, Caccia promised to introduce a private member's bill that would declare the right to a healthy environment as a constitutional right of every Canadian.[102] No such bill was ever introduced.

In 1986, Prime Minister Mulroney's Progressive Conservatives promised to enact a comprehensive new law called the *Canadian Environmental Protection Act*. Environment Minister Tom McMillan claimed it would be the toughest pollution legislation in the Western world and would constitute Canada's first environmental bill of rights.[103] A government report stated that the new law's preamble would acknowledge the right of Canadians to a healthy environment and pledged that Ottawa would take a leadership role in establishing national standards for environmental quality.[104] Public workshops held by Environment Canada reached consensus on including the right to a healthy environment in the new law.[105]

When the Progressive Conservatives introduced Bill C-74, the *Canadian Environmental Protection Act (CEPA)*, in 1987, it failed to include a bill of rights. At least a dozen opposition MPs decried this omission and expressed support for amending Bill C-74 to incorporate an environmental bill of rights.[106] According to the Opposition, the minister of environment had "promised an environmental bill of rights and instead delivered some elegant prose in the preamble which really has no legal status at all."[107] NDP MP Nelson Riis asserted that the overwhelming majority of Canadians wanted an environmental bill of rights. Riis said, "We all agree that Canadians have the right to a healthy environment. If there is any country in the world that is in a position to provide that, it must be Canada."[108]

However, calls to include an environmental bill of rights in the new law were rejected by Environment Minister Tom McMillan, who warned that it would be unwise to endorse "the principle of an environmental bill of rights that simply takes a whole area of public policy, puts it in the laps of the courts, and tells the judiciary to sort it out."[109] When the *Canadian Environmental Protection Act* was eventually enacted, in 1988, it included no environmental bill of rights but only very limited procedural rights to request investigations and initiate lawsuits. In an interesting twist, the federal Department of Justice apparently advised Minister McMillan that environmental rights "would be ineffective without constitutional status."[110]

Tom McMillan's flip-flop on the desirability of environmental rights was dramatic. In response to Charles Caccia's environmental bill of rights motion in 1981, McMillan had stated that "I think we do indeed need a bill of environmental rights which, among other things, would state clearly and explicitly that the citizen has the right to a healthy environment, that government has an obligation to protect the environment ... and that government's first priority in accepting or rejecting any proposal must be the protection of the public interest as far as environmental matters are concerned."[111] McMillan outlined a detailed vision of an environmental bill of rights, including

- application to both levels of government
- paramountcy of the right to a healthy environment over other legislation
- reduced discretion in environmental laws (requiring, rather than permitting, the government to act)
- standing for citizens to defend the environment before tribunals and courts
- mandatory environmental impact assessments, including public hearings
- full access to environmental information
- public participation in setting environmental standards
- right to pursue class actions for environmental damage

- an environmental ombudsperson
- and placing the burden of proof on polluters and manufacturers to demonstrate that their actions or products do not harm the environment.[112]

Yet not one of these provisions was included in *CEPA* when McMillan introduced it and presided over its enactment.

As Charles Caccia stated in 1988, referring to the evolution of *CEPA*, "This legislation has a history of retreats, contradictions, and flip-flops."[113] Tom McMillan was an outspoken advocate of an environmental bill of rights, and then an opponent. In 1988, after listening to a long speech by Caccia on the flaws of Bill C-74, Lynn McDonald, an NDP MP, pointed out that he should have introduced an environmental bill of rights when he was minister of the environment.[114]

Despite the failure to include an environmental bill of rights in *CEPA*, the concept continued to have champions. While in opposition during the early 1990s, the federal Liberal Party promised to introduce an environmental bill of rights that would guarantee citizens the right to a healthy environment, the opportunity to participate in decision making, and the power to use the courts to ensure that federal environmental laws were obeyed and enforced.[115] In a document authored by future prime minister Paul Martin, the Liberal Party stated, "As we reform the economy from an environmental perspective, so must we do for the legal system. At present, the legal system in Canada discourages citizens from bringing lawsuits in the public interest against polluters to make them accountable for the damages they cause. This can be remedied by legislating an Environmental Bill of Rights that entitles Canadians to a healthy environment by guaranteeing: the right to use courts to ensure that federal environmental laws are properly obeyed and enforced; and the right to participate fully in the federal government's environmental decision-making."[116]

In 1993, Liberal MP Ethel Blondin put forward a motion urging the government to "develop a comprehensive environmental Charter of rights."[117] *Creating Opportunity: The Liberal Plan for Canada*, the Liberal Party policy platform for the federal election released later in 1993, recognized that "individual Canadians are far ahead of their governments in their desire for environmental protection ... A new Liberal government will build on this public awareness and give individuals new tools to protect the environment and to participate in environmental decision-making."[118] The document endorsed the proposal for a legal right to sue those breaking environmental laws.

The Liberal promises regarding substantive and procedural environmental rights were never fulfilled and were not reiterated in subsequent Liberal election platforms. In 1995, the House of Commons Standing Committee on Environment and Sustainable Development recommended that "the Government of Canada develop comprehensive federal legislation respecting the environmental rights of Canadians and Canadian workers."[119] *CEPA* underwent a mandatory review process between 1993 and 1999. Although the revised *Canadian Environmental Protection Act, 1999*, retains several ineffective procedural rights (involving requests for investigations and prosecutions), it remains silent on substantive environmental rights. Environmental laws subsequently enacted or amended by the Liberals failed to address the inability of Canadian citizens to ensure that environmental laws were effectively enforced.[120]

Recently before Parliament was Bill C-469, the *Canadian Environmental Bill of Rights*, which included explicit recognition of the right to a healthy environment.[121] The bill was drafted by lawyers from Ecojustice on behalf of Friends of the Earth and the Sierra Club of Canada in 2008 and introduced by NDP MP Linda Duncan as a private member's bill in 2009. The bill set out five primary purposes:

- safeguarding the right of present and future generations of Canadians to a healthy and ecologically balanced environment
- confirming that Ottawa has a public trust duty to protect the environment
- ensuring all Canadians have access to environmental information, effective mechanisms for participating in environmental decision making, and access to justice
- providing legal protection for environmental whistle-blowers (employees who act to protect the environment and may be subject to reprisals by their employer)
- enhancing public confidence in the implementation of environmental law.

At the heart of the *Canadian Environmental Bill of Rights* was recognition of the right to live in a healthy and ecologically balanced environment. The majority of the bill consisted of procedural tools designed to fulfill this right, mandating the federal government to make environmental information available in a reasonable, timely, and affordable fashion (section 10) and to ensure opportunities for effective, timely, and informed public participation in decision making related to laws, regulations, and policies (sections 11-12). Bill C-469 contained a suite of provisions designed to increase the enforcement of Canadian environmental laws by authorizing concerned citizens, NGOs, and communities to

- apply to the commissioner of environment and sustainable development asking the responsible minister to conduct a review of existing or proposed laws, regulations, and policies in order to protect the environment (section 13)
- request investigations into potential violations of environmental law (sections 14-15)
- file environmental protection lawsuits against the federal government for violating the right to a healthy environment, failing to enforce an environmental law, or failing to protect the public trust (sections 16-21)
- and file a civil lawsuit against anyone (individual, business, or government) who violated a federal environmental law or regulation (section 23).

Bill C-469 also required the auditor general to examine all proposed laws and regulations to determine whether they were consistent with its provisions. Finally, the bill would have amended the *Canadian Bill of Rights* to include the right to a healthy and ecologically balanced environment. The *Canadian Bill of Rights* is a law passed by the Diefenbaker government in 1960 and should not be confused with the *Charter of Rights and Freedoms*, which has constitutional status. The *Canadian Bill of Rights* is widely regarded as having little influence on the fulfillment of human rights in Canada, although a case can be made that it elevated the public profile of human rights and served as a stepping-stone to the eventual enactment of the *Charter*.

The main strengths of the *Canadian Environmental Bill of Rights* were its recognition of the right to live in a healthy environment, democracy-enhancing procedural rights – giving citizens a greater role in the environmental decisions that affect their lives – and its potential to improve environmental enforcement.[122] It represented a potentially important step toward accountability and making Parliament's environmental laws more effective. Despite its strengths, however, a legislative *Canadian Environmental Bill of Rights* would be substantially weaker – both legally and in terms of reflecting Canadian values – than a constitutionally entrenched counterpart. Unlike the constitution, the *Canadian Environmental Bill of Rights* would not override other legislation; nor would it apply to provincial, territorial, municipal, or Aboriginal governments. One of its key limitations was that it applied primarily to federal decisions, federally regulated projects, and federal lands and waters. However, it represented a possible milepost on the road to constitutional recognition of the right to a healthy environment and could have spurred the enactment of similar laws at the provincial level.

In 2010, with opposition parties out-voting the government, the *Canadian Environmental Bill of Rights* passed second reading and was referred to the House of Commons Standing Committee on Environment and Sustainable Development for review. After hearing from many expert witnesses, the committee slightly modified Bill C-469 and returned it to the House for third reading in February 2011. However, the bill died on the order paper when Parliament was dissolved for the election in May 2011. The *Canadian Environmental Bill of Rights* would have to be reintroduced at first reading in a future Parliament.

The Right to a Healthy Environment at the Provincial/ Territorial Level

In Quebec, Ontario, the Yukon, the Northwest Territories, and Nunavut, citizens enjoy limited environmental rights set forth in legislation:

- Quebec included the right in its *Environmental Quality Act* in 1978 and more recently in its provincial *Charter of Human Rights and Freedoms* (2006).
- Ontario passed the *Environmental Bill of Rights* in 1993.
- The Yukon included the right in the *Environment Act* in 1991.
- The NWT passed its *Environmental Rights Act* in 1988.
- Nunavut adopted all the NWT's legislation, including the *Environmental Rights Act*, when it became a territory in 1999.

None of these laws deal with substantive rights to clean air, clean water, or a healthy environment. Instead, they focus on a narrow range of procedural rights, such as the right of access to information, to be notified of certain regulatory changes, and to request investigations.

Unsuccessful attempts to legislate environmental rights have occurred in British Columbia, Alberta, and Saskatchewan. The New Democratic Party introduced the earliest proposal for a provincial bill of environmental rights in the BC legislature in 1971.[123] It was never enacted; nor was a similar proposal from the BC Social Credit Party in 1973 or a more comprehensive version introduced by the NDP in 1994.[124] The 1994 environmental bill of rights proposed by BC's NDP government included the following provisions:

> 30(1). Every resident of British Columbia has the right to a healthy environment and a right to protect the environment and the public trust from any adverse effects by any legal means. (2). The Government of British Columbia has a duty, as trustee, to conserve and protect the environment of British Columbia.

The bill was dropped because BC's powerful loggers' union claimed that it would be of "no value to most citizens" but "would be a huge benefit to overzealous green groups who would undoubtedly use it to tie up all kinds of economic activity on the basis of vague and wooly accusations."[125] Alberta (1979) and Saskatchewan (1982, 1992) also considered environmental bills of rights but failed to convert these proposals into law.[126]

Quebec

Quebec, in 1978, was the first province to legislate environmental rights. The specific provision, found in Quebec's *Environmental Quality Act,* states, "Every person has the right to a healthy environment and to its protection, and to the protection of the living species inhabiting it, to the extent provided for by this act and the regulations, orders, approvals, and authorizations issued under any section of this act."[127] Because of its restrictive wording, this provision is generally regarded as having had modest impact.[128] However, it has led to increased public access to the judicial system by eliminating the requirement for a traditional legal interest to gain standing, and at least three dozen cases decided by Quebec courts have mentioned it.[129]

In 2006, Quebec amended its provincial *Charter of Human Rights and Freedoms* to include the right to a healthy environment: "Every person has a right to live in a healthful environment in which biodiversity is preserved, to the extent and according to the standards provided by law."[130] This amendment significantly expanded the scope of environmental rights for Quebec's citizens because it applied to all provincial environmental legislation, not only the *Environmental Quality Act.* Quebec's *Charter of Human Rights and Freedoms* is a quasi-constitutional law in that it requires all legislation passed by the provincial government to be consistent with its provisions. The explicit reference to biodiversity makes it the most eco-centric of the provincial/territorial environmental rights legislation. The law authorizes civil actions for damages and injunctive relief (interim or permanent) for violations of enumerated rights. There have already been a substantial number of cases in which Quebec courts have cited this right to a healthy environment.[131] Sophie Thériault and David Robitaille assert that Quebec's *Charter of Human Rights and Freedoms* requires the provincial government to establish a strong legislative and policy framework for fulfilling this right.[132] However, as provincial legislation it does not have full-fledged constitutional status, unlike the *Canadian Charter of Rights and Freedoms.*

Ontario

In Ontario, the Canadian Environmental Law Association first articulated the need for legislated environmental rights in the early 1970s.[133] A series of provincial environmental bills of rights were introduced by both the Liberals and the NDP, primarily while those parties were in opposition, in 1979, 1980, 1981, 1982, 1987 (twice), 1989, and 1990.[134] Finally, in 1994, Ontario's *Environmental Bill of Rights, 1993 (EBR)* came into force. Its preamble asserts that "the people of Ontario have a right to a healthful environment," and its section 2(1) states that

> The purposes of this Act are,
> (a) to protect, conserve and, where reasonable, restore the integrity of the environment by the means provided in this Act;
> (b) to provide sustainability of the environment by the means provided in this Act; and
> (c) to protect the right to a healthful environment by the means provided in this Act.

The procedural provisions of Ontario's *Environmental Bill of Rights* have produced varying rates of engagement from citizens. Tens of thousands of Ontarians have commented on proposed government actions, standards, or policies.[135] Twenty to thirty requests are made annually for reviews of provincial laws, regulations, or policies, and one in seven is acted upon, although this rate has risen in recent years.[136] Of the ten to fifteen requests made annually for investigations into alleged violations of environmental laws, one in three results in an investigation and enforcement action.[137] Of the ten to twelve applications made each year for leave to appeal environmental or natural resource approvals, roughly 20 percent are granted.[138] On the other hand, in seventeen years there have only been two citizen suits for violations of environmental laws or damage to public resources, two public nuisance lawsuits, and one use of the whistle-blower provision.[139] Ontario's Environmental Review Tribunal has made decisions affirming and applying the right to a healthy environment.[140]

Opinions regarding the effectiveness of the *EBR* are polarized. Environmental lawyer Joseph Castrilli said Ontario "opted for an environmental rights regime in name only."[141] Other lawyers have observed that "the Ontario *Environmental Bill of Rights* is a peculiar and paradoxical piece of legislation. Notwithstanding its title, the *EBR* grants members of the public no explicit substantive environmental rights, and even the procedural rights which the Act provides are subject to very significant limitations."[142]

The *EBR* does have its defenders, with one author suggesting that it is "the most sweeping and complex collection of statutory rights and obligations with respect to government environmental decision-making in any jurisdiction in North America."[143] There is certainly an unprecedented volume of information available through the public registry, including technical details of approvals for specific facilities. The creation of an environmental commissioner of Ontario has contributed to an elevated profile for environmental policy issues. The commissioner believes that the *EBR* makes Ontario a leader in public participation, citizen empowerment, and government accountability.[144] More recently, it was argued that the *EBR* has increased transparency, enabled citizens to meaningfully engage governments, and influenced the outcome of public policy decisions.[145]

Despite the protection provided by the *EBR*, the environmental commissioner of Ontario reported in 1996 that "the ministries are making remarkable changes to environmental safeguards either behind closed doors or with minimal public participation. This is a clear and unacceptable departure from the goals and purposes of the *Environmental Bill of Rights*."[146] In 2004, lawyer Richard Lindgren of the Canadian Environmental Law Association wrote a compelling indictment regarding the first decade of the law's operation:

> While occasional *EBR* "success" stories exist at the local level, there is little or no evidence at the provincial level that the *EBR* has directly led to the conservation of natural resources, protection of biological diversity, or provision of environmental sustainability ... Indeed, the available evidence suggests that despite the existence of the *EBR*, Ontario is still experiencing serious environmental crises, public health concerns, and threats to our quality of life. For example, during the past decade, Ontario has suffered the Walkerton Tragedy, the Plastimet fire, numerous chemical spills, increasing smog alerts, rampant urban sprawl, leaking landfills, energy shortages, climate change impacts, endangered/threatened species of flora and fauna, and intense resource management conflicts over water-takings, for-

estry practices, and aggregate/mining operations. In addition, annual reports from the Commission for Environmental Cooperation have consistently placed Ontario at or near the top of North American jurisdictions with the largest volume of releases of pollutants to air, land and water.[147]

Criticism of the *EBR*'s effectiveness continues to mount.[148] In 2011, the Canadian Environmental Law Association requested a formal review of the *EBR*, with the goal of strengthening the legislation. The environmental commissioner of Ontario concurred with the need to improve the *EBR*, noting in 2011 that an array of problems, such as the failure to post major proposals on the Environmental Registry, "hinder the public's right to exercise their rights under the *EBR*, and point to a lack of respect by the responsible ministries for the legislation and its users."[149]

Yukon

In 1991, the Yukon passed a new *Environment Act* providing, in section 6, that "the people of the Yukon have the right to a healthful natural environment."[150] The natural environment is comprehensively defined, and citizens are provided with legal remedies for breaches of the law. The act imposes public trust obligations on the territorial government, requiring it to protect the environment from impairment and authorizing citizens to file lawsuits if the government fails to fulfill its responsibilities as trustee. The act also establishes a range of procedural rights including whistle-blower protection, the ability to request an investigation, bring a private prosecution, make a complaint, access government information, and request the review of a regulation.[151] The strengths of the act are undermined by its section 9, which provides a plethora of defences, including the fact that a harmful activity was licensed by the territorial or federal government. Few cases have cited the *Environment Act*.[152] A 2010 audit of government performance under the *Environment Act* concluded that the Yukon government had ignored some portions of the act.[153]

Northwest Territories and Nunavut

In 1991, the Legislative Assembly of the Northwest Territories adopted the *Environmental Rights Act*. In its preamble, the act states, "The people of the Northwest Territories have the right to a healthy environment and a right to protect the integrity, biological diversity and productivity of ecosystems in the Northwest Territories."[154] The act allows a resident to bring a court action against any person releasing any contaminant into the environment, enhances access to information, authorizes private prosecutions, enables requests for investigation, and provides whistle-blower protection. When Nunavut was established in 1999, the new territory adopted the existing laws and regulations of the Northwest Territories, meaning that Nunavut has an identical *Environmental Rights Act*. However, these laws have not been used frequently in either territory.

Conclusion

The constitutional right to a healthy environment has never been the subject of a concerted campaign by environmental groups; nor has it ever been championed by a prime minister or other leading political figure. As a result, it has never become a prominent subject of public debate in Canada. As of today, neither the Canadian constitution nor any federal legislation, regulation, policy, or program explicitly recognizes the fundamental human right to live in a healthy environment. Numerous proposals, both constitutional and legislative, have failed since the early 1970s. Prime Ministers Trudeau and Mulroney passed up the opportunity to include substantive environmental provisions in their constitutional reforms, despite broad public support. Politicians have tended to embrace the idea of environmental rights while in opposition and then either sat on their hands while in power or reversed course and actively opposed recognition of these rights.

The consequence is that Canada is a patchwork quilt, where Quebec is the only province that recognizes the right to a healthy environment in its human rights legislation. Quebec, Ontario, and the three territories recognize the right in environmental legislation, whose effectiveness, unfortunately, appears to be limited. Citizens of British Columbia, Alberta, Saskatchewan, Manitoba, New Brunswick, Nova Scotia, Prince Edward Island, and Newfoundland and Labrador have no explicit legally recognized right to live in a healthy environment. The *Canadian Environmental Bill of Rights* (Bill C-469) represented a potential legislative breakthrough but died on the order paper when Parliament was dissolved in 2011.

More than forty years have passed since the idea of entrenching the right to a healthy environment in the constitution was first proposed in Canada. Had Canada endorsed the concept at the time, it would have been at the forefront globally in recognizing this newly emerging human right. Instead, Canada is now an international laggard, as the majority of nations have incorporated environmental rights and responsibilities into their constitutions.

4
Green Constitutions in Other Countries

> The search for wisdom is not to be circumscribed by national boundaries.
>
> – Peter Hogg, *Constitutional Law of Canada*

Unbeknownst to most Canadians, a remarkable shift toward constitutional recognition of the importance of environmental protection has taken place around the world and is ongoing. When Pierre Trudeau began discussing the repatriation of the Canadian constitution in 1968, no constitutions anywhere incorporated the right to live in a healthy environment and only a handful imposed modest environmental responsibilities on governments (such as those of Italy and Madagascar).

However, almost every year since 1971, at least one nation has written or amended its constitution to introduce or strengthen provisions related to environmental protection.* The first broad provisions focusing on the protection of the environment appear in the constitutions of Switzerland (1971), Greece (1975), Papua New Guinea (1975), India (1976), and Portugal (1976). Portugal and Spain (1978) were the first countries to recognize the right to live in a healthy environment. Between 1970 and 1982, the peak years of Canada's constitutional debate, twenty-eight nations – in Europe, Asia, Latin America, and Africa – wrote environmental provisions into their constitutions. Between 1983 and 1992, when further constitutional amendments were a hot topic of discussion in Canada, another forty-three countries enacted constitutional provisions requiring environmental protection.

---

* All of the information on national constitutions in this chapter is from D.R. Boyd, *The Environmental Rights Revolution: A Global Study of Constitutions, Human Rights, and the Environment* (Vancouver: UBC Press, 2012).

The wave of constitutional changes was driven by the end of colonialism in Africa, the end of military dictatorships in Latin America, the end of the communist empire in Eastern Europe, and the ongoing process of constitutional modernization in long-standing democracies, such as Norway and France. In some countries, public pressure caused environmental amendments. For example, in Switzerland in 1971, a petition with more than 100,000 signatures led to a referendum authorizing constitutional changes to ensure a strong federal role in environmental protection. In some countries, political leadership is a driving force, as in France where President Jacques Chirac worked tirelessly from 2001 to 2005 to secure passage of the *Charter for the Environment*.

Today, more than three-quarters of the world's national constitutions (147 out of 193) include explicit references to environmental rights and/or environmental responsibilities (see Appendix A).[1] This includes the majority of nations belonging to the OECD, the Commonwealth, and La Francophonie, all organizations to which Canada belongs. It also includes the majority of nations in Europe, Latin America, Asia-Pacific, Africa, and the Middle East/Central Asia (see Figure 4.1).

The peak year for the incorporation of environmental rights and responsibilities into national constitutions was 1992, with new environmental provisions included in sixteen constitutions in that year alone. Not coincidentally, 1992 was a peak year in terms of global attention to environmental issues, marked by the Earth Summit in Rio, which attracted an unprecedented number of heads of state to an international environmental meeting. And yet the Charlottetown Accord, brokered by political elites and put to the people of Canada that same year, contained only a feeble reference to sustainable development (described in Chapter 3).

Broken down by decade, the incorporation of environmental protection provisions in national constitutions is as follows:

Pre-1970 – 5
1971-79 – 18
1980-89 – 22
1990-99 – 68
2000-09 – 27
2010-12 – 7

A year-by-year breakdown is provided in Table 4.1.

Figure 4.1

Nations with environmental protection provisions in their constitutions

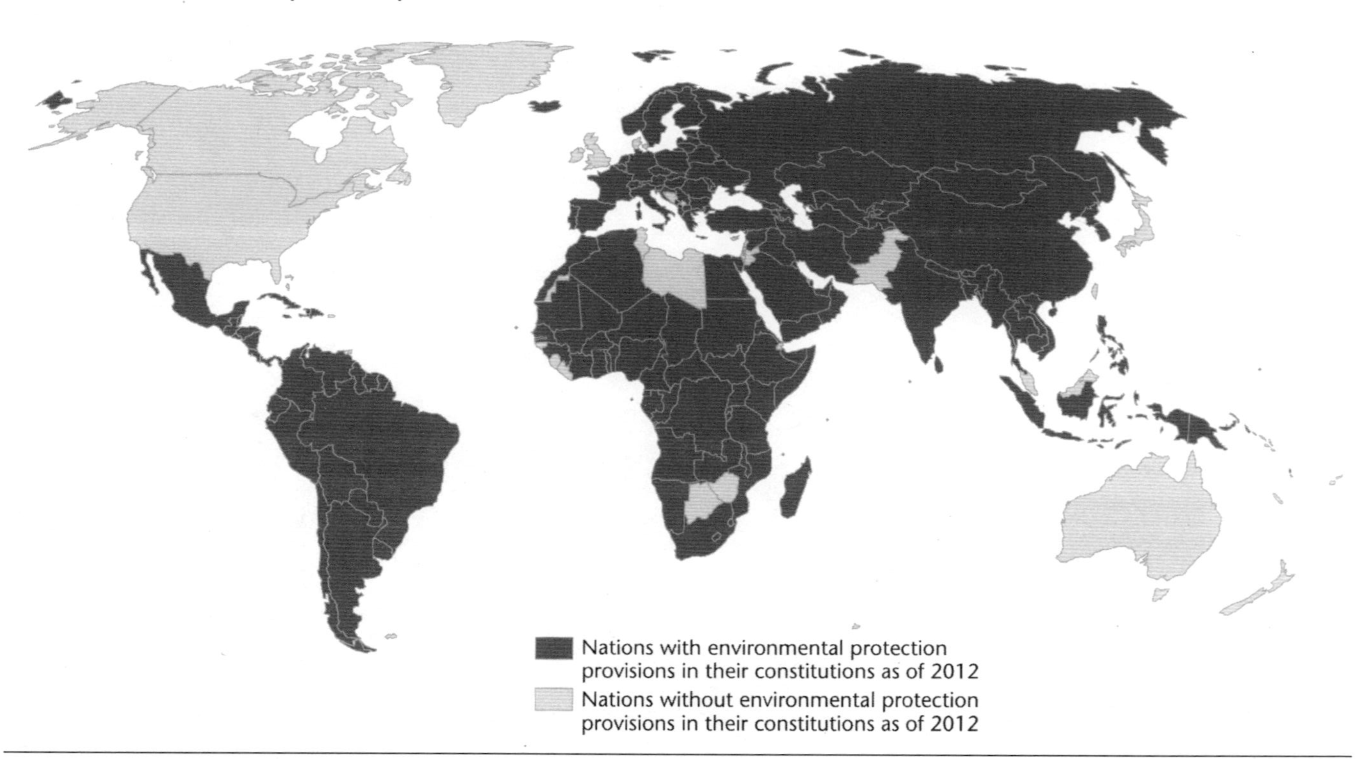

Table 4.1

Year environmental provisions first included in national constitutions

Year	Countries
1948	Italy
1959	Madagascar
1962	Kuwait
1964	Malta
1965	Guatemala
1971	Switzerland, United Arab Emirates
1972	Panama
1973	Bahrain, Syrian Arab Republic
1974	San Marino
1975	Greece, Papua New Guinea
1976	Cuba, India, Portugal
1977	Tanzania
1978	Spain, Sri Lanka, Thailand, Yemen
1979	Iran, Peru
1980	Chile, Guyana, Vanuatu, Vietnam
1981	Belize, Palau
1982	China, Equatorial Guinea, Honduras, Turkey
1983	El Salvador, Netherlands
1984	Austria, Ecuador
1986	Nicaragua
1987	Haiti, Philippines, South Korea, Suriname, Sweden
1988	Brazil
1989	Hungary
1990	Benin, Croatia, Guinea, Mozambique, Namibia, Sao Tome and Principe
1991	Bulgaria, Burkina Faso, Colombia, Gabon, Laos, Macedonia, Mauritania, Slovenia, Zambia
1992	Angola, Cape Verde, Czech Republic, Estonia, Ghana, Lithuania, Mali, Mexico, Mongolia, Norway, Paraguay, Saudi Arabia, Slovak Republic, Togo, Turkmenistan, Uzbekistan
1993	Andorra, Cambodia, Kyrgyzstan, Lesotho, Russia, Seychelles
1994	Argentina, Belarus, Belgium, Costa Rica, Germany, Malawi, Moldova, Tajikistan
1995	Armenia, Azerbaijan, Ethiopia, Finland, Georgia, Kazakhstan, Uganda
1996	Algeria, Cameroon, Chad, Gambia, Niger, Oman, South Africa, Ukraine, Uruguay
1997	Eritrea, Poland
1998	Albania, Latvia, North Korea
1999	Nigeria, Venezuela
2000	Côte d'Ivoire (Ivory Coast), Indonesia

►

Table 4.1

Year	Countries
2001	Comoros, Senegal
2002	Bolivia, Congo-Brazzaville, East Timor
2003	Qatar, Romania, Rwanda
2004	Afghanistan, Central African Republic, Somalia
2005	Burundi, Democratic Republic of the Congo, France, Iraq, Sudan, Swaziland
2006	Nepal, Serbia
2007	Egypt, Luxembourg, Montenegro
2008	Bhutan, Maldives, Myanmar
2010	Dominican Republic, Kenya
2011	Bangladesh, Jamaica, Morocco, South Sudan
2012	Iceland

What are the countries that, like Canada, have bucked this global trend? Among the forty-six UN nations whose constitutions are silent on the matter of environmental protection, there are several overlapping political, geographic, and legal patterns. The United Kingdom is one of these nations, as are twenty-nine former British colonies.[2] Twenty-four of the forty-six are small island states, most of whom were British colonies.[3] Although the constitutions of most former British colonies contain bills of rights, they adopt the classic liberal approach to human rights – a focus on civil and political rights, and no protection for economic, social, and cultural rights (except for property). This caution regarding constitutional recognition of social and economic rights has persisted in former British colonies, including Canada.[4] Like Canada, almost all the English-speaking nations of the Americas (eleven out of thirteen) lack environmental provisions in their constitutions.[5] The constitutions of these nations include few, if any, references to economic, social, or cultural rights. The exceptions are Belize (constitutional environmental provisions are limited to the preamble) and Jamaica (the right to a healthy environment was added in 2011).[6] In contrast, all twenty-two of the non-English-speaking nations in the Americas have incorporated environmental protection provisions into their constitutions.[7]

National legal systems provide another pattern that partially explains the variation in the presence of constitutional environmental provisions. The UN's 193 member-states can be divided into fifteen categories according to the type of legal system.[8] There is a striking difference between common and civil law nations in the extent to which they incorporate environmental provisions into their constitutions. Of the twenty-three nations employing predominantly common law systems, only three have constitutional environmental provisions.[9] In contrast, among the seventy-seven nations with civil law systems, seventy-three have environmental provisions in their constitutions.[10] It is interesting to note that Quebec is the only Canadian province with a civil law system and that Quebec's *Charter of Human Rights and Freedoms* includes the right to a healthy environment. Among the twenty-five nations with mixed legal systems that combine civil law and customary law, twenty-three have environmental provisions in their constitutions.[11] The remaining types of legal systems fall between the civil and common law extremes in terms of protecting the environment.[12]

It is often mistakenly observed that every constitution enacted or amended since 1970 has included environmental rights or responsibilities.[13] In fact, among the nations whose constitutions remain silent on the matter of environmental protection, many have written or amended their constitutions since 1970 without including environmental provisions despite varying degrees of public pressure to do so. Canada is one example; Ireland is another. In 1996, an expert committee tasked with reviewing Ireland's constitution recommended inclusion of a government duty to protect the environment.[14] The Irish constitution has been amended ten times since then but still lacks any environmental provisions. In other nations, such as the United States and Denmark, it is extremely difficult to amend the constitution. Senator Gaylord Nelson, founder of the first Earth Day, proposed the following amendment to the US constitution in 1970: "Every person has the inalienable right to a decent environment. The United States and every State shall guarantee this right."[15] However, constitutional amendments in the USA are rarely passed because of the difficulty in securing two-thirds approval of the House of Representatives and the Senate as well as three-quarters of the states within a seven-year period. Of roughly ten thousand constitutional amendments proposed in the USA since 1789, only twenty-seven have been ratified. In summary, whereas 147 nations have included environmental rights and/or responsibilities in their constitutions, 42 of the remaining 46 (including Canada) have bypassed the opportunity to do so despite carrying out other constitutional reforms since the early 1970s.

Types of Environmental Provisions

Constitutional provisions related to environmental protection can be grouped into five categories, including government's responsibility to protect the environment, substantive rights to environmental quality, procedural environmental rights, individual responsibility to protect the environment, and a miscellaneous "catch-all" category of diverse provisions. Each of these five categories is discussed in greater detail below.

Government's Environmental Duties

The most common form of constitutional provision related to environmental protection is the government duty, found in 142 constitutions (see Appendix A). For example, in the *Instruments of Government Act,* which is part of Sweden's constitution, article 2 succinctly states: "The public institutions shall promote sustainable development leading to a good environment for present and future generations."[16]

Portugal's constitution sets out the duty in more detail:

> Art. 66(2) In order to ensure enjoyment of the right to the environment within an overall framework of sustainable development, acting via appropriate bodies and with the involvement and participation of citizens, the state shall be charged with:
>
> a) Preventing and controlling pollution and its effects and the harmful forms of erosion;
> b) Conducting and promoting town and country planning with a view to a correct location of activities, balanced social and economic development and the enhancement of the landscape;
> c) Creating and developing natural and recreational reserves and parks and classifying and protecting landscapes and places, in such a way as to guarantee the conservation of nature and the preservation of cultural values and assets that are of historic or artistic interest;
> d) Promoting the rational use of natural resources, while safeguarding their ability to renew themselves and maintain ecological stability, with respect for the principle of inter-generational solidarity;
> e) Acting in cooperation with local authorities, promoting the environmental quality of rural settlements and urban life, particularly on the architectural level and as regards the protection of historic zones;
> f) Promoting the integration of environmental objectives into the various policies of a sectoral nature;
> g) Promoting environmental education and respect for environmental values;

h) Ensuring that tax policy renders development compatible with the protection of the environment and the quality of life.

In the majority of nations, the government's duty is explicitly articulated. In a handful of constitutions, there is no provision directly articulating the government's obligation to protect the environment, but there is recognition of the right to live in a healthy environment.[17] In these cases, the basic human rights concept that there can be no right in the absence of a corresponding duty can be used to infer that the government has an obligation to protect the environment.[18]

Substantive Environmental Rights

Ninety-four national constitutions recognize that citizens have a substantive right to live in a healthy environment (see Figure 4.2 and Appendix A), illustrated by this example in Norway's constitution (1992):

> Article 110(b) Every person has a right to an environment that is conducive to health and to natural surroundings whose productivity and diversity are preserved. Natural resources should be made use of on the basis of comprehensive long-term considerations whereby this right will be safeguarded for future generations as well.

The environmental rights entrenched in constitutions are universal (held by all individuals in a nation) with the exception of El Salvador, where the right to a healthy environment appears to be limited to children, and the Maldives, where the right appears to be limited to Muslims (a restriction discussed below). The constitutions of Burundi, Madagascar, and Mauritania are unusual because they do not explicitly mention the right to a healthy environment but rather incorporate by reference all of the rights recognized in the *African (Banjul) Charter on Human and Peoples' Rights*, which includes "the right to a general satisfactory environment."[19]

Broken down by decade, the incorporation of provisions recognizing the right to a healthy environment in national constitutions is as follows:

1970-79 – 4
1980-89 – 13
1990-99 – 47
2000-09 – 23
2010-12 – 7

Figure 4.2

Nations recognizing the constitutional right to a healthy environment

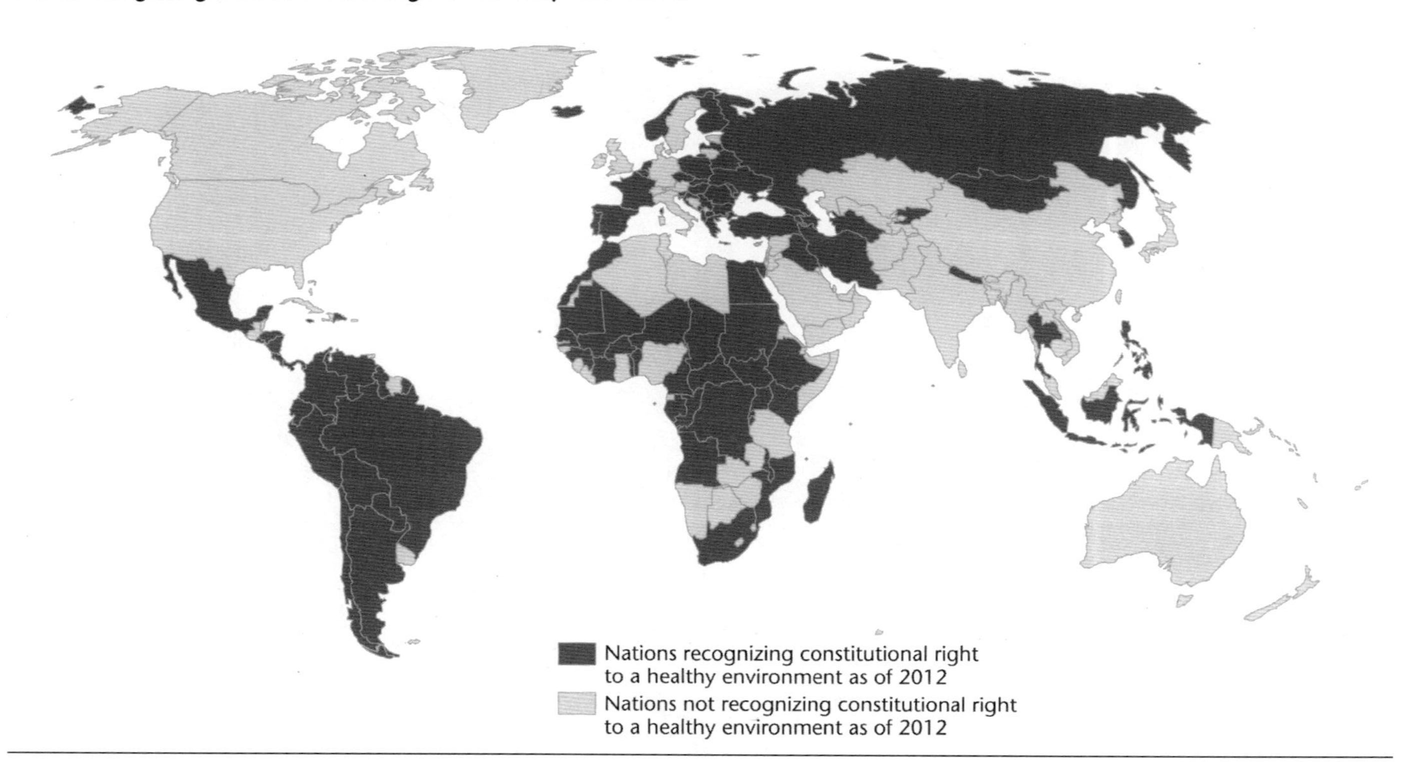

As was the case with environmental provisions generally, the peak year for constitutional recognition of the right to a healthy environment was 1992. A timeline of the right's incorporation in national constitutions is provided in Table 4.2. Sixty-four of the ninety-four constitutions that include substantive environmental rights use the language of a healthy environment or an environment that is not harmful to health. Twenty-three also describe the right in terms of an ecologically balanced environment, language that could assuage, to some extent, concerns about the anthropocentric focus of human rights. A wide variety of other words and phrases are used to describe the right to a healthy environment, including (with their frequency in parentheses) fit or adequate for human development or well-being (ten), preserved/protected (seven), clean (six), safe (six), favourable (five), satisfying/satisfactory (six), natural (three), unpolluted (two), sound (two), free from contamination (two), sustainable (two), good (two), diverse (two), harmonious (two), wholesome (one), lasting (one), human (one), pleasant (one), and benevolent (one).[20] Some of this variability may be a result of inconsistent translation.

Like other constitutional guarantees of human rights, the right to a healthy environment is not absolute. There are four types of provisions that can limit all or a subset of the rights recognized in a given constitution: generic limits, restrictions during emergencies, acknowledgment that rights will be fulfilled on the basis of progressive implementation, and limits on who is eligible to enjoy constitutional rights. More than one of these limitations can be found in a single constitution.

First, constitutions may include generic provisions that authorize restrictions on all human rights in order to meet the public interest in security, order, health, and/or the exercise of other rights. These provisions are similar to section 1 of Canada's *Charter*, which states that rights and freedoms are "subject only to such reasonable limits prescribed by law as can be demonstrably justified in a free and democratic society." Second, constitutions may expressly authorize restrictions on the exercise of rights during emergencies such as wars, invasions, and natural disasters. These emergency provisions either enumerate specific rights that can be suspended or identify specific rights that cannot be restricted even during times of crisis. Third, in some nations with limited financial resources, the right to a healthy environment and other social and economic rights are limited by the concept of progressive implementation, which recognizes that individual countries have different capacities for respecting, protecting, and fulfilling these rights. For example, Turkey's constitution asserts, "The State shall fulfill its duties as laid

Table 4.2

Year right to a healthy environment first included in national constitutions

Year	Countries
1976	Portugal
1978	Spain
1979	Iran, Peru
1980	Chile, Guyana
1982	Honduras, Turkey
1983	El Salvador, Netherlands, Panama
1984	Ecuador
1986	Nicaragua
1987	Philippines, South Korea
1988	Brazil
1989	Hungary
1990	Benin, Croatia, Guinea, Mozambique, Sao Tome and Principe
1991	Bulgaria, Burkina Faso, Colombia, Gabon, Macedonia, Mauritania, Slovenia
1992	Angola, Cape Verde, Czech Republic, Mali, Mongolia, Norway, Paraguay, Slovak Republic, Togo
1993	Andorra, Kyrgyzstan, Russia, Seychelles
1994	Argentina, Belarus, Belgium, Costa Rica, Malawi, Moldova
1995	Armenia, Azerbaijan, Ethiopia, Finland, Georgia, Uganda
1996	Cameroon, Chad, Niger, South Africa, Ukraine
1997	Poland
1998	Albania, Latvia
1999	Mexico, Venezuela
2000	Côte d'Ivoire, Indonesia
2001	Comoros, Senegal
2002	Bolivia, Congo-Brazzaville, East Timor, Greece
2003	Romania, Rwanda
2004	Central African Republic
2005	Burundi, Democratic Republic of the Congo, France, Iraq, Sudan
2006	Nepal, Serbia
2007	Egypt, Montenegro, Thailand
2008	Maldives, Turkmenistan
2010	Dominican Republic, Kenya, Madagascar
2011	Jamaica, Morocco, South Sudan
2012	Iceland

down in the Constitution in the social and economic fields within the capacity of its financial resources, taking into consideration the priorities appropriate with the aims of these duties." Fourth, provisions seemingly unrelated to the right to a healthy environment may restrict the application of the right. For example, non-Muslims in the Maldives do not appear to have equal constitutional rights, including the right to a healthy environment.[21]

The location and classification of the right to a healthy environment within a constitution can also influence its implementation, enforceability, and judicial interpretation. In fifty-eight out of ninety-four constitutions, the right to a healthy environment is articulated in the same section or chapter as other fundamental human rights. Theoretically, this will result in similar treatment for all the human rights identified as fundamental, although, in practice, legal developments may not always reflect words on paper or the intent of the constitution's framers. In seventeen constitutions, the right to a healthy environment is grouped together with economic, social, and cultural rights, a classification that is sometimes viewed as of secondary importance compared to civil and political rights. Eleven nations describe the right to a healthy environment in a section of their constitutions that sets out general provisions or guiding objectives and principles of state policy. This may diminish the legal strength of the environmental right. In three constitutions (Cameroon, the Comoros, and Mauritania), the right to a healthy environment is found in the preamble, where it would generally be of limited practical value. However, these three constitutions place all human rights in the preamble and explicitly state that it is an integral part of the constitution. In two constitutions (Colombia, Democratic Republic of the Congo), the right to a healthy environment is included in a chapter called "Collective Rights," which follows a chapter enumerating social, economic, and cultural rights. Three nations have unique constitutional arrangements for the right to a healthy environment: Argentina includes it in a section called "New Rights and Guarantees," Egypt in a section called "Public Rights," and France in the *Charter for the Environment*. The unusual location of the right within these constitutions could potentially affect its interpretation. In Canada, Aboriginal rights are found in the *Constitution Act, 1982*, rather than the *Charter*, but this distinction does not appear to have significantly affected their interpretation.

PROCEDURAL ENVIRONMENTAL RIGHTS

Thirty-one national constitutions provide procedural rights specifically related to environmental protection, including the right to information, to participate in decision making, and to access the judicial system to challenge government decisions, unconstitutional laws, or alleged violations of individual rights (see Appendix A). The Czech Republic's constitution provides an example: "Article 35(2) Everybody is entitled to timely and complete information about the state of the environment and natural resources."

Many constitutions incorporate generic procedural rights that apply to a broad spectrum of issues including the environment. As well, in many nations procedural rights are already available to citizens because of existing laws and policies, although constitutional affirmation will generally strengthen the individual's position. In almost every case, procedural environmental rights are included in constitutions that also contain a substantive right to live in a healthy environment.

Procedural environmental rights are most commonly found in constitutions from Eastern Europe and Latin America. In some countries, this may be due to the historical suppression of environmental information by autocratic regimes. For example, in the Ukraine, a compelling motivation for the inclusion of guaranteed access to environmental information in the constitution was the Chernobyl nuclear disaster, where vital information about high radiation levels was withheld from the public.[22]

Some constitutions also create an independent office with responsibility for monitoring human rights violations. This can take the form of an independent human rights commission, an ombudsman, or a defender of human rights. For instance, El Salvador has a procurator for the defence of human rights.[23] There is a wide variability in the powers available to these human rights bodies and officers, ranging from preparing reports to initiating litigation intended to protect citizens' rights and ordering reparation for rights that have been violated. In general, these officials can act on complaints received from citizens or initiate their own investigations. Namibia's constitution specifically empowers the ombudsman to investigate problems related to environmental damage.[24]

In Canada, procedural rights are, to some extent, found in federal and provincial legislation, such as laws governing access to information. However, the right to participate in environmental decision making varies widely between provinces and from statute to statute, as do rules governing citizens' access to justice.[25] These legislative provisions would be stronger and more consistent if supported by constitutional recognition of the right to a healthy environment.

Individual Environmental Duties

Individual responsibility for protecting the environment is provided in eighty-four constitutions (see Appendix A). For instance, France's *Charter for the Environment* (2005) states,

> Article 2. Every person has the duty to take part in the preservation and the improvement of the environment. Article 3. Each person shall, in the conditions provided for by law, foresee and avoid the occurrence of any damage which he or she may cause to the environment or, failing that, limit the consequences of such damage.

There are six nations where constitutions establish an individual duty to protect the environment but neither establish an individual right to a healthy environment nor impose environmental obligations upon the state.[26] This seems to run counter to the fundamental idea that constitutions are intended to provide constraints on government power.[27] Constitutions are generally enforceable against the state, not individuals. It is unclear what legal purpose is served by the constitutionalization of individual environmental duties. These provisions appear to be symbolic, hortatory, and educational, confirming that everyone has a part to play in protecting the environment from human-imposed damage and degradation. Canada's *Charter* makes no reference to any individual responsibilities, focusing exclusively on individual rights.

Other Environmental Protection Provisions

Not surprisingly, given the diverse legal systems of the world, there is a broad variety of other constitutional environmental provisions, ranging from generic to highly detailed. Among the most common in this catch-all category are authorizations of restrictions on the use of private property in order to protect the environment, prohibitions on importing toxic, hazardous, or nuclear waste, recognition of the right to clean water, and symbolic value statements regarding the importance placed on protecting the environment. In a handful of constitutions, provisions related to environmental protection are extremely comprehensive, with a level of detail that in most nations would be more typical of environmental legislation.

Many constitutions authorize limits on the exercise of private property rights as justified by protecting the public interest, which generally is not defined but refers to a suite of considerations including environmental concerns. For example, the constitution of Andorra states that "no one shall be deprived of his or her goods or rights, unless upon justified consideration of the public interest, with just compensation by or pursuant to a law."[28] At least fifteen constitutions specifically restrict the use of private property when that use could cause environmental damage. For example, the constitution of Romania states, "The right to own property implies an obligation to comply with duties relating to environmental protection."[29] Jamaica's 2011 *Charter of Fundamental Rights and Freedoms* clarifies that property rights shall not affect the making or operation of any law "reasonably required for the protection of the environment." Another fifteen nations (all former British colonies) share a weak constitutional provision that could authorize environmental limits on property rights. The inclusion of both property rights and the right to a healthy environment in a constitution will create conflicts that require careful balancing by legislatures, bureaucracies, and courts. However, constitutions that explicitly authorize environmental constraints on the use of private property provide helpful guidance to lawmakers, civil servants, and judges, and may contribute to overcoming the historical privileging of private interests over the common good.

A handful of nations, employing a very different constitutional model, spell out environmental policies in extensive detail, closer to what ordinarily, in Canada or the USA, would be found in environmental legislation. For example, Switzerland's constitution includes specific provisions about zoning, water, forests, nature reserves, fishing, hunting, protecting alpine ecosystems, energy policy, and biotechnology. Portugal's constitution requires the government to ensure "that tax policy renders development compatible with the protection of the environment and the quality of life."[30] Among the many environmental clauses in Ecuador's new constitution are a prohibition on genetically modified organisms, reversal of the legal burden of proof so that those accused of causing environmental harm must prove that their actions caused no such harm, a mandate that uncertainties regarding the interpretation of environmental laws be resolved in favour of Nature, and a requirement for the promotion of non-motorized forms of transport in urban areas, particularly through the building of cycling routes.[31] Brazil's constitution requires "a prior environmental impact study, which shall be made public, for the installation of works or activities which may cause significant degradation of the environment."[32] In Argentina, the constitution requires the federal government to "dictate laws containing a minimum budget necessary for protecting the environment."[33]

Many African nations have provisions in their constitutions dealing with environmental issues of concern to their citizens or unique to their history.

For example, Benin, Chad, the Democratic Republic of the Congo, and Niger prohibit the importation of toxic or hazardous waste. Uganda and Malawi have specific references to the protection of biological diversity. Several Oceanic nations (such as Micronesia and Palau) prohibit nuclear testing or the deployment of nuclear weapons within their territories.

Latin America has been a leader in constitutional innovation, with numerous novel provisions related to environmental protection. In Brazil, Colombia, and several other nations, the constitution empowers an independent agency, the Ministerio Publico, to protect collective interests, including the environment. These agencies conduct investigations and prosecutions but do so at arm's length from the state, giving them a high degree of autonomy in enforcing environmental laws against powerful actors. Constitutions throughout Latin America provide for expedited forms of legal action, known variously as the *amparo*, writ of protection, and *tutela*. Although the precise procedure varies from nation to nation, they have in common a relaxation or simplification of the legal process that lowers costs, reduces delays, and dramatically increases access to the judicial system in constitutional cases.[34] The right of amparo dates back to the Mexican constitution of 1857 and has been adopted in almost every Spanish-speaking nation in Latin America.[35]

In 2008, Ecuador became the first nation in the world to provide explicit constitutional recognition of the rights of Nature, followed by Bolivia in 2009.[36] Ecuador's constitution states,

> Chapter Seven: Rights of Nature
>
> Article 71. Nature or Pacha Mama, where life plays and performs, is entitled to full respect, existence, and the maintenance and regeneration of its vital cycles, structure, functions, and evolutionary processes. Any person, community, or nation may require the public authority to comply with the rights of nature. The principles enshrined in the Constitution will be used to apply and interpret these rights, as appropriate. The State will encourage individuals, legal persons, and collective entities to protect nature and promote respect for all the elements that form an ecosystem.
>
> Article 72. Nature is entitled to restoration. This restoration is independent of the obligation of the State and persons or companies to compensate individuals and groups that depend on affected natural systems. In cases of severe or permanent environmental impact, including those linked to the exploitation of nonrenewable natural

resources, the State shall establish the most effective mechanisms to achieve the restoration, and take appropriate measures to eliminate or mitigate adverse environmental consequences.

Article 73. The State will apply precautionary and restrictive measures to activities that could lead to species extinction, destruction of ecosystems, or the permanent alteration of natural cycles. The import of organisms and organic and inorganic material that may ultimately alter the national genetic heritage is prohibited.

Article 74. Individuals, communities, peoples and nations are entitled to benefit from the environment and natural resources that allow them to live well. Environmental services are not subject to appropriation; their production, delivery, use and development are regulated by the State.

Whether and to what extent granting legal rights to Nature will have practical consequences remains to be seen, although it does address concerns that rights-based approaches are unduly anthropocentric.[37] Canada's constitution has been criticized for its failure to recognize the rights of non-human forms of life.[38]

More than forty nations include constitutional references to the rights, health, or well-being of future generations. Almost all these references appear in the context of provisions addressing environmental concerns. For example, in Brazil's constitution, "The Government and the community have a duty to defend and preserve the environment for present and future generations."[39] The constitutions of Bhutan and Portugal refer to the closely related concept of intergenerational equity.[40]

Finally, a growing number of constitutions address the right to an adequate supply of clean water. South Africa is perhaps best known for incorporating this right into its constitution, as follows:

27. Health care, food, water, and social security
    (1) Everyone has the right to have access to ...
        (b) sufficient food and water ...
    (2) The state must take reasonable legislative and other measures, within its available resources, to achieve the progressive realization of each of these rights.

Constitutional provisions requiring the protection and/or provision of clean water are found in at least twenty nations.

The Enforceability of Constitutional Environmental Provisions

Enforceability is an essential aspect of constitutional provisions, for it ensures accountability when rights are violated or responsibilities go unfulfilled. A simple definition of enforceability is the ability of an individual, group, or other organization to access the legal system to resolve a constitutional complaint.[41] In Canada, the *Charter* clearly grants any person the right to go to court when his or her constitutional rights have been infringed or denied.[42] In general, the authorization or prohibition of legal redress relate to broader aspects of the constitution but apply equally to the environmental provisions. In a few cases, they are specifically linked to a constitution's environmental provisions. An example authorizing legal action is found in article 20 of Chile's constitution: "The action for the protection of fundamental rights *[recurso de protección]* shall always lie in the case of Article 19(8), when the right to live in an environment free from contamination has been affected by an illegal act or omission imputable to an authority or specific person." Conversely, an example of an explicit limit on enforceability is found in Nepal's constitution, which imposes extensive duties on the government to protect the environment but subsequently makes it clear that these duties are not enforceable: "Article 36. Questions not to be Raised in Courts: (1) No questions shall be raised in any court as to whether provisions contained in this Part are implemented or not."

In the absence of enforceability, governments may evade their responsibility to protect the environment, and affected individuals may be deprived of a remedy for violations of their right to a healthy environment. Although unenforceable constitutional provisions are toothless tigers, they may still influence interpretation and decision making, and they offer moral, symbolic, and educational value.

Both internal and external factors affect the enforceability of constitutional provisions. Internal factors refer to explicit guarantees or limits within the text of a constitution. External factors encompass a broad range of legal, social, political, economic, and cultural considerations. For instance, lack of financial resources may act as a de facto bar to enforceability for poor communities, who are often disproportionately affected by pollution.[43] Another external limit may be the extreme conservatism of a nation's judiciary or even its unfamiliarity with judicial review of government action. For example, judicial review was introduced into Japan's legal system by the post–Second World War rewriting of the Japanese constitution but continues to have limited effect due to societal and judicial conservatism.[44]

The vast majority of constitutional provisions entrenching the right to live in a healthy environment and government's duty to protect the environment are, prima facie, enforceable. Some nations (such as Belarus) go even further than authorizing enforcement of human rights by individuals and groups, providing constitutional guarantees of legal aid (free legal assistance) for efforts to protect rights.[45]

In thirteen nations, certain rights, including the right to a healthy environment, may be invoked only according to specific conditions determined by law. This is described as a constitutional provision that is not "self-executing." For instance, in Spain, the right to a healthy environment is subject to the following restriction in article 53(3): "Recognition, respect and protection of the principles recognized in Chapter III shall guide legislation, judicial practice and actions by the public authorities. They may only be invoked before the ordinary courts in accordance with the legal provisions implementing them." This clause limits the ability of citizens and NGOs to file lawsuits based directly on their constitutional right to a healthy environment, requiring them to rely on other legal provisions.

There are fifteen nations where the enforceability of government duties to protect the environment appears to be explicitly precluded. Each of these countries has constitutional environmental provisions that are expressed in terms of "Directive Principles of State Policy." For example, in Gambia the directive principles include protecting the environment for posterity and cooperating in preserving the global environment. However, Gambia's constitution explicitly states that "these principles shall not confer legal rights or be enforceable in any court."[46] Olowu describes such guiding principles as "worthless platitudes because of their inherently emasculated constitutional status."[47] The environmental provisions in the 1992 Charlottetown Accord were similar to directive principles, in that they were explicitly unenforceable.

In six nations, progressive implementation is another factor that could restrain the enforceability of government's duty to protect the environment. Where a constitution includes this government duty but specifically states that it is subject to the availability of financial resources and other national priorities, it is less likely that a court will enforce the duty by substituting its policy judgment for that of the government. For instance, Gabon's constitution provides that "the State, according to its possibilities, shall guarantee to all, notably to the child, the mother, the handicapped, to aged workers and to the elderly, ... a preserved natural environment."[48] Because of Canada's level of affluence, incorporating progressive implementation into its constitution would be highly unusual. All the rights set forth in the *Charter* are fully binding on Canadian governments.

The enforceability of environmental provisions cannot be determined with certainty by examining constitutional texts in isolation. Significant differences can exist between enforceability on paper and enforceability in practice. For example, the constitution of India makes rights enforceable. However, it contains no explicit right to a healthy environment, and government's duties to protect the environment are found among the explicitly unenforceable Directive Principles of State Policy.[49] Nevertheless, courts in India have consistently, and in some cases dramatically, circumvented the plain words of the constitution, building a body of jurisprudence that interprets the directive principle regarding environmental protection as legally binding. Indian jurisprudence serves as a compelling example of the unpredictability of constitutional law and a powerful reminder not to rely upon abstract conclusions regarding the enforceability of particular constitutional provisions. As Beatty observes, "Even though most constitutions now contain provisions guaranteeing some set of social and economic rights, it is rare that the particular way they are written in the text is the critical or determining factor in how cases are resolved."[50]

The issue of enforceability is particularly important in the Canadian context. As discussed in Chapter 3, concern about the purportedly unenforceable nature of social, economic, and environmental rights was among the factors that led to their exclusion from Canada's constitution. Other nations did not reach the same conclusion, and Chapter 5 examines their experiences with the implementation and enforcement of these rights, providing potentially useful lessons for Canada.

The Implicit Constitutional Right to a Healthy Environment

In at least eight of these ninety-four countries, courts recognized an implicit constitutional right to a healthy environment prior to amendments that explicitly incorporated it into the constitution.[51] These nations include Argentina, Costa Rica, El Salvador, Greece, Kenya, Nepal, Peru, and Romania. The courts' general rationale is that the right to a healthy environment is a fundamental element of, or a prerequisite to, constitutionally protected rights such as the right to life. For example, according to a prominent and oft-cited Argentine judgment, "The right to live in a healthy environment is a fundamental attribute of people. Any aggression to the environment ends up becoming a threat to life itself and to the psychological and physical integrity of the person, which is based on ecological balance."[52] Similarly, a judgment from the Costa Rican Supreme Court stated, "Life is only possible when it exists in solidarity with nature, which nourishes and sustains us – not only with regard to food, but also with physical well-being. It constitutes a right that all citizens possess to live in an environment free from contamination. This is the basis of a just and productive society."[53] In a subsequent decision, Costa Rica's Supreme Court affirmed that the right to a healthy environment emanated from the constitutional right to life and from the state's obligation to protect nature. The court added that without recognition of the rights to health and to the environment, the right to life would be severely limited.[54]

In at least twelve additional countries currently lacking an explicit constitutional right to a healthy environment, supreme or constitutional courts have held that such a right is implicit in other constitutional rights and therefore enforceable.[55] These countries include Bangladesh, Estonia, Guatemala, India, Israel, Italy, Malaysia, Nigeria, Pakistan, Sri Lanka, Tanzania, and Uruguay. In general, courts from these nations have also held that the right to live in a healthy environment is an essential element of the right to life or the right to health. In 1991, the Indian Supreme Court held that "the right to live is a fundamental right under Article 21 of the Constitution and it includes the right to enjoyment of pollution-free water and air for full enjoyment of life. If anything endangers or impairs that quality of life in derogation of laws, a citizen has the right to have recourse to Article 32 of the Constitution for removing the pollution of water or air which may be detrimental to the quality of life."[56] In 1987, Italy's Constitutional Court held that on the basis of articles 9 and 32 of the Italian constitution (which address the state's duty to safeguard natural beauty and the right to health), "We must recognize the ongoing efforts to give specific recognition to the protection of the environment as a fundamental human right."[57]

However, it should be noted that courts in some countries – for example, the USA – have rejected the argument that there is an implicit constitutional right to a healthy environment.[58] In a series of lower-level court decisions handed down in 1971 and 1972, American judges closed the door on environmental advocates attempting to pursue this approach.[59]

From a Canadian vantage point, it is persuasive that constitutional and supreme courts in at least twenty nations have ruled that the right to a healthy environment is an implicit and essential element of the constitutional right to life. The Supreme Court of Canada regularly employs comparative law and has done so in several leading environmental decisions. For example, in the

Hudson case, which dealt with municipal regulation of pesticides, the court cited two Indian Supreme Court decisions on the precautionary principle.[60] In a number of cases, plaintiffs in Canada have put forward the argument that "the right to life, liberty, and security of the person" in section 7 of the *Charter* includes an implicit right to a healthy environment (see Chapter 8). To date, courts have rejected this argument, although at least one prominent case is ongoing.[61]

Conclusion

Constitutional environmental provisions are now the norm throughout most of the world, including Western and Eastern Europe, Asia, Latin America, and Africa. As of 2012, 147 out of 193 national constitutions incorporate environmental rights and/or responsibilities (see Figure 4.3). Canada is among the dwindling number of countries that have not greened their constitutions. The right to live in a healthy environment enjoys explicit recognition in ninety-four constitutions and implicit constitutional recognition (via court decisions) in at least another twelve countries. No other social or economic right has achieved such a broad level of constitutional recognition in such a short period of time.[62] By comparison, the right to health is recognized in seventy-four constitutions, and the right to food in twenty-one.[63] The constitutional right to a healthy environment is now common in Europe, Latin

Figure 4.3

Prevalence of environmental protection provisions in national constitutions

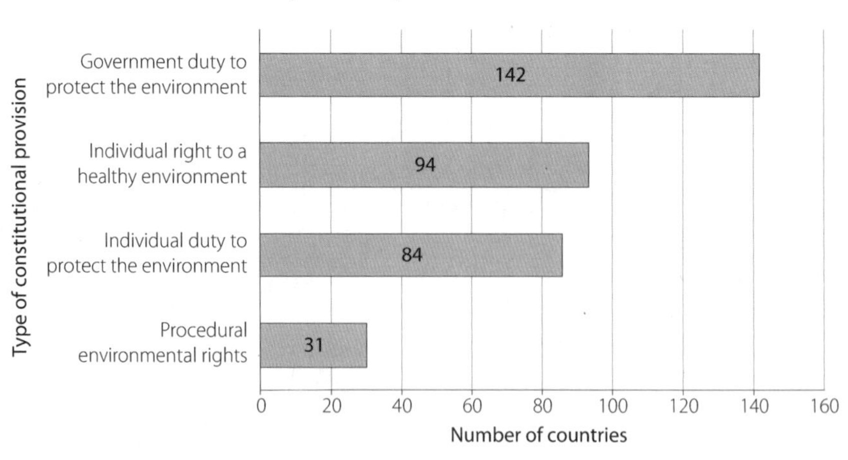

America, Africa, and to a lesser extent, Asia. In most constitutions, the right is treated in much the same way as any other fundamental human right, as enforceable but subject to some limitations.

The constitutionalization of environmental protection began in the 1970s, but the trend continues today. New constitutions enacted in 2010 in Kenya and the Dominican Republic include the rights to a healthy environment and to water, and they feature extensive provisions related to environmental protection.[64] Jamaica's new *Charter of Fundamental Rights and Freedoms,* enacted in 2011, includes the right to a healthy environment, as do the new constitutions of Morocco and South Sudan.[65] The recent constitutional amendments in Kenya and Jamaica carry additional importance because both nations, like Canada, are former British colonies with common law legal systems, where the right to a healthy environment has made minimal inroads to date. Even in the United Kingdom, a joint committee composed of members of both Parliament and the House of Lords recently proposed the inclusion of the "right to a healthy and sustainable environment" in a new bill of rights.[66] Northern Ireland's Human Rights Commission also included environmental rights and responsibilities among its recommendations for a bill of rights.[67] Iceland used crowd-sourcing to draft a new constitution that includes the right to a healthy environment and other strong environmental provisions.[68] Crowd-sourcing involves the use of social media to outsource a specific task to a large undefined group of people, based on the assumption that those with the most relevant expertise and most creative ideas will contribute to solving the task. A broad coalition of Zimbabwean civil society organizations has called for the drafting of a new constitution with a "justiciable Bill of Rights that recognizes civil, political, social, economic, cultural and environmental rights."[69] In 2012, Zambia drafted a new constitution that includes the right to a healthy environment. Parliamentarians in Turkey and Tunisia are engaged in efforts to strengthen the environmental provisions in their constitutions.

Overall, these developments appear to reflect a rapid and worldwide evolution of human values. The same evolution in values has occurred in Canada, yet the Canadian constitution remains silent on the fundamental importance of environmental protection. Whereas other nations are beginning to offer constitutional protection for the rights of Nature, Canada doesn't even recognize the constitutional right of human beings to clean air, fresh water, fertile soil, and healthy ecosystems.

5
Lessons Learned: Implementing Environmental Rights and Responsibilities*

> The most important step in addressing environmental issues is the concrete implementation of public policies ... with an emphasis on prevention and restoration.
>
> – Ricardo Lorenzetti, president of the Supreme Court of Argentina, quoted in *Riachuelo: A Documentary*

For some Canadians, the moral argument that the right to a healthy environment is a fundamental human right that should be enjoyed by all persons may be sufficient to justify constitutional protection. Other Canadians may be convinced by the fact that the right now enjoys constitutional recognition in the majority of the world. These groups share an implicit faith that constitutions, in tandem with legal systems, will ensure the protection and fulfillment of human rights. For other Canadians, the acid test of the worth of constitutional protection for the right to a healthy environment is whether this right will actually enhance Canada's environmental record and improve people's lives.[1] There are legitimate concerns that human rights may be paper tigers and their constitutional recognition nothing more than "cheap talk."[2] Therefore, it is imperative to demonstrate that constitutionalizing the right to a healthy environment in Canada would make a tangible difference, leading to less pollution, healthier people and ecosystems, and overall improved environmental performance.

---

* This chapter is a synthesis of a comprehensive analysis of the practical effects of including environmental rights and responsibilities in constitutions. For the full results of this analysis as well as the methodology employed, please consult Chapters 5-12 and Appendix 1 of my previous book *The Environmental Rights Revolution: A Global Study of Constitutions, Human Rights, and the Environment* (Vancouver: UBC Press, 2012).

Canada is in the fortunate position of being able to draw on the rich experiences of 94 nations that recognize the right to a healthy environment and 147 that include some form of environmental protection requirements in their constitution. Constitutional provisions can have both legal and extra-legal effects. The former include influencing legislation, public policy, institutions, and court decisions, whereas the latter include the evolution of public opinion, attitudes, values, behaviour, and culture. Examples of positive legal effects identified in Chapter 2 and explored in this chapter include stronger environmental laws and policies, advance screening of new laws, a barrier to environmental rollbacks, increased enforcement of environmental laws, higher levels of citizen participation in making the environmental decisions that affect their lives, progress in alleviating environmental injustice, a level playing field for environmental, social, and economic factors in decision making, and increased government and corporate accountability for protecting the environment. Practical experience with the right to a healthy environment is debunking many of the criticisms and potential drawbacks described in Chapter 2. Two important critiques – that it may be undemocratic and/or ineffective – continue to raise substantive concerns.

Regarding extra-legal effects, this chapter examines the essential question of whether constitutional environmental rights and responsibilities affect environmental performance. Among the criteria used to answer this question are the ecological footprint, international rankings of environmental performance, and progress in reducing air pollution and tackling greenhouse gas emissions. If a clear link exists between constitutional provisions requiring environmental protection and the environmental performance of a country, this provides powerful evidence that Canada should prioritize constitutional change, particularly in light of our strong values and weak track record.

The Advantages of Constitutional Environmental Rights

Stronger Environmental Laws

Extensive evidence shows that constitutional recognition of the right to a healthy environment exerts a positive influence on the subsequent enactment and improvement of national environmental laws. In at least seventy-eight of the ninety-four nations where this right is explicitly recognized, environmental laws were strengthened – after the greening of the constitution – to incorporate substantive, and in many cases procedural, environmental rights. This includes all nations in Eastern Europe where the right is recognized (nineteen out of nineteen); almost all nations in Latin America and the

Caribbean (sixteen of eighteen), Western Europe (eight of ten), and Asia (twelve of fourteen); and a majority in Africa (twenty-three of thirty-three).

The OECD confirms that the incorporation of environmental provisions in European constitutions led to "major revision and amplification of environmental policies ... and facilitated the development of inspection, monitoring, and enforcement."[3] In Portugal, as the OECD observes, "The Constitution designates protection of the environment and conservation of natural resources as being among the *essential tasks of the Portuguese State,* and sets out the State's obligations regarding the prevention and control of pollution and its effects."[4] Portugal's *Framework Law on the Environment,* enacted in 1987 (a decade after the greening of the constitution), reiterates the right to a healthy and ecologically balanced environment, outlines the state's responsibility to protect the right, guarantees public participation in decision making, ensures access to courts to prevent environmental harm, seek compensation, or compel government action, and encourages the formation of, and participation in, environmental groups.[5] Spain's constitution recognized the right to a healthy environment more than three decades ago (1978), but it continues to exert a major influence on the development of environmental legislation. For example, the *Environmental Responsibility Law* and the *Law on Natural Heritage and Biodiversity,* both passed in 2007, make repeated reference to article 45 of the constitution (the right to a healthy environment).[6]

In some countries, the constitutional right to a healthy environment has become a unifying legal principle, permeating not only national framework laws but the entire body of environmental law and policy. This is most clearly the case in Argentina, a nation with a federal governance structure similar to that of Canada. The reform of Argentina's constitution in 1994 to include the right to a healthy environment "triggered the need for a new generation of environmental legislation."[7] After 1994, Argentina passed a new comprehensive environmental law (which "sought to make the constitution a reality"), a law governing access to environmental information, and minimum standard laws on issues ranging from industrial waste to clean water.[8] The national constitution also caused a cascade effect, as provincial constitutions were amended to incorporate the right to a healthy environment, and provincial environmental laws were altered to identify the right as a guiding principle.[9] The constitutional right to a healthy environment also had a comprehensive effect on environmental law and policy in other countries including Brazil, Colombia, Costa Rica, the Philippines, Portugal, and South Africa. A similar transformation is now under way in France, following the enactment of the *Charter for the Environment* in 2005.[10]

Among the small number of nations where no constitutional influence on environmental laws could be discerned are those whose constitutional environmental provisions are very recent (Dominican Republic 2010, Madagascar 2010, Jamaica 2011, Morocco 2011, South Sudan 2011, and Iceland 2012) and countries wracked by civil war and other overriding social, economic, or political crises (e.g., Democratic Republic of the Congo). Ten of the sixteen nations where there is no evidence of constitutional influence on environmental laws are in Africa. However, Kenya's 2010 constitution offers an innovative idea intended to overcome this kind of legislative lethargy, mandating that new environmental laws to implement constitutional commitments must be enacted within four years.[11] An extension is available in extenuating circumstances if approved by Kenya's Parliament, but it is only for one year and is non-renewable.

Constitutional provisions are clearly not the only factor contributing to improved environmental laws. For example, the European Union's accession process had a major influence on environmental legislation in Eastern Europe. Other key factors include public pressure, the migration of ideas and legislative approaches from other jurisdictions, and international assistance from agencies such as the UN Environment Programme and the International Union for the Conservation of Nature (IUCN). However, the conclusion that constitutions have had a strong influence on national environmental laws is supported by the consistent inclusion of direct references to the constitution in those laws, the explicit legislative acknowledgment of the right to a healthy environment, and the enactment of related procedural rights. This conclusion is shared by legal experts and organizations including the OECD and the UN Economic Commission for Europe.

The positive influence of the constitutional right to a healthy environment and other constitutional environmental provisions on legislation has been largely overlooked, with most of the scholarly literature focusing on litigation. Yet constitutional provisions may have their greatest impact by contributing to the enactment of stronger legislation. Studies indicate that legislation is more effective than litigation in achieving environmental protection.[12] Legislators can act proactively, whereas courts, by their very nature, can only respond to cases brought to them. Legislation benefits from the existence of institutions, such as environmental ministries or departments, with resources, experience, and technical expertise. As well, if implemented and enforced, legislation tackles all instances of a problem and applies nationally, as opposed to the generally ad hoc nature of litigation, where the effects may be limited to the parties. For example, legally binding national air quality standards should, if adequately implemented and enforced, result in cleaner air throughout an entire country. In contrast, a lawsuit will generally focus on improving air quality in a specific location or region. To be sure, litigation can have radiating effects, which are the indirect consequences that ripple outward through the legal system and into society.[13] Litigation can also be part of a broader strategy and is valued for its "mobilization potential," high public profile, and ability to demand a formal response from government.[14] But radiating effects occur under limited circumstances, whereas legislation is generally intended to have the equivalent of radiating effects.

Advance Screening of New Laws and Regulations

Constitutional recognition of the right to a healthy environment requires that all prospective laws and regulations be screened to ensure that they are consistent with the government duty to respect, protect, and fulfill the right. In some nations, this is a formal process. For example, in France, the Constitutional Council reviews proposed legislation prior to its enactment. In other countries, the screening process is informal. For instance, in Colombia, the close supervision of the Constitutional Court has compelled legislators to consider constitutional case law when drafting the content of new legislation.[15]

Safety Net

In addition to providing an impetus for strengthening environmental laws, the constitutional right to a healthy environment has been used to close gaps in environmental law. Costa Rica and Nepal offer clear examples of courts ordering governments to enact legislation or regulations that would protect fisheries and reduce air pollution, respectively.[16] The courts did not spell out the details of the laws but merely clarified that certain legislation was an essential element of fulfilling the government's environmental responsibilities. In other nations, courts issued carefully crafted judgments that did not compel but rather influenced states to take action (such as legislation governing public smoking in India, air quality standards in Sri Lanka, and plastic bags in Uganda).[17] Courts do not always side with citizens and NGOs seeking to fill legislative or regulatory gaps. The Supreme Court of the Philippines, despite agreeing that air pollution from motor vehicles was a toxic threat to health, declined to order the government to convert all of its vehicles to compressed natural gas, because it believed this would have interfered with legislative and executive responsibilities.[18]

Prevents Rollbacks

Another legal advantage flowing from constitutionalizing the right to a healthy environment is that it may prevent the future weakening of environmental laws and policies (commonly referred to as rollbacks). Courts have articulated the principle, based on the right to a healthy environment, that current environmental laws and policies represent a baseline that can be improved but not weakened.[19] This concept is called the standstill principle in Belgium and is also recognized in Hungary, South Africa, and many nations in Latin America. In France, the principle is known as the "ratchet effect" or "non regression."[20]

Belgian authorities are precluded from weakening levels of environmental protection except in limited circumstances where a compelling public interest exists.[21] For example, a proposal to accommodate motor racing by weakening standards for air and noise pollution was rejected.[22] Similarly, Hungary's Constitutional Court interpreted the right to a healthy environment as requiring the government to maintain a high level of environmental protection. This level of protection, according to the court, could be diminished only if necessary to fulfill other constitutional rights.[23] Therefore, an attempt to privatize publicly owned forests in Hungary was turned down because of weaker environmental standards governing private land. Hungary's Constitutional Court recognized the greater difficulties and higher costs associated with restoring damaged ecosystems, and ruled that "the implementation of the right to environment requires not only keeping the present level of protection, but also that the state should not step backward towards liability based protection from the preventive measures."[24] The standstill principle recognizes that in society's quest for sustainable development, there is only one viable direction and that is toward stronger environmental laws and policies.

Improved Implementation and Enforcement

Recognition of the constitutional right to a healthy environment can facilitate increased implementation and enforcement of environmental laws. Citizens, communities, and NGOs in Europe, Latin America, and Asia have supplemented the enforcement efforts of the state, drawn attention to violations, and provided an impetus for the allocation of additional resources to environmental monitoring and protection. A leading example is the cooperative approach taken in Brazil, where the public and NGOs can report alleged violations of constitutional rights and environmental laws to the independent

Ministerio Publico, which can then conduct investigations, civil actions, and prosecutions. The constitutional changes in 1988 that empowered the Ministerio Publico to enforce constitutional environmental provisions have resulted in a dramatic increase in enforcement of environmental laws.[25] A Brazilian judge wrote that "hundreds of pages would be needed to mention all the precedents" set by Brazilian courts in recent years dealing with constitutional protection for the environment.[26] In the state of São Paulo alone, between 1984 and 2004, the Ministerio Publico filed over four thousand public civil actions in environmental cases addressing issues ranging from deforestation to air pollution.[27]

Empowered by the recognition of their right to a healthy environment, concerned citizens and communities can also enforce the laws themselves when they are being broken and governments turn a blind eye. There are thousands of reported environmental cases where citizen and community enforcement has supplemented or supplanted the efforts of the state.

Increased Public Involvement

Constitutional environmental provisions have substantially increased the public's role in environmental governance. The right to a healthy environment has been consistently interpreted by legislators, the executive, and the judiciary as including procedural environmental rights – access to information, participation in decision making, and access to justice. Citizens, in ever-increasing numbers, are using these rights. Other major factors contributing to the growing public role in environmental governance include the enhanced importance of civil society, advances in communications technology (particularly the Internet), and in many nations the transition from closed, authoritarian types of government to open, participatory democracy. A key development in terms of access to justice has been the use of the constitutional right to a healthy environment (and legislation implementing this right) to rewrite traditional rules of standing to include collective and diffuse interests. In many nations recognizing the right to a healthy environment, administrative processes and courthouse doors are now open to citizens who lack a traditional economic or personal interest but seek to protect society's collective interest in a healthy environment. As a result, the state appears to have lost its monopoly in terms of representing the public interest.

Several Latin American nations – Argentina, Brazil, Colombia, and Costa Rica – are in a class of their own in terms of enhancing access to justice. Procedural innovations have radically increased the ability of citizens, communities, and environmental NGOs (ENGOs) to seek judicial protection of their constitutional rights, including the right to a healthy environment. Simplified, expedited actions include the amparo, tutela, recurso de protección, direct action of unconstitutionality, popular action, and public civil action. These procedural innovations reduce costs, decrease delays, and minimize risks previously associated with pursuing judicial remedies. India's Supreme Court, with its simple writ petition procedure, is not far behind, and the Philippines, with its groundbreaking writ of *kalikasan* (nature) and special procedural rules for environmental litigation, is moving in the same direction.[28]

Increased Accountability

The increased transparency associated with public participation in environmental governance provides a boost to accountability as does more rigorous implementation and enforcement of environmental laws. One measurable indicator of the influence of the constitutional right to a healthy environment on accountability is court decisions that cite this right. Court decisions based on the right have been made in at least forty-four of ninety-four nations and are increasing in frequency and importance. This includes almost all surveyed countries in Western Europe (eight out of ten), most nations in Latin America and the Caribbean (thirteen of eighteen) and Eastern Europe (twelve of nineteen), a minority of nations in Asia (six of fourteen), but only a few in Africa (five of thirty-three). In at least twelve other nations, courts have ruled that the right to a healthy environment is implicit in other constitutional rights and therefore directly enforceable.[29] The number of reported cases per country ranges from one (Malawi) to hundreds in some Latin American, Asian, and European countries. In total, thousands of reported cases are available, led by Colombia, Costa Rica, Brazil, Argentina, India, the Philippines, the Netherlands, Belgium, and Greece. The assertion that constitutional environmental rights are enforceable in "only a few" or a "handful" of countries is clearly no longer accurate.[30] The recent nature of some constitutional environmental rights and difficulties in accessing the jurisprudence of at least forty-five nations mean that these statistics underestimate the full extent of litigation based on the right to a healthy environment. In many nations, not all court decisions are published, meaning that a substantial proportion of litigation is not easily accessible to researchers. For example, Kravchenko and Stec both identify the difficulty of locating judicial decisions from Eastern Europe.[31]

Data from Latin America, Europe, and India indicate that the majority of lawsuits based on the constitutional right to a healthy environment are successful.[32] In Brazil, environmental public civil actions were successful in 67.5 percent of cases.[33] In Colombia, the applicants were successful in 53 percent of the *acciones populares* related to drinking water based on the right to a healthy environment brought between 1991 and 2008.[34] In Costa Rica, roughly 66 percent of cases asserting violations of the right to a healthy environment were successful.[35] Jariwala estimated that nearly 80 percent of environmental cases brought in India succeeded.[36] These statistics should assuage concerns that environmental activists will attempt to block economic development by filing ill-conceived and frivolous lawsuits, as such litigation would result in low success rates.

Courts have ruled that the constitutional right to a healthy environment imposes three duties upon government: to respect the right by not infringing it through state action; to protect it from infringement by third parties (which may require regulations, implementation, and enforcement); and to take actions to fulfill it (such as by providing environmental services including clean water, sanitation, and waste management). As well, courts have consistently held that laws, regulations, and administrative actions that violate the right will be struck down. The Netherlands provides a limited exception, as courts are not permitted to review the constitutionality of legislation.

An examination of the numbers on a regional basis shows that enforcement of the constitutional right to a healthy environment is common in Latin America and Western Europe, is becoming more frequent in parts of Eastern Europe and Asia (particularly South Asia), and remains rare in Africa. Twenty-seven of the forty-five nations for which no court decisions are available are in Africa. This regional pattern is consistent with Epp's hypothesis about the civil and political rights revolution, which stipulates that certain conditions must be present before courts can play a significant role in defending human rights.[37] The presence of these conditions – which include clear constitutional provisions, the rule of law, an independent judiciary, and legal infrastructure supportive of rights-based litigation (lawyers, NGOs, networks, and funding) – appears to be positively correlated with the extent of court decisions about the right to a healthy environment in each of the five regions. Clear constitutional articulation of the right (as in, for example, Argentina, Brazil, Colombia, and Costa Rica) will generally lead to a larger role for courts than an ambiguous provision (such as that of Spain). India and other nations with an implicit constitutional right to a healthy environment are exceptions to this generalization. The absence of the rule of law, in combination with daunting social, economic, and political problems, dramatically reduces the potential influence of the constitutional right in much of Africa, although Kenya, South Africa, and Uganda offer hope that the situation can be reversed.

It is uncommon for courts to decide that the constitutional right to a healthy environment is not directly enforceable, although this is the case in the Czech Republic, Paraguay, the Slovak Republic, South Korea, and Spain. In most of these nations, the courts are constrained by constitutional language specifying that the right can be enforced only pursuant to enabling legislation (that is, the right is not self-executing). However, these countries are exceptions to the general rule that the constitutional right to a healthy environment is directly enforceable. Even in nations where it does not appear to be directly enforceable or self-executing, it can still play a significant role in litigation, as demonstrated by the experiences of Andorra, Belgium, and France. Overall, constitutional principles related to the right to a healthy environment "have created the right conditions for courts of law ... to begin to play a more prominent role in protecting the environment."[38]

It is vital to note that public interest litigation based on the constitutional right will be successful only if the government is proven to be violating the constitution through its actions or omissions. Protecting human rights from violations by the state is a legitimate role for the judiciary in a constitutional democracy. What is novel about judicial protection of the right to a healthy environment is that it can impose a positive duty on the state to take preventive or remedial action. In this sense, judicial protection of the right is distinct from the court's historical role in protecting individuals and their property from state interference. Courts are protecting a collective public interest, historically the prerogative of the legislature. By constitutionalizing the right to a healthy environment, both the public and the judiciary are newly empowered to hold governments accountable for defending the environment. Landmark court decisions regarding the restoration of the Matanza-Riachuelo River in Argentina and of Manila Bay in the Philippines are leading examples.[39] In both cases, a generation of political leaders repeatedly promised to clean up these environmental disasters but took few concrete steps. Litigation brought by concerned citizens, based on their constitutional right to a healthy environment, led to strict and detailed court-imposed obligations that have proven difficult for political leaders to avoid. In both these cases, concerns about the non-enforcement of past court orders led courts to create independent monitoring bodies, impose special reporting requirements, and establish substantial penalties for non-compliance.[40]

Addressing Environmental Justice

The constitutional right to a healthy environment should, in theory, promote environmental justice by ensuring a minimum standard of environmental quality for all members of society. Although evidence reveals that environmental laws have improved extensively, few prioritize the people most affected by environmental degradation – the poor, ethnic minorities, and other populations vulnerable to discrimination. However, some politically weak and marginalized communities have enjoyed success in the courts in enforcing their right to a healthy environment. Many cases, particularly in Latin America, deal with the provision of clean water, sewage treatment, and adequate waste management, concerns more likely to confront the poor than the middle or upper classes. An Argentine case involving Chacras de la Merced, a poor community whose drinking water was being contaminated by inadequate wastewater treatment in an upstream municipality, illustrates the potential for using the right to a healthy environment to advance justice.[41] After political efforts to resolve the problem were unsuccessful, residents engaged a non-profit environmental law firm to file a lawsuit asserting a violation of the constitutional right to a healthy environment. Agreeing that the right had been violated, the court ordered the government to upgrade the wastewater treatment plant and, in the interim, provide a supply of clean water to the residents of Chacras de la Merced. The court-ordered infrastructure improvements were completed, and in an interesting development, the municipality passed a bylaw mandating that all future sewage and sanitation tax revenues must be reinvested in upgrading and maintaining the sewage system.[42] Many poor residents in Argentina, Colombia, Costa Rica, and other nations enjoy clean drinking water today because the constitutional right to a healthy environment compelled governments to make necessary investments in infrastructure and protecting water supplies. In South Africa, constitutionalizing the right to water contributed to the complete rewriting of water laws and policies as well as major investments in infrastructure. Nelson Mandela described the extension of clean drinking water to millions of South Africans (predominantly black and poor) since the mid-1990s as "amongst the most important achievements of democracy in our country."[43]

There are many other examples of courts addressing environmental injustices by defending people's right to live in a healthy environment. Citizens in countries as diverse as Russia, Romania, Chile, and Turkey brought lawsuits based on their right to a healthy environment and received compensation for damage to their health caused by industrial pollution.[44] Because of litigation based on their constitutional environmental rights, people in the

Peruvian village of La Oroya are finally receiving medical treatment for their long-term exposure to lead and other heavy metals emitted by a nearby smelter.[45] There are some situations where systemic changes are being produced by constitutions, legislation, and litigation. In Brazil, litigation based on the constitutional right to a healthy environment resulted in a new government policy that all citizens have the right to a core minimum of essential environmental services including clean water, adequate sanitation, and proper waste management.[46] The comprehensive court-ordered cleanup and restoration of the Matanza-Riachuelo watershed in Argentina and Manila Bay in the Philippines will lead to improved living conditions for millions of people.

On the other hand, it is often difficult for the communities most affected by environmental degradation to influence law and policy-making processes or take advantage of their constitutional rights. Barriers include limited awareness of their rights, lack of financial resources, lack of access to legal assistance, and distrust of the judicial system. Some critics claim that environmental litigation brought by middle-class litigants to enforce their right to a healthy environment worsens the plight of the poor. For example, the closure or relocation of polluting factories in India is alleged to have displaced workers and caused adverse socio-economic effects.[47] More broadly, there are unresolved questions about leakage, wherein legislation, litigation, or other societal forces displace environmentally harmful activities from relatively wealthy nations to poorer countries or regions.[48]

Level Playing Field

Another advantage of the constitutional right to a healthy environment is the prospect of a level playing field with competing social and economic rights. The strengthening of environmental laws represents a significant advance in that direction. Environmental legislation often constrains the exercise of property rights, recognizing that the public interest should take precedence over private interests in some circumstances. In many nations where environmental rights are articulated in constitutions, courts have rejected challenges against environmental laws or administrative decisions in which plaintiffs alleged that their property rights were violated. Courts have referred to constitutional protection of the environment as a compelling rationale that can justify the infringement of private property rights.[49] For example, the Slovenian Constitutional Court upheld a tax on water pollution based on the constitutional interest in environmental protection.[50] In Belgium, "Courts are no longer inclined, when facing conflicting interests, to automatically sacrifice environmental interests in favor of economic interests."[51] South Korea and

Israel are rare examples of nations where courts have ruled that property rights continue to trump the constitutional right to a healthy environment.[52]

Rights can and do collide, in complex multi-faceted disputes. The constitutional right to a healthy environment is not applied as a systematic trump card. Governments and courts go to great efforts to balance competing rights and conflicting social priorities. For example, in a Turkish case involving air pollution from coal-fired power plants, the courts ordered the installation of pollution abatement equipment instead of requiring the plants to be closed.[53] Some would argue that courts have not gone far enough to level the playing field, particularly in cases involving powerful economic interests, such as the Sardar Sarovar Dam in India, the Camisea natural gas project in Peru, or genetically modified crops in France.[54] On the other hand, the constitutional right to a healthy environment played an instrumental role in the Greek Council of State's repeated decisions to strike down approvals for the Acheloos water diversion project, the Finnish Supreme Administrative Court's decision blocking the Vuotos hydroelectric project, Costa Rican court decisions blocking offshore oil and gas development, the Ecuadorean Constitutional Court's rejection of the Baba Dam, Hungarian and Russian court decisions preventing the privatization of public forests, and the Thai Supreme Court's decision to block dozens of petrochemical projects.[55] These cases involved powerful actors and major economic consequences, yet courts took bold decisions based on constitutional environmental provisions.

Finally, the constitutionalization of the right to a healthy environment can have a systematic effect on the exercise of discretion by legislators, judges, and public authorities, pushing countless decisions in a more ecologically sustainable direction. At a minimum, constitutional provisions requiring environmental protection should ensure a better balancing of competing interests than has been the case in the past.

Education

Among the many laws spurred, at least in part, by the constitutionalization of environmental protection are national laws related to environmental education in, for instance, Armenia, Brazil, the Philippines, and South Korea.[56] Courts in Argentina, India, and the Philippines have issued creative orders requiring governments to develop and implement environmental education programs.[57] In France, the *Charter for the Environment* has reportedly revitalized environmental education.[58] As well, extensive efforts have been made by international agencies to educate judges, enforcement agencies, prosecutors, and other groups involved in the implementation and enforcement of environmental laws about the right to a healthy environment.

Disadvantages of Constitutional Environmental Rights

Vague, Absolute, and Redundant?

The argument has been made that the constitutional right to a healthy environment is too vague to be implemented and protected effectively. Yet at least seventy-eight national legislatures and courts in at least fifty-six nations have managed to interpret and implement the right, as hundreds of laws and thousands of court decisions demonstrate. There is an occasional exception, such as a 2008 Supreme Court decision in Paraguay that suggested the impreciseness of the right was one reason for deferring to the legislature.[59] The variety of adjectives used to describe the right – such as healthy, clean, safe, favourable – does not appear to influence the outcome of litigation. Concerns that the right would be applied in an absolutist fashion have not been borne out in any of the nations whose constitutions recognize it. Neither legislatures nor courts have used environmental rights to systematically trump other rights, opting instead for careful balancing. The extensive reliance upon the right to a healthy environment by legislators, citizens, communities, NGOs, and judges should put to rest the notion that it duplicates the protection offered by other human rights or existing environmental laws. As the Supreme Court of the Philippines observed in a pioneering judgment, the right to a healthy environment "is no less important than any of the civil or political rights ... [but] belongs to a different category of rights altogether, for it concerns nothing less than self-preservation and self-perpetuation."[60]

Anthropocentric?

Among the seventy-eight nations where legislation has been influenced by constitutional environmental provisions, many laws intended to protect forests, oceans, wildlife, and biodiversity have been enacted. Although the argument can be made that anthropocentric motives prompt the conservation and preservation of Nature, a growing number of these laws also include recognition of the intrinsic value of the natural world. In some cases this recognition is implicit, whereas in others it is explicit. For example, one of the general principles of Costa Rica's *Law of Biodiversity* is "respect for all forms of life. All living things have the right to live, independently of actual or potential economic value."[61]

Citizens, ENGOs, and prosecutors have brought many successful lawsuits to protect Nature itself – national parks, dolphins, sharks, lakes, forests, rivers, birds, sea turtles, salamanders, and other species.[62] As Lynda Collins proposed, the right to a healthy environment is being "understood as encompassing both human-centered and eco-centric aspects, as in an environment that is both healthy for humans and healthy in its own right (e.g., a healthy lake, a healthy forest, a healthy ecosystem)."[63] In light of the enactment of new environmental laws and the rulings of courts, the constitutional right to a healthy environment, though technically a human right, is having positive spillover effects for Nature. As well, there is an emerging trend toward explicit recognition of the rights of Nature, exemplified by the constitutions of Ecuador (2008), Bolivia (2009), and Iceland (2012). Inspired by these constitutional developments, a number of local governments have enacted bylaws that recognize legal rights for ecosystems.[64]

Non-Justiciable?

The argument that the right to a healthy environment, like other social and economic rights, should not be justiciable because policy decisions are the sole purview of the legislature is also refuted by the evidence from other nations. This objection is largely extinguished by the willingness of courts to take a principled and pragmatic approach to the question of rights, balancing the interests of the individual with those of society in the context of specific facts and circumstances. There are only a handful of countries – the Czech Republic, Spain, Paraguay, the Slovak Republic, and South Korea – where courts have declined to enforce the constitutional right to a healthy environment. Beatty concludes that recent "jurisprudence shows that a lot of judges think that the legal enforcement of social and economic rights isn't so different from the protection that is provided by the more traditional political and civil guarantees."[65] The same could be said regarding legal enforcement of environmental rights. Courts do not generally dictate environmental policy, save in exceptional circumstances, but they do critically scrutinize government policies and actions to determine whether they offer adequate protection for constitutional rights. A case involving the restoration of the Matanza-Riachuelo River in Argentina illustrates how today's judiciaries can undermine the objection that courts are not an appropriate arena for addressing polycentric disputes. Argentina's Supreme Court opened its doors to multiple parties and *amici curiae* (friends of the court), held public hearings, and engaged independent experts (for further details of this case, see Chapter 7).[66]

The Supreme Court of the Philippines employed a similar approach in the *Manila Bay* case (also described in Chapter 7).[67]

Open the Floodgates to Litigation?

Constitutionalizing the right to a healthy environment does result in additional cases being brought to court. In some nations with very open rules regarding standing and expedited procedures for cases involving constitutional rights – such as Argentina, Brazil, Colombia, Costa Rica, and India – courts face a daunting caseload, resulting in backlogs and delays.[68] However, cases based on the right to a healthy environment represent a very small fraction of the total number of constitutional cases in any given nation, according to empirical evidence from Europe and Latin America.[69] Environmental lawsuits tend to have a relatively high success rate, negating the related argument that frivolous and vexatious lawsuits will proliferate if standing and procedural rules are relaxed.

Undemocratic?

The first drawback of constitutionalizing the right to a healthy environment that finds some support in the experiences of other countries involves potentially undemocratic consequences. For the most part, courts are well aware of the separation of powers and act judiciously to avoid crossing the line into legislative and executive action. In some nations, however, judges have taken an activist stance in interpreting and applying social, economic, and environmental rights. Excessive judicial activism can remove contentious issues from the democratic arena and create a risk that governments responsible for environmental protection will be unable to properly establish priorities or allocate resources. The most notorious example is the Supreme Court of India, which has been accused of crossing the line in several high-profile cases, involving motor vehicles in Delhi, pollution of the Ganges River, and forest conservation.[70] Some of the court's orders in these controversial cases have trespassed into the legislative or executive realms. In the forest conservation case, the original lawsuit focused on illegal logging in one region. The Supreme Court expanded the case to cover all of India's forests and forest policies, leading to literally thousands of interlocutory applications related to forestry within the parameters of one case.[71] On the other hand, the Indian Supreme Court's actions can be defended on the basis of government's persistent failure to implement and enforce its environmental laws, as mandated by the constitution.

There are two compelling rebuttals to the charge that the constitutional right to a healthy environment is undemocratic. The first lies in the expansion and enforcement of procedural environmental rights. Improving access to information and participation in environmental decision making can actually enhance democracy by enabling more people to play a hands-on role in shaping the policies and decisions that affect their lives.[72] The constitutional right to a healthy environment is contributing to democracy by providing a robust legal basis for the enjoyment of these procedural rights. In general, constitutional recognition of environmental rights in Latin America and Europe, and to a lesser extent in other regions, has "created a vehicle for new and more democratic relations to resolve conflicts between the state and civil society."[73]

The second rebuttal is that excessive judicial activism is rare and must be distinguished from cases where courts are fulfilling their legitimate roles as constitutional guardians. Constitutions empower courts to safeguard human rights, so the judiciary is exercising one of its basic functions by protecting the right to a healthy environment. South Africa has gained worldwide renown for the seemingly constructive democratic dialogue between judges and legislators, with courts telling governments that they must make best efforts to fulfill social, economic, and environmental rights (such as housing and water) without necessarily spelling out in detail how to do so, except in compelling circumstances (for example, requiring nationwide provision of nevirapine to pregnant women with HIV/AIDS). Corder and other experts have concluded that "an admirable balance has been struck between activism and restraint" in South African courts.[74] The Supreme Court of the Philippines is also praised for combining judicial caution with a willingness to passionately defend constitutional rights, including environmental rights.[75]

Ineffective?

The second substantive criticism directed at constitutionalizing the right to a healthy environment is that it will be ineffective because it fails to address the underlying political economy of environmental degradation. There is undoubtedly some truth to this claim, as neither constitutions nor human rights can magically solve deep-rooted societal problems related to capitalism, globalization, and the growing gap between rich and poor. However, experience indicates that the right can act as a countervailing force to some of the factors identified as key drivers of unsustainability, including deregulation and privatization. For example, the standstill doctrine (described earlier in this chapter) effectively blocks deregulation. Courts from Costa Rica to

Russia have struck down efforts to privatize Nature, from forests to the seabed.[76] In fact, Costa Rica's Constitutional Court has even reversed the process of privatization by mandating the expropriation of privately owned land that provides critical habitat for endangered sea turtles.[77] Critics should bear in mind that the main reason environmental legislation is ineffective is a lack of implementation and enforcement. Constitutionalizing the right to a healthy environment, as demonstrated by the experiences of other nations, provides multiple means for improving implementation and enforcement.

Critics of constitutional rights argue that civil and political rights have been appropriated by societal elites to entrench and extend their power (for example, corporations have used the right to free speech to strike down government regulation of advertising).[78] However, the right to a healthy environment has been used predominantly to advance public, not private, interests. The only prominent example to the contrary is a South African case, where the Fuel Retailers Association used the right to protect its members from competition by successfully challenging the approval of a new gas station.[79] In general, the right to a healthy environment and other constitutional environmental provisions impose positive obligations on the state and are thus pro-government rather than anti-government. In Latin America, and particularly in the leading nations of Argentina, Brazil, Colombia, and Costa Rica, constitutional litigation (including but not limited to the right to a healthy environment) is beginning to alter some of the structural inequalities and power relations that are at the heart of unsustainability.[80] Recent constitutions in Bolivia and Ecuador include strong environmental provisions and share the broader aspiration of contributing to a more just and sustainable society.

Constitutions and Environmental Performance

Stronger environmental laws, increased public participation, and ecologically literate court decisions that hold governments accountable are merely means toward the ultimate objectives of reducing environmental degradation and improving human well-being. The question of whether or not the constitutional right to a healthy environment affects environmental performance requires an assessment of outcomes such as changes in air quality, water quality, and the level of pressure on natural resources. Many factors can influence environmental performance including geographic size, population density, wealth, economic structure, degree of urbanization, income inequality, international trade profile (types of imports and exports), public opinion, history, climate, natural resource endowment, strength of environmental policy, and socio-economic status.[81] It is difficult to disentangle the effects of constitutional provisions related to the environment from these other factors. The time frame required to observe differences in environmental performance flowing from the implementation of constitutional provisions is difficult to establish and will vary from nation to nation depending on legislative and judicial processes as well as political, social, economic, and cultural factors. For example, it will take time to strengthen environmental legislation, create and implement detailed regulations, and enhance the capacity of the public service. Similarly, it will take time for concerned citizens or civil society to identify violations of constitutional rights or duties and then file lawsuits. The judicial process, including appeals, can contribute to additional delay. All of these factors could result in a significant lag before constitutional provisions related to the environment have an effect. Despite these challenges, recent research indicates that nations with environmental rights and responsibilities enshrined in their constitutions

- have smaller per capita ecological footprints (both among 150 nations globally and within five broad geographic regions including Africa, the Americas, Asia-Pacific, Europe, and the Middle East/Central Asia)
- rank higher on environmental performance measured by a suite of twenty-nine indicators (based on a Simon Fraser University study using OECD data for thirty nations)
- rank higher on environmental performance measured by a suite of fifteen indicators (among seventeen similar nations assessed by the Conference Board of Canada)
- are more likely to have ratified international environmental agreements
- and have achieved deeper cuts in emissions of nitrogen oxides, sulphur dioxide, and greenhouse gases.

The Ecological Footprint

The ecological footprint measures how much of the regenerative capacity of the biosphere is used by human activities.[82] Defined as "the area of biologically productive land and water required to produce the resources consumed and to assimilate the wastes generated by humanity, under the predominant management and production practices in any given year," the ecological footprint is ascertained primarily from UN statistics.[83] Calculations of the footprint include the area of land and water needed to produce crops, livestock, fish, wood products, and energy, as well as the area needed to absorb the carbon dioxide produced by burning fossil fuels. Footprints are compared

Table 5.1

Constitutional provisions and ecological footprints

	Nations without EPIC	Nations with duty	Nations with duty/rights	Regional average
Africa	1.8 (*n* = 11)	1.4 (*n* =13)	1.3 (*n* = 23)	1.4 (*n* = 47)
Asia-Pacific	3.7 (*n* = 8)	1.3 (*n* = 9)	2.0 (*n* = 6)	2.3 (*n* = 23)
Americas	4.2 (*n* = 5)	2.3 (*n* = 4)	2.4 (*n* = 15)	2.8 (*n* = 24)
Middle East/ Central Asia	4.8 (*n* = 6)	2.5 (*n* = 8)	1.6 (*n* = 7)	2.9 (*n* = 21)
Europe	5.6 (*n* = 4)	4.8 (*n* = 7)	3.9 (*n* = 24)	4.3 (*n* = 35)
Global average	3.6 (***n*** = 34)	2.3 (***n*** = 41)	2.4 (***n*** = 75)	2.6 (***n*** = 150)

Note: All mean ecological footprint measurements are given in hectares per capita.
EPIC – Environmental provisions in constitutions
Duty – Government has obligation to protect the environment
Rights – Individuals have right to live in a healthy environment

with biological capacity to determine whether a nation is living within its means or whether the Earth can sustain a particular nation's or individual's level of impact. Overshoot (exceeding biocapacity) at the national level is not necessarily unsustainable, as international trade provides a means of appropriating biocapacity from other nations. However, overshoot at the global level is inherently unsustainable.

Data from the Global Footprint Network were used to compare the ecological footprints of 150 nations.[84] Overall, the 34 countries without environmental protection provisions in their constitutions had a larger ecological footprint, averaging 3.58 hectares per capita, whereas the 116 nations with environmental protection provisions in their constitution had a smaller footprint, averaging 2.36 hectares per capita (see Table 5.1). Analysis demonstrated that the differences are statistically significant. Canada had a footprint of 7.07 hectares per capita, the seventh largest in the world. The footprints of nations with constitutional environmental provisions were smaller in each of the five global regions including Africa, the Americas, Asia-Pacific, Europe, and the Middle East/Central Asia.

Simon Fraser University Rankings

Researchers at Simon Fraser University compared the environmental performance of thirty nations belonging to the OECD on a suite of twenty-nine indicators.[85] The indicators included energy consumption, energy intensity, water consumption, greenhouse gas emissions, sulphur oxides, nitrogen oxides, volatile organic compounds, carbon monoxide, ozone-depleting substances, municipal waste, nuclear waste, pesticide use, fertilizer use, livestock, timber harvest, capture fisheries, fisheries as percent of world catch, distance travelled, number of species at risk, percent of species at risk, protected areas, timber harvest to forest growth ratio, environmental pricing, renewable energy including hydro, renewable energy excluding hydro, recycling of municipal waste, pollution abatement and control expenditures, municipal sewage treatment, and official development assistance. The OECD regularly publishes comprehensive environmental data for its member nations and employs an extensive due diligence process to ensure reliability and comparability of data.[86]

The OECD comparison is distinct from the ecological footprint approach in several ways. First, the footprint data involved a heterogeneous group of 150 nations large and small, rich and poor. The 30 OECD nations were more homogeneous, including 27 wealthy industrialized nations and 3 newly industrializing countries (Mexico, Poland, and Turkey). Second, the OECD data included a mixture of pressure, state, and response indicators, whereas the ecological footprint was exclusively focused on pressure indicators. Although there was some overlap between the two studies, the reliance on different indicators was likely to result in differing assessments of environmental performance.[87]

A clear pattern is evident from the environmental ranking of OECD nations (see Table 5.2). Fourteen of the fifteen top-performing nations have constitutions that include protection for the environment. Denmark is the sole exception. The Danish constitution has not been revised since 1953 because it is extremely difficult to amend, though Denmark's environmental policies are heavily influenced by those of its progressive Scandinavian neighbours. Conversely, among the seven nations with the worst environmental records, only Belgium has constitutional provisions related to the environment. Belgium's constitutional environmental provisions are weak, and the small country is densely populated and heavily industrialized. Canada ranked an embarrassing twenty-eighth out of thirty nations. The average ranking of the twenty nations with environmental rights and/or responsibilities in their constitutions was 12.2 (where 1 was the top-performing nation and 30 was the worst-performing nation), whereas the average ranking of the ten nations with constitutions silent on the environment was 21.8. The difference in performance is statistically significant.

Table 5.2

Constitutions and environmental performance of OECD nations

OECD environmental ranking		Government duty to protect	Government duty and individual right
1.	Turkey	Y	Y
2.	Switzerland	Y	N
3.	Denmark	N	N
4.	Poland	Y	Y
5.	Slovak Republic	Y	Y
6.	Germany	Y	N
7.	Austria	Y	N
8.	Sweden	Y	N
9.	Italy	Y	N
10.	Netherlands	Y	Y
11.	Portugal	Y	Y
12.	Czech Republic	Y	Y
13.	Mexico	Y	Y
14.5T.	Norway	Y	Y
14.5T.	Hungary	Y	Y
16.	Japan	N	N
17.	Finland	Y	Y
18.5T.	France	Y	Y
18.5T.	United Kingdom	N	N
20.	Greece	Y	Y
21.	Spain	Y	Y
22.	Luxembourg	N	N
23.	South Korea	Y	Y
24.	Iceland	N	N
25.5T.	New Zealand	N	N
25.5T.	Australia	N	N
27.	Ireland	N	N
28.	Canada	N	N
29.	Belgium	Y	Y
30.	United States	N	N

T = Tie

Y = Yes, constitution includes specified environmental provision

N = No, constitution does not include specified environmental provision

CONFERENCE BOARD OF CANADA RANKINGS

The Conference Board of Canada compared the performance of seventeen wealthy industrialized countries across six domains including environment, economy, education and skills, health, innovation, and society.[88] The board selected these nations from among thirty-eight that were deemed "high income" by the World Bank. According to the board, these countries are likely to have achieved a high and sustainable quality of life, and are therefore an appropriate comparison group. The board then applied three filters: removing nations with populations smaller than 1 million (Iceland and Luxembourg), eliminating those with an area smaller than 10,000 square kilometres (Singapore), and dropping those whose per capita income was below the mean income (based on a five-year average of GDP per capita). In effect, this screening process partially controlled for the effects of population, geographic size, and economic wealth.

The board's environmental comparison examined fifteen indicators in six areas: air quality, waste, water quality and quantity, natural resource management, biodiversity and conservation, and climate change and energy efficiency. Within these broad areas, the board focused on what it described as "outcome" indicators, which measured what nations were achieving, rather than the type or extent of effort being undertaken. There was some degree of overlap with Simon Fraser University's OECD comparison, as six of the board's indicators were identical.[89]

Again, a clear pattern can be observed by looking at the board's environmental performance rankings (see Table 5.3). Eight of the nine top-ranked nations have environmental protection provisions in their constitutions. Conversely, six of the eight lowest-ranked nations did not. Canada ranked a dismal fifteenth out of seventeen nations. The average ranking of the seven nations with no constitutional protection for the environment was 12.6 (where 1 was the top-performing nation and 17 the worst-performing nation). In contrast, the average ranking for the ten nations with environmental rights and/or responsibilities was 6.5. Analysis confirmed that the difference in environmental performance is statistically significant.

CONVENTIONS AND TREATIES

Another metric that can be used to assess the environmental performance of nations is the extent of participation in international environmental agreements. There are more than a thousand of these in place today.[90] Signing and ratifying such agreements is, at least on its face, a reflection of commitment

Table 5.3

Constitutions and the Conference Board of Canada's environmental rankings

Conference Board ranking	Government duty to protect	Government duty and individual right
1. Sweden	Y	N
2. Finland	Y	Y
3. Norway	Y	Y
4. Switzerland	Y	N
5. United Kingdom	N	N
6. France	Y	Y
7. Germany	Y	N
8. Italy	Y	N
9. Austria	Y	N
10. Ireland	N	N
11. Denmark	N	N
12. Belgium	Y	Y
13. Netherlands	Y	Y
14. Japan	N	N
15. Canada	N	N
16. Australia	N	N
17. United States	N	N

Y = Yes, constitution includes specified environmental provision
N = No, constitution does not include specified environmental provision

to improved environmental protection, despite concerns about the enforceability of international law.[91] Because of the general lack of coercive enforcement mechanisms in international environmental law, it can be argued that ratification does not necessarily imply a commitment to comply with the terms of an agreement. For example, it has been suggested that Canada's ratification of the *Kyoto Protocol* in 2002 was a symbolic gesture, rather than an indication of a genuine intent to reduce greenhouse gas emissions.[92]

For some agreements, such as the *Vienna Convention on the Protection of the Ozone Layer* and the associated *Montreal Protocol on Substances That Deplete the Ozone Layer*, international participation is universal. The following assessment examines the ratification status of five major environmental treaties and protocols that do not enjoy universal participation:

- the *Kyoto Protocol to the United Nations Framework Convention on Climate Change*
- the *Stockholm Convention on Persistent Organic Pollutants*
- the *Cartagena Protocol on Biosafety to the United Nations Convention on Biological Diversity*
- the *Rotterdam Convention on the Prior Informed Consent Procedure for Certain Hazardous Chemicals and Pesticides in International Trade*
- and the *Ban Amendment to the Basel Convention on the Control of Transboundary Movements of Hazardous Wastes and Their Disposal.*

The *Kyoto Protocol* commits a group of industrialized nations to self-imposed limits on greenhouse gas emissions.[93] The *Stockholm Convention* bans or severely restricts the manufacturing, use, and release of more than a dozen

TABLE 5.4

Constitutions and ratification of international environmental treaties

Nation	Constitutional Duty	Constitutional Right	*Kyoto*	*Stockholm*	*Cartagena*	*Rotterdam*	*Ban*
Sweden	Yes	No	Y	Y	Y	Y	Y
Finland	Yes	Yes	Y	Y	Y	Y	Y
Norway	Yes	Yes	Y	Y	Y	Y	Y
Switzerland	Yes	No	Y	Y	Y	Y	Y
United Kingdom	No	No	Y	Y	Y	Y	Y
France	Yes	Yes	Y	Y	Y	Y	Y
Italy	Yes	No	Y	N	Y	Y	Y
Austria	Yes	No	Y	Y	Y	Y	Y
Germany	Yes	No	Y	Y	Y	Y	Y
Ireland	No	No	Y	N	Y	Y	Y
Denmark	No	No	Y	Y	Y	Y	Y
Belgium	Yes	Yes	Y	Y	Y	Y	Y
Netherlands	Yes	Yes	Y	Y	Y	Y	Y
Japan	No	No	Y	Y	Y	Y	N
Canada	No	No	Y	Y	N	Y	N
Australia	No	No	Y	Y	N	Y	N
United States	No	No	N	N	N	N	N

Y = Yes, the agreement has been ratified
N = No, the agreement has not been ratified

persistent toxic substances.[94] The *Cartagena Protocol* is intended to protect biological diversity from the risks associated with living genetically modified organisms.[95] The *Rotterdam Convention* requires exporting nations to obtain the prior informed consent of importing nations for trade in designated toxic substances.[96] The *Ban Amendment to the Basel Convention* is intended to restrict international trade in hazardous waste.[97]

Eleven of the seventeen OECD nations in the Conference Board of Canada's study have signed and ratified all five of these international environmental laws (see Table 5.4). Of the ten whose constitutions require environmental protection, nine ratified all five; only Italy failed to ratify one of the agreements. In contrast, of the seven nations without environmental provisions in their constitutions, only Denmark and the UK ratified all five, whereas Australia, Canada, Ireland, Japan, and the USA failed to ratify at least one. The USA stands out because of its failure to ratify any of the five agreements included in this assessment. Canada and Australia each failed to ratify two of the five. Canada is the only country that has publicly reneged its commitment under *Kyoto* and sabotaged the implementation of the *Rotterdam Convention* by blocking the addition of asbestos to the list of hazardous substances governed by the agreement. Overall, this comparison suggests that nations whose constitutions require environmental protection are more likely to ratify international environmental agreements. Other explanations are possible, however, such as the added complexity of achieving ratification in federal nations such as Australia, Canada, and the USA.

Air Pollution and Climate Change

Thus far, the quantitative evidence has consisted of snapshots of environmental performance at a given point in time. Examining patterns of performance over time while taking into account the enactment of constitutional environmental provisions is also essential. The following assessment focuses on three specific indicators: emissions of nitrogen oxides, sulphur dioxide, and greenhouse gases (GHGs). Air pollution has been the focus of remedial efforts in all the major industrialized nations since prior to 1980. The OECD has published relatively reliable data for nitrogen oxide and sulphur dioxide emissions for the period 1980-2005. UN data on greenhouse gas emissions are available for a shorter time period (1990-2009), because climate change did not appear on the public policy radar screen until the late 1980s.[98] Time-series data were analyzed for the seventeen relatively large and wealthy nations used in the Conference Board of Canada's rankings. For purposes of the comparative analysis, France was included among the nations without environmental protection provisions in their constitutions because its *Charter for the Environment* did not come into force until 2005.

Nitrogen Oxide Emissions

Nitrogen oxides (NOx) are produced by the combustion of fossil fuels and contribute to acid precipitation, ozone, smog, and particulate matter. Exposure to elevated levels of nitrogen oxides can contribute to eye, nose, and throat irritation, shortness of breath, respiratory illness, aggravation of asthma, decreased lung function, increased risk of respiratory infection, and reduced lung growth in children.[99]

When one examines the progress of the seventeen wealthy industrialized nations in reducing emissions of NOx, an interesting pattern again emerges (see Table 5.5). Among the eight nations with no environmental provisions in their constitutions, including Canada, total NOx emissions fell an average of 3.1 percent over the twenty-five-year period from 1980 to 2005. The average annual decrease in NOx emissions among these nations was 0.1 percent.

During the same period, total NOx emissions declined by an average of 32.3 percent among the nine nations with constitutional environmental protection. The average annual decrease among these countries was 1.5 percent. In other words, NOx emissions fell ten times faster between 1980 and 2005 in nations whose constitutions required environmental protection. Among the seven nations that introduced environmental protection provisions in their constitutions during this time span (Austria, Belgium, Finland, Germany, Netherlands, Norway, and Sweden), NOx emissions declined by an average of 1.1 percent per year prior to the incorporation of the provisions and by an average of 1.9 percent per year afterward. In Switzerland and Sweden, the rate of decline in NOx emissions also accelerated after their constitutions' environmental provisions were strengthened in 1999 and 2002, respectively. There are other potential factors in the widespread decline of NOx emissions, including technological advances and the *UN Convention on Long-Range Transboundary Air Pollution* (to which fifteen of these seventeen states became parties in the early 1980s).[100]

Sulphur Dioxide Emissions

Sulphur dioxide emissions are generated by the production, processing, and combustion of fossil fuels, as well as by metal smelting and refining. Sulphur dioxide contributes to acid precipitation, which damages forests, soils, and aquatic ecosystems. It also reacts with other air pollutants to form particulate

Table 5.5

Constitutions and changes in nitrogen oxide emissions

		Change in NOx emissions (%)	Average annual change (%)
No environmental provisions in constitutions			
Australia	1990-2005	12.9	0.86
Canada	1980-2005	21.4	0.86
Denmark	1980-2005	−31.9	−1.28
France	1980-2005	−26.7	−1.07
Ireland	1980-2005	58.9	2.36
Japan	1990-2005	−6.4	−0.43
United Kingdom	1980-2005	−32.1	−1.28
United States	1980-2005	−20.9	−0.84
Average		−3.1	−0.10
Constitutional duty for government to protect the environment			
Austria	1980-2005	−8.5	−0.34
Germany	1990-2005	−47.4	−3.16
Italy	1980-2005	−29.7	−1.19
Sweden	1980-2005	−54.8	−2.19
Switzerland	1980-2005	−56.1	−2.24
Average		−39.3	−1.82
Constitutional duty for government to protect the environment and individual right to live in a healthy environment			
Belgium	1990-2005	−26.8	−1.79
Finland	1980-2005	−33.3	−1.33
Netherlands	1980-2005	−41.1	−1.64
Norway	1980-2005	7.1	0.28
Average		−23.5	−1.12
Combined average of nations with EPIC		−32.3	−1.51

EPIC = Environmental provisions in constitution

matter. Exposure to sulphur dioxide can cause severe problems for people with asthma and is linked to increased risks of lung cancer and chronic bronchitis.[101]

Between 1980 and 2005, the nine nations with environmental provisions in their constitutions achieved an impressive average total reduction in sulphur dioxide emissions of 84.8 percent, an average reduction of 3.8 percent per year (see Table 5.6). In comparison, the eight nations with no constitutionalized environmental protection provisions achieved an average total

TABLE 5.6

Constitutions and changes in sulphur dioxide emissions

		Change in SO_2 emissions (%)	Average annual change (%)
No environmental provisions in constitutions			
Australia	1990-2005	53.7	3.6
Canada	1980-2005	−55.5	−2.2
Denmark	1980-2005	−95.1	−3.8
France	1980-2005	−86.1	−3.4
Ireland	1980-2005	−68.5	−2.7
Japan	1990-2005	−40.7	−1.6
United Kingdom	1980-2005	−85.6	−3.4
United States	1980-2005	−44.2	−1.8
Average		−52.8	−1.9
Constitutional duty for government to protect the environment			
Austria	1980-2005	−93.4	−3.7
Germany	1990-2005	−86.0	−5.7
Italy	1980-2005	−87.0	−3.5
Sweden	1980-2005	−92.1	−3.7
Switzerland	1980-2005	−86.5	−3.5
Average		−89.0	−4.0
Constitutional duty for government to protect the environment and individual right to live in a healthy environment			
Belgium	1990-2005	−59.4	−4.0
Finland	1980-2005	−88.3	−3.5
Netherlands	1980-2005	−87.3	−3.5
Norway	1980-2005	−83.0	−3.3
Average		−79.5	−3.6
Combined average of nations with EPIC		−84.8	−3.8

EPIC = Environmental provisions in constitution

reduction of 52.8 percent (an average annual reduction of 1.9 percent). These results are consistent with the other empirical evidence examined in this chapter, as nations with constitutional provisions requiring environmental protection demonstrate superior environmental performance.

Greenhouse Gas Emissions

Climate change was recognized as a global environmental problem in the late 1980s. In 1992, the *UN Framework Convention on Climate Change* was established, and in 1997, the *Kyoto Protocol* instigated legal commitments for

Table 5.7

Constitutions and changes in greenhouse gas (GHG) emissions

Nation	Change in GHG emissions, 1990-2009 (%)	Average annual change (%)
No environmental provisions in constitution		
Australia	30.4	1.5
Canada	17.0	0.9
Denmark	−10.2	−0.5
France	−7.7	−0.4
Ireland	13.8	0.7
Japan	−4.5	−0.2
United Kingdom	−26.9	−1.3
United States	7.2	0.4
Average	2.4	0.1
Constitutional duty for government to protect the environment		
Austria	2.4	0.1
Germany	−26.3	−1.3
Italy	−5.4	−0.3
Sweden	−17.2	−0.9
Switzerland	−2.2	−0.1
Average	−9.7	−0.5
Constitutional duty for government to protect the environment and individual right to live in a healthy environment		
Belgium	−13.2	−0.7
Finland	−5.7	−0.3
Netherlands	−6.1	−0.3
Norway	3.1	0.2
Average	−5.5	−0.3
Combined average of nations with EPIC	−7.8	−0.4

EPIC = Environmental provisions in constitution

emission reductions by most industrialized nations. Between 1990 and 2009, the eight countries without environmental protection provisions in their constitutions saw total GHG emissions increase by an average of 2.4 percent, an average annual increase of 0.1 percent (see Table 5.7).[102] In comparison, the nine nations with environmental provisions in their constitutions saw total GHG emissions decrease by an average of 7.8 percent (equal to an average annual decrease of 0.4 percent). In other words, total GHG emissions in nations without constitutional environmental provisions continued to grow, whereas total GHG emissions in nations with constitutional environmental provisions decreased by an amount exceeding the average commitment under the *Kyoto Protocol*. Again, there are many other factors contributing to variability in greenhouse gas emissions, including economic trends, population growth, and technological advances.

It is tempting to suggest that constitutional environmental provisions are responsible for superior performance in reducing GHG emissions. Instead, there are reasons to believe that GHG emission trends illustrate the difficulty of reaching quick conclusions about cause and effect. Although the *UN Framework Convention on Climate Change* was created in 1992, the *Kyoto Protocol* was not completed until 1997 and did not come into force until 2005. Thus, there was no binding obligation under international law to reduce GHG emissions until the end of the period for which emission trends were assessed. In many nations, potentially effective laws and policies to reduce emissions were not established until the later years in the 1990-2009 period, or are still lacking. The largest reductions in GHG emissions were caused by factors unrelated to environmental protection. In the United Kingdom, fuel switching (from coal to natural gas) was the key factor, whereas the reunification of East and West Germany had a major effect on German GHG emissions. Despite the correlation between constitutional provisions related to environmental protection and reductions in GHG emissions between 1990 and 2009, there may not be a causal relationship.

Conclusion

Constitutional rights and responsibilities can spur stronger, more comprehensive environmental laws and create unprecedented opportunities for public participation in environmental decision making. Legislatures in at least seventy-eight countries (out of ninety-four) have strengthened environmental laws as a result of constitutional recognition of the right to live in a healthy environment. Litigation can be used to compel governments to enact, implement, and enforce laws, and to exercise their discretion in more environmentally friendly ways. Courts in at least fifty-six countries have made decisions that interpret and enforce the right to a healthy environment. The constitutional basis of environmental laws can insulate them to some degree from legal and political challenges, potentially contributing to greater certainty in their application. Increasing the enforcement of environmental laws, and applying them more consistently, can lead to enhanced respect for the environment and for the rule of law.

The evidence reviewed in this chapter indicates that nations with environmental provisions in their constitutions have smaller ecological footprints, rank higher on comprehensive indices of environmental indicators, are more likely to ratify international environmental agreements, and made faster progress in reducing emissions of nitrogen oxides, sulphur dioxide, and greenhouse gases than nations without such provisions. This positive relationship was consistent in a heterogeneous group of 150 nations from across the world and in 2 smaller, more homogeneous groups of countries (30 OECD nations and 17 large, wealthy democracies). The consistency of the correlation between constitutional protection for the environment and superior environmental performance across three indices and four indicators provides persuasive, albeit not conclusive, evidence of substantial influence. There are other potential explanations for this pattern. For example, it might be that the causal relationship works in the other direction – a nation with strong environmental policies and broad public support for environmental protection may be more likely to entrench constitutional provisions related to environmental protection. In such circumstances, the costs of implementing constitutional environmental responsibilities would be perceived as small. However, when the consistent relationship between constitutional provisions and superior environmental performance is combined with the evidence of stronger legislation, enhanced opportunities for public participation, and increasing enforcement of environmental laws, the case for entrenching environmental protection in Canada's constitution must be regarded as compelling.

The impact of constitutional environmental rights and responsibilities is not uniform across or within all regions. Africa lags behind in implementation due to the extensive social, economic, and political problems facing large swaths of that continent. There is high variability between nations within Eastern Europe and Asia, with a positive correlation between the overall health of democracy and the extent of public participation in environmental governance. Where authoritarian regimes maintain power, as in Turkmenistan, constitutional environmental provisions are more symbolic than effective. Where democracy is more robust, as in the Philippines and Slovenia, constitutional environmental provisions are more influential. Given the strength of the rule of law in Canada, a healthy civil society, and relatively strong levels of democracy, economic wealth, and social stability, constitutional environmental rights and responsibilities could be expected to have a substantially beneficial effect on Canada's environmental laws, jurisprudence, and most importantly, performance.

6 International Law and Environmental Rights

> The emergence of individual environmental rights marks perhaps the most significant shift in the focus of international environmental law.
>
> – Patricia Birnie, Alan Boyle, and Catherine Redgwell, *International Law and the Environment*

This chapter examines the evolution of international recognition of the right to a healthy environment, Canada's flip-flop from proponent to opponent of the right, and the implications for Canada of developments in this field of international law. Despite Canada's ongoing refusal to recognize the right to a healthy environment, it is possible that the right and a legally binding obligation to protect it now exist pursuant to international law. Even if these rights and obligations are not yet enforceable, international law could have a profound influence on the adoption and impact of the right to a healthy environment in Canada.

Most of this book focuses on the constitutional right to a healthy environment because human rights are largely implemented and enforced at the national level. As Richard Hiskes, author of *The Human Right to a Green Future,* observes, "Any human right, environmental or otherwise, is always operative mainly at the national level in the legal sense, even if morally or politically the language used to characterize it is more universal or at least global in scope."[1] Nevertheless, international law still may be significant, for several reasons, including its normative role, its influence on domestic legislation and judicial decision making, and the possible emergence of binding obligations.

It is well established that international law influences national law.[2] For many decades, it has provided an impetus for Canadian environmental laws.[3]

The *Migratory Birds Convention Act,* originally passed in 1917, was required to fulfill Canada's commitment under a bilateral agreement with the USA to protect waterfowl and other birds that were being over-hunted. The *Species at Risk Act* was enacted in 2002, in part to fulfill Canada's international obligations pursuant to the 1992 *Convention on Biological Diversity.* International law also affects the substantive content of Canadian environmental laws, as illustrated by the incorporation of the precautionary principle in federal and provincial laws beginning in the late 1990s.[4]

The Supreme Court of Canada has repeatedly used international law to assist in determining the law within Canada, particularly in cases involving the *Charter,* human rights, or environmental protection.[5] The court endorsed the following passage from a textbook on statutory interpretation: "The legislature is presumed to respect the values and principles enshrined in international law, both customary and conventional. These constitute a part of the legal context in which legislation is enacted and read. In so far as possible, therefore, interpretations that reflect these values and principles are preferred."[6] Scholars assert that the influence of international law extends beyond binding treaties and customary international law to "an array of international normative statements that may not legally bind Canada but that Canadian courts may nonetheless find relevant to the interpretation of a domestic statute."[7] In other words, judicial reliance on non-binding international declarations or resolutions is discretionary and will vary according to their persuasive value.[8]

In the environmental context, international legal principles played key roles in six major Supreme Court decisions in the past twenty-five years, involving marine pollution, environmental assessment, interpretation of environmental legislation, the precautionary principle, and liability for contaminated sites.[9] In a case where a logging company challenged the federal *Ocean Dumping Control Act,* the court relied in part on international law governing marine pollution to justify the legislation.[10] In the *Imperial Oil* case dealing with contaminated sites, the court's unanimous decision cited the non-binding *Rio Declaration* and referred to international legal norms including the polluter pays principle, intergenerational equity, and sustainable development.[11] The *Friends of the Oldman River* and *Hydro-Québec* decisions cite the report of the World Commission on Environment and Development (also known as the Brundtland Report).[12] In *Canadian Pacific,* the court relied on the World Commission on Environment and Development's Report of the Experts Group on Environmental Law as an interpretive aid.[13] The *Hudson* decision upholding a municipal pesticide bylaw refers to the *Bergen Ministerial Declaration on Sustainable Development* (1990) for a formulation of the precautionary principle.[14]

Given Canada's current refusal to recognize the right to a healthy environment, it is surprising that Canada once championed international recognition of the right. When the world's nations decided to establish a global response to environmental problems in the late 1960s, Canadian Maurice Strong was chosen to lead the pioneering global environmental conference, in Sweden. Jack Davis, Canada's first minister of environment, was a vice-president of that 1972 Stockholm conference. The ensuing *Stockholm Declaration* provided the first formal recognition of the right to a healthy environment and the accompanying responsibility:

> Principle 1
> Man has the fundamental right to freedom, equality and adequate conditions of life, in an environment of a quality that permits a life of dignity and well-being, and he bears a solemn responsibility to protect and improve the environment for present and future generations.
>
> Principle 2
> The natural resources of the earth including the air, water, land, flora and fauna and especially representative samples of natural ecosystems must be safeguarded for the benefit of present and future generations through careful planning or management, as appropriate.[15]

During the negotiation and development of the *Stockholm Declaration*, Canada advocated unsuccessfully for a stronger expression of the right to live in a healthy environment.[16]

In 1989, Canada signed the *Hague Declaration*, along with twenty-three other nations. The declaration recognizes "the right to live in dignity in a viable global environment, and the consequent duty of the community of nations vis-à-vis present and future generations to do all that can be done to preserve the quality of the environment."[17] Like the *Stockholm Declaration*, it is not legally binding.

As noted in Chapter 3, during the early 1990s, Prime Minister Brian Mulroney actively campaigned for a legally binding global agreement that recognized the right to live in a healthy environment. After his departure,

Canada reversed course and began to oppose international recognition of certain human rights including the right to a healthy environment and the right to water.

A glaring example of this about-face occurred under Prime Minister Jean Chrétien. Canada is one of the fifty-six members of the UN Economic Commission for Europe (UNECE), a body that promotes international co-operation on economic, social, and environmental issues. In the 1990s, the UNECE began negotiations for an agreement that would recognize the right to a healthy environment and establish a suite of procedural rights essential to fulfilling it. During these negotiations, Canada openly opposed the explicit recognition of environmental rights.[18] Fortunately, its arguments were ignored by dozens of European and Asian nations who, in 1998, agreed to the *Aarhus Convention on Access to Information, Public Participation in Decision-Making and Access to Justice in Environmental Matters.*[19] The *Aarhus Convention* refers repeatedly to the right to a healthy environment and has been ratified by forty-four countries plus the European Community. Despite ratifying other UNECE treaties on environmental matters, Canada refuses to ratify *Aarhus,* claiming inaccurately that Canadian legislation already meets or exceeds the procedural safeguards it requires.[20]

The remainder of this chapter reviews the state of international law related to environmental rights – conventions (treaties), customary international law, and general principles of law. Each of these sources of international law can establish legal obligations that bind Canada.

Conventional International Law

Global Human Rights Treaties

When the world's foundational human rights treaties were being negotiated, environmental problems had not yet gained global prominence. Thus, it comes as little surprise that no explicit references to the right to a healthy environment are found in the 1948 *Universal Declaration of Human Rights,* the 1966 *International Covenant on Civil and Political Rights,* or the 1966 *International Covenant on Economic, Social and Cultural Rights (ICESCR).* However, the *Universal Declaration of Human Rights,* which is the backbone of international human rights law despite not being drafted as a legally binding agreement, includes the rights to life and health.[21] Many experts believe that the right to a healthy environment is an implicit yet essential component of these rights.[22] As reported in Chapter 4, this approach has been adopted by at least twenty national courts in countries whose constitutions did not explicitly include the right to a healthy environment (with the right being explicitly added to the constitutions of eight of these nations in subsequent amendments).

The most authoritative expression of the right to health, which directly refers to the environment, is found in the *ICESCR*, which Canada ratified in 1976:

> Article 12. (1) The States Parties to the present Covenant recognize the right to the enjoyment of the highest attainable standard of physical and mental health.
> (2) The steps to be taken by the States Parties in the present Covenant to achieve the full realization of this right shall include those necessary for ...
> (b) The improvement of all aspects of environmental and industrial hygiene.[23]

Article 12(2)(b) is interpreted as referring to environmental health, defined as preventing or reducing environmental risk factors that harm or threaten to harm people's health.[24] For example, the UN Committee on Economic, Social and Cultural Rights asserts that the right to health "includes, *inter alia*, ... the requirement to secure an adequate supply of safe and potable water and basic sanitation; to prevent and reduce the population's exposure to harmful substances such as radiation and harmful chemicals or other detrimental environmental conditions that directly or indirectly impact upon human health."[25] The same UN committee also noted that states violate their duty to protect the right to health if they fail to "enact or enforce laws to prevent the pollution of water, air and soil by extractive and manufacturing industries."[26] According to other experts, environmental obligations stemming from the right to health in the *ICESCR* include

- abstaining from environmental and industrial policies detrimental to health
- not withholding environmental information
- adopting legislation to protect people against environmental activities that could harm their health
- ensuring dissemination of adequate information on environmental risks
- taking measures to ensure, safeguard, and promote a healthy environment
- and providing basic water and sanitation services.[27]

The implicit right to a healthy environment in the *ICESCR* is particularly important because a new *Optional Protocol* establishes a procedure for enforcing rights, similar to the well-established complaints mechanism under the *International Covenant on Civil and Political Rights.* However, Canada has not yet ratified the *Optional Protocol to the ICESCR,* and it is not yet in force.

Three international human rights treaties – the *Convention on the Rights of the Child,* the *Convention on the Elimination of All Forms of Discrimination against Women,* and the *Geneva Conventions* governing state conduct in times of war – indirectly suggest that a minimum level of environmental quality is a basic human right. The *Convention on the Rights of the Child,* as part of children's right to health, guarantees "the provision of adequate nutritious foods and clean drinking water, taking into consideration the dangers and risks of environmental pollution."[28] It also requires that children's education include "the development of respect for the natural environment."[29] The *Convention on the Elimination of All Forms of Discrimination against Women* requires governments to ensure that women "enjoy adequate living conditions, particularly in relation to ... sanitation, electricity, and water supply."[30] The *Geneva Conventions* and related protocols governing humanitarian standards during wars explicitly set forth an obligation to provide prisoners of war and internees with potable drinking water.[31] It would be contradictory and illogical if prisoners of war somehow enjoyed greater rights than ordinary civilians, or if greater rights were applicable in times of war than in peace. An *Additional Protocol to the Geneva Conventions,* finalized in 1977, imposes a duty on governments to protect the environment from "widespread, long-term and severe damage" even during war.[32] Canada is a party to all three of these conventions and their associated protocols.

Regional Human Rights Treaties

Although there is no binding global treaty explicitly recognizing the right to a healthy environment, four regional treaties do recognize this right, including human rights agreements in Africa, Latin America, and the Middle East, plus the *Aarhus Convention,* which covers Europe and parts of Asia. In total, these regional agreements are binding upon at least 118 nations.[33] The right to a healthy environment is also recognized in the non-binding *Charter of Civil Society of the Caribbean Community,* adopted by 15 nations.[34] To date there are no comparable agreements in Asia or Oceania, although the draft *Asian Human Rights Charter* incorporates the right to a healthy environment, and the Association of Southeast Asian Nations has ratified a charter that includes references to human rights and the environment.[35]

The Americas

The inter-American human rights system was born in 1948, with the adoption of the *American Declaration of the Rights and Duties of Man.*[36] In 1969, the *American Convention on Human Rights* was adopted, entering into force in 1978.[37] In 1988, parties to the *American Convention* agreed to the *Additional Protocol to the American Convention on Human Rights* (known as the *San Salvador Protocol*), which provides that

> 11(1) Everyone shall have the right to live in a healthy environment and to have access to basic public services.
> 11(2) The state parties shall promote the protection, preservation, and improvement of the environment.[38]

The *San Salvador Protocol* entered into force in 1999. However, only sixteen of the twenty-four parties to the *American Convention* have ratified it.[39] Although article 11 seems to be a strong articulation of the right to live in a healthy environment, it is weakened by several other articles. Article 1 provides for the progressive, rather than immediate, implementation of the protocol's rights. Article 19(6) does not include the right to a healthy environment among the rights whose violation can give rise to individual petitions. As a result, citizens who believe their right to a healthy environment has been infringed are precluded from bringing a case before the Inter-American Commission unless other rights are also violated.[40] Because of these provisions, some experts criticize the *San Salvador Protocol* as being weak.[41]

Despite belonging to the Organization of American States, Canada has ratified neither the *American Convention on Human Rights* nor the *San Salvador Protocol.* The jurisdiction of the Inter-American Court of Human Rights is limited to nations that have ratified the *American Convention* and accepted the court's optional jurisdiction. However, the Inter-American Commission on Human Rights issues reports and hears cases regarding all thirty-five members of the Organization of American States, meaning that cases can be brought against Canada if the right to a healthy environment and other rights are allegedly violated and procedural requirements have been fulfilled (such as exhausting domestic legal remedies).[42]

Africa

The 1981 *African (Banjul) Charter on Human and Peoples' Rights* is the earliest regional human rights treaty to explicitly recognize the right to live in a healthy environment: "Article 24. All peoples shall have the right to a general satisfactory environment favorable to their development."[43] Fifty-three nations are parties to the *African Charter*.[44] The reference to "All peoples" in article 24 led Birnie and Boyle to suggest that the *African Charter* protects only a collective right rather than an individual right.[45] However, the African Commission on Human and Peoples' Rights has interpreted it as encompassing both.[46]

Europe

Despite its reputation for environmental leadership, Europe lagged behind Africa and the Americas in crafting an agreement that explicitly acknowledges the right to live in a healthy environment. The *European Convention for the Protection of Human Rights and Fundamental Freedoms* (1950) and the *European Social Charter* (1961) both predate the modern environmental era and are silent on the matter of environmental rights. The European Union's *Charter of Fundamental Rights*, proclaimed in 2000, states that "a high level of environmental protection and the improvement of the quality of the environment must be integrated into the policies of the Union and ensured in accordance with the principles of sustainable development."[47] However, it does not explicitly recognize the right to live in a healthy environment, an omission criticized by NGOs and legal experts. Neither the 1999 *Treaty of Amsterdam* (revising the *Maastricht Treaty* of the European Union), nor the as-yet unratified *European Constitution* recognize the right to live in a healthy environment.[48] In 2010, the Committee of Ministers of the Council of Europe rejected a proposal from their own Parliamentary Assembly to add a protocol recognizing the right to a healthy environment to the *European Convention on Human Rights*.[49]

Although the right to a healthy environment is not included in the basic European human rights agreements, the preamble of the 1998 *Aarhus Convention* recognizes "that adequate protection of the environment is essential to human well-being and the enjoyment of basic human rights, including the right to life itself." It adds "that every person has the right to live in an environment adequate to his or her health and well-being, and the duty, both individually and in association with others, to protect and improve the environment for the benefit of present and future generations." Article 1 of the convention states, "Objective: In order to contribute to the protection of the right of every person of present and future generations to live in an environment adequate to his or her health and well-being, each Party shall guarantee the rights of access to information, public participation in decision-making, and access to justice in environmental matters in accordance with the provisions of this Convention."[50] *Aarhus* is regarded as globally significant in its recognition of environmental rights.[51] As Pallemaerts observes, "The *Aarhus Convention* is the first multilateral environmental agreement whose main purpose is to impose on its contracting parties obligations toward their own citizens."[52] In this sense, *Aarhus* represents a hybrid of environmental law and human rights law. It has been ratified by forty-four nations in Europe and Asia, as well as by the European Union.

Middle East

Article 38 of the *Arab Charter on Human Rights* explicitly acknowledges the right to a healthy environment: "Every person has the right to an adequate standard of living for himself and his family, which ensures their well-being and a decent life, including food, clothing, housing, services and the right to a healthy environment. The States Parties shall take the necessary measures commensurate with their resources to guarantee these rights."[53] Ten nations have ratified the *Arab Charter*, which entered into force in 2008 and provides for the creation of an Arab Human Rights Committee to review reports from state parties.[54] The committee does not have the authority to receive petitions or complaints from individuals or NGOs. An Arab Court on Human Rights is being discussed but is not yet established.

Customary International Law

Customary international law, described by the *Statute of the International Court of Justice* as evidence of a general practice accepted as law, has two key elements.[55] The first is objective evidence of state practice, which must be consistent over time and across the majority of nations, although not necessarily uniform. The second element is subjective evidence that states perceive their conduct as responding to legal obligations, a concept known as *opinio juris*. This is comparable to the way in which proving guilt of some crimes requires evidence of both *actus reus* (the criminal act) and *mens rea* (the intention to commit the crime). Evidence of customary international law is provided by constitutions, legislation, regulations, government policy documents and statements, opinions of official legal advisors, diplomatic correspondence, treaty ratifications, the practice of international institutions, and UN General Assembly resolutions relating to legal questions.[56] Judicial decisions (from national and international courts and tribunals) and teachings of legal experts can also influence customary international law.[57]

An important advantage of customary international law over conventional international law is that it can bind all states, even without their consent. As is often observed, "The inactive are carried along with the active."[58] A convention, in contrast, is binding only on parties that ratify it. Only persistent objectors, meaning nations that actively and consistently deny the applicability or existence of a rule of customary international law, may not be bound by it.[59]

On the other hand, customary international law is complex and controversial because it is unwritten and open to conflicting interpretation. Janis writes, "The determination of customary international law is more an art than a scientific method."[60] The distinction between what a state does and what it believes is inherently problematic, as discerning the latter can be difficult. The problem has been addressed by assuming that state practice reflects an underlying intent, and by relying on statements of belief and other positive evidence as a substitute for actual beliefs.[61] There is an ongoing dispute among legal scholars as to whether state practice or opinio juris should be given greater weight in assessing the status of customary international law.[62] Other weaknesses of customary international law include the practical difficulty of demonstrating widespread or consistent practice in a world with approximately two hundred nations, the lengthy duration of time required to establish evidence of consistent practice, and the lack of institutions to adjudicate disputes or enforce the law.

Many international declarations and resolutions have endorsed the right to a healthy environment, including

- the 1972 *Stockholm Declaration*
- the 1989 *Hague Declaration on the Environment*
- resolutions approved by the UN General Assembly from 1990 to 2012
- the Council of Europe's *Dublin Declaration* in 1990
- the 1990 *Cairo Declaration on Human Rights in Islam*
- repeated resolutions from the UN Commission on Human Rights
- the *Earth Charter*, a unique international agreement, drafted by civil society rather than states
- the 2007 *Male' Declaration on the Human Dimension of Global Climate Change*
- and the 2010 draft Universal Declaration of the Rights of Mother Earth.[63]

Although not binding, international declarations and resolutions can influence both state behaviour and the evolution of binding law.[64] On the other hand, the right to a healthy environment was not included in the *Rio*

Declaration on Environment and Development, which was produced at the 1992 Earth Summit; nor was it endorsed at the 2002 World Summit on Sustainable Development.[65] Critics argue that a mere proliferation of declarations cannot be equated with a legally binding right to a healthy environment.[66]

International recognition of the right to a healthy environment has also been endorsed by a slew of legal experts, including

- the World Commission on Environment and Development (also known as the Brundtland Commission)
- the UN special rapporteur on human rights and the environment, whose final report included a *Draft Declaration of Principles on Human Rights and the Environment*
- a Global Judges Symposium
- the International Law Association
- the IUCN's Commission on Environmental Law and the International Council of Environmental Law
- an international group of experts brought together in 1999 by the UN Educational, Scientific and Cultural Organization and the UN high commissioner for human rights
- the Institute of International Law
- and groups of experts assembled in 2002 and 2009 by the UN high commissioner for human rights and the UN Environment Programme.[67]

Experts in international law have also produced a series of declarations endorsing the right to a healthy environment, including

- the 1999 *Bizkaia Declaration on the Right to the Environment*
- the *Limoges Declarations* (1990, 2001, 2011)
- and the *Draft International Declaration on Human Rights and Environment* (2002).[68]

International Courts and Commissions

> The people of both Hungary and Slovakia are ... entitled to the preservation of their human right to the protection of their environment ... The protection of the environment is ... a vital part of contemporary human rights doctrine, for it is a *sine qua non* for numerous human rights such as the right to health and the right to life itself ... Damage to the environment can impair and

> undermine all the rights spoken of in the *Universal Declaration* and other human rights instruments.
>
> – Judge Weeramantry, International Court of Justice, *Gabčíkovo-Nagymaros Project*

Almost all global and regional human rights institutions, including the UN Human Rights Committee, the Inter-American Court of Human Rights, the Inter-American Commission on Human Rights, the European Court of Human Rights, the European Committee of Social Rights, and the African Commission on Human and Peoples' Rights, have developed jurisprudence that links environmental degradation to human rights violations. Air and water pollution, toxic waste, deforestation, and excessive noise have been implicated in violations of the rights to life, health, property, information, and respect for private life, family life, and the home. According to Kiss and Shelton, "International courts and other treaty bodies have expanded or reinterpreted these guarantees in light of environmental concerns, despite the lack of explicit reference to environmental rights in most human rights instruments."[69] The following discussion briefly reviews the key environment/human rights decisions from both global and regional courts and commissions, illustrating the emergence and evolution of the right to a healthy environment. Taken as a whole, these decisions indicate that the right is now widely recognized at international law, either explicitly or as an implicit but essential element of other rights.

INTER-AMERICAN COMMISSION ON HUMAN RIGHTS

The Inter-American Commission on Human Rights (IACHR) has issued recommendations in a number of situations where environmental degradation has affected human rights, including several cases where petitioners alleged a violation of their right to a healthy environment. Most of the cases involved adverse impacts upon Indigenous people. The IACHR first established a link between environmental quality and the right to life in 1985, determining that a highway and authorizations for natural resource exploitation in Brazil violated the rights of Yanomani Indians to health, life, liberty, personal security, and free movement.[70] In a similar situation involving the effects of oil and gas development on Yanomani people in Ecuador, the IACHR concluded that toxic chemicals were contaminating the Yanomani's water, air, and soil, jeopardizing their health and their lives.[71] The IACHR observed that "the realization of the right to life, and to physical security and integrity is necessarily related to, and in some ways dependent upon, one's physical environment. Accordingly, where physical contamination and degradation pose a persistent threat to human life and health, the foregoing rights are implicated ... Conditions of severe environmental pollution, which may cause serious physical illness, impairment and suffering on the part of the local populace, are inconsistent with the right to be respected as a human being."[72]

Although the recommendations of the IACHR are non-binding, they are expected to influence government policies and actions. As well, if a state fails to follow the IACHR's recommendations, the commission can ask the Inter-American Court to issue an enforcement order. Scott argues that because of a lack of implementation, the commission's recommendations regarding Brazil and Ecuador have not improved conditions for Indigenous people and their lands.[73] Both Yanomani cases predate the *San Salvador Protocol*, where the right to a healthy environment is explicitly recognized.

Several cases brought after the *San Salvador Protocol* came into force raised the right to a healthy environment but were decided on the basis that environmental degradation violated other human rights. In 2000, the Association of Lhaka Honhat Aboriginal Communities alleged that a highway being built in Argentina would violate its rights to life and to a healthy environment. The IACHR requested that Argentina conduct meaningful consultation.[74] In 2003, the Maya Indigenous Communities of the Toledo District alleged that logging and oil concessions in Belize violated their right to a healthy environment as part of their rights to life and health. The Maya also alleged violations of their rights to property, religious freedom, family protection, and cultural life, and their right to participate in government decision making. The IACHR held that environmental damage from logging was part of a broad suite of actions that violated the right to property of the Maya and determined that addressing the other alleged human rights violations was unnecessary.[75] In a second 2003 case, a mine contaminated a small Indigenous community in Peru with toxic sludge containing arsenic, lead, mercury, and cadmium. The IACHR requested that Peru implement provisional measures to protect human health, including conducting an environmental assessment and removing the toxic waste.[76] In 2005, a petition filed by Inuit people from Canada and the USA alleged that climate change violated their human rights, including the right to live in a healthy environment, but the petition was declared inadmissible on technical grounds.[77]

Currently pending before the IACHR are three additional petitions linking environmental degradation to human rights. The Cacataibo people, residents of a remote region in the Peruvian Amazon, filed a petition seeking to block oil and gas exploration in their territory.[78] In 2006, the residents of La Oroya, a Peruvian town contaminated by the operation of a lead smelter, won a case in Peru's Constitutional Court, on the basis that a number of their rights were being violated, including the right to a healthy environment. The government did not comply with the court's order, so the residents filed a petition with the IACHR. The IACHR requested that the Peruvian government immediately provide specialized medical treatment to residents of La Oroya who were suffering poor health linked to air, water, and soil pollution.[79] In 2009, the IACHR agreed to adjudicate the case.[80] In 2010, it asked Guatemala to suspend a mining project and prevent environmental contamination threatening the water supply of eighteen Maya communities.[81]

The United States appears to be the only nation that expressly denies the existence of the right to a healthy environment in both domestic and international law. In a case before the IACHR, the USA argued first that the right does not exist, and then in the alternative that even if the right were in fact part of customary international law, it did not apply to Americans, because the US government had persistently objected to its recognition.[82]

The Inter-American Court of Human Rights

Like the IACHR, the Inter-American Court of Human Rights has decided a number of cases involving the effect of environmental degradation on human rights.[83] Again, most of the cases have involved Indigenous communities, and none of the court's decisions have directly addressed the right to a healthy environment. For example, in 2001, the court held that Nicaragua's decision to grant timber licences to a foreign company without considering the dependence of Indigenous Awas Tingni on the land in question violated their human rights.[84] The case represented the first time that the Inter-American Court, relying on the *San Salvador Protocol*, made the connection between environmental degradation and human rights. The court ordered Nicaragua to abstain from permitting any resource extraction activities within the area occupied and used by the Awas Tingni. In 2008, the government of Nicaragua awarded the Awas Tingni community title to 73,000 hectares of its land, marking a major step forward in the resolution of the case.

In 2003, the Kichwa Peoples of the Sarayaku Indigenous Community accused Ecuador of allowing foreign oil companies to carry out activities on ancestral lands without consent or due process.[85] The IACHR asked Ecuador to take provisional steps to protect protestors, secure the Indigenous people's special relationship with their land, and investigate criminal acts against the Kichwa. Ecuador refused to cooperate, so the IACHR went to the Inter-American

Court to seek assistance in enforcing the provisional measures. The court ordered Ecuador to comply with the IACHR's recommendations.[86] The case is now awaiting the court's decision on the merits.[87]

The Yakye Axa are an Indigenous people who were resettled and are seeking a return to their ancestral lands in Paraguay. Their traditional lands have been sold to multinational corporations. In 2005, the Inter-American Court found that Paraguay had violated the Yakye Axa's right to life, interpreting "right to life" broadly as encompassing other rights including the right to a healthy environment.[88] A similar case involving the Sawhoyamaxa Indigenous Community produced the same outcome.[89]

The most recent environmental decision of the Inter-American Court came in 2007, in the Twelve Saramaka Clans case, involving the government of Suriname's actions in granting mining and logging concessions in the traditional territory of the Saramaka people. The court found that serious environmental damage had occurred, violating the Saramaka's right to property (in the collective sense) and their right to judicial protection (since the domestic legal system of Suriname failed to recognize the legitimate legal interest represented by collective title).[90]

European Court of Human Rights

Despite the absence of an explicit right to a healthy environment in the *European Convention on Human Rights*, the European Court of Human Rights (ECHR) has decided many cases where victims of environmental degradation or hazards relied on human rights in their search for redress.[91] In environmental cases, the ECHR has relied on the following rights:

- right to life (article 2)
- right to a fair trial (article 6)
- right to respect for private and family life, and home (article 8)
- freedom of expression (article 10)
- right to peaceful assembly (article 11)
- right to an effective remedy (article 13)
- right to peaceful enjoyment of property (article 1 of the First Protocol)
- and the implicit right to a healthy environment.

The ECHR's breakthrough in protecting human rights from environmental harm came in 1994 in the *Lopez Ostra* case, in which it determined that "severe environmental pollution may affect individuals' well-being and prevent them from enjoying their homes in such a way as to affect their private and family life adversely without, however, seriously endangering their health."[92] The case involved foul odours and smoke from a waste treatment plant located near a family's home. Sands wrote that the *Lopez Ostra* decision implies a general right to a healthy environment in Europe.[93]

Since the *Lopez Ostra* decision, many cases have found violations of article 8 on the basis of environmental hazards, including toxic emissions from a fertilizer factory, air pollution from a steel plant, excessive noise, the operation of a hazardous waste treatment facility, air pollution and vibration from a highway, pollution from coal mining, and the use of sodium cyanide in gold mining.[94] In contrast, in several cases involving allegations of excessive noise from airports, the ECHR did not find that article 8 was violated. The court held that the measures taken by states in relation to noise abatement were within the margin of appreciation (deference accorded to government decision-makers), and in these circumstances it was not for the court to substitute its assessment of what might constitute the best policy.[95]

In a Turkish case *(Oneryildiz)*, at least twenty-six people died because of an explosion at a municipal dump/landfill site, and the evidence indicated that governments knew for years about the serious danger of such an event. Although the right to a healthy environment was mentioned, the case was decided on the basis of violations of the rights to life, effective remedies, and peaceful possession of property. From an environmental perspective, *Oneryildiz* established a positive obligation upon states to protect life from "industrial activities, which by their very nature are dangerous, such as the operation of waste-collection sites."[96] In the words of the ECHR, "The positive obligation to take all appropriate steps to safeguard life for the purposes of Article 2 entails above all a primary duty on the State to put in place a legislative and administrative framework designed to provide effective deterrence against threats to the right to life."[97]

Article 6 of the *European Convention* guarantees that everyone has the right to a fair hearing, and it has been used to provide procedural safeguards in environmental cases. In *Zander*, the lack of a judicial review process available to a Swedish citizen wishing to challenge a permit for a neighbouring waste treatment facility was found to violate article 6.[98] In *Okyay*, the ECHR found a violation of article 6 because the Turkish government failed to enforce court orders, based on environmental damage, to halt pollution from three thermal power plants. The court orders had been upheld on appeal by Turkey's Supreme Administrative Court. The case turned on whether the applicants could establish that they had a civil right relevant to the operation of the power plants despite their acknowledgment that they had suffered no physical or economic harm. Because their right to live in a healthy environment was protected by the Turkish constitution, the ECHR held that they had a civil right for purposes of article 6. In addition, it referred to "relevant international texts on the right to a healthy environment."[99] In the *Taskin* case, the court found a violation of article 6, again based on the constitutional right to a healthy environment, because Turkish authorities circumvented court orders that quashed operating permits for a gold mine.[100]

The ECHR has also made seemingly contradictory observations regarding the right to a healthy environment. In *Hatton*, a case involving excessive noise from Heathrow Airport in the UK, the majority of judges wrote, "There is no explicit right in the *Convention* to a clean and quiet environment, but where an individual is directly and seriously affected by noise or other pollution, an issue may arise under Article 8."[101] The dissenting judges wrote, "Article 8 of the *Convention* guarantees the right to a healthy environment," including "protection against nuisance caused by harmful chemicals, offensive smells, agents which precipitate respiratory ailments, noise, and so on"; they added that the majority judgment "seems to us to deviate from the above developments in the case-law and even to take a step backwards."[102]

In *Kyrtatos*, the ECHR ruled that urban development that harmed a swamp, damaging birds and other protected species, did not constitute interference with article 8.[103] The court reiterated its position that the crucial element in determining whether environmental damage interferes with article 8(1) is the existence of a harmful effect on a person's private or family sphere and not simply the general deterioration of the environment. In a perplexing statement, however, the court added that "it might have been otherwise if, for instance, the environmental deterioration complained of had consisted in the destruction of a forest area in the vicinity of the applicants' house, a situation which could have affected more directly the applicants' own well-being."[104] One might ask why the legal outcome for destroying a forest would differ from that for destroying a swamp. In *Fadeyeva*, a Russian air pollution case, the court reiterated that "Article 8 has been relied on in various cases involving environmental concern, yet it is not violated every time that environmental deterioration occurs: no right to nature preservation is as such included among the rights and freedoms guaranteed by the *Convention*."[105]

Recent decisions in *Tatar*, *Atanasov*, and *Grimkovskaya* clarify the scope of the ECHR's interpretation of the right to a healthy environment. In *Tatar*, a Romanian case dealing with the dangers of using sodium cyanide for mining, the court observed that the right to a healthy environment was protected in both the Romanian constitution and Romanian environmental legislation. It concluded that the state's failure to take positive actions to prevent an environmental disaster violated "the rights to life, private and family life and, more generally, to the enjoyment of a healthy and protected environment."[106] In *Atanasov,* dealing with the reclamation of a tailings pond from a copper mine, the ECHR found evidence of pollution but no proof of direct impact on the applicant or his family and reiterated that there was no right to nature preservation.[107] In *Grimkovskaya,* the court found that the cumulative effect of noise, vibrations, and air and soil pollution from a re-routed motorway directly harmed the applicant and violated article 8.[108]

As Shelton points out, "Environmental rights have found a place in the European system, despite the lack of reference to them in the Convention."[109] Boyle also concludes that the ECHR's case law entrenches environmental rights, although only for individuals directly affected by environmental degradation and not for nature itself.[110]

In Europe, an "inter-institutional dynamic has prompted a frantic race to the 'top,'" with the result that the "rights revolution is transforming the judicial landscape at breakneck speed."[111] In essence, Europe's regional and national courts are competing with each other to push the envelope of human rights jurisprudence, with no court wanting to be left behind. Because the regional law created by European courts is effectively superior to national law, the jurisprudence of the ECHR has a powerful effect, which grows larger in reach as the EU adds nations from Eastern Europe. In environmental cases, the ECHR consistently refers to the constitutional right to a healthy environment in countries from which cases originate (such as Romania, Russia, and Turkey).[112] In effect, the European Court has become the final appellate court for violations of the right to a healthy environment that are either not recognized by domestic courts or not enforced by national authorities.[113] The ECHR's recognition of the right to a healthy environment may create a ripple effect throughout Europe. Although most European nations already recognize the right at the domestic level, some do not. For nations that lack explicit constitutional recognition of the right, such as Switzerland, the emerging case law of the ECHR may hold the key to recognition of this right, because of the court's influence on national courts.[114]

European Committee of Social Rights

The European Committee of Social Rights, established in 1998 to address violations of the *European Social Charter,* recently endorsed the right to a healthy environment for the first time. In *Marangopoulos,* a case asserting that the Greek government was failing to adequately address air pollution from coal mining, the committee determined that the right to a healthy environment was an integral aspect of the right to health.[115] Trilsch described *Marangopoulos* as one of the most important decisions of the European Committee of Social Rights to date, as it "places the right to a healthy environment in the mainstream of human rights."[116]

African Commission on Human and Peoples' Rights

The African Commission on Human and Peoples' Rights has issued one major decision that focuses specifically on the impact of environmental degradation on human rights; a more recent decision involves Indigenous people and the protection of the environment.[117] In *Social and Economic Rights Action Center (SERAC) et al. v. Nigeria,* the commission concluded that the failure of Nigeria's government to prevent toxic pollution from oil development activities violated two rights in the *African Charter:* the right to health and the right to a healthy environment. The Nigerian government argued that the social, cultural, and environmental rights in the *African Charter* were vague and incapable of legal enforcement. The commission rejected this claim, instead offering a comprehensive interpretation of the right to a healthy environment. It concluded that article 24 "imposes clear obligations upon a government ... to take reasonable measures to prevent pollution and ecological degradation, to promote conservation, and to secure an ecologically sustainable development and use of natural resources."[118] Kiss and Shelton note that "the Commission gives the right to environment meaningful content by requiring the state to adopt various techniques of environmental protection, such as environmental impact assessment, public information and participation, access to justice for environmental harm, and monitoring of potentially harmful activities."[119] Shelton describes this decision as "landmark, like the decisions of the Inter-American Commission on Human Rights in its investigations of Ecuador and Brazil," in that it offers "a blueprint for merging environmental protection, economic development, and guarantees of human rights."[120] Despite the seemingly powerful decision, there apparently has been little change on the ground in Nigeria.[121] As noted earlier, the African Commission's decisions are neither legally binding nor enforceable.

The United Nations Human Rights Committee

The UN Human Rights Committee was established to monitor the implementation of the *International Covenant on Civil and Political Rights (ICCPR).* Individuals can file communications with the committee asserting violations of their rights but only if their nation has ratified the *Optional Protocol to the*

ICCPR.[122] There will also be a process for adjudicating complaints alleging violations of the human rights identified in the *International Covenant on Economic, Social and Cultural Rights (ICESCR)* but not until the *Optional Protocol to the ICESCR* comes into force.[123]

Only a handful of the more than one thousand communications submitted to the UN Human Rights Committee since 1976 have involved allegations of environmental degradation.[124] For example, a group of Sri Lankan citizens filed a communication asserting that their right to life, including a healthy environment, had been violated by the construction of a major expressway. The committee found their claim to be inadmissible on technical grounds.[125]

In one of the most prominent environmental cases decided by the committee, residents of Port Hope (Ontario) alleged that, by authorizing the deposit of nuclear waste near their homes, the Canadian government and the Atomic Energy Control Board threatened their right to life. The committee ruled against the residents based on their failure to exhaust domestic remedies, a common prerequisite to gaining access to international courts, commissions, and tribunals. However, the committee noted that the case raised serious issues about the state's obligation to protect the right to life and suggested that the residents would have a remedy under section 7 of Canada's *Charter of Rights and Freedoms.*[126] Decisions of the UN Human Rights Committee are relevant to the interpretation of the *Charter* because Canada is a party to the *International Covenant on Civil and Political Rights* and because these decisions are interpretations by distinguished jurists of language, concepts, and ideas embodied in the *Charter.*[127]

General Principles of Law

An argument can also be made that the right to live in a healthy environment now constitutes a general principle of international law and is therefore binding upon Canada. This category of international law is composed of legal principles that are so basic and fundamental that they are reflected in the legislation and jurisprudence of the majority of legal systems. Examples include the right to life and the concept of *res judicata* (a "matter already judged" is not subject to being litigated again by the same parties). Determining general principles of law is a matter of comparative analysis of national laws and jurisprudence.[128] Although this source of international law may sound straightforward, in reality it is complex and subjective. How many nations must adhere to a principle before it qualifies as a general principle? Malone and Pasternack state that "when a sufficient number of domestic constitutions recognize the same right, then the right can be considered a general principle of law recognized by civilized nations."[129] However, there is no golden rule or even rule of thumb as to what constitutes "a sufficient number" of nations.

Of the 193 UN members, 94 have constitutions that recognize the right to a healthy environment. An additional 12 have recognized an implicit right to a healthy environment through decisions of their Constitutional or Supreme Court. On the basis of regional treaties, 118 UN member nations recognize the right to a healthy environment. After adjusting for double counting, 143 of 193 UN nations recognize the right to a healthy environment in either a constitution or a legally binding regional treaty.[130] Six additional countries belong to the Council of Europe, whose members are subject to the jurisprudence of the European Court of Human Rights (ECHR).[131] The ECHR recognizes that the right to a healthy environment is implicit in the *European Convention on Human Rights.* If one includes the Small Island States, who signed the *Male' Declaration on the Human Dimension of Global Climate Change,* 90 percent of UN nations (174 out of 193) recognize the right to a healthy environment.[132]

Among nations whose constitutions do not specifically refer to the right to a healthy environment, some have nevertheless incorporated the right into national law. For example, although Kazakhstan's constitution does not explicitly mention the right, the new Kazakh *Environmental Code* contains an expansive articulation of its substantive and procedural aspects. The Kazakh government's report to the Aarhus Convention Compliance Committee acknowledges citizens' environmental rights.[133] If national legislation is included, the total increases to 92 percent (177 out of 193).[134] Ninety-two percent of the nations of the world is a very strong majority, and suggests that the right to a healthy environment is close to becoming, if it is not already, a general principle of international law (see Figure 6.1).

The sixteen nations that do not yet recognize that their citizens possess a legal right to live in a healthy environment include Afghanistan, Australia, Brunei Darussalam, Cambodia, Canada, China, Japan, Kuwait, Laos, Lebanon, Malaysia, Myanmar, New Zealand, North Korea, Oman, and the United States. Even in some of these laggard countries, there are subnational jurisdictions that recognize the right to a healthy environment, including five provinces and territories in Canada, six American states (state constitutions in Hawaii, Illinois, Massachusetts, Montana, Pennsylvania, and Rhode Island), and a growing number of cities (such as Montreal, Pittsburgh, and Santa Monica).

Figure 6.1

Nations recognizing the right to a healthy environment

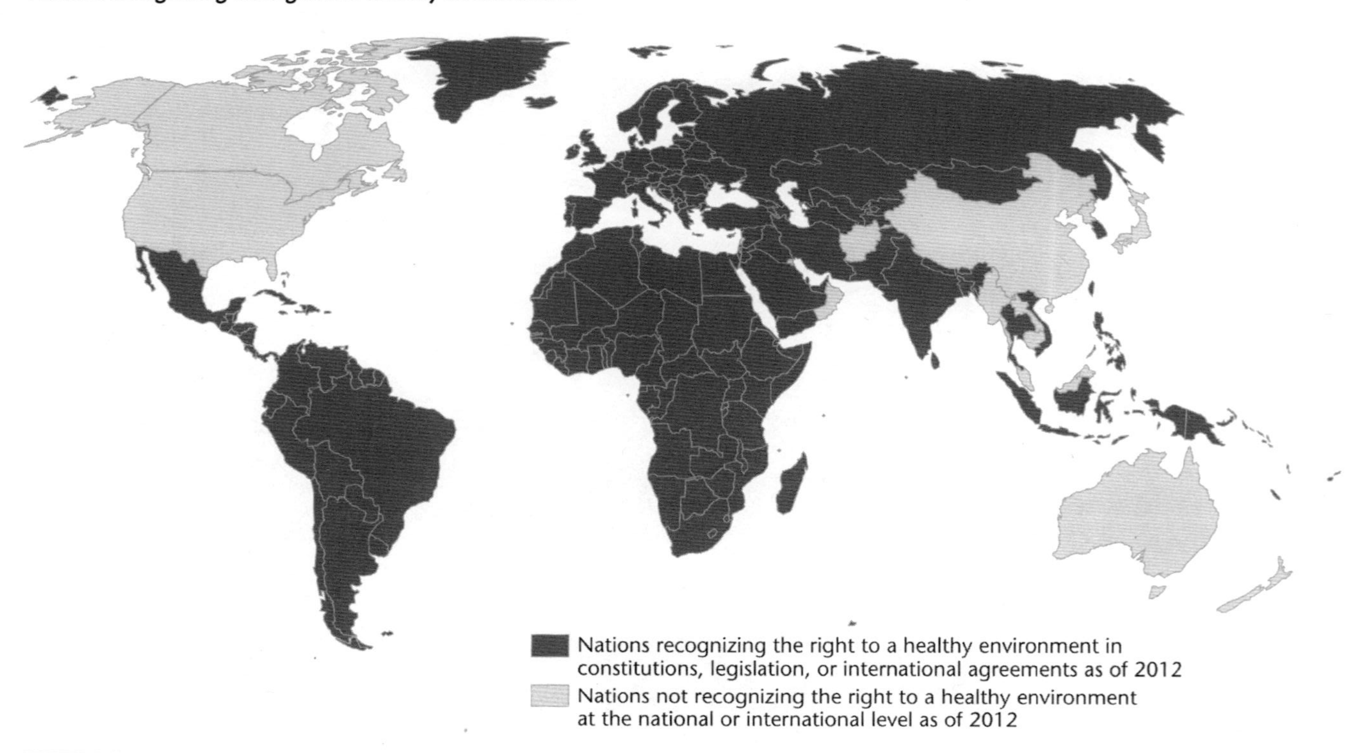

Conclusion

Recognition of the right to a healthy environment at the global and regional levels has grown by leaps and bounds in recent decades. The right is implicit in the *International Covenant on Economic, Social and Cultural Rights* (to which Canada is a party) and explicit in regional treaties covering Europe, part of Asia, the Americas, Africa, and the Middle East. International human rights tribunals in these regions have built a substantial body of decisions interpreting and enforcing the right to a healthy environment. Many non-binding declarations and resolutions have endorsed the right, including some that Canada endorsed. Overall, the majority of the world's nations, regional human rights tribunals, international law organizations, scholarly publications, and international environmental law experts agree that a human right to a healthy environment does exist.[135] Therefore, one may reasonably conclude that the right has surpassed the thresholds necessary for recognition as customary international law and a general principle of law.

International recognition of the right to a healthy environment has influenced legal developments within nations by affecting constitutions, legislation, and jurisprudence. The *Stockholm Declaration* is cited as an inspiration for many nations that subsequently rewrote their constitutions to include environmental rights and responsibilities.[136] International environmental law was a factor in the decisions of countries such as Argentina, Brazil, Finland, and Georgia to provide constitutional recognition of the right to a healthy environment.[137] There are many examples of international law influencing decisions about the right to a healthy environment in national court systems. For example, the *Stockholm Declaration* influenced the Supreme Court of India's decisions protecting the constitutional right to a healthy environment.[138] The right to a healthy environment in the *African Charter* led Kenyan and Nigerian courts to make important rulings, finding the right to be an essential part of the constitutional right to life, although not explicitly articulated as such in either the Kenyan or Nigerian constitutions.[139] Costa Rican courts have cited the *San Salvador Protocol* in cases involving the constitutional right to a healthy environment.[140]

Canada is not immune to these developments, yet as Nickie Vlavianos concludes, the application of human rights law in the environmental context in Canada remains "in its infancy."[141] The pressure on Canadian governments to recognize and respect the right to a healthy environment will inevitably increase as advocates use international law to strengthen their arguments. Canadians who believe that their right to a healthy environment is being violated may pursue cases in domestic courts, using international law to buttress their position. If they are unsuccessful in domestic courts, international recourse may be available. Cases could be brought against Canada before the Inter-American Commission on Human Rights for violating the right to a healthy environment or before the UN Human Rights Committee for environmental hazards that allegedly violate the right to life guaranteed by the *International Covenant on Civil and Political Rights.* If and when Canada ratifies the *Optional Protocol to the International Covenant on Economic, Social and Cultural Rights,* cases could be filed alleging that environmental hazards violate the right to health. The international legal landscape has undergone a sea change that Canada cannot continue to ignore.

7
What Difference Would the Right to a Healthy Environment Make in Canada?

> Whether we have an environmental bill of rights or a patchwork quilt of symbolic gestures will determine whether our laws are intended to protect the environment or pay lip service to it.
>
> – John Swaigen, *Environmental Rights in Canada*

The Government of Canada's position is that existing laws, policies, and programs are sufficient to ensure that Canadians breathe clean air, drink safe water, and live in a healthy environment. However, the evidence of Canada's appalling environmental record and the extensive adverse health effects presented in Chapter 1 make a mockery of this claim. The suggestion that Canadian governments already protect the right to a healthy environment is refuted year after year by tens of thousands of premature deaths, millions of illnesses, billions of dollars in preventable health care expenditures, hundreds of endangered species, and dismal ratings on international comparisons of environmental performance. Given this context, how would constitutional recognition of environmental rights and responsibilities make a tangible difference in Canada?

This chapter draws upon the experiences of other nations to demonstrate that constitutional recognition of environmental rights and responsibilities in Canada would probably lead to a series of systemic improvements including

- stronger environmental laws and policies
- improved implementation and enforcement of environmental laws and policies
- new barriers to weakening environmental laws
- better access to information, enhanced opportunities to participate in decision making, and guaranteed access to justice

- and greater emphasis on ecological tax shifting (imposing taxes on activities that inflict environmental harm while simultaneously decreasing the tax burden on beneficial activities such as employment and investment).

As well, acknowledging that Canadians enjoy a constitutional right to live in a healthy environment could produce superior outcomes on a range of specific issues:

- protecting human health by reducing air pollution and tackling industrial pollution hot spots
- ensuring access to safe drinking water for all Canadians and accelerating the cleanup and restoration of the Great Lakes
- addressing climate change by reducing greenhouse gas emissions and strengthening rules regarding offshore drilling
- and conserving biological diversity through stronger protection for endangered species and their habitat.

It is impossible to predict with certainty the consequences that would flow from constitutional recognition of the right to a healthy environment in Canada. Forecasting the future is fraught with difficulties. Although the experiences of other nations may not be directly transferable to Canada, they provide the best available evidence of the potential implications of constitutional environmental rights and responsibilities.

Systemic Improvements

Stronger Environmental Laws

For several decades, polls have consistently indicated that Canadians want stronger laws to protect the environment.[1] Yet the international comparisons summarized in Chapter 1 demonstrate the weakness of Canadian laws, standards, and guidelines governing air quality, drinking water, food safety, greenhouse gas emissions, and protection of biodiversity.

Constitutional recognition of the right to a healthy environment provides a powerful catalyst for stronger environmental laws. In seventy-eight of ninety-four nations where this right enjoys constitutional status, environmental laws were subsequently strengthened to focus on fulfilling it. In some cases, such as in Argentina, Brazil, Colombia, Costa Rica, France, the Philippines, Portugal, and South Africa, the entire environmental governance paradigm shifted from minimizing damage to securing the right to a healthy environment.

A comparison can be drawn with the process that occurred in Canada during the early 1980s after the *Charter of Rights and Freedoms* was enacted. Federal and provincial governments conducted a comprehensive review of existing laws and regulations, attempting to make all changes necessary to comply with the rights guaranteed in the *Charter*. As well, all laws passed after 1982 are pre-screened by government lawyers to ensure that they are consistent with the *Charter*.

Similarly, recognition of the constitutional right to a healthy environment in Canada would trigger a comprehensive review of existing laws, policies, and standards. Given their relative weakness, many of these instruments would have to be strengthened. For example, unenforceable air and water quality guidelines that are substantially weaker than binding standards in other industrialized nations would be impossible to defend, as would the continued approval of pesticides not permitted in other jurisdictions because of health and environmental concerns. To raise several specific examples, the Canada Wide Standard for sulphur dioxide would have to be strengthened as it currently allows four times the lawful level in the USA and is merely a guideline, whereas the US standard is legally binding. The Canadian rule allowing lead, a dangerous neurotoxin, in fruit juices at twenty times higher than the concentration permitted in water would have to be strengthened to protect children. The registration of atrazine, a pesticide banned throughout the European Union because of serious concerns about adverse health and environmental effects but still among the most heavily used pesticides in Ontario, would have to be revoked. All new laws related to environmental protection and the management of activities with potentially adverse environmental impacts would undergo rigorous pre-screening to ensure that they were consistent with the right to a healthy environment. Over time, these legal changes would probably lead to substantial improvements in Canada's environmental performance.

ENVIRONMENTAL ENFORCEMENT

Despite a litany of promises from politicians, enforcement of environmental laws in Canada ranges from lackadaisical to non-existent.[2] When the *Canadian Environmental Protection Act (CEPA)* was introduced in 1987, Environment Minister Tom McMillan touted it as "the toughest environmental legislation in the western world."[3] But what good is a tough environmental law if it is rarely enforced? The total amount of fines imposed under *CEPA* from 1988 through 2010 was $2,466,352.[4] By comparison, the Toronto Public Library collected more in overdue book fines during a single year ($2,685,067 in 2009).[5] Federal enforcement of environmental laws in the USA dwarfs enforcement in Canada. In 2010, the US Environmental Protection Agency hammered lawbreakers with over $150 million in fines and administrative penalties, and secured court judgments requiring defendants to pay $64 million in fines.[6] The agency also sent executives or managers from corporate polluters and despoilers to prison for seventy-two years and forced lawbreakers to invest over $12 billion to comply with their legal obligations.

"Law and order" governments in Canada like to portray themselves as tough on crime. During the federal election campaign in 2008, the Conservatives promised a "crackdown on environmental crime" and subsequently enacted the *Environmental Enforcement Act*.[7] Penalties for the most serious environmental crimes are up to $1 million for individuals, $6 million for corporations, and $12 million for repeat offenders. These potential fines are reminiscent of Ontario's *Toughest Environmental Penalties Act, 2000*, enacted by Premier Mike Harris and his Conservative government, which raised potential fines for environmental violations to $10 million.[8] Huge potential fines are meaningless when there are no enforcement officers to carry out investigations and lay charges. The Harris government had already eviscerated the Ministry of Environment's capacity to enforce the law, slashing its budget from $290 million in 1995 to $165 million in 1998.[9] By 2000, Ontario's Ministry of Environment employed 41 percent fewer people than it did in 1994-95 (58 percent fewer if contract and temporary job assignments are included).[10] Although the federal government has hired additional environmental enforcement personnel since 2007, the amount of enforcement has declined further from levels that were already abysmally low.[11]

Myriad violations of environmental laws occur every day in Canada. From coast to coast, air is being polluted, water and soil contaminated, and natural habitat destroyed. Data obtained through freedom of information requests by the environmental law organization Ecojustice (after long battles to gain access) document that governments turn a blind eye to thousands of breaches of federal and provincial environmental laws every year.[12]

The experience of other nations shows that incorporating environmental rights and responsibilities into the constitution results in improved implementation and enforcement of environmental laws and policies. More resources are allocated, citizens become more involved, and the level of prosecutions increases. A leading example is Brazil, where amendments to the constitution in 1988 incorporated the right to a healthy environment, empowered the Ministerio Publico (an arm's-length enforcement agency whose previous mandate had been limited to criminal matters) to conduct investigations and enforce environmental laws, and created new forms of legal action to protect the environment.[13] The result was a dramatic increase in environmental enforcement. If environmental rights and responsibilities had constitutional status in Canada, it is likely that enforcement would improve substantially.

Prevent Environmental Law Rollbacks

Between 2006 and 2010, the minority Conservative government led by Prime Minister Stephen Harper quietly sabotaged several important Canadian environmental laws and eliminated key programs intended to address climate change. The extent of the damage to date pales in comparison to the environmental havoc wrought by US president George W. Bush during his eight years in office.[14] However, the majority Conservative government has signalled its intention to dramatically weaken environmental protection through budget cuts, devastating changes to the *Fisheries Act* and other laws, the elimination of key research programs, and the eradication of the National Round Table on the Environment and Economy.[15]

In the 2008-09 budget, the Conservative government weakened several key elements of the *Navigable Waters Protection Act*, eliminating mandatory environmental assessments for major developments on Canadian rivers (such as bridges, booms, dams, and causeways) and exempting some types of works and some types of waterways from requiring permits.[16] Whether there will be an environmental assessment now depends on the discretion of the minister of transport. The changes to the *Navigable Waters Protection Act* also authorize the use of Ministerial Orders to make a wide range of decisions – such as potentially excluding projects on major rivers from requiring approval – without any public notice or consultation. The Federation of Canadian Municipalities described these powers as broad and arbitrary.[17] A Senate committee concluded that there was inadequate consultation and that the revised act "provides too much discretionary power."[18] The government ignored these critiques, claiming that the changes were made to address the economic downturn by streamlining the approval process for infrastructure and natural resource projects.

In the 2010 budget, the *Canadian Environmental Assessment Act* was weakened by exempting infrastructure projects from assessment, reassigning responsibility for assessing energy projects to the National Energy Board and the Canadian Nuclear Safety Commission, and increasing the environment minister's discretion to determine the scope of a project for purposes of environmental assessment.[19] The latter change effectively reversed a Supreme Court of Canada decision that rejected the federal government's attempt to artificially narrow the scope of environmental assessment.[20] The anticipated beneficiaries of the weaker environmental assessment process include the oil and gas, mining, and nuclear industries. According to environmental lawyer Dianne Saxe, these changes "make it less likely that cumulative impacts will be evaluated, such as climate change."[21]

Again, in the 2012 budget, the Conservatives made damaging changes to the *Canadian Environmental Assessment Act*, imposing short time periods for the completion of assessments, transferring decision-making powers to provincial and territorial governments, limiting public participation, and exempting thousands of smaller projects from review.[22] *Fisheries Act* changes will eviscerate key habitat protection provisions. The Minister will be authorized to exempt some industrial activities and to decide that some water bodies do not deserve the act's protection. The *Species at Risk Act* will also be weakened to allow pipeline projects to destroy endangered species and their habitat. These environmental rollbacks were intended to accelerate the approval of controversial mega-projects such as the proposed Northern Gateway pipeline and its associated supertankers for exporting tar sands oil to China.

What is particularly nefarious about the changes to these essential environmental laws is their undemocratic nature. The amendments were not subject to the regular process of public debate and scrutiny by the appropriate parliamentary committees. Instead, they were hidden in lengthy budget implementation laws (the 2008-09, 2010, and 2012 budget laws consisted of 528, 880, and 421 densely written pages, respectively). This pernicious tactic, borrowed from the USA, offered several advantages to a minority government – it avoids contentious public debate and prevents the Opposition from voting against the bill because it is considered a confidence motion whose defeat would trigger an election. Environmental lawyer Stephen Hazell argued forcefully that "Canada's environmental assessment law should be publicly debated in the House of Commons Environment Committee, not weakened through quick-and-dirty amendments buried in budget bills."[23] To the Conservative government, public debate was undesirable because 80 percent of Canadians support stronger environmental laws, not weaker laws.

Environmental rollbacks also occur at the provincial level. Environmental laws and regulations were weakened and extensive budget cuts occurred in

Ontario under Premier Mike Harris during the 1990s, including changes that contributed to the Walkerton contaminated water disaster that killed seven people and made thousands ill.[24] In British Columbia, rollbacks weakened pesticide regulations, pulp mill pollution standards, logging practices, provincial environmental assessment legislation, and air quality rules.[25] For example, a regulation that required all beehive burners in the province to cease operations by the end of 1995 was repealed. Beehive burners produce prodigious volumes of air pollution and have been banned in the USA since the early 1970s. As of 2011, dozens of BC's beehive burners were still in operation, with the deadline for their closure extended to 2016.[26] Another example of a provincial rollback involves regulation of mercury emissions in Nova Scotia. In 2005, Canadian environment ministers established so-called Canada Wide Standards for mercury emissions from power plants, which are the largest source of mercury emissions in Canada. The *Nova Scotia Air Quality Regulations* were supposed to require a 70 percent reduction by 2010, but the target date has been pushed back to 2014.[27]

The existence of a constitutional right to a healthy environment could throw a roadblock in front of these environmental rollbacks. In a number of nations where this right is recognized (Belgium, France, Hungary), legislatures are not allowed to weaken levels of environmental protection. Existing environmental laws and standards represent a baseline that can be improved but not weakened. Thus, undemocratic actions such as the weakening of the *Canadian Environmental Assessment Act, Navigable Waters Protection Act, Fisheries Act,* and provincial environmental rules could be prevented or held to be unconstitutional if Canada recognized the constitutional right to a healthy environment. As Canadian legal experts point out, a constitution "expresses the basic character and qualities of a nation-state, and state actors are inhibited from taking action undermining that character."[28]

Ecological Tax Shifting

It is widely recognized that restructuring the tax system can have a powerful influence in promoting a shift toward sustainability.[29] Unfortunately, Canada lags far behind other nations, particularly in Europe, in reaping the benefits of environmental taxes.[30] There is substantial public opposition to new taxes, and politicians have done a poor job of explaining the virtues of tax shifting. In 2008, Prime Minister Harper claimed that a carbon tax would "wreak havoc on Canada's economy, destroy jobs, [and] weaken business."[31] In fact, nations such as Norway, Sweden, Finland, and the Netherlands have used taxes on carbon dioxide emissions, air pollutants, pesticides, and chemicals for decades, with impressive results. They not only outperform Canada with respect to environmental protection, but also rank ahead of it in terms of economic competitiveness.[32] Evidence demonstrates that strong environmental standards and taxes spur innovation.[33] One factor contributing to Canada's failure to shift taxes onto pollution is uncertainty about constitutional jurisdiction.[34]

In countries where the constitution recognizes the right to a healthy environment and government's duty to protect the environment, ecological tax shifting enjoys enhanced support. The support may be explicit, as in Portugal, where the constitution states,

> Art. 66(2) In order to ensure enjoyment of the right to the environment within an overall framework of sustainable development, acting via appropriate bodies and with the involvement and participation of citizens, the state shall be charged with ...
>
> h) Ensuring that tax policy renders development compatible with the protection of the environment and the quality of life.

In other nations, constitutional support for ecological tax shifting is implicit. The right to a healthy environment has been used to justify environmental taxes and to defend them from attacks claiming that they violate property rights or are beyond a particular government's powers. For example, in a case challenging the legality of a tax on water pollution, Slovenia's Constitutional Court held that the relevant provisions of the *Environmental Protection Act* were valid, based on the constitutional right to a healthy environment.[35] In Spain, courts have also relied on the right to a healthy environment to justify environmental taxes.[36]

Protecting Human Health

Air Pollution

Air pollution inflicts widespread and devastating impacts on human health in Canada. The Canadian Medical Association reports that more than twenty thousand premature deaths annually are attributable to air pollution, through a combination of cardiovascular and respiratory diseases.[37] One in two Canadians lives in an area where he or she is exposed to unsafe levels of air pollution.[38] François Reeves, a cardiologist in Montreal, observed, "I can often tell how busy my day will be based on the air-quality rating."[39] In recent decades, the proportion of Canadian children suffering from asthma quadrupled to more than 12 percent, making asthma the leading cause of absence from school.[40]

Before being elected in 2006, the federal Conservatives promised a Clean Air Act and tough new regulations to improve air quality in Canada, including a pledge to cut industrial air pollution 50 percent by 2010. The promise was repeated in 2008, with the timeline for the 50 percent reduction bumped back to 2015. As of 2012, there is still no Clean Air Act, no new regulations limiting industrial air pollution, and no improvements in air quality.

As noted in Chapter 5, wealthy industrialized nations with constitutional environmental rights and responsibilities (such as Germany, the Netherlands, Norway, Sweden, and Switzerland) have been more effective in improving air quality. Between 1980 and 2005, emissions of nitrogen oxides and sulphur dioxide fell much faster in these countries than in their counterparts without similar constitutional provisions. It is common for constitutional entrenchment of environmental protection to spur the enactment or strengthening of air quality laws and regulations. For example, constitutional recognition of the right to a healthy environment in the Philippines led to a strong *Clean Air Act* (1999) that expanded upon both the substantive and procedural aspects of the right:

> S. 4. *Recognition of Rights.* Pursuant to the above-declared principles, the following rights of citizens are hereby recognized and the State shall seek to guarantee their enjoyment:
> (a) The right to breathe clean air;
> (b) The right to utilize and enjoy all natural resources according to the principles of sustainable development;
> (c) The right to participate in the formulation, planning, implementation, and monitoring of environmental policies and programs and in the decision-making process;
> (d) The right to participate in the decision-making process concerning development policies, plans, programs, projects, or activities that may have adverse impact on the environment and public health;
> (e) The right to be informed of the nature and extent of the potential hazard of any activity, undertaking, or project and to be served timely notice of any significant rise in the level of pollution and the accidental or deliberate release into the atmosphere of harmful or hazardous substances;

(f) The right of access to public records that a citizen may need to exercise his or her rights effectively under this Act;
(g) The right to bring action in court or quasi-judicial bodies to enjoin all activities in violation of environmental laws and regulations, to compel the rehabilitation and cleanup of affected areas, and to seek the imposition of penal sanctions against violators of environmental laws; and
(h) The right to bring action in court for compensation of personal damages resulting from the adverse environmental and public health impact of a project or activity.

Basing their decisions on the constitutional right to a healthy environment, Supreme Courts in Argentina, Brazil, India, Nepal, and Sri Lanka have forced governments to enact or strengthen air quality regulations.[41] For instance, in Brazil, a lawsuit brought by São Paulo's Ministerio Publico and an ENGO forced the government to enact stronger standards for diesel fuel.[42] In Portugal, a court decided that a gas station could not be built beside an elementary school, because the constitutional right to a healthy environment justified preventive action to ensure clean air.[43] Courts in Colombia, Costa Rica, Ecuador, Greece, Thailand, and other countries have ordered industries generating excess air pollution to clean up their operations.[44]

Constitutional recognition of the right to a healthy environment could spur the enactment of strong, legally enforceable air quality standards in Canada, improving protection of both human health and the environment. Clean air advocates would have a persuasive basis for arguing that Canadian air quality rules should be as good as or better than the rules being implemented in Europe and the USA. It would be more difficult for governments to defend the status quo, which treats Canadians as second-class citizens. If Canadian governments refused to accelerate efforts to improve today's inadequate air quality, concerned individuals or communities would have recourse to the courts to seek protection of their constitutional right to a healthy environment.

Industrial Pollution Hot Spots

Constitutionalizing the right to a healthy environment could improve the quality of life in Canadian communities that are subjected to disproportionate quantities of pollution. There are many toxic hot spots in Canada, such as the Sydney tar ponds, Fort McKay and Fort Chipewyan downstream of the tar sands, Hamilton, Uranium Lake, Boat Harbour, the Giant Mine, Kitimat, and Taylor.[45] Perhaps the most notorious example is Sarnia, Ontario, known as Canada's Chemical Valley. More than sixty major chemical, petroleum-refining, and petrochemical facilities are located in a twenty-five-kilometre radius, spewing over 130 million kilograms of toxic substances into the air annually, including pollutants that cause cancer, cardiovascular disease, respiratory illness, and a host of other adverse health effects ranging from organ damage to birth defects.[46] It should be noted that corporations provide self-reported pollution data to Environment Canada, and independent audits indicate that the figures can be grossly underestimated. For example, estimated benzene emissions reported to the National Pollutants Release Inventory by oil and gas companies were 60 percent lower than actual emissions measured by independent researchers.[47]

The World Health Organization recently reported that Sarnia has the worst air quality in Canada.[48] To put Sarnia's air pollution in perspective, consider that, in 2005, industrial facilities in this community pumped out more toxic air pollution than the entire provinces of Manitoba, Saskatchewan, or New Brunswick. Among the leading substances of concern are toluene and mercury, chemicals known to impair the neurological development of fetuses, infants, and children; dioxins, one of the most dangerous carcinogenic substances ever encountered; benzene, another carcinogen; and the air contaminants associated with smog. Studies show elevated rates of hospital admissions among Sarnia residents for respiratory and cardiovascular disease, compared to residents of nearby Windsor and London.[49] Sarnians also have higher than normal rates of cerebral palsy.[50]

Members of the Aamjiwnaang First Nation live on a small reserve surrounded by Sarnia's industrial plants and suffer from a litany of health problems. A Health Canada study found elevated rates of death, disease, and hospitalization among them.[51] Leukemia rates for women aged twenty-five to forty-four were double the provincial average, whereas the proportion of men with Hodgkin's disease was 80 percent higher than the overall rate for Ontario.[52] More than one in five Aamjiwnaang children has asthma. One in four struggles with learning or behavioural problems. Four in ten women reported having a miscarriage or stillbirth. A survey of more than four hundred residents identified a nightmarish list of health impacts, including cancer, asthma, severe and chronic headaches, learning disabilities, and skin rashes. The most commonly cited health impact was fear – of the outdoors, of the frequent warning sirens signalling a spill or unexpected release, and of problems not reported by industry.[53] A peer-reviewed scientific study recorded a disturbing disparity in the number of baby boys born in the area.[54] Since the early 1990s, the proportion of male babies born on the Aamjiwnaang reserve fell from normal levels (slightly more than half of all births) to less than 35 percent of births in the five years from 1999 to 2003. Researchers suspect that this dramatic change may be caused by exposure to chemicals that disrupted the reproductive systems of people in this community.

Despite extensive evidence chronicling the health and environmental damage imposed on local residents, corporations continue to expand operations at Sarnia, adding to the pollution burden. Governments continue to give industry the green light without studying cumulative effects or the unfair distribution of pollution. Ontario recently approved an increase in toxic emissions from a Suncor refinery. Unlike in the USA and other nations, no law or policy in Canada requires industry or government to assess whether a proposed industrial project or expansion poses a disproportionate threat to the health of a vulnerable population or exacerbates pre-existing pollution inequities.

In contrast, citizens in a diverse range of nations – Brazil, Colombia, Costa Rica, India, Italy, the Philippines, Russia, Spain, and Thailand – have been able to force governments and industry to clean up pollution hot spots by wielding the constitutional right to a healthy environment to achieve stronger laws, stricter standards, and more effective enforcement. For example, Thailand's Supreme Administrative Court ordered a halt to dozens of industrial projects in Map Ta Phut, a heavily industrialized area similar to Sarnia.[55] Map Ta Phut is home to 117 industrial plants, including 45 petrochemical factories, 8 coal-fired power plants, 12 chemical fertilizer factories, and 2 oil refineries. Air quality in the region is poor. The basis of the court's judgment was the failure to conduct health assessments, violating people's constitutional right to live in a healthy environment. Seventy-six new projects worth billions of dollars in total were stopped by an injunction, and eleven projects were subsequently given the green light when the court determined that they would not impose significant health or environmental effects.[56] In Brazil, the city of Cubatao used to be notorious for extreme levels of pollution released from industrial facilities, earning it the nickname "Valley of Death" and a place on top-ten lists of the world's most polluted locations. Since the constitutional changes in Brazil in 1988 that recognized the right to a healthy environment, many charges have been laid against offending polluters and more than $1.2 billion has been spent to clean up Cubatao's air, water, and land, with positive results.[57] Cubatao, in a newly industrializing nation, has made more progress in tackling excessive industrial pollution than Sarnia, in one of the world's wealthiest countries.

If the right to a healthy environment were constitutionally protected in Canada, the residents of Sarnia, Fort Chipewyan, Sydney, and other communities who bear a disproportionate share of the burden of pollution would have much stronger tools available in their struggle for environmental justice.

Fresh Water

Safe Drinking Water for All Canadians

An adequate supply of clean water is a vital prerequisite for life, health, dignity, and the realization of other human rights. Unfortunately, inadequate investments in water infrastructure and the lack of national standards for water quality jeopardize the health of Canadians.[58] There are still many rural communities in Canada that do not have access to safe drinking water.[59] First Nations people living on reserves are the most likely to suffer serious water quality problems.[60] More than a hundred First Nations face ongoing boil water advisories (out of roughly six hundred First Nations in Canada).[61] Even more disturbing is the fact that the federal government estimates that there are five thousand homes in First Nations communities (representing more than twenty thousand residents) that lack running water and indoor toilets.[62] Many of these deplorable situations have been dragging on for years.[63] Examples of First Nations communities where, as of 2012, the majority of residents still lack running water and indoor toilets include Pikangikum in Ontario; Kitcisakik in Quebec; St. Theresa Point, Wasagamack, Red Sucker Lake, and Garden Hill in Manitoba; and Little Buffalo in Alberta.[64] The lack of access to safe drinking water has adverse physical and psychological effects. Ottawa admits that "the incidence of waterborne diseases is several times higher in First Nations communities, than in the general population, in part because of the inadequate or non-existent water treatment systems."[65]

In contrast, constitutional provisions explicitly requiring the protection and/or provision of clean water are found in at least twenty nations and are increasingly prevalent in new constitutions. The Dominican Republic and Kenya recognized the right to water in new constitutions enacted in 2010, as did Morocco in 2011 and Iceland in 2012.[66] In South Africa, explicit constitutional recognition of the right to water has had a significant effect on water laws and policies, and has contributed to major investments in infrastructure.[67] Recognition of the constitutional right to water is credited with spurring the extension of potable water to ten million South Africans (predominantly black and poor) in ten years.[68] In Uruguay, the constitutional provision guaranteeing the right to clean water also prohibits privatization of the water supply. UN data show that 100 percent of Uruguayans enjoy access to improved sources of drinking water, consistent with their constitutional right.[69]

In a number of nations where there is no explicit constitutional right to water – including Argentina, Belgium, Brazil, Costa Rica, Colombia, India, Indonesia, Nepal, and Pakistan – courts have held that the right to water is an implicit but enforceable constitutional right.[70] These courts based their decisions on the fact that access to safe drinking water is a fundamental prerequisite to the enjoyment of other human rights, including the right to life and the right to live in a healthy environment. For example, in Argentina, grounding their stance on the constitutional right to a healthy environment, courts have ordered governments to provide communities with potable water, construct drinking water treatment facilities, provide medical treatment for individuals harmed by contaminated drinking water, and carry out environmental remediation of polluted watersheds.[71] In Brazil, litigation based on the constitutional right to a healthy environment has produced a policy that all Brazilians have the right to a core minimum of environmental services including water and sanitation.[72]

A survey conducted by the Trudeau Foundation in 2010 found that 96 percent of Canadians agree that the human right to water should be recognized and protected.[73] However, Canada is among a handful of nations leading opposition to international recognition of the right to water and sanitation.[74] At the UN Commission on Human Rights in 2002 and 2003, Canada was the only country to vote against resolutions recognizing the right to water and sanitation.[75] In 2008, Canada played a key role in blocking a motion by Germany and Spain to officially recognize water as a human right at the UN Human Rights Council.[76] In 2010, the UN General Assembly passed a resolution recognizing the right to water, with 124 nations voting in favour, none against, and 41 abstaining. Canada was among the nations that abstained.[77] Later in 2010, the UN Human Rights Council confirmed that "the human right to safe drinking water and sanitation is derived from the right to an adequate standard of living and is inextricably related to the highest attainable standard of physical and mental health, as well as the right to life and human dignity."[78]

Constitutional recognition of the right to a healthy environment could serve as an impetus for Canadian governments to treat the lack of safe drinking water in Aboriginal communities as the urgent humanitarian crisis that it is, requiring an immediate investment in infrastructure, training for system operators, and legal standards. All Canadians could benefit from increased investment in drinking water and wastewater treatment infrastructure and the enactment of binding national standards for drinking water quality.

Cleanup and Restoration of the Great Lakes

Straddling the Canada-US border, the Great Lakes are among the world's largest bodies of fresh water, and they provide drinking water and recreational opportunities for millions of Canadians. Yet the Great Lakes suffer from extensive damage inflicted when few people gave a second thought to dumping toxic substances into the environment, because nature's capacity for absorption and resilience seemed infinite. The days of ecological naïveté are behind us now. There have been four decades of on-again, off-again efforts to clean up and restore the Great Lakes since the notorious "death" of Lake Erie, dating back to the *Canada-US Great Lakes Water Quality Agreement* signed by Prime Minister Trudeau and President Nixon in 1972.

Despite lofty promises, progress has been slow. Concentrations of highly toxic and long-lasting PCBs are still approximately a hundred times higher than agreed-upon water quality objectives. High levels of pollution tend to be concentrated in poor communities, whereas wealthy regions enjoy low levels of pollution.[79] The Great Lakes are the subject of fish consumption advisories warning that eating fish can cause birth defects and other serious health effects. Communities living near hazardous waste sites in the Great Lakes region suffer from elevated levels of infant mortality, premature births, low birth weights, and cancer. Only modest progress has been made by the Canadian government to fulfill the objectives regarding restoration of areas of concern identified by the *Great Lakes Water Quality Agreement*. After several decades, only three out of seventeen areas of concern have been sufficiently restored to be delisted.[80]

One of the major reasons that Canadian progress has been painfully slow is the ongoing refusal to dedicate adequate resources to this problem. In 1994, Canada announced a $125 million Great Lakes cleanup initiative. In 2001, a follow-up audit by the commissioner of the environment and sustainable development found that less than 12 percent of the funding for this initiative ever materialized.[81] From 1990 to 2010, the federal government invested approximately $7 million per year in Great Lakes cleanup projects.[82] The 2010 budget provided Environment Canada with $8 million per year, and the 2011 budget promised an additional $5 million over two years.[83] These amounts are woefully inadequate. The 2011 *Alternative Federal*

Budget produced by the Canadian Centre for Policy Alternatives called for $3.375 billion for Great Lakes restoration over five years.[84] It is estimated that $2.4 billion is required for improving municipal wastewater treatment infrastructure, $150 million for cleanup of contaminated sediment, and $90 million for Hamilton's harbour alone.[85]

Recent developments in Argentina and the Philippines, two nations with far less economic wealth than Canada, demonstrate the power of the constitutional right to a healthy environment to produce superior progress in cleaning up polluted water bodies and ecosystems. In 2004, a group of concerned Argentine citizens sued the national government, the provincial government, and the City of Buenos Aires, along with forty-four industrial facilities, for polluting the Riachuelo River, asserting a violation of their right to a healthy environment. Millions of people, many of them poor, live near the Riachuelo, one of the most polluted rivers in South America. In 2006, Argentina's Supreme Court ordered the government to conduct an environmental assessment of the state of the river and initiate an environmental education program. The court also required all the polluting industries to provide information about their wastewater treatment equipment, programs, and practices.[86] In 2007, the Supreme Court ordered the government to draft a comprehensive cleanup and restoration plan for the river. Recognizing the limits of its own expertise in evaluating this plan, the court commissioned an independent evaluation by scientists at the University of Buenos Aires. The expert review and comments from both the plaintiffs and non-government organizations identified extensive weaknesses in the draft plan. The court also convened five public hearings to ensure that broad-based community participation informed its judgment. In response, the Argentine government established a new river basin authority, which must implement a comprehensive action plan, coordinate and harmonize activities, and control and monitor environmental compliance.[87]

In 2008, the Supreme Court issued a comprehensive final ruling in the case, in which it ordered

- inspections of all polluting enterprises and creation and implementation of wastewater treatment plans, all on a strict schedule
- closure of all illegal dumps, redevelopment of landfills, and cleanup of the riverbanks
- improvement of the drinking water, sewage treatment, and storm-water discharge systems in the river basin

- development of a regional environmental health plan, including contingencies for possible emergencies
- supervision, by the federal auditor general, of the budget allocation for implementation of the restoration plan
- formation of a committee of NGOs involved in the litigation to monitor compliance with the court's decision
- ongoing judicial oversight of the implementation of the plan, with a federal court judge empowered to resolve any disputes related to the court's decision
- and notice that any violations of the timelines established by the court would result in daily fines against the president of the Matanza-Riachuelo Watershed Authority (the new intergovernmental body responsible for implementing the restoration plan).[88]

The court's decisions were based on articles 41 and 43 of Argentina's constitution, recognizing the right to a healthy environment and the citizens' power to defend their rights through the judicial system. The remedies are intended to restore past damage as well as prevent future degradation of the river system. Argentina's Supreme Court "made it clear that extraordinary measures may be required on the side of judges where environmental issues and interests are at stake."[89]

Substantial on-the-ground progress has already been made. The World Bank has approved US$2 billion in financing for the Matanza-Riachuelo Basin Sustainable Development Project, which it acknowledges was triggered by the decision of the Supreme Court of Argentina and is intended to contribute to compliance with that court's order.[90] The Argentine government will increase the number of environmental inspectors in the region from 3 to 250.[91] Progress made by mid-2011 included provision of clean drinking water to 1 million people, a new sewage treatment system serving half a million, 167 polluting companies closed, 134 garbage dumps closed, and the creation of 139 sampling points for monitoring water, air, and soil quality.[92] The Supreme Court continues to hold quarterly public hearings in which it questions the federal environment minister and the head of the watershed authority on progress toward fulfilling the court's order. International scholars have hailed the litigation for its "remarkable policy impact" and positive social impact on previously marginalized communities.[93] As the World Bank observed, there have been previous pledges to restore the Matanza-Riachuelo watershed, but the Supreme Court ruling ensures an unprecedented degree of political and legal accountability.[94]

In 2008, the Supreme Court of the Philippines released a strikingly similar judgment in the *Concerned Residents of Manila Bay* case, also based on the right to a healthy environment. According to the court,

> The importance of the Manila Bay as a sea resource, playground, and as a historical landmark cannot be over-emphasized. It is not yet too late in the day to restore the Manila Bay to its former splendor and bring back the plants and sea life that once thrived in its blue waters. But the tasks ahead, daunting as they may be, could only be accomplished if those mandated, with the help and cooperation of all civic-minded individuals, would put their minds to these tasks and take responsibility. This means that the State, through petitioners, has to take the lead in the preservation and protection of the Manila Bay.
>
> The era of delays, procrastination, and *ad hoc* measures is over. Petitioners must transcend their limitations, real or imaginary, and buckle down to work before the problem at hand becomes unmanageable. Thus, we must reiterate that different government agencies and instrumentalities cannot shirk from their mandates; they must perform their basic functions in cleaning up and rehabilitating the Manila Bay.[95]

The court ordered twelve government agencies to develop a comprehensive plan, within six months, to rehabilitate and restore Manila Bay to a level of water quality adequate for all kinds of recreation. More specifically, it ordered responsible agencies to

- install and operate sewage treatment facilities
- clean up hazardous and toxic wastes
- prevent pollution from ships
- develop adequate facilities and programs for the proper disposal of solid waste
- remove structures that obstruct the free flow of waters into Manila Bay
- revitalize marine life by reintroducing indigenous aquatic species
- require septic and sludge companies to use adequate treatment facilities
- prevent all forms of illegal fishing
- establish a comprehensive environmental education program
- and allocate a budget sufficient to carry out the restoration plan.

The court adopted the extraordinary remedy of "continuing mandamus," giving itself ongoing supervision of the implementation of the restoration plan with the goal "of ensuring that its decision would not be set to naught by administrative inaction or indifference."[96] Government agencies are required, by court order, to submit quarterly progress reports. In conclusion, the court stated that the responsible government agencies "cannot escape their obligation to future generations of Filipinos to keep the waters of the Manila Bay as clean and clear as humanly possible. Anything less would be a betrayal of the trust reposed in them."[97]

In 2009, the Supreme Court also established an expert advisory committee – composed of two members of the court and three scientists – to review the government's reports and ensure that progress was satisfactory. At the committee's request, the court issued a further order in 2011 including more detailed instructions to the government agencies responsible for implementing the original order, such as deadlines for specific activities and additional reporting requirements.[98] The Department of Environment and Natural Resources is implementing a plan intended to clean fourteen river systems and reduce pollutants entering Manila Bay by 50 percent by 2015.

Both the similarities and the differences between Canada's Great Lakes, Argentina's Riachuelo River, and Manila Bay in the Philippines are striking. In all three cases, generations of political leaders promised to clean up these badly damaged ecosystems but took few concrete steps. Canada, despite its far greater economic wealth, continues to allocate inadequate attention or resources to restoring the Great Lakes. Concerned citizens and ENGOs are frustrated by their inability to compel faster progress. In Argentina and the Philippines, citizens empowered by their constitutional right to live in a healthy environment succeeded in holding governments accountable. Government agencies and corporations were ordered to perform cleanup, restoration, and pollution prevention activities that will cost billions of dollars. The legal processes leading to these decisions were open and flexible, and they relied on independent experts for scientific assistance. The courts incorporated innovative mechanisms to ensure compliance, including third-party supervision, mandatory progress reports, and substantial fines for non-compliance. P.B. Velasco Jr. (associate justice, Supreme Court of the Philippines) responded to criticism of the *Manila Bay* judgment by stating that "it is not judicial activism when courts carry out their constitutionally assigned function of judicial review and in the process enjoin those charged with implementing a law to so implement the law."[99]

Climate Change

Greenhouse Gas Emissions

Canada's performance on climate change is widely acknowledged to be among the worst in the industrialized world. Pursuant to the *Kyoto Protocol*, Canada pledged to reduce emissions to 6 percent below 1990 levels by 2012. Instead, Canadian emissions rose 24 percent.[100] Prime Minister Harper's government rejected Canada's international obligations under the *Kyoto Protocol* and put forward a much less ambitious commitment under the non-binding *Copenhagen Accord*. Environment Canada reported that given the weakness of present climate policies, by 2020 Canadian emissions will probably be 29 percent above our modest *Copenhagen* commitment.[101] Canada still provides an estimated $1.4 billion in subsidies to fossil fuel companies, despite their environmental destruction and enormous profits. Canada has resisted recognition of the fact that climate change has implications for the full enjoyment of human rights.[102] An increasing proportion of Canada's oil comes from the pollution-intensive tar sands, contaminating air and water, threatening the health of communities downwind and downstream, and producing prodigious volumes of greenhouse gas (GHG) emissions.

Constitutional uncertainty has contributed to Canada's inaction.[103] Alastair Lucas warns that "there is at least a likelihood that the federal government lacks constitutional authority to legislate national standards and the necessary framework for a national emissions trading system."[104] As well, Canadian courts have been reluctant to hold Ottawa accountable, in cases involving emissions from the tar sands and failure to comply with the *Kyoto Protocol Implementation Act*.[105]

The wealthy industrialized nations whose constitutions include environmental rights and responsibilities have a significantly better record in controlling GHG emissions. Countries that have articulated the ambitious goal of eventually becoming zero-carbon and have begun moving in that direction (Costa Rica, Norway, Sweden) all enjoy constitutional environmental provisions. For example, Sweden has reduced GHG emissions to 20 percent below 1990 levels while experiencing economic growth at a pace comparable to that of Canada since that time.

Efforts to address climate change in Canada would benefit from recognition of the constitutional right to a healthy environment and government's corresponding obligation to respect, protect, and fulfill this right. It could tip the balance in myriad legislative, regulatory, administrative, judicial, corporate, and individual decisions related to energy production and use, energy efficiency, and energy conservation. It is unlikely that constitutional recognition of environmental rights and responsibilities would bring an immediate halt to the extraction of oil from the tar sands, as some environmentalists have advocated. However, it could compel the industry to reduce water use, air pollution, greenhouse gas emissions, and releases of toxic substances, and could be used to push for constraints on expansion until cleaner production processes are available.

Offshore Drilling

British Petroleum's catastrophic oil spill in the Gulf of Mexico in 2010 elevated concerns about the controversial practice of deep-water drilling, particularly in marine areas with high ecological values. In Canada, there is a moratorium on oil and gas exploration on the west coast, despite earlier pledges by BC's Liberal government that it would be open for drilling by 2010. However, there is a booming oil and gas industry on the east coast and ongoing development in the Arctic. In light of the Gulf of Mexico disaster, questions have been raised about how much time would be required to drill a relief well should a blowout occur in the Beaufort Sea. The chilling answer is that it could take two to three years because of the short drilling season.[106] Oil would continue to gush for that entire time, mainly into an ocean covered by Arctic ice.

Given this, it is interesting to view the contrasting approach to offshore oil and gas exploration in Costa Rica, Brazil, and Norway – nations that recognize the constitutional right to a healthy environment. Due to ecological concerns, Costa Rica's Constitutional Court struck down Harken Energy's approvals for offshore oil and gas exploration.[107] Costa Rica subsequently rescinded Harken's contract, prompting the company to attempt to sue for $57 billion in damages through the World Bank's International Center for the Settlement of Investment Disputes (ICSID). Costa Rica rejected ICSID's jurisdiction and refused to pay compensation, citing Harken's failure to comply with environmental laws as a breach of the contract. The outcome has been described as a "resounding victory" in Costa Rica's efforts to protect the environment.[108] In Brazil and Norway, offshore oil and gas development is permitted but under more stringent rules than found in Canada or the USA.[109] A small oil spill off the coast of Brazil in 2011 prompted a multi-million-dollar fine and a multi-billion-dollar lawsuit for environmental damages against Chevron by federal prosecutors.[110]

A constitutional right to a healthy environment could have a beneficial influence on Canadian offshore drilling activities and proposals, either through spurring tougher rules, empowering citizens and communities via enhanced access to information and greater roles in decision making, or if all else fails, access to the judicial system.

Conserving Biodiversity

Canada has a mixed record in terms of the conservation of biological diversity, as illustrated by a number of examples. According to the Committee on the Status of Endangered Wildlife in Canada, 36 species have already become extinct or been extirpated from Canada, and another 579 have been designated as being at risk of extinction.[111] The list grows longer every year. Canada ranks a disappointing 111th out of 201 countries in terms of the proportion of land area protected, and fares even worse in protecting marine areas.[112] The federal Department of Fisheries and Oceans allows lakes to be used as tailing ponds for the deposit of mining waste, although this seems to violate the spirit, if not the letter, of the federal *Fisheries Act*.[113] Ottawa's recent rejection of the Prosperity gold mine that would have destroyed Fish Lake in British Columbia was an encouraging exception to this trend, although a revised version of the mine is going through a new environmental assessment process. Some of Canada's iconic national parks are being overrun by commercial development. Industrial activity is still permitted in some provincial parks and protected areas. Ottawa has been sued repeatedly and criticized by courts for failing to implement the *Species at Risk Act*.[114] Alberta and British Columbia still lack endangered species legislation. Reports from independent observers indicate that Canadian fishermen using long-lines to catch tuna and swordfish in the Western Atlantic caught over a thousand loggerhead sea turtles annually between 1999 and 2007, even though the turtles were designated as endangered under Canada's *Species at Risk Act*.[115] The long-line fishery also harms large numbers of globally endangered leatherback turtles and blue sharks. According to experts, simple changes in fishing gear and techniques could prevent this unnecessary by-catch and associated deaths.

In Canada, when economic considerations clash with concerns about biodiversity, the former usually emerge victorious. In nations where the constitution includes the right to a healthy environment and the corresponding responsibility to protect the environment, a better balance is being achieved. Enhanced protection for Nature may be attained through stronger laws, better enforcement of laws, or by citizens using the courts to hold governments accountable to their constitutional commitment. Countries from Costa Rica to Spain have passed strong laws to protect endangered ecosystems and species from harmful human activities, with Costa Rica's comprehensive biodiversity law explicitly recognizing the inherent value of Nature. Panama recently passed a law banning commercial long-lining in order to limit overfishing and to protect sea turtles and sharks.[116] A recent court decision in Ecuador, based on the constitutional rights of Nature, ordered the restoration of a river harmed by road-building activities.[117]

In Europe, legislatures and courts have played a substantial role in using the right to a healthy environment to protect biodiversity: for example, they have protected lakes from development and struck down efforts to privatize forests.[118] Dutch courts have relied on the constitutionalized right to a healthy environment to protect the habitat of an endangered species of salamander and to place greater weight on environmental considerations than on economic concerns.[119] Belgian jurisprudence has also interpreted the right to a healthy environment broadly, not as limited to protecting humans from pollution but also as protecting nature and biodiversity.[120] In Portugal, successful cases based on the constitutional right to a healthy environment have been brought to protect various bird species and their habitat.[121] In Greece, the Council of State (the highest administrative court) repeatedly cancelled permits for a major water diversion project that would have dammed and rerouted the Acheloos River into a different watershed, causing extensive ecological damage.[122]

In Finland, plans to build a hydroelectric dam and reservoir in the headwaters of the Kemijoki River were repeatedly rejected because of the high natural values of the area, internationally renowned as important migratory bird habitat.[123] However, the project was approved in 2000, triggering a legal challenge by opponents of the dam. Based in part on the constitutional right to a healthy environment, the legal challenge was successful. Finland's Supreme Administrative Court stated that the *Water Act* "must be interpreted in light of Article 20 of the constitution, which guarantees the right to a decent environment."[124] The court noted that the constitutional provision was both a prescription to legislators and a principle for interpreting and applying the law. This Finnish case illustrates the important influence that constitutional environmental rights can have on the interpretation of other laws and policies.

Costa Rica's Constitutional Court is a global leader in protecting endangered species and their habitat. Decisions of the court, based on the right to a healthy environment, include

- making it illegal to hunt endangered green turtles

- striking down government authorization of timber harvesting in habitat for the endangered green macaw
- ordering the government to stop the wasteful practice of shark finning
- nullifying a municipal zoning regulation that authorized construction in Las Baulas National Park and ordering the government to expropriate private lands within the park that were slated for tourist development but provided critical habitat for endangered sea turtles
- and ordering the government to enact regulations required for the implementation of the *Fisheries and Aquaculture Act.*[125]

Given the experiences of other nations, it is likely that recognition of the constitutional right to a healthy environment in Canada would improve the odds for the survival and recovery of many endangered species, from sea turtles and killer whales to woodland caribou and piping plovers.

Conclusion

The constitutional right to a healthy environment is not a panacea that will automatically address all of Canada's environmental challenges. However, the examples in this chapter, drawing on the experiences of other countries, demonstrate that it is a potentially powerful tool that could be harnessed to close the glaring gap between the actions and rhetoric of Canadians. Combined with the empirical evidence of environmental performance described in Chapter 5, the examples suggest a high probability that the cumulative effect of constitutionalizing the right to a healthy environment would be an overall strengthening of Canada's environmental performance.

8
Pathways for Greening Canada's Constitution

> Canadians became so accustomed to the mega constitutional game – the great Lockean project of democratically contracting together to adopt a constitution – that it is difficult for them to realize that in these quieter constitutional times since the Meech Lake and Charlottetown Accord debacles, the country's constitutional system has been changing and developing.
>
> – Peter Russell, *Constitutional Odyssey*

The progress of environmental rights in Canada and around the world over the past four decades can be compared to the course of a river. It twists and turns, and the current flows more quickly in some stretches and during some seasons than others. At times there is turbulent white water, and experts will disagree over the best approach to navigation. However, it is almost certain that the water in the river will eventually reach the ocean. The explicit recognition of the right to a healthy environment as a fundamental human right appears to be an inevitable development, representing the evolution of universal human values.

Despite international momentum and a variety of compelling rationales for enshrining the right to clean air, clean water, fertile soil, and a healthy environment in Canada's constitution, the path forward is littered with legal and political obstacles. It is important to recognize that a country's constitution, understood holistically, is composed of four elements:

- the formal written constitution, including direct amendments
- laws that do not alter the formal constitution but create or change major government institutions (e.g., the *Constitutional Amendments Act, Clarity Act*)
- political practices that, over time, evolve into constitutional conventions

- and judicial decisions interpreting the formal constitution and clarifying the principles underlying the constitutional system as a whole (e.g., the *Secession Reference*).[1]

In light of this broad understanding, there are three ways – one legislative and two judicial – that Canada's constitution could be modified to recognize the right to a healthy environment and associated responsibilities. First, a direct constitutional amendment can be sought through the political process, requiring the approval of federal and provincial legislatures. The second option is litigation – seeking a court decision recognizing that the right to a healthy environment is implicit in an existing constitutional provision. The third possibility involves persuading either Ottawa or a provincial/territorial government to ask the courts whether Canada's constitution already includes an implicit right to a healthy environment, using a special procedure called a judicial reference. The second and third options follow different legal paths but could achieve the same result – an indirect constitutional amendment. Many experts have observed that litigation can be an effective instrument for "changing the dynamics of political power and altering the status quo of competing interests."[2] However, for a host of reasons – democratic legitimacy, clarity, symbolic value, legal effects, and practical consequences – a direct constitutional amendment is the most powerful outcome. This chapter will outline the legal and political details of these three pathways.

Option 1: Direct Amendment of Canada's Constitution

Five different procedures are available for directly amending Canada's constitution, including the *Charter of Rights and Freedoms,* as set forth in part V of the *Constitution Act, 1982:*

- the general amending formula requiring a proclamation issued by the governor general and authorized by resolutions from the House of Commons, the Senate, and the legislative assemblies of two-thirds of the provinces representing at least 50 percent of all Canadians (section 38)
- the unanimity formula requiring the consent of the House of Commons, the Senate, and the legislative assemblies of all ten provinces to change specific fundamental aspects of the constitution, such as the amending formula itself or the composition of the Supreme Court of Canada (section 41)

- the bilateral amendment formula, which, in the case of provisions that apply to one or more, but not all, provinces, requires authorization by the House of Commons, the Senate, and the legislative assembly of each province to which an amendment applies (section 43)
- unilateral amendment of certain types of provisions by Parliament (section 44), such as adding representation for Nunavut in the House of Commons and Senate
- and unilateral amendment of certain types of provisions by a provincial legislature (section 45).

The general amending formula in section 38 is the only procedure capable of achieving constitutional recognition of the right to a healthy environment. It puts forward the basic rule requiring the concurrence of Parliament and the legislatures of at least two-thirds of the provinces with at least 50 percent of the population. Two-thirds of the ten provinces is agreed to mean seven provinces.[3] There is a three-year deadline for securing the required resolutions.[4] As of 2012, the provincial populations are such that no single province has a veto under the constitutional amending formula (that is, no province has 50 percent of Canada's population; see Table 8.1). It is important to note that the requirement of Senate approval can be overridden. If 180 days (6 months) pass after the House of Commons adopts its authorizing resolution and the Senate has not concurred, the House may adopt a second resolution, eliminating the need for Senate approval.[5] Critics observe that the amending formula is complex and rigid, and that it makes no provision for public participation.[6]

The difficulties of achieving constitutional amendments were made potentially more daunting by a federal law passed in 1996 in response to the narrowly defeated Quebec referendum. The *Constitutional Amendments Act* provides that resolutions for constitutional changes introduced by a federal minister of the Crown must be supported by Quebec, Ontario, British Columbia, two or more Atlantic provinces with at least 50 percent of the region's population, and two or more Prairie provinces with at least 50 percent of the region's population.[7] In effect, this system gives a veto to Ontario, Quebec, British Columbia, and Alberta (based on current population distributions in the Prairies). Although in theory the *Constitutional Amendments Act* could be amended or repealed by Parliament, some experts believe that it may acquire quasi-constitutional status over time.[8]

Under the *Constitutional Amendments Act*, only federal ministers of the Crown (Cabinet ministers) are prohibited from proposing a motion for a

Table 8.1

Canada's population, by province and territory (2011)

Province/territory	Population	Proportion of population (%)
Ontario	13,373,000	38.8
Quebec	7,979,700	23.1
British Columbia	4,573,300	13.3
Alberta	3,779,400	11.0
Manitoba	1,250,600	3.6
Saskatchewan	1,057,900	3.1
Nova Scotia	945,400	2.7
New Brunswick	755,500	2.2
Newfoundland and Labrador	510,600	1.5
Prince Edward Island	145,900	0.4
Northwest Territories	43,700	0.1
Yukon	34,700	0.1
Nunavut	33,300	0.1
Canada	34,483,000	100.0

Source: Statistics Canada (2011b).

resolution authorizing a constitutional amendment. A government backbencher or an opposition MP could propose such a motion without triggering the vetoes established by the act.[9] Therefore, it may be easier to secure a constitutional amendment in the absence of a majority federal government because resolutions introduced by MPs other than Cabinet ministers could be passed by the House of Commons, and no province would possess a veto.

Alberta and British Columbia have passed laws requiring that provincial referendums be held before constitutional amendment resolutions are introduced in the legislative assembly. Alberta's legislation binds the legislative assembly to act in accordance with the wishes expressed by a majority of the citizens who voted in the provincial referendum.[10] Under BC's law, the government is not legally bound to follow the outcome of the referendum (although refusing to do so could create a political backlash).[11] Peter Russell has suggested that political pressure for a national referendum to ratify major constitutional changes would probably be irresistible.[12]

The general amending formula requires a high degree of national consensus, which may be challenging to achieve in today's regionally fractured political landscape. Yet it is inconceivable that a constitution enshrined in

1982 will be treated as though written in stone and immune to revisions required to reflect social, scientific, and cultural advances. In fact, amending Canada's constitution is by no means an impossible proposition. The constitution has been amended at least eleven times since 1982, including two direct changes to the *Charter*. The general amending formula was used in 1983 to amend section 25 of the *Charter*, establishing additional guarantees and commitments relating to Aboriginal peoples.[13] Section 16(2) of the *Charter* was amended in 1993 to enhance the equality of English- and French-speaking communities in New Brunswick. Remarkably, despite the heightened tensions between Ottawa and the separatist Parti Québécois government, these two parties successfully negotiated a bilateral constitutional amendment relating to education and denominational schools.[14] The some-but-not-all-provinces procedure (section 43) has been used seven times (four amendments involving Newfoundland, one involving PEI, one involving New Brunswick, and one involving Quebec). In 2011, the constitutional rules governing the allocation of seats in the House of Commons were amended.[15] As Warren J. Newman notes, "By any reasonable standard, these are not insignificant accomplishments."[16]

On the other hand, dozens of other efforts to amend the constitution on specific issues have failed since 1982.[17] The federal Progressive Conservatives proposed a property rights amendment in 1983 that was defeated in the House of Commons. Similar property rights amendments were the subject of legislative resolutions in British Columbia, New Brunswick, and Ontario. Prime Minister Mulroney made an effort in 1984-85 to limit the powers of the Senate. The proposed amendment was supported by the majority of provinces but opposed by the Quebec and Manitoba governments. After a provincial election in Ontario replaced the Conservatives with the Liberals, Ontario sided with Quebec and Manitoba. As a result, the amendment died. A proposal by the federal Progressive Conservatives to recognize the rights of unborn children was defeated in the House of Commons in 1987. NDP MP Svend Robinson proposed removing the reference to God from the preamble of the *Charter* in 1999, but his proposal went nowhere. The right to a healthy environment enjoys much greater public consensus than any of the unsuccessful subjects of constitutional reform.

Moving Forward on a Direct Amendment

There are several options for amending Canada's constitution to recognize the right to a healthy environment, ranging from simple to comprehensive:

- clarifying that the right to "life, liberty, and security of the person" in section 7 of the *Charter* includes the right to clean air, safe water, and a healthy environment
- adding a stand-alone right to a healthy and ecologically balanced environment, either in the "Fundamental Freedoms" section of the *Charter* or in a new section of the *Charter*
- or incorporating a detailed *Charter of Environmental Rights and Responsibilities* into Canada's constitution, emulating the approach taken by France in its *Charter for the Environment* (see Appendix B).

A proposal to include the right to a healthy environment or other environmental provisions in the constitution can be initiated by a resolution passed in the House of Commons, the Senate, or the legislative assembly of any province.[18] In other words, there are twelve different political entities that could kick-start the process of greening Canada's constitution. As the Supreme Court of Canada has observed, this power of initiative reflects a basic democratic principle by "conferring a right to initiate constitutional change on each participant in Confederation."[19] Of particular interest in the context of potential environmental provisions, the Supreme Court then stated, "The existence of this right imposes a corresponding duty on the participants in Confederation to engage in constitutional discussions in order to acknowledge and address democratic expressions of a desire for change in other provinces."[20] In other words, once either Ottawa or a provincial government initiates the constitutional amendment procedure, all parties are under an obligation to come to the negotiating table and bargain in good faith.[21] Once the right to a healthy environment is the subject of a single legislature's resolution, all the federal and provincial governments would be engaged, and the clock would begin ticking toward the three-year deadline.

One of the largest obstacles to achieving a constitutional amendment recognizing the right to a healthy environment is the problem of linkage.[22] Past efforts to address Quebec's constitutional concerns have triggered an unmanageable avalanche of demands from other political actors.[23] These demands include expanding provincial powers, reforming the Senate, recognizing social and economic rights, and addressing the aspirations of Aboriginal people. The Meech Lake and Charlottetown Accords foundered under the weight of comprehensive constitutional reform packages. The eleven successful amendments, in contrast, have been focused on narrow topics. The potential linkage to constitutional property rights is also raised as an argument against seeking entrenchment of the right to a healthy environment.[24] Several heated battles have already been fought to prevent the addition of protection for property rights to the *Charter*. The argument that entrenching property rights in the constitution would undermine environmental regulation played a prominent role in the debates.

As noted earlier, the failures of Meech Lake and Charlottetown created a widespread perception that prospects for constitutional change in Canada are dim. As Newman observed, "The trauma attendant upon the failure of that agreement [Meech Lake] to be ratified by formal constitutional amendment has had an incalculable impact on our national psyche and on the way in which our political actors approach the question of constitutional reform."[25] However, Ronald Watts argues persuasively that it would be an error to assume "that the only kind of significant change to the federal system is comprehensive constitutional change."[26] Watts suggests that a preferable approach would be to proceed by pragmatic and incremental adjustments. He refers to Australia, Germany, and Switzerland as examples of federal countries where "substantial change and even transformation has been achieved ... by incremental piecemeal constitutional adjustment and even more by pragmatic political adaptation."[27]

In conclusion, comprehensive constitutional reform is likely to be so unwieldy as to almost guarantee failure. Narrow, focused changes that enjoy high levels of public support – a description that fits the right to a healthy environment – appear to have much better prospects for success.

Option 2: Litigation

The second option for attempting to constitutionalize the right to a healthy environment is through a lawsuit arguing that some specific form of ecological harm (such as air pollution) violates a right that is already explicitly protected by the *Canadian Charter of Rights and Freedoms*. The crux of the argument would be that there is an implicit constitutional right to a healthy environment, most likely vis-à-vis section 7 of the *Charter*, which states that "everyone has the right to life, liberty and security of the person and the right not to be deprived thereof except in accordance with the principles of fundamental justice."[28] In essence, this approach is analogous to the litigation that led the Supreme Court of Canada to determine that sexual orientation was implicitly included in the *Charter*'s section 15 equality provision and that discrimination on the basis of sexual orientation was therefore unlawful.[29]

Many lawyers and scholars have suggested that the words of section 7 referring to "life, liberty and security of the person" are sufficiently broad to be interpreted as encompassing the right to a healthy environment.[30] For example, as early as 1983, Colin Stevenson argued, "If section 7 purports to protect rights to life, liberty, and security of the person, surely this must also be taken to include a right to a clean environment."[31] According to Dianne Saxe, "If a healthy environment is a necessary precondition for human life and bodily integrity, then the human right to life and bodily integrity must entail a right to a healthy environment."[32] More recently, Lynda Collins reviewed Supreme Court of Canada jurisprudence and concluded that "it is clear that s. 7 may provide redress in cases of serious state-sponsored environmental harm."[33] On the other hand, Alastair Lucas wrote that "it is possible, but unlikely, that environmental rights may be enforced directly under the Canadian *Charter of Rights and Freedoms*."[34]

In theory, it could also be argued that certain kinds of pollution or environmental destruction violate freedom of religion (section 2(a) of the *Charter*) or that disproportionate pollution harming a specific identifiable group violates the *Charter*'s equality guarantee (section 15). John Borrows wrote a clear and compelling argument for acknowledging Indigenous spiritual beliefs related to the living Earth under the auspices of section 2(a) but concluded that it was unlikely to succeed in the conservative Canadian court system.[35] Because the section 7 arguments appear to be the strongest, they will be the focus of discussion in this chapter.

The appropriate scope of section 7 of the *Charter* is one of the most contested issues in Canadian constitutional law, as it raises "a wide array of difficult moral and ethical issues."[36] Many different types of claims have been launched based on the right to life, liberty, and security of the person, including concerns about cruise missile testing, the siting of a landfill, the inadequacy of provincial welfare programs, and the legality of a Quebec law prohibiting private health insurance.[37] Most of the successful challenges launched under section 7 have been related to government actions that violated an individual's right to life, liberty, and security of the person in the context of the administration of justice, particularly the criminal justice system. However, more recent cases, including the *Chaoulli* decision on private health insurance, have confirmed that section 7 applies in a broader range of circumstances.

According to the Supreme Court of Canada, a claimant asserting a violation of section 7 must prove two main elements:

- that a deprivation of the right to life, liberty, and security of the person has occurred
- and that the deprivation is not in accordance with the principles of fundamental justice.[38]

The "deprivation" can relate to any or all of the three interests identified in section 7 – life, liberty, and security of the person.[39] The right to life has been described as the right, freedom, or ability to maintain one's existence.[40] The right to liberty "encompasses ... those matters that can properly be characterized as fundamentally or inherently personal such that, by their very nature, they implicate basic choices going to the core of what it means to enjoy individual dignity and independence."[41] The right to security of the person includes both physical and psychological components: "Security of the person in s. 7 encompasses notions of personal autonomy (at least with respect to the right to make choices concerning one's own body), control over one's physical and psychological integrity which is free from state interference, and basic human dignity."[42] The Supreme Court has ruled that the right to security of the person can be violated by laws or government actions that increase risks to health (for example, where delays in obtaining abortions result in an increased probability of serious harm).[43]

In many cases, the Supreme Court of Canada has commented on the high degree of importance ascribed to protecting the right to bodily integrity (as an element of security of the person). One line of cases involves strip searches, body cavity searches, and taking blood, hair, and tissue samples from criminal suspects.[44] In the words of the court, "Canadians think of their bodies as the outward manifestation of themselves. It is considered to be uniquely important and uniquely theirs. Any invasion of the body is an invasion of the particular person. Indeed, it is the ultimate invasion of personal dignity and privacy."[45] Another line of cases interpreting the right to bodily integrity comes from the medical context, such as the right to refuse medical treatment and manufacturers' duty to disclose dangers inherent in the use of their products (as in the potential for breast implants to rupture).[46] Therefore, it seems logical that the intrusive presence of harmful levels of toxic substances (such as mercury or PCBs) in a person's body could also be considered a violation of the right to bodily integrity and therefore a potential violation of section 7.[47]

A contentious issue is whether section 7 is, or ought to be, the basis for positive state obligations, such as guaranteeing adequate living standards or a healthy environment.[48] Efforts to broaden the application of section 7 to incorporate social, economic, and environmental rights have not succeeded, although the Supreme Court has deliberately left the door open. On behalf of the majority in the *Gosselin* case, which dealt with reduced welfare payments for young people in Quebec, Chief Justice McLachlin wrote,

> Nothing in the jurisprudence thus far suggests that s. 7 places a positive obligation on the state to ensure that each person enjoys life, liberty or security of the person. Rather, s. 7 has been interpreted as restricting the state's ability to deprive people of these. Such a deprivation does not exist in the case at bar. One day s. 7 may be interpreted to include positive obligations. It would be a mistake to regard s. 7 as frozen, or its content as having been exhaustively defined in previous cases. The question therefore is not whether s. 7 has ever been – or will ever be – recognized as creating positive rights. Rather, the question is whether the present circumstances warrant a novel application of s. 7 as the basis for a positive state obligation to guarantee adequate living standards. I conclude that they do not. I leave open the possibility that a positive obligation to sustain life, liberty, or security of person may be made out in special circumstances. However, this is not such a case.[49]

Justices Arbour and L'Heureux-Dubé, dissenting in *Gosselin,* argued that section 7 established a positive obligation on the state to make provision for everyone's basic needs.[50] The decision in *Chaoulli,* striking down Quebec's prohibition of private health insurance, may have marked a new era in the Supreme Court's interpretation of section 7, suggesting that the court is willing to take a broader, more flexible approach.[51]

The legal attributes of a potentially successful section 7 case can be ascertained by reviewing past jurisprudence on this and other *Charter* rights. First, applicants must meet the test for standing – either a directly affected interest (e.g., adverse health effects) or public interest standing, which is at the court's discretion. A court's decision on public interest standing depends on whether the applicant has a genuine interest, the case presents a serious legal issue, and there are no other effective means to bring the issue before the court. Second, there must be government action that is alleged to violate the right to life, liberty, and security of the person. Government involvement could take the form of an investment, a project on Crown land, or the issuance of a permit or licence authorizing some kind of activity. Third, there must be a relatively direct causal nexus between the government action and the alleged harm. In two previous section 7 cases, adverse health effects from cruise missile testing that allegedly increased the risk of war, and inadequate liability regimes for nuclear power facilities that allegedly increased the risk of accidents, were considered too speculative. Fourth, the deprivation of the right to life, liberty, and security of the person must be contrary to the "principles of fundamental justice." According to the Supreme Court, if a rule or principle is to constitute a principle of fundamental justice for the purposes of section 7, it must

- be a legal principle about which there is significant societal consensus that it is fundamental to the way in which the legal system ought fairly to operate
- and be identified with sufficient precision to yield a manageable standard against which to measure deprivations of life, liberty, or security of the person.[52]

Fifth, once a claimant has established a violation of section 7 of the *Charter*, the onus shifts to the government to justify the infringement under section 1, which states that "the *Canadian Charter of Rights and Freedoms* guarantees the rights and freedoms set out in it subject only to such reasonable limits prescribed by law as can be demonstrably justified in a free and democratic society."[53] The Supreme Court has stated that "a violation of section 7 will be saved by section 1 only in cases arising out of exceptional conditions, such as natural disasters, the outbreak of war, epidemics and the like."[54] Thus, it is highly unlikely that a government could successfully justify an environmental hazard that violated an individual's right to life, liberty, or security of the person.

In at least ten previous cases, litigants have attempted to rely on section 7 to challenge environmental harms. These cases (described in Appendix C) involved claims that the section was violated by

- cruise missile testing in northern Canada
- inadequate liability limits for nuclear reactors, increasing the likelihood of nuclear proliferation and nuclear accidents
- adverse health effects from a proposed municipal waste incinerator
- adverse health effects from a proposed landfill
- fluoridation of public water supplies
- the approval and use of toxic pesticides
- and pollution from proposed oil and gas wells.[55]

Although none of these cases were successful, the Supreme Court of Canada and other courts have been careful to leave the door open for future cases that might produce a different result. The track record of failure may appear discouraging, but this reflects the evolutionary process of law. Often a series of unsuccessful cases will be brought before victory is ultimately achieved. A classic example involves segregated schooling in the USA pursuant to the "separate but equal" doctrine, which was challenged in lawsuits for decades before the US Supreme Court issued its landmark judgment in *Brown v. Board of Education* in 1954.[56]

There are four reasons for cautious optimism if and when a compelling case asserting an implicit right to a healthy environment reaches the Supreme Court of Canada. First, the court has a strong track record in environmental cases. Second, it has explicitly referred to the right to a safe environment in several cases. Third, it frequently relies on international and comparative law (the decisions of other national courts) in interpreting the *Charter*, and both of these sources of law support recognition of an implicit right to a healthy environment. Fourth, the court describes the constitution as a "living tree" and emphasizes the need to interpret the document progressively over time to meet changing circumstances.

In a series of cases dating back to the 1970s, the Supreme Court of Canada has repeatedly demonstrated an understanding of the need for stronger legal protection of the environment. In 1978, in a case dealing with garbage dumped in a creek, the court stated that the prevention of pollution "is a matter of great public concern."[57] In the *Sparrow* case involving Aboriginal fishing rights, the court ruled that legitimate conservation concerns must always be the overriding priority in fisheries management, even where constitutionally protected Aboriginal rights are involved.[58] In *Friends of the Oldman River*, the Supreme Court found that Ottawa had failed to follow its own rules governing environmental assessment and stated that "the protection of the environment has become one of the major challenges of our time."[59] In *Hydro-Québec*, the court upheld the constitutionality of the *Canadian Environmental Protection Act* and stated that protecting the environment was a matter of "super-ordinate public importance."[60] In *Hudson*, the court upheld a municipal pesticide bylaw, endorsed the precautionary principle as a key element of environmental management, and stated, "Our common future, that of every Canadian community, depends on a healthy environment."[61] In a case involving Imperial Oil's liability for cleaning up a contaminated site in Quebec, the court strongly endorsed the polluter pays principle.[62] In a 2004 case involving damage to forests, the court repeatedly referred to the fundamental value of environmental protection and suggested that the law must evolve to assist in realizing this value.[63] In 2008, the Supreme Court endorsed the awarding of damages in an environmental class action lawsuit based on dust and foul odours from a cement plant.[64]

Second, and perhaps even more importantly, in 1995 the Supreme Court made the following observation in an environmental case:

> It is clear that over the past two decades, citizens have become acutely aware of the importance of environmental protection, and of the fact that penal consequences may flow from conduct which harms the environment ... Everyone is aware that individually and collectively, we are responsible for preserving the natural environment. I would agree with the Law Reform Commission of Canada, *Crimes Against the Environment*, *supra*, which concluded at p. 8 that:
>
>> ... a fundamental and widely shared value is indeed seriously contravened by some environmental pollution, a value which we will refer to as the *right to a safe environment*.
>>
>> To some extent, this right and value appears to be new and emerging, but in part because it is an extension of existing and very traditional rights and values already protected by criminal law, its presence and shape even now are largely discernible. Among the new strands of this fundamental value are, it may be argued, those such as *quality of life*, and *stewardship* of the natural environment. At the same time, traditional values as well have simply expanded and evolved to include the environment now as an area and interest of direct and primary concern. Among these values fundamental to the purposes and protections of criminal law are the *sanctity of life*, the *inviolability and integrity of persons*, and the *protection of human life and health*. It is increasingly understood that certain forms and degrees of environmental pollution can directly or indirectly, sooner or later, seriously harm or endanger human life and human health.[65]

The Supreme Court reiterated this statement in a 1997 case.[66] As well, in a 2003 Quebec case dealing with pollution, the court commented extensively on "the fundamental right to the preservation of the quality of the environment."[67] Most recently, in a decision that upheld a noise bylaw in Montreal, the court endorsed the statement that "the citizens of a city, even a city the size of Montréal, have the right to a healthy environment."[68] The Supreme Court's repeated references to the right to a safe or healthy environment establish a body of precedents that bode well for future efforts to expand the scope and impact of this right in Canada.

The Federal Court of Appeal also referred positively to the individual's right to a safe environment in a case where it quashed the registration of a toxic pesticide.[69] Another leading Canadian case (decided by the Newfoundland Court of Appeal) referred to "the rights of future generations to the protection of the present integrity of the natural world," from which it surely follows that current generations must possess a similar right.[70]

Third, Canadian courts are relatively open to considering principles and precedents from other jurisdictions.[71] Courts around the world are engaged in a dialogue concerning similar legal questions, a phenomenon known as transjudicialism.[72] As described earlier, the argument that other constitutional rights should be interpreted as including an implicit right to a healthy environment has been accepted by courts in at least twenty nations.[73] These include Argentina, Bangladesh, Costa Rica, El Salvador, Estonia, Greece, Guatemala, India, Israel, Italy, Kenya, Malaysia, Nigeria, Nepal, Pakistan, Peru, Romania, Sri Lanka, Tanzania, and Uruguay. On the other hand, in several cases during the 1970s, US courts rejected the argument that there is an implicit constitutional right to a healthy environment.[74] Of course, the decisions of foreign courts are persuasive rather than binding on Canadian courts.

There is also extensive international jurisprudence supporting the argument that environmental hazards can violate the right to life, from tribunals including the Inter-American Commission on Human Rights, the Inter-American Court of Human Rights, the European Court of Human Rights, the European Committee of Social Rights, the African Commission on Human and Peoples' Rights, and the UN Human Rights Committee (see Chapter 6 for details). A strong argument can be made that the right to a healthy environment is now a general principle of law as well as customary international law. This substantial and growing body of international law clearly supports Canadian recognition of an implicit constitutional right to a healthy environment.

Fourth, as the Supreme Court of Canada has stated, Canada's constitution is intended to be a living tree, "drafted with an eye to the future," and it must "be capable of growth and development over time to meet new social, political and historical realities often unimagined by its framers."[75] The Supreme Court has also repeatedly stated that the interpretation of the

Charter should be "a generous rather than a legalistic one, aimed at fulfilling the purpose of the guarantee and securing for individuals the full benefit of the *Charter*'s protection."[76]

Moving Forward on Litigation

Any concerned citizen, ENGO, or community could file a lawsuit targeting a specific government action, arguing that the implicit right to live in a healthy environment in section 7 of the *Charter* is being violated. For example, potential cases could challenge

- the approval and use of pesticides that have been banned in other nations (such as atrazine, a pesticide that contaminates groundwater and is known to disrupt the hormone system of humans and other animals)
- the inadequate regulation of toxic substances that are found in the bodies of Canadians (a phenomenon known as the chemical body burden)
- voluntary air quality guidelines that fail to protect Canadians' health and are substantially weaker than comparable national standards in other countries
- drinking water guidelines that are unenforceable, fail to protect health, and are substantially weaker than comparable national standards in other countries
- industrial facilities that are having demonstrable adverse health effects on local communities
- or other situations where the government is involved in the production or approval of an activity or product resulting in an environmental hazard that has harmed or is likely to harm human health (such as asbestos mining and export).

Each potential case would involve difficulties with respect to both the scientific evidence and the associated legal issues. It is challenging to establish a causal link between the source of a pollutant and demonstrable adverse health effects.[77] Identifying, financing, and preparing the litigation would probably involve an extensive time period and substantial costs. Notwithstanding the challenges, environmental lawyer Jerry V. DeMarco analyzed the Supreme Court jurisprudence summarized above and concluded that "there is an open invitation for innovative litigation aimed at protecting the rights and interests of present and future generations in a healthy environment. Given the greater understanding of the relationships between a clean environment and human health and well-being, this evolution may also end up incorporating a role for the *Charter* in safeguarding today's society and our children."[78]

There is at least one lawsuit currently under way in Canada invoking the implicit constitutional right to a healthy environment. On behalf of two members of the Aamjiwnaang First Nation in Sarnia (Canada's Chemical Valley), lawyers with Ecojustice filed a lawsuit in 2010 arguing that chemical pollution was violating sections 7 and 15 of the *Charter*.[79] The lawsuit against Ontario's Ministry of the Environment challenges a government decision to approve an increase in air pollution from a Suncor petroleum refinery. In a nutshell, the Aamjiwnaang argue that by permitting additional releases of sulphur dioxide, nitrogen oxides, hydrogen sulfide, particulate matter, and benzene into what is already one of the most heavily polluted areas of Canada, the government has violated their right to life, liberty, and security of the person.[80] There is solid medical evidence that these pollutants cause an array of negative health effects including cancer, cardiovascular disease, respiratory disease, and damage to reproductive, neurological, and developmental systems. The Aamjiwnaang people suffer from elevated rates of cancer and asthma, a skewed birth ratio, and far below average life expectancy.[81] Their case is strengthened by the fact that the increased levels of pollution were negotiated and approved in secret (violating principles of fundamental justice). The lawsuit also asserts a violation of equality rights under section 15 of the *Charter*, arguing that members of the Aamjiwnaang First Nation already suffer from a disproportionate burden of air pollution, which would be exacerbated by the approved increase.

Option 3: A Judicial Reference

The third option for achieving constitutional recognition of the right to a healthy environment involves the judicial reference, a uniquely Canadian legal process through which governments seek legal advice from courts, often on controversial issues. Judicial references involve important questions of law concerning the interpretation of the constitution, the constitutionality or interpretation of any federal or provincial legislation, or any other important legal question. A key feature is that governments are able to ask courts to answer hypothetical questions in the absence of a dispute between parties. As one judge wrote, the "very reason why [judicial reference] legislation (giving governments the power to refer any matter to the court for an opinion) has been enacted is to overcome the general principle that courts will not entertain claims that are hypothetical or merely academic."[82]

References can be initiated by either the federal government or any provincial or territorial government. Federally initiated judicial references (through the governor-in-council or Cabinet) go directly to the Supreme Court of Canada.[83] Provincially initiated references (through the lieutenant-governor-in-council or Cabinet) go to the appropriate provincial Court of Appeal.[84] The Yukon follows the same process as the provinces.[85] In the NWT and Nunavut, the reference procedure is slightly different, in that the Minister of Justice refers questions to the NWT Supreme Court and Nunavut Court of Justice, respectively.[86] Decisions from provincial and territorial courts in judicial references can be appealed to the Supreme Court of Canada as of right, meaning permission for leave to appeal is not required.[87]

The relevant court determines how the reference will actually proceed: what material should be presented, who should participate, and how long the process will take. In all cases, interested groups and individuals can apply to the courts to participate as intervenors. Where the government of any province has a special interest in a question put in a reference, the attorney general of the province must be notified in order that he or she may participate.

Throughout Canada's history, judicial references have tackled many important issues and accordingly have a strong degree of both legal legitimacy and public acceptance.[88] As several experts observed, "The process has been widely accepted and the reference opinions have withstood the test of time as well as any of the thousands of decisions Canadian courts have rendered."[89] In theory, reference judgments are advisory opinions only and are not legally binding, yet in practice they establish precedents and are followed by governments.[90] Arguments against references are that they involve abstract legal questions better answered in the context of specific factual controversies, that interested parties may not be involved, and that they constitute an elitist process.[91]

There have been more than seventy references by the federal government to the Supreme Court since the first one in 1892. Among the most prominent in recent decades have been the *Anti-Inflation Act Reference* (1976), the *Senate Reference* (1980), the *Newfoundland Continental Shelf Reference* (1984), the *Manitoba Language Rights Reference* (1984), the *Reference Re Ng Extradition* (1991), the *David Milgaard Conviction Reference* (1991), the *Reference re Quebec Secession* (1998), the *Reference re Same-sex Marriage* (2004), and the *Reference re Securities Act* (2011). The Supreme Court has also heard dozens of references initiated by provincial governments including the *Constitutional Patriation Reference* (1981), the *Quebec Veto Reference* (1982), the *Provincial Court Judges Reference* (1997), and the *Firearms Act Reference* (2000).

The Persons Case

Perhaps the most famous judicial reference in Canadian history was the so-called Persons case.[92] In 1927, five Canadian women – Henrietta Muir Edwards, Nellie McClung, Louise McKinney, Emily Murphy, and Irene Parlby – sent a petition to the federal government requesting that the question "Does the word 'persons' in section 24 of the *British North America Act, 1867*, include female persons?" be submitted to the Supreme Court of Canada via the reference procedure. The federal Cabinet honoured their request, and the Supreme Court infamously ruled that although women were persons in a general sense, the phrase "qualified persons" in section 24 of the *British North America Act* did not include them.[93]

The Supreme Court's decision was appealed to the Judicial Committee of the Privy Council in England, at the time the highest court of appeal for Canada. In 1929, Lord Sankey, lord chancellor of the Privy Council, announced the decision that women are included in the phrase "qualified persons" and as such are eligible to become members of the Senate. The Privy Council decision recognized "that the exclusion of women from all public offices is a relic of days more barbarous than ours. And to those who would ask why the word 'persons' should include females, the obvious answer is, why should it not?"[94] Although technically concerned with the eligibility of women to sit in the Senate, the decision had broad implications for women's right to equality in Canada.[95]

The Persons case is also important because it articulated, for the first time, the "living tree doctrine," which says that a constitution is organic and must be read in a broad and liberal manner so as to adapt it to changing times.[96] In the words of the Judicial Committee of the Privy Council, Canada's constitution is intended to be "a living tree capable of growth and expansion within its natural limits."[97] The Supreme Court of Canada had ruled that the word "persons" must be interpreted in a manner consistent with the original intent of the drafters of the *British North America Act* in 1867. The Judicial Committee of the Privy Council rejected that "original meaning" or "frozen rights" approach.

Moving Forward on a Judicial Reference

The Persons case offers a compelling precedent for the right to a healthy environment. An environmental group or coalition could formally request that the federal government initiate a reference to the Supreme Court to determine whether the right is implicit in the constitution. A government must approve every reference before it can be initiated but can do so at the request of other parties. In the past, references have been commenced at the behest of individuals, NGOs, businesses, and foreign governments.[98] For example, in addition to the Persons case, a 1946 reference about the rights of persons of Japanese descent was initiated by pressure from an NGO called the Co-operative Committee on Japanese Canadians.[99]

Seeking a reference could generate considerable public attention for the concept of a constitutional right to a healthy environment. The Persons case was preceded by petitions and letters from hundreds of thousands of Canadians supporting the appointment of women to the Senate. If Ottawa refused to initiate the process, provincial and territorial governments could be approached. It seems plausible that at least one provincial or territorial government would be willing to initiate a reference, assuming it could be convinced that political benefits might be reaped. Ultimately, if a court (ideally the Supreme Court) issued a positive ruling, the right to a healthy environment would enjoy unprecedented constitutional recognition in Canada. If a court issued a negative ruling, this could provide additional momentum for a campaign to secure the direct amendment of the constitution, as the court's judgment could be portrayed as out of sync with the values of the overwhelming majority of Canadians.

As a hypothetical example, a reference on the right to a healthy environment could ask the following types of questions:

- Does section 7 of the *Charter* include an implicit right to live in a healthy environment as part of the right to life, liberty, and security of the person?
- Does the presence of mercury, PCBs, or other contaminants of concern found in the blood, fat, or other body tissue of Canadians violate section 7 of the *Charter*?
- Do Canadian governments have a constitutional duty to ensure clean air, safe water, and other elements of a healthy environment?

It is certain that large numbers of interested groups from across the political spectrum would apply for permission to participate in such a case as intervenors, thus ensuring that the Supreme Court heard submissions from a broad range of Canadians. For example, in the 2004 *Reference re Same-sex Marriage*, the court heard arguments from twenty-nine individuals and groups in addition to the federal government.[100]

Conclusion

To reiterate, there are three pathways to constitutional recognition of the right to a healthy environment:

- a direct amendment to Canada's constitution
- a lawsuit asserting that a specific environmental harm is violating the implicit right to a healthy environment in section 7 of the *Charter*
- or a judicial reference by one or more governments asking courts to determine whether section 7 of the *Charter* includes an implicit right to a healthy environment.

Each approach has pros and cons. They are not mutually exclusive. None guarantees a successful outcome. Directly amending the constitution would have the greatest impact legally, practically, and symbolically but is widely perceived, by both the public and political elites, as tantamount to impossible. Although this perception is inaccurate, it creates a major barrier. One government would have to be persuaded to play a leadership role by passing a resolution proposing the constitutional amendment. Then the clock would begin ticking, with a three-year deadline. The political challenge is daunting, as the support of the House of Commons and at least seven provinces must be obtained within three years.

The two legal options – litigation and a judicial reference – would seek the same result, a court ruling that the right to a healthy environment is implicitly included in the right to life, liberty, and security of the person and therefore enjoys constitutional protection. At the risk of stating the obvious, litigation is always expensive, time consuming, and rife with uncertainty. On the plus side, these legal options would avoid the linkage problem, preventing other interests from piggybacking on the amendment of the *Charter* to push for other constitutional reforms. However, opponents – both government and industry – would be expected to mount a vigorous campaign to defeat either of these types of legal proceedings.

Lawsuits asserting a violation of the implicit right to a healthy environment face considerable factual, scientific, and legal hurdles. As in almost any legal action, there are both positive and negative precedents. Past efforts to persuade Canadian courts that section 7 of the *Charter* ought to be broadly construed so as to encompass the right to a healthy environment have failed. The challenges facing the Aamjiwnaang case (and other future section 7 lawsuits) should not be underestimated. Yet this approach has been remarkably successful in many other nations and enjoys support in international law. Given the enlightened jurisprudence of the Supreme Court of Canada in environmental cases, this option has significant potential. As environmental issues continue to be a pressing concern to Canadians, it seems likely that the question of whether the *Charter* includes an implicit right to a healthy environment will eventually be placed squarely before the Supreme Court. The Aamjiwnaang case could conceivably do so within the next five years.

Assuming that a willing government could be found, the reference procedure would be faster and less expensive than starting a lawsuit. A reference would also be less complicated because it would avoid factual disputes and focus strictly on legal questions. NGOs campaigning for a reference could harness the popular appeal of the Persons case. If the federal government could not be persuaded to initiate the reference procedure, more time would be needed because provincial/territorial references must go to courts of appeal before proceeding to the more authoritative Supreme Court of Canada. As with the litigation option, a reference faces substantial uncertainty despite the precedents from other nations, international law, and the Supreme Court's strong track record in environmental cases.

Thirty years after the *Charter* was enacted, increasing pressure for environmental reform of Canada's constitution appears inevitable, particularly given international developments in this field. In light of ongoing environmental problems, extensive negative health effects, and concern about the future of Canada's magnificent natural heritage, Canadians can be expected to demand that their basic right to breathe clean air, drink safe water, and live in a healthy environment be granted constitutional recognition.

9
Prospects for Change

> We need to inculcate the concept that every citizen has a right to a safe and healthy environment. Our failure to persuade people on this has been the principal failure of the environmental movement.
>
> – Robert F. Kennedy Jr., "Thoughts on Environmental Rights and Ownership"

The prospects for achieving substantial constitutional reform in Canada are widely perceived to be bleak. The scars inflicted by the nail-biting Quebec referendums and the failures of the Meech Lake and Charlottetown Accords linger. For many years, as Peter Russell wrote in his book *Constitutional Odyssey*, "using the 'c' word was a guaranteed conversational turn-off at Canadian dinner tables."[1] There is no question that in Canada's legal system it is difficult to amend the constitution. Political and legal developments over the past fifteen years have made it seem even more challenging, yet eleven amendments have already occurred. A national poll conducted in 2011 revealed that more than 60 percent of Canadians are amenable to amending the constitution, suggesting that the scars of the past are finally healing.[2] More inspiring is a public opinion poll conducted in 2010 that found 96 percent of Canadians believe the right to clean water should be guaranteed as a human right for all Canadians.[3] In light of the enduring popularity of the *Charter*, the consistently strong environmental concerns expressed by Canadians, and the almost unanimous public support for the right to water, it seems likely that constitutional recognition of the right to a healthy environment would receive tremendous support.

The most powerful path forward is to directly amend Canada's constitution to incorporate the right to a healthy environment. This approach is the most compelling in terms of long-term influence on Canadian values, as our experience with the *Charter* demonstrates. This is the most potent approach legally. It has the greatest symbolic value. The alternative route – judicial recognition of an implicit right to a healthy environment – would still be a major victory and could spur a direct amendment. However, it would be naive to suggest that amending the constitution to include environmental rights and responsibilities – either directly or indirectly – will be easy or straightforward. As Swaigen and Woods wrote in 1981, "The difficulties of arguing for, designing, and implementing a right that will have an inevitable positive impact on environmental quality should not be underestimated."[4] Few major achievements are easy. But as Robert F. Kennedy said during a 1966 speech in South Africa,

> There is no basic inconsistency between ideals and realistic possibilities – no separation between the deepest desires of heart and of mind and the rational application of human effort to human problems. It is not realistic to solve problems and take action unguided by ultimate moral aims and values, although we all know some who claim that it is so. In my judgment, it is thoughtless folly. For it ignores the realities of human faith and of passion and of belief; forces ultimately more powerful than all the calculations of our economists or of our generals. Of course to adhere to standards, to idealism, to vision, in the face of immediate dangers takes great courage and takes self-confidence. But we also know that only those who dare to fail greatly, can ever achieve greatly.[5]

Adversaries of constitutional change enjoy the powerful force of inertia. Political opposition will inevitably be marshalled, led by vested interests that perceive a threat to their activities. Some corporations, industry associations, and provincial governments will issue dire warnings about the potential damage to Canada's economy, the spectre of a deluge of litigation, and the prospect of courts making or overturning decisions that rightly belong in democratically elected hands. Critics will argue that Canada already has extensive measures in place to safeguard human rights and the environment. Industry's vitriolic opposition to the proposed *Canadian Environmental Bill of Rights* (Bill C-469) offered a preview of the negativity and intensity that would probably characterize its reaction to a proposed constitutional amendment.[6] Representatives from the Canadian Chamber of Commerce, the Canadian Association of Petroleum Producers, and other industry groups warned that Bill C-469 would freeze capital investment in Canada and inflict economic chaos while serving the interests of a small number of "special interest" groups. The experience of other countries with constitutional environmental rights and responsibilities and Canada's own experience with the *Charter* demonstrate that none of these arguments are persuasive.

Even some supporters of environmental rights may fear opening a Pandora's box of constitutional amendments that could worsen prospects for improving Canada's environmental record. However, the Meech Lake and Charlottetown boondoggles offer valuable lessons for future constitutional reform efforts.[7] Linkage, especially related to Quebec issues, would need to be rigorously avoided, as this would complicate and delay matters to the extent that the proposal would bog down. It would also take strategic and sustained effort to prevent the proposal from being linked to other constitutional changes, such as entrenching property rights or transferring federal responsibility for environmental protection to the provinces. Canada's constitution must not be viewed as written in stone, proposed amendments must not be viewed as taboo, and progress must not be barred by obsessions with the unsuccessful battles of the past.

Canadian political parties are divided about the desirability of according constitutional status to the right to a healthy environment. There are two national parties – the New Democrats and the Greens – that support amending the constitution to recognize environmental rights and responsibilities. The New Democrats propose "creating a legal framework to ensure that people have the right to live in a healthy environment with access to natural spaces."[8] Lawyer John Swaigen, in response to a request from NDP MP Nathan Cullen, provided a draft constitutional amendment on the right to a healthy environment.[9] In 2005, the Green Party of Canada proposed an amendment to Canada's *Charter of Rights and Freedoms* to enshrine basic environmental rights including the right to clean air, soil, and water. The pledge was incorporated into the party's election platform in 2006.[10] In 2010, the Green Party again promised to amend "the *Canadian Charter of Rights and Freedoms* to enshrine the right of future Canadians to an ecological heritage that includes breathable air and drinkable water."[11]

The governing Conservatives are opposed to recognizing the right to a healthy environment and have demonstrated a disturbing degree of hostility toward existing federal environmental responsibilities by weakening laws, cutting staff and budgets, and reneging on international commitments.[12] The Liberals have not taken a position on greening Canada's constitution, although previous leaders Stéphane Dion and Michael Ignatieff did not respond positively to suggestions that they champion the measure.[13]

Some of Canada's past political leaders view constitutional amendment as impractical. Marc Lalonde, who served as minister of justice and attorney general, and who played other roles in Liberal governments headed by Pierre Trudeau, responded to questions about the right to a healthy environment by saying that governments prefer to "let sleeping dogs lie."[14] Retired judge Barry Strayer, who was Pierre Trudeau's legal advisor for fifteen years during the era of constitutional reform, also sees constitutional recognition of environmental rights or responsibilities as unlikely.[15] Strayer's reasons include opposition from provincial governments, concerns about transferring environmental policy decisions from elected legislators to unelected judges, the difficult choices that could face judges in environmental cases, and constitutional fatigue.

Other political pundits and constitutional experts are more optimistic. Roy Romanow is the former Saskatchewan premier who played a key role in negotiating the 1981 Kitchen Accord that paved the way for patriation of Canada's constitution. In his book *Canada Notwithstanding,* Romanow wrote that "the need for constitutional reform has not been lessened by the limited success of 1981. Significant numbers of unresolved constitutional dilemmas await attention."[16] With the advantage of hindsight, Romanow regrets the earlier failure to address the environment and "would fight for the recognition of the right to a healthy environment if given another chance."[17]

Scholars are divided. One of Canada's leading constitutional law experts, Peter Hogg, believes that future changes to the constitution will be difficult to achieve yet are needed to give effect to new and evolving values.[18] Garth Stevenson acknowledges that the present "constitutional impasse" makes formal amendment almost impossible yet finds it "hard to believe that either the federal distribution of powers or the *Canadian Charter of Rights and Freedoms* is so perfect that it might not require some modification over the next 50 or 100 years."[19] Another leading constitutional law expert, Dale Gibson, believes that it is only a matter of time until the right to a healthy environment is entrenched in the *Charter.*[20] Lorraine Weinrib describes constitutions as "organic instruments" that must continue to evolve in concert with societal values.[21]

Environmental law experts are also divided about the prospects for constitutional reform. A lengthy 1999 law review article on environmental rights in Canada failed even to mention constitutional environmental rights, focusing exclusively on legislative rights.[22] Environmental lawyer William Andrews, who wrote about the importance of recognizing the constitutional right to a healthy environment back in the 1980s, feels that the present odds of achieving a *Charter* amendment are "slim to none" because of the need for widespread political consensus and the probability that other issues would be added, leading to the linkage problem.[23] However, John Swaigen, the environmental lawyer who felt that environmental rights and responsibilities were too "far out" to achieve constitutional status in the 1970s, believes that the time has come and that a constitutional amendment is now an "achievable reality."[24]

History is replete with lessons about the danger of describing future political developments as impossible – from the fall of the Berlin Wall and the dissolution of the Soviet Union to the end of apartheid in South Africa. In the context of greening constitutions, France provides an inspiring example for Canada. In 1995, soon after becoming president, Jacques Chirac provoked the ire of environmental groups by insisting that France resume nuclear testing at Mururoa Atoll in French Polynesia. Yet in 2001, Chirac unveiled a proposal for a *Charter for the Environment* that incorporated constitutional recognition of the right to live in a healthy environment, the obligation to protect the environment, the precautionary principle, and other key ecological principles (see Appendix B).[25] Chirac's proposal was greeted with skepticism from environmental groups and opposition from the business community.[26] Pundits suggested he was merely trying to secure green votes in the 2002 election.[27] Chirac ignored the critics and enthusiastically championed his proposal:

> I have called for France to have an Environmental Charter incorporated into our Constitution. The right to a quality environment will hence be protected in the same way as the rights of man and the citizen stated in the declaration of 1789 and the economic and social rights laid down in the Preamble to the 1946 Constitution.
>
> The Charter was drafted following a major national public debate and has been submitted to Parliament. It states the place of Man in his natural environment, without which he would not be able to survive, and the detrimental consequences of excessive pressure on natural resources.
>
> It declares everyone's right to live in a balanced environment that is not harmful to their health. It calls on everyone, and first and

> foremost the State, to adopt an attitude of responsibility based on education, information, prevention, precaution and compensation for the sake of future generations. This text raises great hopes. I am aware of the questions that such a move could raise and I understand them, but I believe that the adoption of this Charter will represent a huge step forward for France ... A benchmark text that will inspire France's national, European and international policies for decades to come.[28]

In 2005, the French Congress (including both the National Assembly and the Senate) approved the *Charter for the Environment* by a landslide vote of 531 to 23.[29] Although it was anticipated that the charter would increase the prominence of environmental issues in French law, David Marrani asserts that despite its recent vintage, "it has developed beyond all predictions."[30] The charter is influencing legislation, court decisions, government policy, and even the French education system.[31] In 2011, France cited the charter in becoming the first nation in the world to ban hydraulic fracturing, or fracking, the environmentally destructive method of extracting oil or natural gas from underground rock formations. The Constitutional Council evaluated the consistency of a new law on genetically modified organisms and a proposed carbon tax with the charter.[32] The Council of State (the highest administrative court in France) has based more than a dozen decisions on the charter, on issues ranging from nuclear power to the protection of mountain lakes.[33] The French experience suggests that a combination of public pressure and political leadership can overcome constitutional inertia, even in the face of cynicism and opposition from societal elites.

More than 145 nations – from Argentina to Zambia – have deliberately expressed their commitment to environmental protection through constitutional changes in the past four decades. This trend continues, as in the past three years the Dominican Republic, Iceland, Jamaica, Kenya, Morocco, and South Sudan have adopted new constitutions recognizing the right to a healthy environment. Proposed constitutions for Egypt, Nepal, and Tunisia also include the right, as does a proposed bill of rights for the United Kingdom. The majority of the nations whose constitutions mandate environmental protection enjoy stronger environmental laws, better enforcement of those laws, enhanced government and corporate accountability, improved access to environmental information, and higher levels of public participation in decision making. Even more compelling is evidence that, compared to nations whose constitutions are silent on green issues, nations with environmental provisions in their constitutions have smaller ecological footprints, perform better on comprehensive rankings of environmental performance, have reduced air pollution much faster, are more effectively addressing climate change, and are more likely to ratify international environmental treaties. Most importantly, these constitutional provisions are making a substantial contribution to improving people's lives and well-being. Benefits include improved access to safe drinking water, cleaner air, more effective sanitation and waste management practices, and healthier ecosystems.

Over 90 percent of the world's nations accept that the right to a healthy environment is an essential human right. The right is now well entrenched in international law. Thus, it is anomalous for Canada to be among the final heel-dragging hold-outs, given that protection of the environment is such a fundamental Canadian value. The most basic option would be to amend the existing section 7 of the *Charter* by adding the following clarification:

> 7.1 Everyone has the right to live in a healthy and ecologically balanced environment, including clean air, safe water, fertile soil, nutritious food, and vibrant biodiversity.

This approach offers the advantage of fitting within the current style of the Charter, which is concise and focused exclusively on individual rights. Government's duty to protect the environment is implicit, and it is left to citizens, legislatures, and courts to fill in the details. A second option would be to take a more comprehensive approach. This option would be comparable to the extensive provisions of the Charter dealing with official languages (sections 16-23).

A draft Canadian Charter of Environmental Rights and Responsibilities (below) is offered as a starting point for discussion. It draws on the insights, innovations, and experiences of other nations but is uniquely Canadian. It could be incorporated into the existing *Charter* or added to the handful of documents that collectively make up Canada's constitution:

The Canadian Charter of Environmental Rights and Responsibilities

The people of Canada understand that:

The beauty, vastness, and diversity of Nature are at the heart of the Canadian identity;

We are stewards of a sacred trust, safeguarding Canada's unique and magnificent natural heritage on behalf of the world;

The air we breathe, the water we drink, and the food we eat make us part of, and dependent upon, the environment;

The choices we make to meet our needs must not compromise the capacity of future generations and other peoples to satisfy their own needs;

Our future health, well-being, and prosperity depend on reducing our pressure on the Earth's ecosystems and living graciously within Nature's limits;

Therefore, we proclaim:

1 Everyone has the right to live in a healthy and ecologically balanced environment, including clean air, safe water, fertile soil, nutritious food, and vibrant biodiversity.
2 Everyone has a responsibility to protect and, where possible, restore the environment.
3 Everyone has the right to information about the state of the environment, the right to participate in making decisions that affect the environment, and the right of access to judicial remedies in response to violations of their right to live in a healthy environment.
4 Governments at all levels, according to their jurisdiction under the *Constitution Act, 1867*, are trustees who share the responsibility for protecting and restoring the environment, for the benefit of present and future generations.
5 Government laws, regulations, policies, and decisions shall apply the polluter pays principle, so that any individual, private enterprise, or public entity that damages the environment is responsible for paying for the full costs of restoring, rehabilitating, or paying compensation for damages inflicted.
6 Government laws, regulations, policies, and decisions shall follow the precautionary principle, so that where there is evidence of potentially significant environmental harm, a lack of scientific certainty shall not be used to avoid or delay the implementation of effective and efficient measures to prevent or mitigate the harm.
7 Governments shall ensure that the costs of pollution and environmental damage are fairly distributed, that existing environmental injustices are alleviated, and that the benefits of environmental goods and services are enjoyed equitably.

8 Educational programs at all levels, from preschool to university, must contribute to the implementation of the rights and responsibilities defined by this Charter.

9 The rights of future generations and Nature shall be respected by governments when enacting laws or regulations, making decisions, developing policies, and implementing programs or budgets.

10 Canada shall comply with the principles articulated in this Charter when engaged in negotiations or actions at the international level.

This draft charter most closely resembles France's *Charter for the Environment,* which has already had a substantial impact since its enactment in 2005.[34] Both set forth the rationale for constitutional change as a response to pressing national and global ecological challenges. Both articulate substantive and procedural environmental rights and responsibilities. The draft Canadian Charter of Environmental Rights and Responsibilities addresses the complex question of constitutional jurisdiction by clarifying that governments at all levels are trustees for environmental protection within their fields of responsibility. It also identifies a number of established legal principles – polluter pays, precaution, environmental justice, and intergenerational equity – and elevates them to constitutional status to ensure that they guide government decision making. Inspired by Indigenous law as well as recent constitutional changes in Bolivia, Ecuador, and Iceland, it also recognizes the rights of Nature. Like the French charter, it emphasizes the critical role of education. Finally, Canada would be constitutionally bound to act in an environmentally responsible manner on the international stage, reversing a recent pattern of obstructing negotiations and violating commitments.

The constitution belongs to the people of Canada, not to governments. Political elites no longer have a monopoly on constitutional reform. Canadians have a direct interest in participating in, and contributing to, proposed changes. As Alan Cairns concluded, "The *Charter* has permanently and drastically altered constitutional politics in Canada."[35] The call for recognition of the right to a healthy environment should come from the people and be for the people, instead of emerging from behind the closed doors of a first ministers' meeting. The process of enshrining environmental rights and responsibilities in the constitution should be open, transparent, and democratic, including approval in a national referendum. It would be consistent with the deep affection, even reverence, that Canadians have for the natural beauty and splendour of this great country to give voice to their pride through the constitution. To motivate governments to take action on this issue will require the committed support of Canadians of all ages, all backgrounds, all provinces and territories, and all political persuasions. It will require the support of environmental groups, unions, businesses, Aboriginal people, opinion leaders, soccer moms, youths, seniors, activists, new Canadians, farmers, blue-collar workers, white-collar workers, and green-collar workers. A grassroots movement could push for recognition of environmental rights at all levels – municipal, regional, provincial/territorial, and federal. Five provinces and territories already recognize the right to a healthy environment. The city of Montreal passed a pioneering municipal charter that includes environmental rights and responsibilities.[36] Local victories could establish momentum toward the ultimate goal of constitutional recognition. The prime minister and the premiers must put aside philosophical differences and demonstrate genuine leadership. The right to a healthy environment should be a unifying constitutional issue because it focuses on our common desire to protect Canada's magnificent natural heritage rather than on potentially divisive differences such as language and multiculturalism.

Would constitutional recognition of environmental rights and responsibilities really make a substantial difference in Canada? For the people of Sydney, Nova Scotia, who have suffered from the negative health and environmental impacts of the infamous tar ponds for decades without effective cleanup, the answer is yes. For residents of Sarnia, Ontario, who live in the midst of Canada's most notorious concentration of industrial polluters, the answer is yes. For communities with unsafe drinking water, the answer is yes. For individuals suffering from respiratory difficulties because of poor air quality, the answer is yes. For endangered species pushed to the brink of extinction by reckless human activities, the answer is yes. For every Canadian who believes that the environment is important and ought to be taken better care of, whether to protect our health, the planet's health, or the interests of future generations, the answer is yes.

The simple reality is this: Canada cannot become a sustainable nation with existing laws and institutions. Our laws must be amended to recognize the ironclad and irrevocable laws of nature. Our society needs to shift its focus toward improving our quality of life and reducing inequality rather than myopically seeking to increase the GDP. Our economy must be transformed from the linear (burning fossil fuels, consuming resources, and creating waste) to the circular – using renewable energy to power a society where everything can be reused, recycled, or composted. Our financial system needs to get the prices right by incorporating the full costs of goods and services. Taxes need to be shifted away from beneficial activities, such as work and investment, to damaging actions such as waste and pollution. The focus of our health care system must move from treatment to prevention. Our schools need to make ecological literacy a priority on par with reading and writing. The archaic first-past-the-post electoral system needs to be replaced with a system that honours all votes and offers more representative democracy.

Constitutional protection for the environment, especially the right to a healthy environment, is an integral part of this suite of systemic changes. It has the potential to transform Canada's legal system and alter our vision of the world, bringing us closer to the elusive goal of achieving sustainability. It would mark a change of course, an admission that we have not been up to the task, and a meaningful, enforceable promise to do better in the future. The right to a healthy environment recognizes our most common link, that we all share this beautiful country we are so fortunate to call home. This right comes with a reciprocal responsibility – to protect the environment for our children, grandchildren, future generations, and other species. Entrenching environmental rights and responsibilities in the constitution would force Canadians to make sustainability a genuine priority, resulting in changes that would make Canada a greener, cleaner, wealthier, healthier, happier nation in the long run.

Appendices

Appendix A
Environmental Protection Provisions in National Constitutions

Country	Substantial Environmental Right	Procedural Environmental Right	Individual Environmental Responsibility	Government Environmental Duty
Afghanistan	No	No	No	Yes
Albania	Y	Y	N	Y
Algeria	N	N	Y	N
Andorra	Y	N	N	Y
Angola	Y	N	N	Y
Antigua and Barbuda	N	N	N	N
Argentina	Y	Y	Y	Y
Armenia	Y	N	Y	Y
Australia	N	N	N	N
Austria	N	Y	N	Y
Azerbaijan	Y	Y	Y	Y
Bahamas	N	N	N	N
Bahrain	N	N	N	Y
Bangladesh	N	N	N	Y
Barbados	N	N	N	N
Belarus	Y	Y	Y	Y
Belgium	Y	N	N	Y
Belize	N	N	N	Y
Benin	Y	N	Y	Y
Bhutan	N	N	Y	Y
Bolivia	Y	Y	Y	Y
Bosnia and Herzegovina	N	N	N	N
Botswana	N	N	N	N
Brazil	Y	Y	Y	Y
Brunei Darussalam	N	N	N	N
Bulgaria	Y	N	Y	Y
Burkina Faso	Y	Y	Y	Y
Burundi	Y	N	N	Y
Cambodia	N	N	N	Y
Cameroon	Y	N	Y	Y
Canada	N	N	N	N
Cape Verde	Y	N	Y	Y
Central African Republic	Y	N	N	Y
Chad	Y	N	Y	Y
Chile	Y	Y	N	Y
China	N	N	N	Y
Colombia	Y	Y	Y	Y
Comoros	Y	N	Y	Y
Congo-Brazzaville	Y	N	Y	Y

▶

◀ Appendix A

Country	Substantial Environmental Right	Procedural Environmental Right	Individual Environmental Responsibility	Government Environmental Duty
Congo, Democratic Republic of	Y	N	Y	Y
Costa Rica	Y	Y	N	Y
Côte d'Ivoire	Y	N	Y	Y
Croatia	Y	N	Y	Y
Cuba	N	N	Y	Y
Cyprus	N	N	N	N
Czech Republic	Y	Y	Y	Y
Denmark	N	N	N	N
Djibouti	N	N	N	N
Dominica	N	N	N	N
Dominican Republic	Y	Y	Y	Y
East Timor	Y	N	Y	Y
Ecuador	Y	Y	Y	Y
Egypt	Y	N	Y	Y
El Salvador	Y	N	N	Y
Equatorial Guinea	N	N	N	Y
Eritrea	N	N	N	Y
Estonia	N	N	Y	N
Ethiopia	Y	Y	Y	Y
Fiji	N	N	N	N
Finland	Y	N	Y	Y
France	Y	Y	Y	Y
Gabon	Y	N	N	Y
Gambia	N	N	Y	Y
Georgia	Y	Y	Y	Y
Germany	N	N	N	Y
Ghana	N	N	Y	Y
Greece	Y	N	N	Y
Grenada	N	N	N	N
Guatemala	N	N	N	Y
Guinea	Y	N	N	Y
Guinea-Bissau	N	N	N	N
Guyana	Y	N	Y	Y
Haiti	N	N	Y	Y
Honduras	Y	N	N	Y
Hungary	Y	N	N	Y
Iceland	Y	Y	Y	Y
India	N	N	Y	Y
Indonesia	Y	N	N	Y
Iran	Y	N	N	Y

▶

◀ Appendix A

Country	Substantial Environmental Right	Procedural Environmental Right	Individual Environmental Responsibility	Government Environmental Duty
Iraq	Y	N	N	Y
Ireland	N	N	N	N
Israel	N	N	N	N
Italy	N	N	N	Y
Jamaica	Y	N	Y	Y
Japan	N	N	N	N
Jordan	N	N	N	N
Kazakhstan	N	N	Y	Y
Kenya	Y	Y	Y	Y
Kiribati	N	N	N	N
Korea, North	N	N	N	Y
Korea, South	Y	N	Y	Y
Kuwait	N	N	N	Y
Kyrgyzstan	Y	N	N	Y
Laos	N	N	Y	N
Latvia	Y	Y	N	Y
Lebanon	N	N	N	N
Lesotho	N	N	N	Y
Liberia	N	N	N	N
Libya	N	N	N	N
Liechtenstein	N	N	N	N
Lithuania	N	N	Y	Y
Luxembourg	N	N	N	Y
Macedonia	Y	N	Y	Y
Madagascar	Y	N	Y	Y
Malawi	Y	N	N	Y
Malaysia	N	N	N	N
Maldives	Y	N	Y	Y
Mali	Y	N	Y	Y
Malta	N	N	N	Y
Marshall Islands	N	N	N	N
Mauritania	Y	N	N	Y
Mauritius	N	N	N	N
Mexico	Y	N	N	Y
Micronesia	N	N	N	N
Moldova	Y	Y	Y	Y
Monaco	N	N	N	N
Mongolia	Y	N	Y	Y
Montenegro	Y	Y	Y	Y
Morocco	Y	N	N	Y
Mozambique	Y	N	Y	Y

▶

APPENDIX A

Country	Substantial Environmental Right	Procedural Environmental Right	Individual Environmental Responsibility	Government Environmental Duty
Myanmar	N	N	Y	Y
Namibia	N	N	N	Y
Nauru	N	N	N	N
Nepal	Y	N	N	Y
Netherlands	Y	N	N	Y
New Zealand	N	N	N	N
Nicaragua	Y	N	N	Y
Niger	Y	N	Y	Y
Nigeria	N	N	N	Y
Norway	Y	Y	N	Y
Oman	N	N	N	Y
Pakistan	N	N	N	N
Palau	N	N	N	Y
Panama	Y	N	Y	Y
Papua New Guinea	N	N	Y	N
Paraguay	Y	N	N	Y
Peru	Y	N	N	Y
Philippines	Y	N	N	Y
Poland	Y	Y	Y	Y
Portugal	Y	Y	Y	Y
Qatar	N	N	N	Y
Romania	Y	N	Y	Y
Russia	Y	Y	Y	Y
Rwanda	Y	N	Y	Y
Saint Kitts and Nevis	N	N	N	N
Saint Lucia	N	N	N	N
Saint Vincent and the Grenadines	N	N	N	N
Samoa	N	N	N	N
San Marino	N	N	N	Y
Sao Tome and Principe	Y	N	Y	Y
Saudi Arabia	N	N	N	Y
Senegal	Y	N	N	Y
Serbia	Y	Y	Y	Y
Seychelles	Y	N	Y	Y
Sierra Leone	N	N	N	N
Singapore	N	N	N	N
Slovak Republic	Y	Y	Y	Y
Slovenia	Y	N	Y	Y
Solomon Islands	N	N	N	N

►

Appendix A

Country	Substantial Environmental Right	Procedural Environmental Right	Individual Environmental Responsibility	Government Environmental Duty
Somalia	N	N	Y	Y
South Africa	Y	N	N	Y
South Sudan	Y	N	Y	Y
Spain	Y	N	Y	Y
Sri Lanka	N	N	Y	Y
Sudan	Y	N	Y	Y
Suriname	N	N	N	Y
Swaziland	N	N	Y	Y
Sweden	N	N	N	Y
Switzerland	N	N	N	Y
Syrian Arab Republic	N	N	Y	Y
Tajikistan	N	N	Y	Y
Tanzania	N	N	Y	Y
Thailand	Y	Y	Y	Y
Togo	Y	N	N	Y
Tonga	N	N	N	N
Trinidad and Tobago	N	N	N	N
Tunisia	N	N	N	N
Turkey	Y	N	Y	Y
Turkmenistan	Y	N	N	Y
Tuvalu	N	N	N	N
Uganda	Y	N	Y	Y
Ukraine	Y	Y	Y	Y
United Arab Emirates	N	N	N	Y
United Kingdom	N	N	N	N
United States	N	N	N	N
Uruguay	N	N	Y	Y
Uzbekistan	N	N	Y	Y
Vanuatu	N	N	Y	N
Venezuela	Y	Y	Y	Y
Vietnam	N	N	Y	Y
Yemen	N	N	Y	Y
Zambia	N	N	N	Y
Zimbabwe	N	N	N	N
Total environmental provisions in constitutions	94	31	84	142

Y = Yes, N = No

Note: For the full text of environmental provisions in national constitutions, please see Appendix 2 of Boyd (2012), which is available online at http://hdl.handle.net/2429/36469.

Appendix B
France's *Charter for the Environment* (2005)

The French people, considering that:

- natural resources and ecosystems have contributed to the emergence of humanity;
- the future and the very existence of humanity are intrinsically linked with its natural environment;
- the environment is the common heritage of all human beings;
- mankind has a growing influence on the conditions of life and on its own evolution;
- biological diversity, personal fulfillment, and progress of human societies are affected by certain types of consumption or production and by the excessive exploitation of natural resources;
- the preservation of the environment must be achieved with the same devotion as other fundamental national interests;
- in order to ensure sustainable development, choices aiming to meet present needs must not compromise the capacity of future generations and other peoples to satisfy their own needs;

Hereby proclaim:

Article 1. Everyone has the right to live in an environment that is both well balanced and favorable to his/her health.

Article 2. Every person has the duty to take part in the preservation and the improvement of the environment.

Article 3. Each person shall, in the conditions provided for by law, foresee and avoid the occurrence of any damage which he or she may cause to the environment or, failing that, limit the consequences of such damage.

Article 4. Every person must, in the conditions provided for by law, contribute to the reparation of damages that he or she causes to the environment.

Article 5. Upon the risk of damage, even when uncertain given current scientific knowledge, that might impact the environment in a serious and irreversible manner, public authorities will ensure, by application of the precautionary principle, the adoption of appropriate provisionary measures aiming to avoid the risk of the damage and to implement evaluation procedures to measure the level of risk.

Article 6. Public policies must promote sustainable development. To this effect, they must take into account the protection and the improvement of the environment and must reconcile these objectives with economic and social development.

Article 7. Every person has the right, under limited conditions defined by law, to access information relative to the environment that is held by public authorities, and to participate in the creation of public decisions that have an impact on the environment.

Article 8. Education and information on the environment must contribute to the implementation of the rights and responsibilities defined by this *Charter*.

Article 9. Research and innovation must bring their participation to the preservation and improvement of the environment.

Article 10. This *Charter* inspires France into action within the European Union and international community.

Appendix C
Environmental Cases and Section 7 of the *Charter of Rights and Freedoms*

The purpose of this appendix is to briefly summarize the factual and legal issues addressed in previous lawsuits alleging that specific environmental harms constituted a violation of section 7 of the *Charter*.

1. Cruise Missile Testing

The *Operation Dismantle* case involved a lawsuit challenging the federal government's decision to allow the United States to conduct cruise missile tests in northern Canada. A coalition of peace and disarmament groups argued that the testing of cruise missiles contributed to the acceleration of the arms race, increased the risk of nuclear war, and therefore violated their *Charter* right to life, liberty, and security of the person. The majority decision of the Supreme Court of Canada, written by Dickson J., found that the potential risk was too "uncertain, speculative, and hypothetical to sustain a cause of action."[1] As a result, the majority of the court did not answer the questions about the interpretation of section 7 of the *Charter*.

In a concurring judgment, Wilson J. speculated about the scope of section 7, recognizing that, hypothetically, some government decisions could violate the *Charter* by creating unacceptable risks to the public or to individuals. The three examples described by Wilson included experiments with nerve gas without an individual's consent, testing cruise missiles with live warheads, and forcing people into military service without passing enabling legislation. Wilson also made it clear that the substantive right embraced by section 7 had limits because many state actions effectively increase or decrease the risks faced by citizens. Examples include policies on speed limits, drunk driving, changes to police budgets, increases or decreases in health care spending, and decriminalization of marijuana. Wilson's decision seemingly opened the door to liberal interpretations of section 7, including potential applications in the area of environmental rights, while at the same time circumscribing the potential boundaries of such applications.

2. Energy Probe's *Nuclear Liability Act* Case

In the early 1990s, Ontario courts decided a case bearing some similarities to *Operation Dismantle*.[2] Energy Probe, a non-governmental organization, argued that the *Nuclear Liability Act*'s limits on the level of liability insurance required by corporations operating nuclear reactors violated section 7. Because liability was capped at an arbitrarily low level, Energy Probe claimed that there was inadequate motivation for nuclear operators to take appropriate safety precautions and there was an incentive for further proliferation of nuclear reactors. These two factors, it was asserted, increased the risk to the public of a nuclear accident.

Ruling on a pre-trial motion, the Ontario Court of Appeal refused to throw out the lawsuit, concluding that the appellants had some possibility of proving that the act violated rights protected by section 7 of the *Charter.*[3] However, the case failed at trial because of the tenuous connection between the legislation in question and the potential harm to individuals from a nuclear accident. The requisite degree of cause and effect was simply not present. According to the court,

> I have great difficulty with a proposition that would bring a government policy decision concerning the use of nuclear power within the scope of s. 7. The government decided to develop atomic energy for peaceful purposes, one being to generate electricity by the use of nuclear power. The government was well aware of the inherent risks but, in its wisdom, proceeded with fostering the development of nuclear reactors by enacting the *Nuclear Liability Act* to deal with the economic consequences of the known risks to the public. Those policy decisions cannot invoke s. 7 security ... Furthermore, the plaintiffs have failed to prove that increased use of nuclear power increases the risk to security of the person. Electricity is produced by various uses of natural resources to produce power: for example, coal and gas, which also have their impact on the environment. The plaintiffs have not provided evidence to show that there is a greater risk to the public of producing electricity by nuclear power than by alternate methods. It is not sufficient for the plaintiffs to allege that there are greater possible consequences to the security of the person because of the *Act.* As Dickson J. stated in *Operation Dismantle:* "Section 7 of the *Charter* cannot reasonably be read as imposing a duty on the government to refrain from those acts which *might* lead to consequences that deprive or threaten to deprive individuals of their life and security of the person. A duty of the federal cabinet cannot arise on the basis of speculation and hypothesis about possible effects of government action."[4]

3. Halifax's Municipal Waste Incinerator

When Halifax decided to build a waste incinerator to deal with municipal waste, a coalition of citizens challenged the decision on various grounds including the alleged violation of section 7. The Municipality of Halifax challenged the standing of the citizens to bring the legal action. The Nova Scotia Supreme Court granted public interest standing to the coalition, on the basis that the question of whether potential harm to the health of humans or the environment infringes section 7 rights is a serious issue that the courts must address.[5] The Nova Scotia Court of Appeal overturned the lower court's decision about standing on the basis that the coalition's application was premature, as an environmental assessment of the waste incinerator was still pending.

4. Oxford County Landfill

The plaintiffs alleged that construction of a landfill site adjacent to their properties would violate section 7 of the *Charter*.[6] The pleadings were struck by the court, partially because the plaintiffs failed to allege damage or injury to their health or security of the person. Potts J., in dissent, argued that the question of whether section 7 was violated by the landfill would depend on the scientific evidence adduced at trial.

5. Fluoridation of Municipal Water Supplies

Two cases alleged that fluoridation of public drinking water created a health risk in violation of section 7 of the *Charter*.[7] Both were decided against the plaintiffs, as the courts found that the health risks posed by fluoridation were "minimal." Both cases seemed to accept that a more serious environmental health risk created by government action would be theoretically capable of constituting a violation of section 7.

6. Approval and Use of Pesticides

Two cases, *Weir* and *Kuczerpa*, raised the section 7 argument in the context of government approvals for pesticide registration and spraying. In *Weir*, Madame Justice Ross described the issue of the scope of section 7 as "of significance to the community at large" but declined to rule on the issue, holding that "a decision with respect to the constitutional question raised should await another case where there is a proper evidentiary foundation."[8]

In *Kuczerpa*, the plaintiff sued the federal minister of agriculture for approving the use of pesticides that allegedly caused "delayed neurotoxicity" and debilitating physical conditions.[9] Unfortunately, the plaintiff, a non-lawyer, represented herself, resulting in extensive difficulties with the pleadings. The Federal Court rejected the application of section 7 of the *Charter* to the facts of the case.

7. Drilling of Sour Oil and Gas Wells

In at least two cases, citizens have presented arguments to Alberta's Energy and Utilities Board that section 7 of the Charter includes a right to a healthy environment, meaning freedom from exposure to harmful pollution discharged from oil or gas wells. Landowners were concerned about the close proximity of proposed wells to their residences. In *Kelly,* Berger J. of the Alberta Court of Appeal granted leave to appeal the Energy and Utilities Board decision, ruling that "it is at least arguable that the Applicants should be entitled to mount an argument on appeal that s. 7 may be invoked."[10] In *Domke,* the Court of Appeal refused to grant leave on the grounds that the evidence in the case was inadequate to establish a section 7 breach.[11]

Notes

CHAPTER 1: CANADA NEEDS CONSTITUTIONAL ENVIRONMENTAL RIGHTS

1 R. Carson, quoted in Cronin and Kennedy (1997, 235). See also Carson (1962, 12-13).
2 Ignatieff (2000, 2001).
3 Cranston (1973).
4 Hayward (2000, 568; 2005).
5 Shue (1996, 23).
6 Birnie and Boyle (2002, 255).
7 Miller (1998, 92).
8 Robertson and Merrills (1989, 259).
9 Kravchenko and Bonine (2008); Boyd (2012).
10 *State v. Acheson* (1991, South Africa).
11 Hayward (2005).
12 Boyd (2006c).
13 Environment Canada, Department of Foreign Affairs and International Trade, Health Canada, and Department of Justice (2006).
14 Bryant, Nielsen, and Tangley (1997); Environment Canada (2001).
15 Global Forest Watch (2003).
16 Mosquin (2000).
17 Angus (1997); Anderssen and Valpy (2004).
18 *Ontario v. Canadian Pacific,* [1995]; *R. v. Hydro-Québec,* [1997]; *114957 Canada Ltée (Spraytech, Société d'arrosage) v. Hudson (Town),* [2001]; *British Columbia v. Canadian Forest Products Ltd.,* [2004].
19 Hoggan and Associates (2009); A. McAllister (2010a).
20 World Values Survey (2010).
21 Environics Research Group (2010).
22 Nanos (2009, 12).
23 Environics International (1999).
24 Gunton and Calbrick (2010).
25 Organisation for Economic Co-operation and Development (2004a).
26 Conference Board of Canada (2011).
27 Emerson et al. (2010).
28 Weibust (2009, 119).

29 A. McAllister (2010b).
30 World Wildlife Fund, Zoological Society of London, and Global Footprint Network (2010).
31 Wood, Tanner, and Richardson (2010, 982).
32 Boyd, Attaran, and Stanbrook (2008).
33 Canadian Press (2009); Gurzu (2010).
34 Editorial Board (2012).
35 Environment Canada (1996).
36 S. Harper, quoted in Hahn (2006).
37 Boyd (2012).
38 Quoted in Mark (2012, 43).
39 Boyd (2003).
40 Boyd (2006a).
41 Organisation for Economic Co-operation and Development (2007).
42 Environment Canada (2010).
43 Canadian Environmental Law Association and Environmental Defence (2010).
44 Boyd (2006d).
45 Christensen (2011); Hrudey (2008).
46 Boyd (2011b).
47 Boyd (2006b).
48 Ibid.
49 World Health Organization (2008).
50 Boyd and Genuis (2008).
51 Conference Board of Canada (2008).
52 Boyd (2007).
53 Conference Board of Canada (2004, 2009).
54 Hawke (2002).
55 Elgie (2007); McDonald (2008).
56 Hodgett (1911); Murray (1912).
57 No author (1961).
58 Canada, *House of Commons Debates* (14 February 1969) 5524 (P.E. Trudeau).
59 Gibson (1970, 57).
60 M. Balf (Thompson Basin Pollution Probe), "Testimony before the Special Joint Committee of the Senate and the House of Commons on the Constitution of Canada," *Minutes of Proceedings and Evidence* 31 (12 January 1971): 23.
61 Canadian Environmental Law Association (1978).
62 MacLaren (1984).
63 Muldoon (1991).
64 *Friends of the Oldman River*, [1992, para. 86].
65 Harrison (1996).
66 Elgie (2007).
67 *Interprovincial Co-operatives Limited*, [1976].
68 *Fowler v. R.*, [1980]; *Northwest Falling Contractors v. R.*, [1980].
69 *Re The Canadian Metal Company Limited and The Queen* (1982).
70 *R. v. Crown Zellerbach*, [1988].

71 *Friends of the Oldman River*, [1992].
72 *114957 Canada Ltée (Spraytech, Société d'arrosage) v. Hudson (Town)*, [2001].
73 *R. v. Hydro-Québec*, [1997, para. 41].
74 Beatty (1998, 58).
75 Illical and Harrison (2007).
76 Amos, Harrison, and Hoberg (2001, 156).
77 *Nuclear Safety and Control Act* (1997).
78 Houck (2009, 283n73).
79 Conference Board of Canada (2008); Emerson et al. (2010); Gunton and Calbrick (2010).
80 *Treaty Establishing the European Economic Community* (1957).
81 Houck (2009, 283).
82 *Single European Act* (1987).
83 Weibust (2009).
84 Law Commission of Canada (2006).
85 Borrows (2010, 289n4).
86 Chartrand (2005, 26).
87 *Mitchell v. M.N.R.*, [2001, para. 10]; *R. v. Van der Peet*, [1996].
88 *UN Declaration on the Rights of Indigenous Peoples* (2007, arts. 5, 11, 27, 40).
89 Borrows (2010, 243-44).
90 Henderson (1996).
91 Borrows (2005, 160).
92 Borrows (2010, 22).
93 Chivian and Bernstein (2008, xii).
94 Mendelsohn (2004, 63).
95 Howe and Russell (2001); Centre for Research and Information on Canada (2002).

CHAPTER 2: THE PROS AND CONS OF THE RIGHT TO A HEALTHY ENVIRONMENT

1 Hayward (2005, 126).
2 *Marbury v. Madison* (1803, 177).
3 *Constitution Act, 1982* (1982, s. 52).
4 Dworkin (1978).
5 Boyd (2003, 2006a, 2006b, 2006d).
6 C.P. Stevenson (1983, 391).
7 Shue (1996).
8 Boyd (2003).
9 C.P. Stevenson (1983, 391).
10 de Sadeleer (2002, 278).
11 Bruch, Coker, and VanArsdale (2007).
12 Canadian Institute for Environmental Law and Policy (2008); Bergeson (2011).
13 Bruch, Coker, and VanArsdale (2007).
14 Stone (1972).
15 Hayward (2005, 129).
16 Dawson (1993, 53).

17 Kelly (2006, 214).
18 Friends of the Earth Canada (2009, 2).
19 Hazell and Worthy (2010).
20 Chiappinelli (1992).
21 Mehta (1997, 354).
22 Stephens (2009, 116).
23 Du Bois (1996, 157).
24 Saxe (1990); Cranor (2006).
25 Estrin and Swaigen (1974, 311).
26 Brandl and Bungert (1992, 87).
27 de Sadeleer (2004).
28 Gosine and Teelucksingh (2008); Agyeman et al. (2009).
29 Bryner (1987, 7).
30 Fredman (2008, 32-33).
31 Cha (2007, 12).
32 Brandl and Bungert (1992, 4-5).
33 Kiss (1993, 559).
34 May (2006, 118).
35 Swaigen and Woods (1981, 200-1).
36 Birnie and Boyle (2002, 255).
37 Webber (1994, 149-50); Handl (2001).
38 Pevato (1999).
39 Saxe (1990, 20).
40 Handl (2001).
41 Kiss and Shelton (2004, 710).
42 Michaels (2008).
43 Anderson (1996b, 224).
44 M. Warawa, "Testimony before House of Commons Standing Committee on Environment and Sustainable Development," *Evidence,* 3rd sess., 40th Parliament (24 November 2010).
45 T. Huffaker, "Testimony before House of Commons Standing Committee on Environment and Sustainable Development," *Evidence,* 3rd sess., 40th Parliament (15 November 2010).
46 *R. v. Keegstra,* [1990].
47 Beatty (2004, 137).
48 Haszeldine (2009).
49 See the website of Norway's Government Pension Fund at http://www.regjeringen.no/.
50 Malone and Pasternack (2006).
51 Atapattu (2006).
52 Boyd (2003); Weibust (2009); Wood, Tanner, and Richardson (2010).
53 Borovoy (1988); Waldron (1993, 2006).
54 Barry (1996).
55 Sax (1971, 237).
56 Brandl and Bungert (1992, 94).

57 Fuller (1978); Manfredi and Maioni (2009); Cameron (2009).
58 *Inverhuron and District Ratepayers' Association v. Minister of Environment et al.*, 2001.
59 *Rhodes et al. v. E.I. DuPont* (2009, 756).
60 Morton and Knopff (2000); Kelly and Manfredi (2009b).
61 Huffaker, "Testimony before House of Commons Standing Committee," 2010.
62 Petter (2009).
63 Hiebert (2010).
64 Dershowitz (2004, 109).
65 *Vriend v. Alberta*, [1998, para. 178].
66 Nedelsky (2008); Hogg and Bushell (1997).
67 Roach (2001, 226).
68 Kelly (2006).
69 Russell (2004, 268).
70 Garner (2004).
71 Davis (1992); Sunstein (1993).
72 Waldron (1999).
73 Fried (1973).
74 Sunstein (1993, 35).
75 Davis (1992).
76 Baderin and McCorquodale (2006); Fredman (2008); Gauri and Brinks (2008).
77 Beatty (2004); Tushnet (2002).
78 *Government of the Republic of South Africa et al. v. Grootboom et al.* (2000); Beatty (2004, 129).
79 Sunstein (2001); Davis (2004, 2008).
80 Ramcharan (2005, 3).
81 Jackman and Porter (2008).
82 Schwartz (1992).
83 Sandel (1982).
84 Glendon (1991).
85 Handl (2001).
86 Weiss (1989, 105).
87 Swaigen and Woods (1981, 199); Boutaud, Gondran, and Brodhag (2006).
88 Raz (1986, 258).
89 Cranston (1973); Nedelsky (2008).
90 Ruhl (1997).
91 Huffaker, "Testimony before House of Commons Standing Committee," 2010.
92 W. Everson, "Testimony before House of Commons Standing Committee on Environment and Sustainable Development," *Evidence*, 3rd sess., 40th Parliament (15 November 2010).
93 Hayward (2005, 100).
94 Alston (1982, 1984).
95 Miller (1998, xi).
96 Environment Canada, Department of Foreign Affairs and International Trade, Health Canada, and Department of Justice (2006).
97 Cancado Trindade (1993).

98 UN General Assembly (1986).
99 Redgwell (1996).
100 Bridge and Laytner (2005).
101 Stone (1972).
102 *Sierra Club v. Morton* (1972).
103 Nash (1989).
104 Sunstein (1999).
105 Tribe (1974); Livingston (1984); Collins (2007).
106 *Law on the Rights of Mother Earth* (2010).
107 *R.F. Wheeler and E.G. Huddle v. Attorney General of the State of Loja* (2011).
108 Shelton (2004b, 22).
109 Redgwell (1996, 87).
110 Rosenberg (1991); Handl (2001).
111 Pound (1917); Bakan (1997).
112 Ruhl (1999, 281).
113 Lazarus (2004, 28).
114 Anderson (1996a, 22); Bakan (1997); Hancock (2003).
115 Galanter (1974); Bakan (1997).
116 Scheingold (1974, 1989).
117 Rosenberg (1991); Arthurs (2003).
118 Petter (2009, 43).
119 Saxe (1990).
120 Swaigen and Woods (1981, 200)
121 Epp (1998, 205).
122 Ibid.; Beatty (2004).
123 Hill, Wolfson, and Targ (2004).
124 Cullet (1995).
125 For pro-*Charter* survey results, see Centre for Research and Information on Canada (2002); Thompson (2010). For anti-*Charter* sentiments, see Nanos (2007).

Chapter 3: The History of Environmental Rights in Canada

1 Chrétien (1990, 283).
2 Trudeau (1961-62, 125).
3 Trudeau (1968, 27).
4 Williams (1985, 115).
5 Barry Strayer (personal communication, 7 January 2011), on file with author.
6 Trudeau (1968, 27).
7 Government of Canada (1969, 14, 16).
8 Canadian Intergovernmental Conference Secretariat (1974).
9 Ibid.
10 Harrison (1996, 72-73).
11 D.V. Heald, "Testimony before the Special Joint Committee of the Senate and the House of Commons on the Constitution of Canada," *Minutes of Proceedings and Evidence* 12 (17 November 1970): 32.
12 MacNeill (1971); Jim MacNeill (personal communication, 4 May 2011).

13 Trudeau (1970).
14 Trudeau (1961, 44-45).
15 Canada, *House of Commons Debates* (14 February 1969) 5524 (P.E. Trudeau).
16 Harrison (1996, 64).
17 Canada, *House of Commons Debates* (23 June 1969) 10548 (R. Harding). See also ibid. (26 January 1971) 2789 (T.C. Douglas).
18 Trudeau (1996, 301).
19 Harrison (1996, 70).
20 Trudeau (1993, 156).
21 Harrison (1996, 63).
22 Trudeau (1993, 253-54).
23 Zolf (1984, 46).
24 Canada, *House of Commons Debates* (24 October 1969) 39 (P.E. Trudeau).
25 Lloyd Axworthy, Tom Axworthy, Ron Graham, Marc Lalonde, Jim MacNeill, and Barry Strayer (personal communications, 2011).
26 Raffan (1998, 76).
27 N. Lyon, "Testimony before the Special Joint Committee of the Senate and the House of Commons on the Constitution of Canada," *Minutes of Proceedings and Evidence* 16 (26 November 1970): 38.
28 M. MacGuigan, "Testimony before the Special Joint Committee of the Senate and the House of Commons on the Constitution of Canada," *Minutes of Proceedings and Evidence* 26 (7 January 1971): 34.
29 Lyon, "Testimony before the Special Joint Committee," 1970, 40-41.
30 J. Egan, "Testimony before the Special Joint Committee of the Senate and the House of Commons on the Constitution of Canada," *Minutes of Proceedings and Evidence* 28 (9 January 1971): 29.
31 M. Balf (Thompson Basin Pollution Probe), "Testimony before the Special Joint Committee of the Senate and the House of Commons on the Constitution of Canada," *Minutes of Proceedings and Evidence* 31 (12 January 1971): 23.
32 O. Paquette, "Testimony before the Special Joint Committee of the Senate and the House of Commons on the Constitution of Canada," *Minutes of Proceedings and Evidence* 31 (12 January 1971): 35.
33 C.L. McLaughlin, "Testimony before the Special Joint Committee of the Senate and the House of Commons on the Constitution of Canada," *Minutes of Proceedings and Evidence* 19 (7 December 1970): 98-99.
34 Molgat and MacGuigan (1972, 91).
35 Ibid., 3.
36 Ibid., 91-92.
37 Canadian Environmental Law Association (1972, 1).
38 Holman and Morley (1971, 15); Brand and Morley (1972, 146).
39 Franson and Burns (1974, 165).
40 Estrin and Swaigen (1978, 459).
41 Williams (1985, 115).
42 Bill C-60, *An Act to Amend the Constitution of Canada,* 3rd sess., 30th Parliament, 1978, s. 4.

43 Ron Graham (personal communication, 7 February 2011).
44 Vigod and Swaigen (1978, 9).
45 Mains (1980, 14).
46 Ibid., 17.
47 D. Davidson, "Testimony before the Special Joint Committee of the Senate and the House of Commons on the Constitution of Canada," *Minutes of Proceedings and Evidence* 32 (6 January 1981): 6.
48 S. Robinson, "Testimony before the Special Joint Committee of the Senate and the House of Commons on the Constitution of Canada," *Minutes of Proceedings and Evidence* 49 (30 January 1981): 8.
49 Ibid., 67.
50 J. Chrétien, "Testimony before the Special Joint Committee of the Senate and the House of Commons on the Constitution of Canada," *Minutes of Proceedings and Evidence* 49 (30 January 1981): 70.
51 Special Joint Committee of the Senate and the House of Commons on the Constitution of Canada, *Minutes of Proceedings and Evidence* 49 (30 January 1981): 8.
52 Canada, *House of Commons Debates* (21 April 1981) 9358 (D. Blackburn).
53 John Swaigen (personal communication, 10 August 2010).
54 Roy Romanow (personal communication, 12 April 2011).
55 Canada, *House of Commons Debates* (27 January 1983) 22258 (J. Fulton).
56 Gibson (1983, 143).
57 Ibid., 125.
58 Law Reform Commission (1985, 67).
59 *Ontario v. Canadian Pacific*, [1995, para. 55]; *R. v. Hydro-Québec*, [1997, para. 124].
60 Gibson (1988, 281-82).
61 Hatherly (1987).
62 World Commission on Environment and Development (1987, 330-32, 348).
63 Walters (1991).
64 Andrews (1988, 263).
65 Canada, *House of Commons Debates* (5 June 1989) 2521 (J. Fulton).
66 Canadian Bar Association (1990, 27).
67 Gertler, Muldoon, and Valiante (1990, 82).
68 Canada, *House of Commons Debates* (10 December 1990) 16485 (J. Fulton).
69 Ibid. (11 December 1990) 16587 (A. McLaughlin).
70 Ibid. (5 June 1991) 1235 (L. Taylor).
71 Ibid., 1238-40 (P. Martin).
72 Ibid., 1241 (L. Bourgault).
73 Rutherford (1991); Gertler and Vigod (1991); Muldoon and Valiante (1991).
74 Ontario Ministry of the Attorney General, Constitutional Law and Policy Division (1991).
75 Government of Canada (1991, vii).
76 Citizens' Forum on Canada's Future (1991, 42, 45).
77 Rutherford and Muldoon (1991).
78 Andrews and Alexander (1991).

79 Nedelsky (2008, 166).
80 Beaudoin and Dobbie (1992, 24).
81 Ibid., 123.
82 Rutherford (1992).
83 Hughes (1992, 79).
84 Ibid., 81.
85 No author (1992, 2).
86 Rutherford (1992).
87 Rutherford and Muldoon (1992, 26).
88 *Hague Declaration on the Environment* (1989).
89 The *Hague Declaration* was signed by Australia, Brazil, Canada, Côte d'Ivoire, Egypt, Federal Republic of Germany, France, Hungary, India, Indonesia, Italy, Japan, Jordan, Kenya, Malta, the Netherlands, New Zealand, Norway, Senegal, Spain, Sweden, Tunisia, Venezuela, and Zimbabwe.
90 Proposal of Canada, UN Doc. A/Conf.151/PC/WGIII/L5, 16 August 1991, quoted in Dejeant-Pons and Pallemaerts (2002, 13n2).
91 B. Mulroney, quoted in Meakin (1992).
92 Meakin (1992).
93 Douglas (1991).
94 Muldoon (1988, 35).
95 Hughes and Iyalomhe (1999, 256).
96 Estrin and Swaigen (1978).
97 Franson and Burns (1974, 171).
98 C. Caccia, Private Member's motion, "Establishment of Environmental Bill of Rights," *Hansard*, 9 July 1981, 11385-89.
99 Canada, *House of Commons Debates* (9 July 1981) 11389 (T. McMillan).
100 Ibid. (10 July 1981) 11405 (T. McMillan).
101 Canadian Environmental Law Research Foundation (1984).
102 Canada, *House of Commons Debates* (22 April 1985) 3942 (C. Caccia).
103 Ibid. (10 October 1986) 290, 292 (T. McMillan).
104 McMillan (1986, 16, 25).
105 Environment Canada (1987).
106 Canada, *House of Commons Debates* (17 September 1987) 9054 (N.Riis); ibid., 9022 (L. McDonald); ibid., 9061 (D. Berger); ibid., 9062 (A. McLaughlin); ibid., 9070 (S. Copps); ibid. (24 September 1987) 9313 (R. Skelly); ibid. (25 September 1987) 9350 (C. Keeper); ibid. (23 October 1987) 10336 (J. Manly); ibid. (20 April 1988) 14658 (I. Waddell); ibid. (2 May 1988) 15006 (S. Langdon); ibid. (4 May 1988) 15135 (D. Heaps).
107 Ibid. (15 September 1987) 9325 (W. Rompkey).
108 Ibid. (5 May 1988) 15148 (N. Riis).
109 T. McMillan, *Minutes of Proceedings and Evidence*, Bill C-74, 2nd sess., 33rd Parliament (3 February 1988): 14-16.
110 Andrews (1988, 264).
111 Canada, *House of Commons Debates* (9 July 1981) 11387 (T. McMillan).
112 Ibid.

113 Canada, *House of Commons Debates* (26 April 1988) 14839 (C. Caccia).
114 Ibid., 14847 (L. McDonald).
115 Martin (1992).
116 Ibid., 22.
117 Canada, *House of Commons Debates* (19 February 1993) 16235-38 (E. Blondin).
118 Liberal Party of Canada (1993, 68).
119 House of Commons Standing Committee on Environment and Sustainable Development (1995, 235).
120 Boyd (2003).
121 Boyd (2010).
122 Ibid.
123 Bill 101, *Environmental Bill of Rights, 1971*, 2nd sess., 29th Parliament, 1971.
124 Bill 79, *Environmental Bill of Rights*, 2nd sess., 30th Parliament, 1973; British Columbia, Draft Environmental Protection Act, 1994, Part 2.
125 International Woodworkers of America to NDP minister of forests Andrew Petter, 12 October 1994, on file with author.
126 Alberta, Bill 222, *The Environmental Bill of Rights*, 1st sess., 19th Legislature, 1979; Saskatchewan, Bill 23, *Environmental Magna Carta Act*, 1st sess., 20th Legislature, 1982; Saskatchewan, Bill 48, *The Charter of Environmental Rights and Responsibilities*, 2nd sess., 22nd Legislature, 1992.
127 *Environmental Quality Act* (1994, s. 19(1)).
128 Corriveau (1995).
129 For example, see *Nadon v. Anjou (Ville)*, [1994]; *Regroupement des citoyens contre la pollution c. Alex Couture inc.* (2008); *Gestion Serge Lafrenière inc. c. Calvé*, [1999]; *Imperial Oil Ltd. v. Quebec (Minister of Environment)*, [2003]. Complete list on file with author.
130 *Charter of Human Rights and Freedoms* (s. 46(1)).
131 For example, see *Carrier c. Québec (Procureur Général)*, 2010; *Drouin c. Ville de Sainte-Agathe-des-Monts*, 2009; *St-Luc-de-Vincennes (Municipalité de) c. Compostage Mauricie inc.*, 2008; *Regroupement des citoyens du quartier St-Georges inc. c. Alcoa Canada ltée*, [2007].
132 Thériault and Robitaille (2011).
133 Estrin and Swaigen (1974).
134 Muldoon and Lindgren (1995, 8-11).
135 Environmental Commissioner of Ontario (1996-2011).
136 Muldoon et al. (2009, 214-15).
137 Environmental Commissioner of Ontario (1996-2011).
138 Muldoon et al. (2009, 214-15).
139 Environmental Commissioner of Ontario (1996-2011).
140 *Johnson v. Director, Ministry of the Environment* (2006).
141 Castrilli (1998, 425).
142 Winfield, Ford, and Crann (1995, 56).
143 Babor (1999, 123).
144 Environmental Commissioner of Ontario (2011).
145 Hersey (2009).

146 Environmental Commissioner of Ontario (1996, 1).
147 Lindgren (2004, 7).
148 Lukasik, McRobert, and Shultz (2006).
149 Environmental Commissioner of Ontario (2011, 118).
150 *Environment Act* (1991).
151 Ibid.
152 *Western Copper Corporation v. Yukon Water Board*, 2010.
153 Yukon Government Audit Services Branch (2010, 8).
154 *Environmental Rights Act* (1988).

CHAPTER 4: GREEN CONSTITUTIONS IN OTHER COUNTRIES

1 The environment-related provisions of all national constitutions can be viewed at http://hdl.handle.net/2429/36469.
2 The twenty-nine former British colonies (including nations that were part of British colonies) are Antigua and Barbuda, Australia, Bahamas, Barbados, Botswana, Brunei Darussalam, Canada, Cyprus, Dominica, Fiji, Grenada, Ireland, Kiribati, Malaysia, Mauritius, New Zealand, Pakistan, Saint Kitts and Nevis, Saint Lucia, Saint Vincent and the Grenadines, Samoa, Sierra Leone, Singapore, Solomon Islands, Tonga, Trinidad and Tobago, Tuvalu, United States, and Zimbabwe.
3 The twenty-four small island nations are Antigua and Barbuda, Bahamas, Barbados, Brunei Darussalam, Cyprus, Dominica, Fiji, Grenada, Ireland, Kiribati, Marshall Islands, Mauritius, Micronesia, Nauru, New Zealand, Saint Kitts and Nevis, Saint Lucia, Saint Vincent and the Grenadines, Samoa, Singapore, Solomon Islands, Tonga, Trinidad and Tobago, and Tuvalu.
4 Olowu (2006).
5 Antigua and Barbuda, Bahamas, Barbados, Canada, Dominica, Grenada, Saint Kitts, Saint Lucia, Saint Vincent and the Grenadines, Trinidad and Tobago, and the USA.
6 Wolfrum and Grote (2012).
7 Argentina, Bolivia, Brazil, Chile, Colombia, Costa Rica, Cuba, Dominican Republic, Ecuador, El Salvador, Guatemala, Guyana, Haiti, Honduras, Mexico, Nicaragua, Panama, Paraguay, Peru, Suriname, Uruguay, and Venezuela.
8 Juriglobe – World Legal Systems Research Group, "Distribution of the United Nations Member States According to Their Legal Systems and Their Various Legal Components," University of Ottawa, 2009, http://www.juriglobe.ca/.
9 The only common law mono-systems with environmental provisions in their constitutions are Belize, Jamaica, and Palau.
10 The only civil law mono-systems without environmental provisions in their constitutions are Bosnia and Herzegovina, Denmark, Liechtenstein, and Monaco.
11 The only mixed civil and customary law nations without environmental provisions in their constitutions are Guinea-Bissau and Japan.
12 The exception is Muslim mono-systems, as all three nations in this category (Afghanistan, Maldives, and Saudi Arabia) have environmental provisions in their constitutions.
13 Shelton (2001); Soveroski (2007).
14 Constitution Review Group (1996).

15 Senate Joint Resolution 169 (1970).
16 All excerpts from national constitutions in this chapter are from Wolfrum and Grote (2012) unless otherwise noted.
17 Belgium, Central African Republic, Comoros, and Senegal.
18 Hohfeld (1923).
19 *African (Banjul) Charter on Human and Peoples' Rights* (1982, art. 24); Wolfrum and Grote (2012).
20 The total of descriptive words and phrases adds up to more than ninety-four because many constitutions use more than one word or phrase to describe the right.
21 Grote (2008a); US Department of State (2009); Wolfrum and Grote (2012).
22 Shemshuchenko (1995).
23 Constitution of El Salvador, arts. 191-94.
24 Constitution of Namibia, art. 91.
25 Friends of the Earth (2009).
26 Algeria, Estonia, Laos, Papua New Guinea, Syrian Arab Republic, and Vanuatu.
27 Monahan (2006, 3).
28 Constitution of Andorra, art. 27(2). Andorra's constitution is not in Wolfrum and Grote (2012) but can be found online at Andorramania, http://www.andorramania.com/.
29 Constitution of Romania, art. 44(7).
30 Constitution of Portugal, art. 66(2)(h).
31 Constitution of Ecuador, arts. 395(4), 397(1), 401, 415.
32 Constitution of Brazil, art. 225(1)(V).
33 Constitution of Argentina, art. 41(3).
34 Brewer-Carias (2009).
35 Grote (2008b).
36 Constitution of Ecuador, art. 71; Constitution of Bolivia, art. 33.
37 Pallemaerts (1994); Redgwell (1996).
38 McKenzie (2002, 22).
39 Constitution of Brazil, art. 225.
40 Constitution of Bhutan, art. 5(4); Constitution of Portugal, art. 66(2)(d).
41 Intergovernmental Working Group (2004, 73).
42 *Canadian Charter of Rights and Freedoms* (1982, s. 24).
43 Bullard (2005).
44 Takahashi (2002).
45 Constitution of Belarus, art. 62.
46 Constitution of Gambia, art. 211.
47 Olowu (2006, 56).
48 Constitution of Gabon, art. 1(8).
49 Constitution of India, arts. 37, 48(A).
50 Beatty (2004, 137).
51 Boyd (2011a).
52 *Margarita v. Copetro* (1993).
53 *Carlos Roberto García Chacón* (1993).
54 *Presidente de la sociedad MARLENE S.A. v. Municipalidad de Tibás Marlene* (1994).

55 Boyd (2011a).
56 *Subhash Kumar v. State of Bihar* (1991).
57 Decision 210/1987, Constitutional Court.
58 Eurick (2001).
59 *Ely v. Velde* (1971); *Environmental Defense Fund v. Corps of Engineers* (1971); *Tanner v. Armco* (1972).
60 *114957 Canada Ltée (Spraytech, Société d'arrosage) v. Hudson (Town)*, [2001].
61 *A. Lockridge and R. Plain v. Director, Ministry of the Environment et al.* (2010).
62 Law and Versteeg (2011, 2012).
63 Kinney and Clark (2004).
64 For the constitution of Kenya, see http://www.nation.co.ke/blob/view/-/687282/data/113655/-/tvxtg2z/-/draft.pdf.
65 Jamaica's 2011 *Charter of Fundamental Rights and Freedoms* can be seen at http://www2.ohchr.org/english/bodies/hrc/docs/ngos/JJSR_Jamaica_HRC103_Annex1.pdf.
66 UK Joint Committee on Human Rights (2008, 59).
67 Northern Ireland Human Rights Commission (2008).
68 Iceland's draft constitution can be seen at the website of Iceland's Constitutional Council at http://stjornlagarad.is/english/.
69 Zimbabwe Lawyers for Human Rights and National Constitutional Assembly (2009, 80).

CHAPTER 5: LESSONS LEARNED

1 Ignatieff (2001); Dershowitz (2004).
2 Farber (2002).
3 Organisation for Economic Co-operation and Development (2004b, 122). See also Organisation for Economic Co-operation and Development (2005, 18).
4 Organisation for Economic Co-operation and Development (2001, 41-42, emphasis in original).
5 *Framework Law on the Environment* (1987).
6 *Environmental Responsibility Law* (2007); *Law on Natural Heritage and Biodiversity* (2007). See also *Law 27/2006*, which deals with procedural environmental rights.
7 Walsh (2007, 505).
8 Sabsay (2003); *General Law on the Environment* (2002); *Minimum Standard Law regarding Industrial Waste* (2002); *Minimum Standard Law regarding Management and Elimination of PCBs* (2002); *Water Law* (2003).
9 An example of a provincial law that incorporates the right to a healthy environment as a guiding principle is Rio Negro's *Environmental Impact Assessment Law* (1998). See also Sabsay (n.d.).
10 Marrani (2009).
11 Constitution of Kenya, art. 261(1), fifth schedule.
12 Rosenberg (1991); Bogart (2002).
13 Galanter (1983).
14 Gloppen (2006).

15 Cepeda Espinosa (2005).

16 *Asociación Interamericana para la Defensa del Ambiente (AIDA) y otros* (2009, Costa Rica); *Suray Prasad Sharma Dhungel v. Godavari Marble Industries and others* (1995, Nepal).

17 *Murli S. Deora v. Union of India* (2001); *Lalanath de Silva v. Minister of Forestry and Environment* (1998, Sri Lanka); *Greenwatch v. Attorney General and National Environmental Management Authority* (2002, Uganda).

18 *H.M. Henares, Jr. et al. v. Land Transportation Franchising and Regulatory Board et al.* (2006, Philippines). See also *Anjum Irfan v. LDA* (2002, Pakistan).

19 Belgian Constitutional Court, no. 135/2006; Constitutional Court, no. 137/2006; Constitutional Court, no. 145/2006; Lavrysen (2007).

20 Prieur (2011).

21 Belgian Constitutional Court, no. 135/2006; Constitutional Court, no. 137/2006; Constitutional Court, no. 145/2006; Lavrysen (2007).

22 *Jacobs v. Flemish Region* (1999); *Venter* (1999).

23 Judgment 28/1994, 1919.

24 Judgment 48/1997; Majtenyi (2006).

25 L.K. McAllister (2005, 2008).

26 Quoted in Passos de Freitas (2003, 62).

27 L.K. McAllister (2008, 99).

28 Supreme Court of the Philippines (2010).

29 Boyd (2011a).

30 May (2006); Bruckerhoff (2008, 625); May and Daly (2009).

31 Kravchenko (2002); Stec (2009).

32 Regarding Europe, see de Sadeleer, Roller, and Dross (2005).

33 Hochstetler and Keck (2007, 55).

34 Defensoría del Pueblo (2009).

35 Boyd (2012).

36 Jariwala (2000).

37 Epp (1998).

38 UN Economic Commission for Latin America and the Caribbean (2002, 163).

39 *Beatriz Silvia Mendoza and others v. National Government and Others* (2008); *Concerned Residents of Manila Bay* (2008).

40 Staveland-Saeter (2011).

41 Picolotti (2005).

42 Ibid.

43 Mandela (2002, 1).

44 *Tatar and Tatar v. Romania* (2009); *Fadeyeva v. Russia* (2005); *Taskin et al. v. Turkey* (2004). For Chile, see "Defensa de los Derechos Humanos: Caso contaminación en Arica," Fiscalía del Medio Ambiente, 2012, http://www.fima.cl/.

45 *Pablo Miguel Fabián Martínez and others v. Minister of Health and Director General of Environmental Health* (2006).

46 Supreme Court of Justice Appeal no. 575.998 (Minas Gervais), 16 November 2004; Supreme Court of Justice Appeal no. 70011759842 (Rio Grande do Sul),

1 December 2005; Supreme Court of Justice Appeal no. 70012091278 (Rio Grande do Sul), 25 January 2006.

47 Alley and Meadows (2004, 15).

48 Ghertner and Fripp (2006).

49 Council of State, 695/1986 (Greece); *N.V. Hazegras v. Flemish Government* (1995, Belgium); *Pedro Viudes v. Ley No. 816/96* (1997, Paraguay); Sioutis (2006); Dougnac Rodriguez (2009).

50 *Pavel Ocepek, Breg pri Komendi* (1999).

51 Lavrysen (2009, 114).

52 *Constitutional Complaint against Article 21 of the Urban Planning Act* (1998, S. Korea); *Adam, Teva ve'Din (Human Being, Nature, and Law) v. Prime Minister of Israel et al.* (2004).

53 *Okyay et al. v. Turkey* (2005).

54 Cullet (2007); Turner (2009).

55 For Greece, see *Hellenic Ornithological Society* (1994) and Council of State, 3478/2000; for Finland, see Koivurova (2004); for Costa Rica, see *M.M. Levy y Asociación Ecologista Limonense v. Ministerio del Ambiente y Energia* (2001); for Ecuador, see *Baba Dam Case* (2008); for Hungary, see Judgment 28/1994; for Russia, see *T.V. Zlotnikova, K.E. Lebedeva et al.* (1998); for Thailand, see Boonlai and Changplayngam (2009); and Ahuja (2009).

56 *Law on Ecological Education of the Population* (2001, Armenia); *National Environmental Education Policy Act* (1999, Brazil); *National Environmental Awareness and Education Act of 2008* (Philippines); *Environmental Education Promotion Act* (2008, South Korea).

57 *Beatriz Silvia Mendoza and others v. National Government and Others* (2008); *M.C. Mehta v. Union of India* (2000); *M.C. Mehta v. Union of India*, AIR 1988 SC 1031; *M.C. Mehta v. Union of India* (1992); *Concerned Residents of Manila Bay* (2008).

58 Marrani (2008).

59 *Federación de Asociación Organización de Afectados por La Represa y Acyreta de Itapua y Misiones* (2008).

60 *Minors Oposa v. Factoran, Jr., Secretary of the Department of the Environment and Natural Resources* (1993).

61 *Law on Biodiversity* (1998, art. 9.1).

62 *Comunidad de Chañaral v. CODELCO* (1988, Chile); *Arco Iris v. Ecuador Mineral Institute* (1993, Ecuador); *Hnuti Duha v. Sumava National Park Authority* (1996, Czech Republic); *Caribbean Conservation Corporation et al. v. Costa Rica* (1999); *Khabisi NO and Another v. Aquarella Investment 83 (Pty) Ltd and Others* (2007, South Africa); Boyd (2012).

63 Collins (2007, 137).

64 Mark (2012).

65 Beatty (2004, 129).

66 *Beatriz Silvia Mendoza and others v. National Government and Others* (2008).

67 *Concerned Residents of Manila Bay* (2008).

68 Arantes (2005); Krishnan (2008).

69 de Sadeleer, Roller, and Dross (2005); L.K. McAllister (2008).

70 For Delhi motor vehicle pollution, see *M.C. Mehta v. Union of India* (2002); for Ganges pollution, see *M.C. Mehta v. Union of India*, AIR 1988 SC 1115; for forest conservation, see *T.N. Godavarman Tirumulpad v. Union of India* (1998).
71 Sharma (2005, 2008).
72 Stephens (2009).
73 Garcia-Guadilla (2006, 14).
74 Corder (2007, 361).
75 Velasco (2009).
76 *M.M. Levy y Asociación Ecologista Limonense v. Ministerio del Ambiente y Energia* (2001); *T.V. Zlotnikova, K.E. Lebedeva et al.* (1998).
77 *A. Cederstav and Others v. National Technical Secretary for the Environment, Municipality of Santa Cruz and Others* (2008).
78 Bakan (1997).
79 *Fuel Retailers Association of South Africa v. Director-General: Environmental Management* (2007).
80 Gargarella, Domingo, and Roux (2006).
81 Jorgenson, Rice, and Crowe (2005).
82 Wackernagel and Rees (1996).
83 Wackernagel et al. (2002, 9266).
84 Ewing et al. (2008).
85 Simon Fraser University Sustainable Planning Research Group (2005).
86 Organisation for Economic Co-operation and Development (2007).
87 Wilson, Tyedmers, and Pelot (2007).
88 Data were updated to reflect the Conference Board's most recent ranking of nations on environmental performance. Conference Board of Canada (2011).
89 Overlapping indicators were VOC emissions, water consumption, municipal waste, low emitting energy production, threatened species, and use of forest resources.
90 Nanda and Pring (2003).
91 Guzman (2008).
92 Simpson, Jaccard, and Rivers (2007).
93 *Kyoto Protocol* (1997).
94 *Stockholm Convention on Persistent Organic Pollutants* (2001).
95 *Cartagena Protocol on Biosafety* (2000).
96 *Rotterdam Convention on the Prior Informed Consent Procedure for Certain Hazardous Chemicals and Pesticides in International Trade* (1999).
97 *Ban Amendment to the Basel Convention on the Control of Transboundary Movements of Hazardous Wastes and Their Disposal* (1995).
98 Organisation for Economic Co-operation and Development (2007).
99 Curtis et al. (2006).
100 *UN Convention on Long-Range Transboundary Air Pollution* (1979). Australia and Japan are not parties.
101 Curtis et al. (2006).
102 Data for GHG emissions have been updated to the most recent available (2009), using "Greenhouse Gas Inventory Data," UN Framework Convention on Climate Change, http://unfccc.int/.

CHAPTER 6: INTERNATIONAL LAW AND ENVIRONMENTAL RIGHTS

1 Hiskes (2009, 70).
2 DeMarco and Campbell (2004).
3 Wood, Tanner, and Richardson (2010).
4 Abouchar (2002).
5 Brunee and Toope (2002); Provost (2008).
6 Sullivan (1994, 330), quoted in *Baker v. Canada (Minister of Citizenship and Immigration)*, [1999, para. 70].
7 Brunee and Toope (2002, 52).
8 Provost (2008, 150).
9 DeMarco and Campbell (2004, 330).
10 *R. v. Crown Zellerbach*, [1988].
11 *Imperial Oil Ltd. v. Quebec (Minister of the Environment)*, [2003].
12 *Friends of the Oldman River*, [1992]; *R. v. Hydro-Québec*, [1997].
13 *Ontario v. Canadian Pacific*, [1995].
14 *114957 Canada Ltée (Spraytech, Société d'arrosage) v. Hudson (Town)*, [2001].
15 *Stockholm Declaration (Declaration of the United Nations Conference on the Human Environment)* (1972).
16 Sohn (1973, 436).
17 *Hague Declaration on the Environment* (1989).
18 Wates (1996).
19 *Aarhus Convention on Access to Information, Public Participation in Decision-Making and Access to Justice in Environmental Matters* (1998).
20 See "*Aarhus Convention*, Status of Ratification," United Nations Economic Commission for Europe, http://www.unece.org/.
21 Kindred and Saunders (2006, 866).
22 Toebes (1999, 257); Weissbrodt and de la Vega (2007, 189).
23 *International Covenant on Economic, Social and Cultural Rights* (1966, art. 12(1-2)).
24 Toebes (1999, 257).
25 UN Committee on Economic, Social and Cultural Rights (2000, para. 15).
26 Ibid., para. 51.
27 Toebes (1999).
28 *Convention on the Rights of the Child* (1989, art. 24(2)(c)).
29 Ibid., art. 29.
30 *Convention on the Elimination of All Forms of Discrimination against Women* (1979, art. 14(2)(h)).
31 *Geneva Convention (III) Relative to the Treatment of Prisoners of War*, Geneva, 12 August 1949, arts. 26, 46; *Geneva Convention (IV) Relative to the Protection of Civilian Persons in Time of War*, Geneva, 12 August 1949, arts. 89, 127.
32 *Protocol Additional to the Geneva Conventions of 12 August 1949, and Relating to the Protection of Victims of International Armed Conflicts (Protocol I)*, 8 June 1977, art. 55.
33 The *African Charter* has been ratified by fifty-three nations, of whom fifty-two are UN members. The *San Salvador Protocol* has been ratified by sixteen countries. The *Arab Charter* has been ratified by at least ten nations (Algeria, Bahrain, Jordan,

Libya, Palestine, Qatar, Saudi Arabia, Syrian Arab Republic, United Arab Emirates, and Yemen). Algeria and Libya have ratified both the *African Charter* and the *Arab Charter*; Palestine is not a UN member. The *Aarhus Convention* has been ratified by forty-four, although the United Kingdom filed a reservation with its ratification in which it refused to acknowledge that there is a substantive right to a healthy environment. All ratification data are current to 1 January 2012.

34 Caribbean Community Secretariat (1997, art. XXIII).

35 *Asian Human Rights Charter* (1998, art. 3(2)), reproduced in Shelton (2008, 1079).

36 *American Declaration of the Rights and Duties of Man* (1948).

37 *American Convention on Human Rights* (1978).

38 *Additional Protocol to the American Convention on Human Rights in the Area of Economic, Social, and Cultural Rights* (1988).

39 "Multilateral Treaties: Signatories and Ratifications," Organization of American States, Department of International Law, 2011, http://www.oas.org/. Four additional nations (Chile, Dominican Republic, Haiti, and Venezuela) had signed the *San Salvador Protocol* but had not ratified it as of 1 January 2012.

40 Although article 11 cannot be enforced through an individual petition, it is arguably incorporated, through article 29 of the *American Convention on Human Rights*, into the existing rights in both the *Convention* and the *American Declaration of the Rights and Duties of Man*.

41 Taillant (2003).

42 The Inter-American Commission recently held a hearing on the petition filed by the Hul'qumi'num Treaty Group against Canada, alleging the violation of various human rights resulting from the expropriation of land and the ongoing environmental destruction caused by widespread clear cutting. Case 12.734, argued 28 October 2011; decision pending as of 1 January 2012.

43 *African (Banjul) Charter on Human and Peoples' Rights* (1982).

44 African Commission on Human and Peoples' Rights, "List of Countries Which Have Signed, Ratified/Acceded to the African Union Convention on African Charter on Human and Peoples' Rights," 2009, http://www.achpr.org/instruments/achpr/ratification/.

45 Birnie and Boyle (2002, 254).

46 *Social and Economic Rights Action Center (SERAC) et al. v. Nigeria (2001).*

47 Article 37, proclaimed by the European Parliament, the Council of the European Union, and the European Commission, 7 December 2000.

48 There are extensive environmental provisions in the draft *European Constitution*, but none refer to a right to a healthy environment.

49 Committee of Ministers, Parliamentary Assembly of the Council of Europe (2010).

50 *Aarhus Convention* (1998).

51 Stec (2003).

52 Pallemaerts (2002, 18).

53 *Arab Charter on Human Rights* (2004, art. 38).

54 The ten nations are Algeria, Bahrain, Jordan, Libya, Palestine, Qatar, Saudi Arabia, Syrian Arab Republic, United Arab Emirates, and Yemen. Rishmawi (2010).

55 Roberts (2001).

56 Brownlie (2003, 6).
57 Currie, Forcese, and Oosterveld (2007).
58 Birnie and Boyle (2002, 15).
59 Currie, Forcese, and Oosterveld (2007, 141).
60 Janis (2003, 44).
61 Brownlie (2003).
62 Roberts (2001, 758).
63 *Stockholm Declaration (Declaration of the United Nations Conference on the Human Environment)* 1972; *Hague Declaration on the Environment* (1989); UN General Assembly (1990, 2010); Council of Europe (1990); Organization of the Islamic Conference (1990); UN Commission on Human Rights (1991, 2001, 2003, 2005); *Earth Charter*, art. 9(a), http://www.earthcharter.org; Alliance of Small Island States (2007); Universal Declaration of the Rights of Mother Earth (2010).
64 Guzman (2008); Boyle (2006).
65 *Rio Declaration on Environment and Development* (1992).
66 Pevato (1999).
67 World Commission on Environment and Development (1987, 348); Ksentini (1994); *Johannesburg Principles on the Role of Law and Sustainable Development* (2003); Schrijver and Weiss (1995, para. 31); Commission on Environmental Law of the IUCN, in cooperation with the International Council of Environmental Law (1995); UN Educational, Scientific and Cultural Organization and the UN High Commissioner for Human Rights (1999); excerpts in Dejeant-Pons and Pallemaerts (2002, 91); UN High Commissioner for Human Rights and UN Environment Programme (2002, para. 15; 2009).
68 UN Educational, Scientific and Cultural Organization and the UN High Commissioner for Human Rights (1999); International Centre of Comparative Environmental Law (1990, 2001, 2011); Center for Human Rights and Environment and the Center for International Environmental Law (2002).
69 Kiss and Shelton (2004, 682).
70 *Case of Yanomani Indians* (1985).
71 Inter-American Commission on Human Rights (1997).
72 Ibid., 88.
73 I.K. Scott (2000).
74 *Association of Lhaka Honhat Aboriginal Communities v. Argentina* (2000).
75 *Maya Indigenous Communities of the Toledo District (Belize Maya)* (2004).
76 *Community of San Mateo de Huanchor and its members v. Peru* (2004).
77 Earthjustice (2005).
78 Documents related to the case are available from the Center for International Environmental Law, http://www.ciel.org/.
79 *Community of La Oroya v. Peru* (2007).
80 *Community of La Oroya v. Peru* (2009).
81 *Maya People of the Sipacapa and San Miguel Ixtahuacán Municipalities v. Guatemala* (2010).
82 *Mossman Environmental Action Now v. United States* (2010).
83 Inter-American Court of Human Rights (2008).

84 *Caso de la Comunidad Mayagna (Sumo) Awas Tingni* (2001).
85 *Kichwa Peoples of the Sarayaku Indigenous Community v. Ecuador* (2004).
86 *Case of the Sarayaku Indigenous Community v. Ecuador* (2004).
87 IACHR Application to the Inter-American Court in the case of *Kichwa Peoples of the Sarayaku Indigenous Community v. Ecuador*, Case 12.465, 26 April 2010.
88 *Case of the Yakye Axa Indigenous Community v. Paraguay* (2005).
89 *Sawhoyamaxa Indigenous Community of the Enxet People v. Paraguay* (2006).
90 *Twelve Saramaka Clans v. Suriname* (2007).
91 The European Commission on Human Rights was disbanded in 1988, and the European Court of Human Rights is now responsible for adjudicating individuals' cases.
92 *Lopez Ostra v. Spain* (1994, para. 51).
93 Sands (1996).
94 *Guerra et al. v. Italy* (1998); *Ledyayeva, Dobrokhotova, Zolotareva et Romashina v. Russia* (2006); *Moreno Gomez v. Spain* (2004); *Giacomelli v. Italy* (2006); *Grimkovskaya v. Ukraine* (2011); *Taskin and Others v. Turkey* (2004); *Dubetska et al. v. Ukraine* (2011); *Tatar and Tatar v. Romania* (2009).
95 *Hatton and Others v. United Kingdom* (2003).
96 *Oneryildiz v. Turkey* (2004, para. 71).
97 Ibid., para. 89.
98 *Zander v. Sweden* (1993).
99 *Okyay et al. v. Turkey* (2005, paras. 51-52).
100 *Taskin and Others v. Turkey* (2004).
101 *Hatton and Others v. United Kingdom* (2003, para. 96).
102 Ibid., dissenting judgment, paras. 2, 4.
103 *Kyrtatos v. Greece* (2003).
104 Ibid., para. 53.
105 *Fadeyeva v. Russia* (2005, para. 68).
106 *Tatar and Tatar v. Romania* (2009, paras. 107, 112).
107 *Atanasov v. Bulgaria* (2011).
108 *Grimkovskaya v. Ukraine* (2011).
109 Shelton (2008, 205).
110 Boyle (2009).
111 Lasser (2009, 1).
112 *Taskin and Others v. Turkey* (2004); *Okyay et al. v. Turkey* (2005); *Fadeyeva v. Russia* (2005); *Tatar and Tatar v. Romania* (2009).
113 Schall (2008).
114 Hottelier and Martenet (2006).
115 *Marangopoulos Foundation for Human Rights v. Greece* (2006).
116 Trilsch (2009, 534).
117 *Social and Economic Rights Action Center (SERAC) et al. v. Nigeria (2001); Centre for Minority Rights Development on behalf of Endorois Community v. Kenya* (2010).
118 *Social and Economic Rights Action Center (SERAC) et al. v. Nigeria* (2001, para. 52).
119 Kiss and Shelton (2004, 716).
120 Shelton (2004a, 206); Chirwa (2002).

121 Ebuku (2007).
122 *Optional Protocol to the International Covenant on Civil and Political Rights* (1976).
123 *Optional Protocol to the International Covenant on Economic, Social and Cultural Rights* (2009).
124 Kiss and Shelton (2004, 683).
125 United Nations Human Rights Committee, Communication no. 1331/2004: Sri Laṇka, CCPR/C/87/D/1331/2004, 14 September 2006.
126 *E.H.P. v. Canada* (1982, para. 8).
127 Hogg (2007).
128 Currie, Forcese, and Oosterveld (2007).
129 Malone and Pasternack (2006, 67).
130 This includes the 94 nations that recognize the right to a healthy environment explicitly in their constitutions, the 11 that recognize the right through high court decisions, and the following 38 that have ratified one of the four regional treaties: Algeria, Austria, Bahrain, Bosnia and Herzegovina, Botswana, Cyprus, Denmark, Djibouti, Equatorial Guinea, Eritrea, Gambia, Germany, Ghana, Guinea-Bissau, Jordan, Kazakhstan, Lesotho, Liberia, Libya, Lithuania, Luxembourg, Malta, Mauritius, Namibia, Qatar, Saudi Arabia, Sierra Leone, Somalia, Suriname, Swaziland, Sweden, Syrian Arab Republic, Tajikistan, Tunisia, United Arab Emirates, Yemen, Zambia, and Zimbabwe.
131 Ireland, Liechtenstein, Monaco, San Marino, Switzerland, and United Kingdom.
132 Antigua and Barbuda, Bahamas, Barbados, Belize, Cuba, Dominica, Fiji, Grenada, Haiti, Kiribati, Marshall Islands, Micronesia, Nauru, Palau, Papua New Guinea, Saint Kitts and Nevis, Saint Lucia, Saint Vincent and the Grenadines, Samoa, Singapore, Solomon Islands, Tonga, Trinidad and Tobago, Tuvalu, and Vanuatu.
133 *Environmental Code* (2007).
134 Three additional nations whose environmental laws explicitly recognize the right to a healthy environment are Bhutan, Uzbekistan, and Vietnam.
135 Boyd (2012, ch. 4).
136 Pallemaerts (2002, 11-12).
137 Hançock (2003); Davies (2007); Sarlet and Fensterseifer (2009).
138 Nimushakavi (2006, 23, 156-57).
139 *P.K. Waweru v. Republic of Kenya* (2006).
140 Sala Constitucional de Costa Rica, resolución no. 2003-04654 (2003); Sala Constitucional de Costa Rica, resolución no. 2007-02154 (2007).
141 Vlavianos (2006, 28).

Chapter 7: What Difference Would the Right to a Healthy Environment Make in Canada?

1 Hoggan and Associates (2009).
2 Boyd (2003); Girard, Day, and Snider (2010); Commissioner of the Environment and Sustainable Development (2011); Ecojustice (2011).
3 Tom McMillan, quoted in Boyd (2003, 101).
4 Girard, Day, and Snider (2010).

5 Lynn Pasternak, Planning Department, Toronto Public Library (personal communication, 14 February 2011).
6 US Environmental Protection Agency (2011).
7 *Environmental Enforcement Act* (2009).
8 *Toughest Environmental Penalties Act, 2000* (2000).
9 Boyd (2003).
10 Ibid.
11 Commissioner of the Environment and Sustainable Development (2011); Ecojustice (2011).
12 Boyd (2003).
13 L.K. McAllister (2008).
14 Kennedy (2004).
15 Canadian Environmental Law Association (2012); Gage (2012). See also the website established by a large coalition of environmental organizations at http://www.envirolawsmatter.ca.
16 *Budget Implementation Act, 2009* (2009); Lake Ontario Waterkeeper (2009).
17 Senate Committee on Energy, the Environment, and Natural Resources (2009, 13).
18 Ibid., 18.
19 *Jobs and Economic Growth Act* (2010, ss. 2153, 2155).
20 *Mining Watch Canada v. Canada (Minister of Fisheries and Oceans)*, [2010].
21 Saxe (2010).
22 Flaherty (2012).
23 S. Hazell, quoted in Ecojustice, "Don't Gut Environmental Assessment Law through Budget Bill, Groups Say," media release, 2 September 2010.
24 Cooper (1999).
25 *Significant Projects Streamlining Act* (2003).
26 *Wood Burner and Incinerator Regulation* (1995).
27 *Nova Scotia Air Quality Regulations* (2010).
28 Mathen (2011, 165).
29 Ekins and Speck (2011).
30 Organisation for Economic Co-operation and Development (2010).
31 S. Harper, quoted in Chase (2008, A1).
32 Conference Board of Canada (2011).
33 Porter and van der Linde (1995); Organisation for Economic Co-operation and Development (2010).
34 Bankes and Lucas (2004); Lucas (2004); Chalifour (2008); Hogg (2008); Hsu and Elliot (2009).
35 *Pavel Ocepek, Breg pri Komendi* (1999).
36 Constitutional Court decisions include Sentencia 247/2007; Sentencia 179/2006; Auto 351/2005; Sentencia 173/2005; Sentencia 194/2004; Sentencia 195/2003. Supreme Court decisions include STS 4076/2008; STS 274/2008; STS 5364/2007; STS 5964/2006.
37 Canadian Medical Association (2008).
38 Boyd (2006a).

39 Reeves (2010).
40 Health Canada (2001).
41 Boyd (2012).
42 Vieira (2008).
43 *Maia Petrol Pump case* (1996).
44 Boyd (2012).
45 Veugelers and Read (1999); Jerrett et al. (2001); Buzzelli et al. (2003).
46 MacDonald and Rang (2007); D.N. Scott (2008).
47 Mittelstaedt (2008); Chambers et al. (2008).
48 World Health Organization (2011).
49 Fung, Lunginaah, and Gorey (2007).
50 Gilbertson (2004).
51 Health Canada (2000).
52 Ibid.
53 MacDonald and Rang (2007).
54 Mackenzie, Lockridge, and Keith (2005).
55 Ahuja (2009); Boonlai and Changplayngam (2009).
56 Ibid.
57 Hochstetler and Keck (2004); L.K. McAllister (2008).
58 Boyd (2006d); Hrudey (2008).
59 Peterson and Torchia (2008).
60 Boyd (2011b).
61 As of 31 March 2012, 121 First Nations in Canada were subject to ongoing boil water advisories. Health Canada (2012); Indian and Northern Affairs Canada (2010).
62 Government of Canada (2004, 84).
63 Polaris Institute with the Assembly of First Nations and the Canadian Labour Congress (2008).
64 Fallding (2010).
65 Government of Canada (2004, 84).
66 Constitution of the Dominican Republic (arts. 15, 61); constitution of Kenya (art. 43(1)(d)); constitution of Morocco (art. 31).
67 *Water Services Act* (1997); *National Water Act* (1998, preamble, art. 4); *Local Government Municipal Structures Act* (1998); *Local Government Municipal Systems Act* (2000); Du Plessis (2011).
68 Smets (2006, 92).
69 World Health Organization and UNICEF (2010).
70 Judgment no. 36/98 (1998); over nine thousand constitutional cases were brought in Colombia between 1991 and 2008 related to the provision of potable drinking water and basic sanitation. Defensoría del Pueblo (2009); Sala Constitucional de Costa Rica, resolución no. 2007-02154 (2007); *AP Pollution Control Board v. M.V. Nayudu* (1999/2001); Narain (2010); *Judicial Review of the Law No. 7 of 2004 on Water Resources* (2005); Belbase and Thapa (2007); in Pakistan, the Supreme Court held that "the right to have water free from pollution and contamination is a right to life itself ... The right to have unpolluted water is the right of every person

wherever he lives." *General Secretary West Pakistan Salt Miners Labour Union v. Director Industries and Mineral Development* (1994, 2061).

71 Chacras de la Merced case, see Picolotti (2005); Paynemil Mapuche Community case, "Ensuring Accountability: Argentina," The Rights to Water and Sanitation, http://www.righttowater.org.uk/; *Beatriz Silvia Mendoza and others v. National Government and Others* (2008).

72 See Supreme Court of Justice Appeal no. 575.998 (Minas Gervais); Appeal no. 70011759842 (Rio Grande do Sul); Appeal no. 70012091278 (Rio Grande do Sul).

73 Environics Research Group (2010).

74 Howatt (2007).

75 Blanchfield (2003).

76 Diebel (2008).

77 Hunter (2010).

78 UN Human Rights Council (2010, 2).

79 Canadian Environmental Law Association and Environmental Defence (2008).

80 Commissioner of the Environment and Sustainable Development (2008).

81 Commissioner of the Environment and Sustainable Development (2001).

82 Commissioner of the Environment and Sustainable Development (2008).

83 Department of Finance (2010, 2011).

84 Canadian Centre for Policy Alternatives (2011, 117).

85 Commissioner of the Environment and Sustainable Development (2008).

86 *Beatriz Silvia Mendoza and others v. National Government and Others* (2006).

87 *Law on the Matanza-Riachuelo Watershed* (2006).

88 *Beatriz Silvia Mendoza and others v. National Government and Others* (2008).

89 Carballo (2009, 285).

90 World Bank (2009).

91 Yang and Percival (2009).

92 Matanza-Riachuelo Watershed Authority (2011).

93 Staveland-Saeter (2011, 48).

94 World Bank (2009, 15).

95 *Concerned Residents of Manila Bay* (2008).

96 Ibid. The court cited *M.C. Mehta v. Union of India,* 4 SC 463 (1987).

97 *Concerned Residents of Manila Bay* (2008).

98 *Metropolitan Manila Development Authority et al. v. Concerned Citizens of Manila Bay et al.* (2011).

99 Velasco (2009, 11).

100 Statistics Canada (2011a).

101 De Souza (2011).

102 Limon (2009, 445).

103 McDonald (2008).

104 Lucas (2004, 186).

105 *Friends of the Earth v. Minister of Environment et al.* (2009); Hazell (2010).

106 Mayeda (2010).

107 *M.M. Levy y Asociación Ecologista Limonense v. Ministerio del Ambiente y Energia* (2001).

108 Carminati (2007).
109 For example, Brazil and Norway both require automatic remote shut-off valves for offshore oil rigs. Doggett and Gardner (2010).
110 "Chevron Faces $10.6bn Brazil Legal Suit over Oil Spill," BBC News, 14 December 2011.
111 Statistics Canada (2011a).
112 Ibid.
113 Gage (2010).
114 *Alberta Wilderness Association v. Canada (Minister of Environment)* (2009); *David Suzuki Foundation et al. v. Canada (Minister of Fisheries and Oceans)* (2012).
115 Brazner and McMillan (2008).
116 Panama's Executive Decree 486, signed by President Ricardo Martinelli on 28 December 2010.
117 *R.F. Wheeler and E.G. Huddle v. Attorney General of the State of Loja* (2011).
118 *T.V. Zlotnikova, K.E. Lebedeva et al.* (1998); Slovenia, Constitutional Court Decision no. U-I-30/95.
119 Council of State, 31 January 1991; Council of State, 18 July 1991; Council of State, 22 April 1991; Council of State, 29 May 1992; Supreme Court, 14 April 1989.
120 Haumont and Bodart (2006).
121 Aragao (2004).
122 Karakostas and Vassilopoulos (1999).
123 Koivurova (2004).
124 Quoted in ibid., 57.
125 *Caribbean Conservation Corporation et al. v. Costa Rica* (1999); Sala Constitucional de Costa Rica, resolución 2002-2486; *A. Cederstav and Others v. National Technical Secretary for the Environment, Municipality of Santa Cruz and Others* (2008); *Asociación Interamericana para la Defensa del Ambiente (AIDA) y otros Recurso de Amparo* (2009).

CHAPTER 8: PATHWAYS FOR GREENING CANADA'S CONSTITUTION

1 Russell (2004).
2 Manfredi (2002, 147).
3 Hogg (2007).
4 *Constitution Act, 1982* (1982, s. 39(2)).
5 Ibid., s. 47.
6 G. Stevenson (2007).
7 *Act Respecting Constitutional Amendments* (1996).
8 Swartz and Heard (1997); Cameron and Krikorian (2008).
9 Hurley (1996).
10 *Constitutional Referendum Act* (2000, ss. 2, 4).
11 *Constitutional Amendment Approval Act* (1996).
12 Russell (2004, 239).
13 *Constitution Amendment Proclamation* (1983).
14 Section 93A was added to the *Constitution Act, 1867*, so that sections 93(1) to (4) no longer apply to Quebec.

15 *An Act to Amend the Constitution Act, 1867, the Electoral Boundaries Readjustment Act and the Canada Elections Act* (2011).
16 Newman (2007, 749).
17 Hurley (1996, 99-136).
18 *Constitution Act, 1982* (1982, s. 46).
19 *Reference re Quebec Secession,* [1998, para. 69].
20 Ibid.
21 Hogg (1999); Dawson (1999, 32).
22 Webber (1994).
23 Cameron and Krikorian (2008, 394).
24 Mulvihill (1988).
25 Newman (2007, 771).
26 Watts (1996, xiv, 114).
27 Ibid., 114.
28 *Canadian Charter of Rights and Freedoms* (1982).
29 *Egan v. Canada,* [1995]; *Vriend v. Alberta,* [1998].
30 C.P. Stevenson (1983); Hatherly (1987); Gage (2003); DeMarco (2004, 2007); Collins (2009).
31 C.P. Stevenson (1983, 413)
32 Saxe (1990, 9).
33 Collins (2009, 21).
34 Lucas (1987, 40).
35 Borrows (2010).
36 Sharpe and Roach (2009, 232).
37 *Operation Dismantle Inc. v. The Queen,* [1985].
38 *Gosselin v. Quebec (Attorney General),* [2002, para. 205]; *R. v. Beare,* [1988, 401].
39 *Singh v. Minister of Employment and Immigration,* [1985, 204-5]; *Re BC Motor Vehicle Act,* [1985].
40 *Canada v. Schmidt,* [1987]; *Kindler v. Canada (Minister of Justice),* [1991]; *Reference Re Ng Extradition,* [1991]; *United States v. Burns,* [2001].
41 *Godbout v. Longueuil (Ville),* [1997, para. 66].
42 *Rodriguez v. British Columbia (Attorney General),* [1993, 520].
43 *R. v. Morgentaler,* [1998].
44 *R. v. Stillman,* [1997, para. 42]; *R. v. Pohoretsky,* [1987, 949].
45 *R. v. Stillman,* [1997, para. 87].
46 *Hollis v. Dow Corning Corp.,* [1995].
47 Gage (2003).
48 Young (2005).
49 *Gosselin v. Quebec (Attorney General),* [2002, paras. 68-69].
50 Ibid., paras. 316, 358.
51 *Chaoulli v. Quebec (Attorney General),* [2005].
52 *R. v. Malmo-Levine; R. v. Caine,* [2003]; *Canadian Foundation for Children, Youth and the Law v. Canada (Attorney General),* [2004].
53 See also *R. v. Oakes,* [1986].

54 *R. v. D.B.*, [2008, para. 89]; *Suresh v. Canada*, [2002, para. 78].
55 *Operation Dismantle Inc. v. The Queen*, [1985]; *Energy Probe v. A.G. Canada* (1994); *Energy Probe v. Canada (Attorney General)* (1989); *Coalition of Citizens for a Charter Challenge v. Metropolitan Authority* (1993); *Manicom et al. v. County of Oxford et al.* (1985); *Locke v. Calgary*, [1993]; *Millership et al. v. British Columbia et al.*, 2003; *Kuczerpa v. The Queen* (1993); *Weir v. Environmental Appeal Board (B.C.) et al.* (2003); *Kelly v. Alberta* (2008); *Domke v. Alberta* (2008).
56 *Brown v. Board of Education* (1954); Kluger (1976).
57 *R. v. Sault Ste. Marie*, [1978, 1326].
58 *R. v. Sparrow*, [1990].
59 *Friends of the Oldman River*, [1992, 16-17].
60 *R. v. Hydro-Québec*, [1997, para. 85]. See also *Western Canadian Shopping Centres Inc. v. Dutton*, [2001, para. 26].
61 *114957 Canada Ltée (Spraytech, Société d'arrosage) v. Hudson (Town)*, [2001, para. 1].
62 *Imperial Oil Ltd. v. Quebec (Minister of the Environment)*, [2003].
63 *British Columbia v. Canadian Forest Products Ltd.*, [2004, para. 155].
64 *St. Lawrence Cement Inc. v. Barrette*, [2008].
65 *Ontario v. Canadian Pacific*, [1995, para. 55, emphasis in original].
66 *R. v. Hydro-Québec*, [1997, para. 124].
67 *Imperial Oil Ltd. v. Quebec (Minister of the Environment)*, [2003, para. 20].
68 *Montréal (City) v. 2952-1366 Québec Inc.* (2005, para. 99).
69 *Pulp, Paper and Woodworkers of Canada, Local 8 v. Canada (Minister of Agriculture, Pesticides Directorate)* (1994).
70 *Labrador Inuit Association v. Newfoundland (Minister of Environment and Labour)* (1997, para. 11), cited in *R. v. BHP Diamonds Inc.* (2002), and *R. v. Abitibi Consolidated Inc.* (2000).
71 Brunee and Toope (2002).
72 Slaughter (1994).
73 Boyd (2011a).
74 Eurick (2001).
75 *Hunter v. Southam*, [1984, 155]; *Manitoba (A.G.) v. Metropolitan Stores (MTS) Ltd.*, [1987, 124].
76 *R. v. Big M Drug Mart Ltd.*, [1985, 344]; *Dunmore v. Ontario (Attorney General)*, [2001].
77 Cranor (2006).
78 DeMarco (2004, 27). See also DeMarco (2006).
79 *A. Lockridge and R. Plain v. Director, Ministry of the Environment et al.* (2010).
80 For additional background on the environmental hazards facing the Aamjiwnaang First Nation, see MacDonald and Rang (2007); D.N. Scott (2008).
81 Mackenzie, Lockridge, and Keith (2005).
82 *Kátlodééche First Nation v. H.M.T.Q. et al.* (2003, para. 31).
83 *Supreme Court Act* (1985, s. 53).
84 For BC, see *Constitutional Question Act* (1996, s. 1); for Alberta, see *Judicature Act* (2000, s. 26); for Saskatchewan, see *Constitutional Questions Act* (1978, ss. 2-7); for Manitoba, see *Constitutional Questions Act* (C.C.S.M., c . C-180, s. 1); for Ontario,

see *Courts of Justice Act* (1990, s. 8); for Quebec, see *Court of Appeal Reference Act* (R.S.Q., c. R-23, s. 1); for New Brunswick, see *Judicature Act* (1973, s. 23); for Nova Scotia, see *Constitutional Questions Act* (1989, ss. 3-8); for Prince Edward Island, see *Judicature Act* (1988, s. 7); for Newfoundland and Labrador, see *Judicature Act* (1990, ss. 13-20).

85 *Constitutional Questions Act* (2002, s. 4).
86 For the Northwest Territories, see *Legal Questions Act* (1988); for Nunavut, see *Legal Questions Act* (1988).
87 *Supreme Court Act* (1985, ss. 2(2) and 36).
88 Strayer (1983, 278); Huffman and Saathoff (1990); Chevrette and Webber (2003).
89 Huffman and Saathoff (1990, 1308).
90 *Reference re References,* [1910].
91 Huffman and Saathoff (1990).
92 *Reference re British North America Act 1867 (UK) Section 24,* [1928].
93 L'Heureux-Dubé (2002).
94 *Edwards v. Canada (Attorney General),* [1930, 128].
95 Mahoney (1982, 234).
96 L'Heureux-Dubé (2000).
97 *Edwards v. Canada (Attorney General),* [1930, 136].
98 *Reference re Employment of Aliens,* [1921]; *Reference re Tariff Board of Commerce,* [1934]; *Reference Re Persons of the Japanese Race,* [1946]; Huffman and Saathoff (1990).
99 *Co-operative Committee on Japanese Canadians v. Attorney General,* [1947].
100 *Reference re Same-sex Marriage,* [2004].

CHAPTER 9: PROSPECTS FOR CHANGE

1 Russell (2004, 228).
2 Bryden (2011).
3 Environics Research Group (2010).
4 Swaigen and Woods (1981, 198-99).
5 Kennedy (1967, 232).
6 W. Everson, "Testimony before House of Commons Standing Committee on Environment and Sustainable Development," *Evidence,* 3rd sess., 40th Parliament (15 November 2010); T. Huffaker, "Testimony before House of Commons Standing Committee on Environment and Sustainable Development," *Evidence,* 3rd sess., 40th Parliament (15 November 2010).
7 Stein (1997).
8 New Democratic Party of Canada (2010, s. 2.1).
9 John Swaigen (personal communication, 7 March 2011).
10 Green Party of Canada (2006, 5, 7).
11 Green Party of Canada (2010, 53).
12 Environment Canada, Department of Foreign Affairs and International Trade, Health Canada, and Department of Justice (2006).
13 Stéphane Dion and senior Ignatieff staff (personal communications, 2008 and 2010).

14 Marc Lalonde (personal communication, 7 March 2011).
15 Barry Strayer (personal communication, 7 January 2011).
16 Romanow (2007, 277).
17 Roy Romanow (personal communication, 12 April 2011).
18 Hogg (2007, 4-38).
19 G. Stevenson (2007, 704-5).
20 Dale Gibson (personal communication, 7 April 2011).
21 Weinrib (1998, 282).
22 Hughes and Iyalomhe (1999).
23 William Andrews (personal communication, 11 March 2011). See also Andrews (2000).
24 Swaigen (2006); John Swaigen (personal communication, 10 August 2010).
25 Ollivier (2001).
26 Ollivier (2003).
27 Ollivier (2001).
28 Chirac (2004).
29 Case (2005).
30 Marrani (2008, 25; 2009).
31 Prieur (2008); Marrani (2008).
32 Decision no. 2008-564.
33 *L'Association France Nature Environnement; Commune d'Annecy; Groupement des Agriculteurs Biologistes et Biodynamistes de Maine-et-Loire.*
34 Marrani (2008, 2009).
35 Cairns (1991, 260).
36 Montreal (City of) (2005).

APPENDIX C

1 *Operation Dismantle Inc. v. The Queen* [1985, para. 3].
2 *Energy Probe v. A.G. Canada* (1994).
3 *Energy Probe v. Canada (Attorney General)* (1989).
4 *Energy Probe v. A.G. Canada* (1994, paras. 76-77).
5 *Coalition of Citizens for a Charter Challenge v. Metropolitan Authority* (1993).
6 *Manicom et al. v. County of Oxford et al.* (1985).
7 *Locke v. Calgary*, [1993]; *Millership et al. v. British Columbia et al.*, 2003.
8 *Weir v. Environmental Appeal Board (B.C.) et al.* (2003, para. 51).
9 *Kuczerpa v. The Queen* (1993).
10 *Kelly v. Alberta* (2008, para. 18).
11 *Domke v. Alberta* (2008); Vlavianos (2008).

References

BOOKS, ARTICLES, AND REPORTS

Abouchar, J. 2002. "The Precautionary Principle in Canada: The First Decade." *Environmental Law Reporter* 32, 12: 11407-20.

Agyeman, J., P. Cole, R. Haluza-Delay, and P. O'Riley, eds. 2009. *Speaking for Ourselves: Environmental Justice in Canada.* Vancouver: UBC Press.

Ahuja, A. 2009. "Thai Environmental Group Takes Aim at More Firms." Reuters, 4 December.

Alley, K.D., and D. Meadows. 2004. "Workers' Rights and Pollution Control in Delhi." *Human Rights Dialogue* 2, 11: 15-17.

Alliance of Small Island States. 2007. "Male' Declaration on the Human Dimension of Global Climate Change." November. Center for International Environmental Law. http://www.ciel.org/Publications/Male_Declaration_Nov07.pdf.

Alston, P. 1982. "A Third Generation of Solidarity Rights: Progressive Development or Obfuscation of International Human Rights Law?" *Netherlands International Law Review* 29: 307-22.

–. 1984. "Conjuring Up New Human Rights: A Proposal for Quality Control." *American Journal of International Law* 78: 607-21.

Amos, W., K. Harrison, and G. Hoberg. 2001. "In Search of a Minimum Winning Coalition: The Politics of Species-at-Risk Legislation in Canada." In *Politics of the Wild: Canada and Endangered Species,* ed. K. Beazley and R. Boardman, 137-56. Oxford: Oxford University Press.

Anderson, M.R. 1996a. "Human Rights Approaches to Environmental Protection: An Overview." In Boyle and Anderson 1996, 1-24.

–. 1996b. "Individual Rights to Environmental Protection in India." In Boyle and Anderson 1996, 199-225.

Anderssen, E., and M. Valpy. 2004. "Face the Nation." In *The New Canada: A Globe and Mail Report on the Next Generation,* ed. E. Anderssen and M. Valpy, 15-25. Toronto: McClelland and Stewart.

Andrews, W.J. 1988. "The Environment and the Canadian Charter of Rights and Freedoms." In *Le droit à la qualité de l'environnement: un droit en devenir, un droit à définer,* ed. N. Duplé, 261-72. Montreal: Québec/Amérique.

–. 2000. "Public Access to Environmental Justice: A Comment Ten Years After." In *Sustainable Development in Canada: Into the Next Millennium,* ed. L.J. Griffiths and P. Houlihan, 105-14. Toronto: Canadian Bar Association.

Andrews, W.J., and L. Alexander. 1991. *Enhancing Environmental Protection in the Canadian Constitution: Comments on the Federal Government's Constitutional Proposals*. Vancouver: West Coast Environmental Law Association.

Angus, I. 1997. *A Border Within: National Identity, Cultural Plurality, and Wilderness*. Montreal and Kingston: McGill-Queen's University Press.

Aragao, A. 2004. "The Application and Interpretation of the Core Environmental Principles by the Portuguese Courts." In Macrory 2004, 159-77.

Arantes, R.B. 2005. "Constitutionalism, the Expansion of Justice and the Judicialization of Politics in Brazil." In Sieder, Schjolden, and Angell 2005, 231-62.

Arthurs, H. 2003. "Constitutional Courage." *McGill Law Journal* 49, 1: 1-23.

Atapattu, S. 2006. *Emerging Principles of International Environmental Law*. Ardsley, NY: Transnational.

Babor, D.D.M. 1999. "Environmental Rights in Ontario: Are Participatory Mechanisms Working?" *Colorado Journal of International Environmental Law and Policy* 10: 121-35.

Baderin, M.A., and R. McCorquodale, eds. 2006. *Economic, Social and Cultural Rights in Action*. Oxford: Oxford University Press.

Bakan, J. 1997. *Just Words: Constitutional Rights and Social Wrongs*. Toronto: University of Toronto Press.

Bankes, N.D., and A.R. Lucas. 2004. "*Kyoto*, Constitutional Law and Alberta's Proposals." *Alberta Law Review* 42, 2: 355-98.

Barry, B. 1996. *Justice as Impartiality*. Oxford: Oxford University Press.

Beatty, D.M. 1998. "Polluting the Law to Protect the Environment." *Constitutional Forum* 9, 2: 55-58.

–. 2004. *The Ultimate Rule of Law*. Oxford: Oxford University Press.

Beaudoin, G., and D. Dobbie. 1992. "A Renewed Canada: The Report of the Special Joint Committee of the Senate and the House of Commons." *Minutes of Proceedings and Evidence* 66 (February 27-28).

Belbase, N., and L.B. Thapa. 2007. "Nepal." In *Environmental Justice and Rural Communities: Studies from India and Nepal*, ed. P. Moore and F. Pastakia, 65-108. Gland, Switzerland: IUCN.

Bergeson, L.L. 2011. "Emerging Nanomaterial Governance Systems: The State of Play." *Molecular Imaging* 10, 1: 17-27.

Birnie, P., and A. Boyle. 2002. *International Law and the Environment*. 2nd ed. Oxford: Oxford University Press.

Birnie, P., A. Boyle, and C. Redgwell. 2009. *International Law and the Environment*. 3rd ed. Oxford: Oxford University Press.

Blanchfield, M. 2003. "Our Painful Vote against Clean Water." *Ottawa Citizen*, 21 September, A4.

Bogart, W.A. 2002. *Consequences: The Impact of Law and Its Complexity*. Toronto: University of Toronto Press.

Boonlai, K., and P. Changplayngam. 2009. "Thai Court Halts Many New Plants in Big Industrial Zone." Reuters, 3 December.

Borovoy, A.A. 1988. *When Freedoms Collide: The Case for Our Civil Liberties*. Toronto: Lester and Orpen Dennys.

Borrows, J. 2005. "Creating an Indigenous Legal Community" (John C. Tait Memorial Lecture in Law and Public Policy delivered at the Faculty of Law, McGill University, 14 October 2004). *McGill Law Journal* 50, 1: 153-72.

–. 2010. *Canada's Indigenous Constitution.* Toronto: University of Toronto Press.

Boutaud, A., N. Gondran, and C. Brodhag. 2006. "(Local) Environmental Quality versus (Global) Ecological Carrying Capacity: What Might Alternative Aggregated Indicators Bring to the Debates about Environmental Kuznets Curves and Sustainable Development?" *International Journal of Sustainable Development* 9, 3: 297-310.

Boyd, D.R. 2003. *Unnatural Law: Rethinking Canadian Environmental Law and Policy.* Vancouver: UBC Press.

–. 2006a. *The Air We Breathe: An International Comparison of Air Quality Standards and Guidelines.* Vancouver: David Suzuki Foundation.

–. 2006b. *The Food We Eat: An International Comparison of Pesticide Regulations.* Vancouver: David Suzuki Foundation.

–. 2006c. "Petition regarding the Right of Canadians to Clean Air, Clean Water, and a Healthy Environment." Petition no. 163, 16 January. Office of the Auditor General of Canada. http://www.oag-bvg.gc.ca/.

–. 2006d. *The Water We Drink: An International Comparison of Drinking Water Standards.* Vancouver: David Suzuki Foundation.

–. 2007. *Prescription for a Healthy Canada: Towards a National Environmental Health Strategy.* Vancouver: David Suzuki Foundation.

–. 2010. "Bill C-469: The Canadian Environmental Bill of Rights." Brief prepared for the House of Commons Standing Committee on Environment and Sustainable Development. 27 October.

–. 2011a. "The Implicit Constitutional Right to a Healthy Environment." *Review of European Community and International Environmental Law* 20, 2: 171-79.

–. 2011b. "No Taps, No Toilets: First Nations and the Constitutional Right to Water in Canada." *McGill Law Journal* 57, 1: 81-134.

–. 2012. *The Environmental Rights Revolution: A Global Study of Constitutions, Human Rights, and the Environment.* Vancouver: UBC Press.

Boyd, D.R., A. Attaran, and M. Stanbrook. 2008. "Asbestos Mortality: A Canadian Export." *Canadian Medical Association Journal* 179, 9: 871-72.

Boyd, D.R., and S. Genuis. 2008. "The Environmental Burden of Disease in Canada: Respiratory Disease, Cardiovascular Disease, Cancer, and Congenital Affliction." *Environmental Research* 106: 240-49.

Boyle, A.E. 2006. "Soft Law in International Law-Making." In *International Law,* ed. M.D. Evans, 141-58. 2nd ed. Oxford: Oxford University Press.

–. 2009. *Human Rights and the Environment: A Reassessment.* Nairobi: UNEP.

Boyle, A.E., and M.R. Anderson, eds. 1996. *Human Rights Approaches to Environmental Protection.* Oxford: Clarendon Press.

Brand, J., and G. Morley, eds. 1972. *As We See It: Proceedings of a Workshop on Canadian Law and the Environment.* Winnipeg: Agassiz Centre for Water Studies.

Brandl, E., and H. Bungert. 1992. "Constitutional Entrenchment of Environmental Protection: A Comparative Analysis of Experiences Abroad." *Harvard Environmental Law Review* 16, 1: 1-100.

Brazner, J.C., and J. McMillan. 2008. "Loggerhead Turtle (Caretta caretta) Bycatch in the Canadian Pelagic Longline Fisheries: Relative Importance in the Western North Atlantic and Opportunities for Mitigation." *Fisheries Research* 91, 2-3: 310-24.

Brewer-Carias, A.R. 2009. *Constitutional Protection of Human Rights in Latin America: A Comparative Study of Amparo Proceedings.* Cambridge: Cambridge University Press.

Bridge, D., and A. Laytner, trans. 2005. *The Animals' Lawsuit against Humanity: An Illustrated 10th Century Iraqi Fable.* Louisville, KY: Fons Vitae.

Brownlie, I. 2003. *Principles of Public International Law.* 6th ed. Oxford: Oxford University Press.

Bruch, C., W. Coker, and C. VanArsdale. 2007. *Constitutional Environmental Law: Giving Force to Fundamental Principles in Africa.* 2nd ed. Washington, DC: Environmental Law Institute.

Bruckerhoff, J.J. 2008. "Giving Nature Constitutional Protection: A Less Anthropocentric Interpretation of Environmental Rights." *Texas Law Review* 86: 616-46.

Brunee, J., and S.J. Toope. 2002. "Hesitant Embrace: The Application of International Law by Canadian Courts." *Canadian Yearbook of International Law* 40: 3-60.

Bryant, D., D. Nielsen, and L. Tangley. 1997. *The Last Frontier Forests: Ecosystems and Economies on the Edge.* Washington, DC: World Resources Institute.

Bryden, J. 2011. "Most Canadians Willing to Re-Open Constitution, Poll Finds." *Toronto Globe and Mail,* 26 May.

Bryner, G.C. 1987. "Constitutionalism and the Politics of Rights." In *Constitutionalism and Rights,* ed. G.C. Bryner and N.B. Reynolds, 7-32. Albany, NY: State University Press.

Bullard, R.D., ed. 2005. *The Quest for Environmental Justice: Human Rights and the Politics of Pollution.* San Francisco: Sierra Club Books.

Buzzelli, M., M. Jerrett, R. Burnett, and N. Finklestein. 2003. "Spatiotemporal Perspectives on Air Pollution and Environmental Justice in Hamilton, Canada, 1985-1996." *Annals of the Association of American Geographers* 93, 3: 557-73.

Cairns, A.C. 1991. *Disruptions: Constitutional Struggles from the Charter to Meech Lake,* edited by D.E. Williams. Toronto: McClelland and Stewart.

Cameron, A.M. 2009. *Power without Law: The Supreme Court of Canada, the Marshall Decisions, and the Failure of Judicial Activism.* Montreal and Kingston: McGill-Queen's University Press.

Cameron, D.R., and J.D. Krikorian. 2008. "Recognizing Quebec in the Constitution of Canada: Using the Bilateral Constitutional Amendment Process." *University of Toronto Law Journal* 58, 4: 389-420.

Canadian Bar Association. 1990. *Report of the Canadian Bar Association Committee on Sustainable Development in Canada: Options for Law Reform.* Ottawa: CBA.

Canadian Centre for Policy Alternatives. 2011. *Alternative Federal Budget.* Ottawa: CCPA.

Canadian Environmental Law Association. 1972. *Public Rights and Environmental Planning.* Toronto: Canadian Environmental Law Research Foundation.

–. 1978. "CELA Asks for Constitutional Guarantee of a Clean Environment." *CELA Newsletter* 3, 5: 70.

–. 2012. "Federal Budget Signals Attack on Canada's Environmental Laws." Media release, 29 March.

Canadian Environmental Law Association and Environmental Defence. 2008. *An Examination of Pollution and Poverty in the Great Lakes Basin.* Toronto: CELA and ED.

–. 2010. *Partners in Pollution 2: An Update on the Continuing Canadian and United States Contributions to Great Lakes–St. Lawrence River Ecosystem Pollution.* Toronto: CELA and ED.

Canadian Environmental Law Research Foundation. 1984. *Preliminary Analysis of Elements of a Federal Environmental Bill of Rights.* Toronto: CELRF.

Canadian Intergovernmental Conference Secretariat. 1974. *The Constitutional Review, 1968-1971: Secretary's Report.* Ottawa: The Secretariat.

Canadian Institute for Environmental Law and Policy. 2008. "Update on a Framework for Canadian Nanotechnology Policy: A Second Discussion Paper." http://www.cielap.org/pdf/2008NanoUpdate.pdf.

Canadian Medical Association. 2008. *No Breathing Room: National Illness Costs of Air Pollution.* Toronto: CMA.

Canadian Press. 2009. "Harper Defends Climate-Change Efforts amid Criticism Canada Is Lagging." 23 September.

Cancado Trindade, A.A. 1993. "Environmental Protection and the Absence of Restrictions on Human Rights." In *Human Rights in the Twenty-First Century: A Global Challenge,* ed. K.E. Mahoney and P. Mahoney, 561-93. Dordrecht, Netherlands: Martinus Nijhoff.

Carballo, J. 2009. "Argentina." In Kotze and Paterson 2009, 269-94.

Caribbean Community Secretariat. 1997. *Charter of Civil Society for the Caribbean Community.* Georgetown, Guyana: CARICOM Secretariat. http://www.caricom.org/.

Carminati, G. 2007. "Is International Trade Really Making Developing Countries Dirtier and Developed Countries Richer?" *UC Davis Business Law Journal* 8, 1: 205-33.

Carson, R. 1962. *Silent Spring.* Boston: Houghton Mifflin.

Case, D. 2005. "Liberté, Egalité, Environment: The French Constitution Gets a Dash of Green." *Daily Grist,* 14 July.

Castrilli, J. 1998. "Environmental Rights Statutes in Canada and the U.S." *Villanova Environmental Law Journal* 9, 2: 349-438.

Center for Human Rights and Environment and Center for International Environmental Law. 2002. *Draft International Declaration on Human Rights and Environment.* Cordoba, Argentina: CHRE.

Centre for Research and Information on Canada. 2002. *The Charter: Dividing or Uniting Canadians?* CRIC Papers 5. Montreal: CRIC.

Cepeda Espinosa, M.J. 2005. "The Judicialization of Politics in Colombia: The Old and the New." In Sieder, Schjolden, and Angell 2005, 67-104.

Cha, J.M. 2007. *Increasing Access to Environmental Justice: A Resource Book for Advocacy and Legal Literacy in South Asia.* Kathmandu: International Centre for Integrated Mountain Development.

Chalifour, N.J. 2008. "Making Federalism Work for Climate Change: Canada's Division of Powers over Carbon Taxes." *National Journal of Constitutional Law* 22, 2: 119-214.

Chalifour, N.J., P. Kameri-Mbote, L.H. Lye, and J.R. Nolon, eds. 2007. *Land Use Law for Sustainable Development.* Cambridge: Cambridge University Press.

Chambers, A.K., M. Strosher, T. Wooten, J. Moncrieff, and P. McCready. 2008. "Direct Measurement of Fugitive Emissions of Hydrocarbons from a Refinery." *Journal of the Air and Waste Management Association* 58: 1047-56.

Chartrand, L.D. 2005. *Accommodating Indigenous Legal Traditions.* Ottawa: Indigenous Bar Association.

Chase, S. 2008. "Tories' 'Recession' Threat Based on Old Numbers." *Toronto Globe and Mail,* 11 September, A1.

Chevrette, F., and G.C.N. Webber. 2003. "L'utilisation de la procédure de l'avis consultatif devant la Cour suprême du Canada: Essai de typologie." *Canadian Bar Review* 82, 3: 757-90.

Chiappinelli, J.A. 1992. "The Right to a Clean and Safe Environment: A Case for a Constitutional Amendment Recognizing Public Rights in Common Resources." *Buffalo Law Review* 40: 597-611.

Chirac, J. 2004. "Statement." Delivered at the Opening Ceremony of the Founding Congress of the World Organization for Cities and Local Government, Paris, 2 May.

Chirwa, D.M. 2002. "A Fresh Commitment to Implementing Economic, Social, and Cultural Rights in Africa: Social and Economic Rights Action Center (SERAC) and the Center for Economic and Social Rights v. Nigeria." *ESR Review* 3, 2: 19-21.

Chivian, E., and A. Bernstein. 2008. *Sustaining Life: How Human Health Depends on Biodiversity.* New York: Oxford University Press.

Chrétien, J. 1990. "Bringing the Constitution Home." In *Towards a Just Society,* ed. T. Axworthy and P.E. Trudeau, 282-309. Markham: Viking.

Christensen, R. 2011. *Waterproof 3: Canada's Drinking Water Report Card.* Vancouver: Ecojustice.

Citizens' Forum on Canada's Future with Keith Spicer. 1991. *Report to the People and Government of Canada.* Ottawa: Minister of Supply and Services.

Collins, L. 2007. "Are We There Yet? The Right to Environment in International and European Law." *McGill International Journal of Sustainable Development Law and Policy* 3, 2: 119-53.

–. 2009. "An Ecologically Literate Reading of the Canadian Charter of Rights and Freedoms." *Windsor Review of Legal and Social Issues* 26, 1: 7-48.

Commission on Environmental Law of the IUCN (in cooperation with the International Council of Environmental Law). 1995. *International Covenant on Environment and Development.* Excerpts in Dejeant-Pons and Pallemaerts 2002, 89-90.

Commissioner of the Environment and Sustainable Development. 2001. *Report of the Commissioner of Environment and Sustainable Development to the House of Commons.* Ottawa: Auditor General.

–. 2008. "Ecosystems – Areas of Concern in the Great Lakes." In *2008 Report of the Commissioner of Environment and Sustainable Development to the House of Commons,* Chapter 7. Ottawa: Auditor General.

–. 2011. "Enforcement of the Canadian Environmental Protection Act, 1999." In *Report of the Commissioner of Environment and Sustainable Development to the House of Commons,* Chapter 3. Ottawa: Auditor General.

Committee of Ministers, Parliamentary Assembly of the Council of Europe. 2010. *Reply to Recommendation 1885: Drafting an Additional Protocol to the European Convention on Human Rights concerning the Right to a Healthy Environment.* Doc. no. 12298, 16 June.

Conference Board of Canada. 2004. *Challenging Health Care System Sustainability: Understanding Health System Performance of Leading Countries.* Ottawa: Conference Board.

–. 2008. *How Canada Performs: A Report Card on Canada.* Ottawa: Conference Board.

–. 2009. *Critical Steps for Canada: Environmental Health Lessons across Borders: Australia, Sweden and California.* Ottawa: Conference Board.

–. 2011. *How Canada Performs: A Report Card on Canada.* Ottawa: Conference Board. http://www.conferenceboard.ca/.

Constitution Review Group, All-Party Oireachtas Committee on the Constitution. 1996. *Report of the Constitution Review Group.* Dublin: Stationery Office.

Cooper, K. 1999. "An Updated Chronology of Changes in Ontario's Environmental Policy." *Intervenor* (Canadian Environmental Law Association) 24, 1: 9-16.

Corder, H. 2007. "South Africa's Top Courts since 1994." In *Judicial Activism in Common Law Supreme Courts,* ed. B. Dickson, 323-62. Oxford: Oxford University Press.

Corriveau, Y. 1995. "Citizen Rights and Litigation in Environmental Law." In *Environmental Rights: Law, Litigation and Access to Justice,* ed. S. Deimann and B. Dyssli, 117-65. London: Cameron May.

Council of Europe. 1990. *Dublin Declaration,* 26 July. Excerpts in Dejeant-Pons and Pallemaerts 2002, 255-56.

Cranor, C.F. 2006. *Toxic Torts: Science, Law, and the Possibility of Justice.* Cambridge: Cambridge University Press.

Cranston, M. 1973. *What Are Human Rights?* London: Bodley Head.

Cronin, J., and R.F. Kennedy Jr. 1997. *The Riverkeepers: Two Activists Fight to Reclaim Our Environment as a Basic Human Right.* New York: Scribner.

Cullet, P. 1995. "Definition of an Environmental Right in a Human Rights Context." *Netherlands Quarterly of Human Rights* 13: 25-35.

–. 2007. *The Sardar Sarovar Dam Project.* Aldershot, UK: Ashgate.

Currie, J.H., C. Forcese, and V. Oosterveld. 2007. *International Law: Doctrine, Practice, and Theory.* Toronto: Irwin Law.

Curtis, L., W. Rea, P. Smith-Willis, E. Fenyves, and Y. Pan. 2006. "Adverse Health Effects of Outdoor Air Pollutants." *Environment International* 32, 6: 815-30.

Davies, S. 2007. "In Name or Nature? Implementing International Environmental Procedural Rights in the Post-Aarhus Environment: A Finnish Example." *Environmental Law Review* 9, 3: 190-200.

Davis, D.M. 1992. "The Case against the Inclusion of Socio-economic Demands in a Bill of Rights Except as Directive Principles." *South African Journal on Human Rights* 8: 475-90.

–. 2004. "Socio-Economic Rights in South Africa: The Record after Ten Years." *New Zealand Journal of Public and International Law* 2, 1: 47-66.

–. 2008. "Socioeconomic Rights: Do They Deliver the Goods?" *International Journal of Constitutional Law* 6, 3-4: 687-711.

Davis, D.M., P. Macklem, and G. Mundlak. 2002. "Social Rights, Social Citizenship, and Transformative Constitutionalism: A Comparative Assessment." In *Labour Law in an Era of Globalization*, ed. J. Conaghan, M. Fischl, and K. Klare, 511-34. Oxford: Oxford University Press.

Dawson, M. 1993. "The Impact of the *Charter* on the Public Policy Process and the Department of Justice." In *The Impact of the Charter on the Public Policy Process*, ed. P. Monahan and M. Finkelstein, 51-60. North York: York University Centre for Public Law and Public Policy.

–. 1999. "Reflections on the Opinion of the Supreme Court of Canada in the Quebec Secession Reference." *National Journal of Constitutional Law* 11: 5-48.

de Sadeleer, N. 2002. *Environmental Principles: From Political Slogans to Legal Rules*. Oxford: Oxford University Press.

–. 2004. "Environmental Principles, Modern and Post-Modern Law." In Macrory 2004, 223-36.

de Sadeleer, N., G. Roller, and M. Dross. 2005. *Access to Justice in Environmental Matters and the Role of NGOs: Empirical Findings and Legal Appraisal*. Groningen: Europa Law.

De Souza, M. 2011. "Jobs Doomed with Slashed Climate Policies." *Ottawa Citizen*, 12 March.

Defensoría del Pueblo. 2009. *Diagnóstico del Cumplimiento del Derecho Humano al Agua en Colombia*. Bogota: Defensoría del Pueblo.

Dejeant-Pons, M., and M. Pallemaerts, eds. 2002. *Human Rights and the Environment: Compendium of Instruments and Other International Texts on Individual and Collective Rights Relating to the Environment in the International and European Framework*. Strasbourg: Council of Europe.

DeMarco, J.V. 2004. "Law for Future Generations: The Theory of Intergenerational Equity in Canadian Environmental Law." *Journal of Environmental Law and Practice* 15, 1: 1-46.

–. 2006. "Developments in Municipal and Environmental Law: The 2005-2006 Term." *Supreme Court Law Review*, 2nd ser., 35: 275-310.

–. 2007. "The Supreme Court of Canada's Recognition of Fundamental Environmental Values: What Could Be Next in Canadian Environmental Law?" *Journal of Environmental Law and Practice* 17, 3: 159-204.

DeMarco, J.V., and M.L. Campbell. 2004. "The Supreme Court of Canada's Progressive Use of International Environmental Law and Policy in Interpreting Domestic Legislation." *Review of European Community and International Environmental Law* 13, 3: 320-32.

Department of Finance. 2010. *Budget 2010: Leading the Way on Jobs and Economic Growth*. Ottawa: Department of Finance.

–. 2011. *Budget 2011: A Low-Tax Plan for Jobs and Growth*. Ottawa: Department of Finance.

Dershowitz, A. 2004. *Rights from Wrongs: A Secular Theory of the Origins of Rights*. New York: Basic Books.

Di Paola, M.E., ed. 2003. *Symposium of Judges and Prosecutors of Latin America: Environmental Compliance and Enforcement*. Buenos Aires: Fundación Ambiente y Recursos Naturales.

Diebel, L. 2008. "Canada Foils UN Water Plan." *Toronto Star*, 2 April. http://www.thestar.com/.

Doggett, T., and T. Gardner. 2010. "US Mulls Requiring Remote Shutoffs for Rigs." Reuters, 3 May.

Douglas, K. 1991. *An Environmental Bill of Rights for Canada*. Ottawa: Library of Parliament Research Branch.

Dougnac Rodriguez, F. 2009. "Reflexiones sobre algunos principios y valores que regulan el medio ambiente en Chile." *Justicia Ambiental* 1: 101-29.

Du Bois, F. 1996. "Social Justice and the Judicial Enforcement of Environmental Rights and Duties." In Boyle and Anderson 1996, 153-75.

Du Plessis, A. 2011. "A Government in Deep Water? Some Thoughts on the State's Duties in Relation to Water Arising from South Africa's Bill of Rights." *Review of European Community and International Environmental Law* 19, 3: 316-27.

Dworkin, R. 1978. *Taking Rights Seriously*. London: Duckworth.

Earthjustice. 2005. *Petition to the IACHR on Human Rights Seeking Relief from Violations Resulting from Global Warming Caused by Acts and Omissions of the United States*. 7 December. http://www.earthjustice.org/library/legal_docs/petition-to-the-inter-american-commission-on-human-rights-on-behalf-of-the-inuit-circumpolar-conference.pdf.

Ebuku, K.S.A. 2007. "Constitutional Right to a Healthy Environment and Human Rights Approaches to Environmental Protection in Nigeria: *Gbemre v. Shell* Revisited." *Review of European Community and International Environmental Law* 16, 3: 312-20.

Ecojustice. 2011. *Getting Tough on Environmental Crime? Holding the Federal Government to Account on Environmental Crime*. Ottawa: Ecojustice.

Editorial Board. 2012. "Frozen Out." *Nature* 483, 6: 6.

Ekins, P., and S. Speck. 2011. *Environmental Tax Reform: A Policy for Green Growth*. Oxford: Oxford University Press.

Elgie, S. 2007. "Kyoto, the Constitution and Carbon Trading: Waking a Sleeping BNA Bear (or Two)." *Review of Constitutional Studies* 13, 1: 67-129.

Emerson, J., et al. 2010. *Environmental Performance Index 2010*. New Haven, CT: Yale Center for Environmental Law and Policy and Columbia University Center for International Earth Science Information Network.

Environics International. 1999. *Public Opinion and the Environment, 1999: Biodiversity Issues*. Opinion poll conducted for Environment Canada.

Environics Research Group. 2010. *Human Rights in Canada Today: A National Opinion Survey*. Prepared for the Trudeau Foundation's 7th Annual Conference on Public Policy, Winnipeg, 18-20 November.

Environment Canada. 1987. *Summary of Workshops: Draft Environmental Protection Act*. Ottawa: Environment Canada.

–. 1996. *The State of Canada's Environment*. Ottawa: Minister of Public Works and Government Services.

–. 2001. *Tracking Key Environmental Issues*. Ottawa: Minister of Public Works and Government Services.

–. 2010. Air Quality Indicators. http://www.ec.gc.ca/.

Environment Canada, Department of Foreign Affairs and International Trade, Health Canada, and Department of Justice. 2006. "Government of Canada's Response to

Environmental Petition 163 Filed by Mr. David R. Boyd." 2 June. Office of the Auditor General of Canada. http://www.oag-bvg.gc.ca/.

Environmental Commissioner of Ontario. 1996-2011. *Annual Reports.* http://www.eco.on.ca.

Epp, C. 1998. *The Rights Revolution: Lawyers, Activists and Supreme Courts in Comparative Perspective.* Chicago: University of Chicago Press.

Estrin, D., and J. Swaigen. 1974. *Environment on Trial: A Citizens' Guide to Ontario Environmental Law.* Toronto: Canadian Environmental Law Association and Canadian Environmental Law Research Foundation.

–. 1978. *Environment on Trial: A Citizens' Guide to Ontario Environmental Law.* 2nd ed. Toronto: Canadian Environmental Law Research Foundation.

Eurick, J.P. 2001. "The Constitutional Right to a Healthy Environment: Enforcing Environmental Protection through State and Federal Constitutions." *International Legal Perspectives* 11, 2: 185-222.

Ewing, B., S. Goldfinger, M. Wackernagel, M. Stechbart, S.M. Rizk, A. Reed, and J. Kitzes. 2008. *The Ecological Footprint Atlas 2008.* Oakland: Global Footprint Network.

Fallding, H. 2010. "No Running Water." *Winnipeg Free Press,* 30 October, A1. http://www.winnipegfreepress.com/.

Farber, D.A. 2002. "Rights as Signals." *Journal of Legal Studies* 31, 1: 83-98.

Flaherty, J.M. 2012. *Jobs, Growth, and Long-term Prosperity: Economic Action Plan 2012.* Ottawa: Public Works and Government Services.

Franson, R.T., and P.T. Burns. 1974. "Environmental Rights for the Canadian Citizen: A Prescription for Reform." *Alberta Law Review* 12, 2: 153-71.

Fredman, S. 2008. *Human Rights Transformed: Positive Rights and Positive Duties.* Oxford: Oxford University Press.

Fried, C. 1973. *Right and Wrong.* Cambridge, MA: Harvard University Press.

Friends of the Earth Canada. 2009. *Standing on Guard: Environmental Rights in Canada, 2009.* Ottawa: FOEC.

Fuller, L. 1978. "The Forms and Limits of Adjudication." *Harvard Law Review* 92, 2: 353-409.

Fung, K., I. Lunginaah, and K.M. Gorey. 2007. "Impact of Air Pollution on Hospital Admissions in Southwestern Ontario, Canada: Generating Hypotheses in Sentinel High Exposure Places." *Environmental Health* 6: 18-34.

Gage, A. 2003. "Public Health Hazards and S. 7 of the *Charter.*" *Journal of Environmental Law and Practice* 13, 1: 1-34.

–. 2010. "Fish Lakes and Tailings Ponds." *Journal of Environmental Law and Practice* 22, 1: 1-38.

–. 2012. "Fisheries Act Amendments Would Be an Attack on Salmon." *Environmental Law Alert,* 19 March. http://wcel.org.

Galanter, M. 1974. "Why the 'Haves' Come Out Ahead: Speculations on the Limits of Legal Change." *Law and Society Review* 9, 1: 95-160.

–. 1983. "The Radiating Effects of Courts." In *Empirical Theories about Courts,* ed. K. Boyum and L. Matter, 117-42. New York: Longman.

Garcia-Guadilla, M.P. 2006. *Environmental Movements, Politics, and Agenda 21 in Latin America.* Geneva: UN Research Institute for Social Development.

Gargarella, R., P. Domingo, and T. Roux, eds. 2006. *Courts and Social Transformation in New Democracies: An Institutional Voice for the Poor?* Aldershot, UK: Ashgate.

Garner, B.A. 2004. *Black's Law Dictionary*. St. Paul, MN: Thomson/West.

Gauri, V., and D.M. Brinks, eds. 2008. *Courting Social Justice: Judicial Enforcement of Social and Economic Rights in the Developing World.* Cambridge: Cambridge University Press.

Gertler, F., P. Muldoon, and M. Valiante. 1990. "Public Access to Environmental Justice." In *Report of the Canadian Bar Association Committee on Sustainable Development in Canada: Options for Law Reform*, 79-97. Toronto: CBA.

Gertler, F., and T. Vigod. 1991. *Submission by the Canadian Environmental Law Association to the Select Committee on Ontario in Confederation: Environmental Protection in a New Constitution.* Toronto: Canadian Environmental Law Association.

Ghertner, D.A., and M. Fripp. 2006. "Trading Away Damage: Quantifying Environmental Leakage through Consumption-Based Life-Cycle Analysis." *Ecological Economics* 63, 2-3: 563-77.

Gibson, D. 1970. *Constitutional Jurisdiction over Environmental Management in Canada.* Ottawa: Government of Canada.

–. 1983. "Environmental Protection and Enhancement under a New Canadian Constitution." In *Canada and the New Constitution: The Unfinished Agenda*, ed. S.M. Beck and C. Bernier, 115-28. Montreal: Institute for Research on Public Policy.

–. 1988. "Constitutional Entrenchment of Environmental Rights." In *Le droit à la qualité de l'environnement: un droit en devenir, un droit à définer*, ed. N. Duplé, 273-300. Montreal: Québec/Amérique.

Gilbertson, M. 2004. "Male Cerebral Palsy Hospitalization as a Potential Indicator of Neurological Effects of Methylmercury Exposure in Great Lakes Communities." *Environmental Research* 95, 3: 375-84.

Girard, A.L., S. Day, and L. Snider. 2010. "Tracking Environmental Crime through CEPA: Canada's Environment Cops or Industry's Best Friend?" *Canadian Journal of Sociology* 35, 2: 219-41.

Glendon, M.A. 1991. *Rights Talk: The Impoverishment of Political Discourse.* New York: Free Press.

Global Forest Watch. 2003. *Canada's Large Intact Forest Landscapes.* Edmonton: Global Forest Watch and World Resources Institute.

Gloppen, S. 2006. "Courts and Social Transformation: An Analytical Framework." In Gargarella, Domingo, and Roux 2006, 35-60.

Gosine, A., and C. Teelucksingh. 2008. *Environmental Justice and Racism in Canada: An Introduction.* Toronto: Emond Montgomery.

Government of Canada. 1969. *The Constitution and the People of Canada.* Ottawa: Queen's Printer.

–. 1991. *Shaping Canada's Future Together.* Ottawa: Minister of Supply and Services.

–. 2004. *Implementation of the International Covenant on Economic, Social, and Cultural Rights: 4th Periodic Report to the UN under Articles 16 and 17 of the Covenant.* E/C.12/4/Add.15.

Green Party of Canada. 2006. *Election Platform 2006.* Ottawa: Green Party of Canada.

–. 2010. *Vision Green*. Ottawa: Green Party of Canada. http://greenparty.ca/files/attachments/Vision.Green_.2010.E.pdf.

Grote, R. 2008a. "The Republic of Maldives: Introductory Note." In Wolfrum and Grote 2012.

–. 2008b. "The United Mexican States: Introductory Note." In Wolfrum and Grote 2012.

Gunton, T., and K.S. Calbrick. 2010. *The Maple Leaf in the OECD: Canada's Environmental Performance*. Study prepared for the David Suzuki Foundation. Vancouver: School of Resource and Environmental Management, Simon Fraser University.

Gurzu, A. 2010. "Climate Change Criticism Reaches New Level: Leaders' Comments Show International Frustration over Canada's Position, Experts Say." *The Hill Times Online*, 19 May. http://www.hilltimes.com/.

Guzman, A.T. 2008. *How International Law Works: A Rational Choice Theory*. Oxford: Oxford University Press.

Hahn, P. 2006. "A Conversation with the Prime Minister." CTV News. 23 December. http://www.ctv.ca/CTVNews/TopStories/20061221/harper_year_end_061221/.

Hancock, J. 2003. *Environmental Human Rights: Power, Ethics, and Law*. Aldershot, UK: Ashgate.

Handl, G. 2001. "Human Rights and Protection of the Environment." In *Economic, Social and Cultural Rights: A Textbook*, ed. A. Eide, C. Krause, and A. Rosas, 303-28. 2nd ed. Dordrecht, Netherlands: Martinus Nijhoff.

Harrison, K. 1996. *Passing the Buck: Federalism and Canadian Environmental Policy*. Vancouver: UBC Press.

Haszeldine, R.S. 2009. "Carbon Capture and Storage: How Green Can Black Be?" *Science* 325, 5948: 1647-52.

Hatherly, M. 1987. "Constitutional Amendment." In *Environmental Protection and the Canadian Constitution*, ed. D. Tingley, 126-30. Edmonton: Environmental Law Centre.

Haumont, F., and J. Bodart. 2006. "Le droit a un environnement sain: Le cas de la Belgique." *Annuaire international des droits de l'homme* 1: 449-78.

Hawke, N. 2002. "Canadian Federalism and Environmental Protection." *Journal of Environmental Law* 14, 2: 185-95.

Hayward, T. 2000. "Constitutional Environmental Rights: A Case for Political Analysis." *Political Studies* 48, 3: 558-72.

–. 2005. *Constitutional Environmental Rights*. Oxford: Oxford University Press.

Hazell, R., and B. Worthy. 2010. "Assessing the Performance of Freedom of Information." *Government Information Quarterly* 27, 4: 352-59.

Hazell, S. 2010. "Improving the Effectiveness of Environmental Assessment in Addressing Federal Environmental Priorities." *Journal of Environmental Law and Practice* 20, 3: 213-32.

Health Canada. 2000. *St. Clair Area of Concern: Health Data and Statistics for Sarnia and Region (1986-1992)*. Great Lake Health Effects Program. Ottawa: Health Canada.

–. 2001. *Respiratory Disease in Canada*. Ottawa: Health Canada.

–. 2012. *First Nations, Inuit and Aboriginal Health: Drinking Water and Wastewater*. Health Canada. http://www.hc-sc.gc.ca/.

Henderson, J.S.Y. 1996. "First Nations' Legal Inheritances in Canada: The Mikmaq Model." *Manitoba Law Journal* 23, 1: 1-31.

Hersey, A. 2009. "Government, Watchdog, and Citizen Engagement: Affecting Environmental Decision Making in Ontario through the Environmental Registry and the Office of the Environmental Commissioner of Ontario." Paper presented at the 2009 Annual Meeting of the Canadian Political Science Association, Ottawa, 27 May.

Hiebert, J.L. 2010. "The Canadian Charter of Rights and Freedoms." In *The Oxford Handbook of Canadian Politics*, ed. J.C. Courtney and D.E. Smith, 54-71. New York: Oxford University Press.

Hill, B.E., S. Wolfson, and N. Targ. 2004. "Human Rights and the Environment: A Synopsis and Some Predictions." *Georgetown International Environmental Law Review* 16, 3: 359-402.

Hiskes, R.P. 2009. *The Human Right to a Green Future: Environmental Rights and Intergenerational Justice.* Cambridge: Cambridge University Press.

Hochstetler, K., and M. Keck. 2004. *From Pollution Control to Sustainable Cities: Urban Environmental Politics in Brazil.* Working Paper CBS-55-04. Oxford: Centre for Brazilian Studies, University of Oxford.

–. 2007. *Greening Brazil: Environmental Activism in State and Society.* Durham, NC: Duke University Press.

Hodgett, C.A. 1911. "The Canadian Commission of Conservation and Public Health." *Journal of the American Public Health Association* 1, 6: 400-5.

Hogg, P.W. 1999. "The Duty to Negotiate." *Canada Watch* 7, 1-2. http://www.yorku.ca/.

–. 2007. *Constitutional Law of Canada.* Toronto: Thomson.

–. 2008. *A Question of Parliamentary Power: Criminal Law and the Control of Greenhouse Gas Emissions.* Backgrounder no. 114. Toronto: C.D. Howe Institute.

Hogg, P.W., and A. Bushell. 1997. "The Charter Dialogue between Courts and Legislatures." *Osgoode Hall Law Journal* 35, 1: 75-124.

Hoggan and Associates. 2009. *Sustainability Research Initiative.* Vancouver: James Hoggan and Associates.

Hohfeld, W.N. 1923. *Fundamental Legal Concepts as Applied in Judicial Reasoning.* New Haven, CT: Yale University Press.

Holman, J., and G. Morley, eds. 1971. *The Last Bottle of Chianti and a Soft Boiled Egg.* Winnipeg: Agassiz Centre for Water Studies.

Hottelier, M., and V. Martenet. 2006. "Le droit de l'homme a un environnement sain: perspectives suisses." *Annuaire international des droits de l'homme* 1: 427-47.

Houck, O.A. 2009. "A Case of Sustainable Development: The River God and the Forest at the End of the World." *Tulsa Law Review* 44, 1: 275-316.

House of Commons Standing Committee on Environment and Sustainable Development. 1995. *It's About Our Health! Towards Pollution Prevention.* Ottawa: Government Services Canada.

Howatt, S. 2007. "A National Disgrace: Canada's Shameful Position on the Right to Water Needs to Change." *Canadian Perspectives* (Council of Canadians) (Spring): 6-7.

Howe, P., and P. Russell, eds. 2001. *Judicial Power and Canadian Democracy.* Montreal and Kingston: McGill-Queen's University Press.

Hrudey, S.E. 2008. "Safe Water? Depends on Where You Live!" *Canadian Medical Association Journal* 178, 8: 975.

Hsu, S.-L., and R. Elliot. 2009. "Regulating Greenhouse Gases in Canada: Constitutional and Policy Dimensions." *McGill Law Journal* 54, 3: 463-516.

Huffman, J.L., and M. Saathoff. 1990. "Advisory Opinions and Canadian Constitutional Development: The Supreme Court's Reference Jurisdiction." *Minnesota Law Review* 74, 6: 1251-1336.

Hughes, E. 1992. "Shaping Canada's Future Together or a Doomed Attempt to Escape from Reality." *Constitutional Forum* 3: 79-81.

Hughes, E., and D. Iyalomhe. 1999. "Substantive Environmental Rights in Canada." *Ottawa Law Review* 30, 2: 229-58.

Hunter, I. 2010. "Canada's Cowardly Vote on the Right to Water." *Victoria Times-Colonist,* 1 August.

Hurley, J.R. 1996. *Amending Canada's Constitution.* Ottawa: Minister of Supply and Services.

Ignatieff, M. 2000. *The Rights Revolution.* Toronto: House of Anansi.

–. 2001. *Human Rights as Politics and Idolatry.* Princeton, NJ: Princeton University Press.

Illical, M., and K. Harrison. 2007. "Protecting Endangered Species in the US and Canada: The Role of Negative Lesson Drawing." *Canadian Journal of Political Science* 40: 367-94.

Indian and Northern Affairs Canada. 2010. *First Nations Water and Wastewater Action Plan, Progress Report April 2009-March 2010.* Ottawa: DIAND.

Inter-American Commission on Human Rights. 1997. *Report on the Human Rights Situation in Ecuador.* OEA/Ser.L/V/II.96, ch. 9.

Inter-American Court of Human Rights. 2008. *Annual Report of the Inter-American Court of Human Rights.* San Jose, Costa Rica: IACHR.

Intergovernmental Working Group for the Elaboration of a Set of Voluntary Guidelines to Support the Progressive Realization of the Right to Adequate Food in the Context of National Food Security. 2004. *Justiciability of the Right to Food.* Rome: FAO.

International Centre of Comparative Environmental Law. 1990. *Déclaration de Limoges.* World Conference of Environmental Law Organizations. Limoges, France: ICCEL.

–. 2001. *Déclaration de Limoges II: Towards a New Environmental Law.* World Conference of Environmental Law Organizations. Limoges, France: ICCEL.

–. 2011. *Recommendations from the 3rd World Conference of Environmental Law Organizations and Lawyers.* Limoges, France: ICCEL.

Jackman, M., and B. Porter. 2008. "The Justiciability of Social and Economic Rights in Canada." In *Social Rights Jurisprudence,* ed. M. Langford, 209-29. Cambridge: Cambridge University Press.

Janis, M.W. 2003. *An Introduction to International Law.* 4th ed. New York: Aspen.

Jariwala, C.M. 2000. "The Directions of Environmental Justice: An Overview." In *Fifty Years of the Supreme Court of India: Its Grasp and Reach,* ed. S.K. Verma and K. Kusum, 469-94. New Delhi: Oxford University Press.

Jerrett, M., R. Burnett, P. Kanaroglou, J. Eyles, N. Finkelstein, C. Giovis, and J.R. Brook. 2001. "A GIS-Environmental Justice Analysis of Particulate Air Pollution in Hamilton, Canada." *Environment and Planning A* 33, 6: 955-73.

Johannesburg Principles on the Role of Law and Sustainable Development. 2003. Adopted at the Global Judges Symposium held in Johannesburg, South Africa, 18-20 August 2002. *Journal of Environmental Law* 15: 107-10.

Jorgenson, A.K., J. Rice, and J. Crowe. 2005. "Unpacking the Ecological Footprint of Nations." *International Journal of Comparative Sociology* 46: 241-60.

Karakostas, I., and I. Vassilopoulos. 1999. *Environmental Law in Greece.* The Hague: Kluwer Law International.

Kelly, J.B. 2006. *Governing with the Charter: Legislative and Judicial Activism and Framers' Intent.* Vancouver: UBC Press.

Kelly, J.B., and C.P. Manfredi, eds. 2009a. *Contested Constitutionalism: Reflections on the Canadian Charter of Rights and Freedoms.* Vancouver: UBC Press.

–. 2009b. "Should We Cheer? Contested Constitutionalism and the *Canadian Charter of Rights and Freedoms.*" In Kelly and Manfredi 2009a, 3-29.

Kennedy, R.F. 1967. *To Seek a Newer World.* New York: Doubleday.

Kennedy, R.F., Jr. 2004. *Crimes against Nature.* New York: HarperCollins.

Kindred, H.M., and P.M. Saunders, eds. 2006. *International Law Chiefly as Applied and Interpreted in Canada.* 7th ed. Toronto: Emond Montgomery.

Kinney, E.D., and B.A. Clark. 2004. "Provisions for Health and Health Care in the Constitutions of the Countries of the World." *Cornell International Law Journal* 37, 2: 285-355.

Kiss, A. 1993. "Concept and Possible Implications of the Right to Environment." In *Human Rights in the Twenty-First Century: A Global Challenge,* ed. K.E. Mahoney and P. Mahoney, 551-59. Dordrecht, Netherlands: Martinus Nijhoff.

Kiss, A., and D. Shelton. 2004. *International Environmental Law.* 3rd ed. Ardsley, NY: Transnational.

Kluger, R. 1976. *Simple Justice: The History of Brown v. Board of Education.* New York: Vintage.

Koivurova, T. 2004. "The Case of Vuotos: Interplay between International, Community, and National Law." *Review of European Community and International Environmental Law* 13, 1: 47-60.

Kotze, L.J., and A.R. Paterson, eds. 2009. *The Role of the Judiciary in Environmental Governance: Comparative Perspectives.* The Hague: Kluwer Law International.

Kravchenko, S. 2002. "New Laws on Public Participation in the Newly Independent States." In Zillman, Lucas, and Pring 2002, 467-503.

Kravchenko, S., and J.E. Bonine. 2008. *Human Rights and the Environment: Cases, Law, and Policy.* Durham, NC: Carolina Academic Press.

Krishnan, J.K. 2008. "Scholarly Discourse, Public Perceptions and the Cementing of Norms: The Case of the Indian Supreme Court and a Plea for Research." *Journal of Appellate Process and Practice* 9, 2: 255-90.

Ksentini, F.Z. 1994. *Review of Further Developments in Fields with Which the Sub-Commission Has Been Concerned: Human Rights and the Environment; Final Report of the UN Sub-Commission on Prevention of Discrimination and Protection of Minorities.* UN Doc. E/CN.4/Sub.2/1994/9. 6 July.

Lake Ontario Waterkeeper. 2009. "Navigable Waters Protection Act Amendments: Comparison Document." Prepared by Lake Ontario Waterkeeper. 11 February. http://www.waterkeeper.ca/documents/2009-02-11.NWPASummary.pdf.

Lasser, M. de S.-O.-l'E. 2009. *Judicial Transformations: The Rights Revolution in the Courts of Europe.* Oxford: Oxford University Press.

Lavrysen, L. 2007. "Presentation of Aarhus-Related Cases of the Belgian Constitutional Court." *Environmental Law Network International Review* 2: 5-8.

–. 2009. "Belgium." In Kotze and Paterson 2009, 85-122.

Law, D.S., and M. Versteeg. 2011. "The Evolution and Ideology of Global Constitutionalism." *California Law Review* 99, 5: 1163-1257.

–. 2012. "The Declining Influence of the United States Constitution." *New York University Law Review* 87, 3: 762-858.

Law Commission of Canada. 2006. *Justice Within: Indigenous Legal Traditions.* Ottawa: Law Commission of Canada.

Law Reform Commission. 1985. *Crimes against the Environment.* Working Paper no. 44. Ottawa: Law Reform Commission.

Lazarus, R. 2004. *The Making of Environmental Law.* Chicago: University of Chicago Press.

L'Heureux-Dubé, C. 2000. "The Legacy of the 'Persons Case': Cultivating the Living Tree's Equality Leaves." *Saskatchewan Law Review* 63, 2: 389-402.

–. 2002. "It Takes a Vision: The Constitutionalization of Equality in Canada." *Yale Journal of Law and Feminism* 14, 2: 363-76.

Liberal Party of Canada. 1993. *Creating Opportunity: The Liberal Plan for Canada.* Ottawa: Liberal Party of Canada.

Limon, M. 2009. "Human Rights and Climate Change: Constructing a Case for Political Survival." *Harvard Environmental Law Review* 33, 2: 439-76.

Lindgren, R.D. 2004. *The Environmental Bill of Rights Turns Ten Years-Old: Congratulations or Condolences?* Toronto: Canadian Environmental Law Association.

Livingston, J. 1984. "Rightness or Rights?" *Osgoode Hall Law Journal* 22, 2: 309-21.

Lucas, A.R. 1987. "Natural Resource and Environmental Management: A Jurisdictional Primer." In *Environmental Protection and the Canadian Constitution,* ed. D. Tingley, 31-43. Edmonton: Environmental Law Centre.

–. 2004. "Legal Constraints and Opportunities: Climate Change and the Law." In *Hard Choices: Climate Change in Canada,* ed. H. Coward and A.J. Weaver, 179-98. Waterloo: Wilfrid Laurier University Press.

Lukasik, L., D. McRobert, and L. Shultz. 2006. "Public Participation Rights, Environmental Policy Struggles & E-Democracy: Lessons Learned during the First 11 Years of Ontario's Environmental Bill of Rights." Paper presented to the International Association of Public Participation Practitioners Conference, Montreal, 10-15 November.

MacDonald, E., and S. Rang. 2007. *Exposing Canada's Chemical Valley: An Investigation of Cumulative Air Pollution Emissions in the Sarnia, Ontario Area.* Toronto: Ecojustice.

Mackenzie, C.A., A. Lockridge, and M. Keith. 2005. "Declining Sex Ratio in a First Nations Community." *Environmental Health Perspectives* 113, 10: 1295-98.

MacLaren, J.P.S. 1984. "Tribulations of Antoine Ratte: A Case Study of the Environmental Regulation of the Canadian Lumbering Industry in the Nineteenth Century." *UNB Law Journal* 33: 203-60.

MacNeill, J.W. 1971. *Environmental Management.* Ottawa: Information Canada.

Macrory, R., ed. 2004. *Principles of European Environmental Law: Proceedings of the Avosetta Group of European Environmental Lawyers.* Amsterdam: Europa Law.

Mahoney, K. 1982. "The Constitutional Law of Equality in Canada." *Maine Law Review* 44, 2: 229-60.

Mains, G. 1980. "Some Environmental Aspects of a Canadian Constitution." *Alternatives* 9, 2: 14-18.

Majtenyi, B. 2006. "The Institutional System of Hungarian Environmental Law." *Gazzetta Ambiente* 5: 149-54.

Malone, L.A., and S. Pasternack. 2006. *Defending the Environment: Civil Society Strategies to Enforce International Environmental Law.* 2nd ed. Washington, DC: Island Press.

Mandela, N. 2002. "No Water, No Future." Speech at the World Summit on Sustainable Development, Johannesburg, 28 August.

Manfredi, C., and A. Maioni. 2009. "Judicializing Health Policy: Unexpected Lessons and an Inconvenient Truth." In Kelly and Manfredi 2009a, 129-44.

Manfredi, C.P. 2002. "Strategic Behaviour and the Canadian Charter of Rights and Freedoms." In *The Myth of the Sacred: The Charter, the Courts and the Politics of the Constitution in Canada,* ed. P. James, D. Abelson, and M. Lusztig, 147-67. Montreal and Kingston: McGill-Queen's University Press.

Mark, J. 2012. "Natural Law." *Earth Island Journal* 27, 1: 40-46.

Marrani, D. 2008. "The Second Anniversary of the Constitutionalisation of the French Charter for the Environment: Constitutional and Environmental Implications." *Environmental Law Review* 10, 1: 9-27.

–. 2009. "Human Rights and Environmental Protection: The Pressure of the Charter for the Environment on French Administrative Courts." *Sustainable Development Law and Policy* 10, 1: 52-57.

Martin, P. 1992. *The Environment: A Liberal Vision.* Ottawa: Liberal Party of Canada.

Matanza-Riachuelo Watershed Authority (Autoridad de Cuenca Matanza Riachuelo). 2011. *Plan Integral de Saneamiento Ambiental.* Buenos Aires: ACUMAR. http://www.acumar.gov.ar/.

Mathen, C. 2011. "'The question calls for an answer and I propose to answer it': The *Patriation Reference* as Constitutional Method." *Supreme Court Law Review,* 2nd ser., 54: 143-66.

May, J.R. 2006. "Constituting Fundamental Environmental Rights Worldwide." *Pace Environmental Law Review* 23, 1: 113-82.

May, J.R., and E. Daly. 2009. "Violating Fundamental Environmental Rights Worldwide." *Oregon Review of International Law* 11, 2: 365-439.

Mayeda, A. 2010. "Drilling Oil-Spill Relief Well off Canada's Arctic Coast Would Take Three Years: Regulators." *Postmedia News,* 1 August.

McAllister, A. 2010a. *A Backyard Field Guide to Canadians.* Vancouver: McAllister Opinion Research.

–. 2010b. *Global Thought Leader Survey.* Vancouver: McAllister Opinion Research.

McAllister, L.K. 2005. "Public Prosecutors and Environmental Protection in Brazil." In *Environmental Issues in Latin America and the Caribbean,* ed. A. Romero and S. West, 207-29. New York: Springer.

–. 2008. *Making Law Matter: Environmental Protection and Legal Institutions in Brazil.* Stanford, CA: Stanford University Press.

McDonald, L. 2008. "Constitutional Change to Address Climate Change and Non-renewable Energy Use." *Constitutional Forum* 17, 3: 113-21.

McKenzie, J. 2002. *Environmental Politics in Canada: Managing the Commons into the Twenty-First Century.* Don Mills: Oxford University Press.

McMillan, T. 1986. *The Right to a Healthy Environment: An Overview of the Proposed Environmental Protection Act.* Ottawa: Environment Canada.

Meakin, S. 1992. *The Rio Earth Summit: Summary of the United Nations Conference on Environment and Development.* Document BP-317E. Ottawa: Depository Services Program, Government of Canada. http://publications.gc.ca/.

Mehta, M.C. 1997. "Making the Law Work for the Environment." *Asia Pacific Journal of Environmental Law* 2, 4: 349-59.

Mendelsohn, M. 2004. "Birth of a New Ethnicity." In *The New Canada: A Globe and Mail Report on the Next Generation,* ed. E. Anderssen and M. Valpy, 59-65. Toronto: McClelland and Stewart.

Michaels, D. 2008. *Doubt Is Their Product: How Industry's Assault on Science Threatens Your Health.* Oxford: Oxford University Press.

Miller, C. 1998. *Environmental Rights: Critical Perspectives.* London: Routledge.

Mittelstaedt, M. 2008. "Oil Refineries Drastically Underestimate Release of Emissions, Study Says." *Toronto Globe and Mail,* 6 September.

Molgat, G.L., and M. MacGuigan. 1972. *Final Report of the Special Joint Committee of the Senate and the House of Commons on the Constitution of Canada.* Ottawa: Queen's Printer.

Monahan, P.J. 2006. *Constitutional Law.* 3rd ed. Toronto: Irwin Law.

Montreal (City of). 2005. *Montreal Charter of Rights and Responsibilities.* http://ville.montreal.qc.ca/.

Morton, F.L., and R. Knopff. 2000. *The Charter Revolution and the Court Party.* Peterborough: Broadview Press.

Mosquin, T. 2000. "Status and Trends in Canadian Biodiversity." In *Biodiversity in Canada: Ecology, Ideas, and Action,* ed. Stephen Bocking, 59-80. Peterborough: Broadview Press.

Muldoon, P. 1988. "The Fight for an Environmental Bill of Rights." *Alternatives* 15, 2: 33-39.

–. 1991. *Environment and the Constitution: Submission to the Standing Committee on the Environment.* Toronto: Canadian Environmental Law Association.

Muldoon, P., and R. Lindgren. 1995. *The Environmental Bill of Rights: A Practical Guide.* Toronto: Emond Montgomery.

Muldoon, P., A. Lucas, R.B. Gibson, and P. Pickfield. 2009. *An Introduction to Environmental Law and Policy in Canada.* Toronto: Emond Montgomery.

Muldoon, P., and M. Valiante. 1991. *Environmental Rights and the Constitution: Toward an Environmental Democracy.* Toronto: Pollution Probe.

Mulvihill, P. 1988. "Would Constitutional Property Rights Inhibit Environmental Protection?" *Alternatives* 15, 2: 5-8.

Murray, T.A. 1912. *The Prevention of the Pollution of Canada's Surface Waters.* Ottawa: Canada's Commission of Conservation.

Nanda, V.P., and G. Pring. 2003. *International Environmental Law and Policy for the 21st Century.* Ardsley, NY: Transnational.

Nanos, N. 2007. "Charter Values Don't Equal Canadian Values: Strong Support for Same-Sex Marriage and Property Rights." *Policy Options* 28, 1 (February): 50-55.

–. 2009. "Canadians Overwhelmingly Choose Water as Our Most Important Natural Resource." *Policy Options* 30, 7 (July-August): 12-15.

Narain, V. 2010. "Water as a Fundamental Right: The Perspective from India." *Vermont Law Review* 34, 4: 917-26.

Nash, R.F. 1989. *The Rights of Nature: A History of Environmental Ethics.* Madison: University of Wisconsin Press.

Nedelsky, J. 2008. "Reconceiving Rights and Constitutionalism." *Journal of Human Rights* 7: 139-73.

New Democratic Party of Canada. 2010. "Our Vision for Canada: Building a Clean and Sustainable Economy." Ottawa: NDP.

Newman, W.J. 2007. "Living with the Amending Procedures: Prospects for Future Constitutional Reform in Canada." In *A Living Tree: The Legacy of 1982 in Canada's Political Evolution,* ed. G. Mitchell, Z. Peach, D.E. Smith, and J.D. Whyte, 747-80. Markham: LexisNexis Canada and Saskatchewan Institute of Public Policy.

Nimushakavi, V. 2006. *Constitutional Policy and Environmental Jurisprudence in India.* New Delhi: Macmillan India.

No author. 1961. "Administrative and Jurisdictional Factors: Plenary Session." In *Resources for Tomorrow: Proceedings of the Conference.* Vol. 3. Ottawa: Queen's Printer.

No author. 1992. *Consensus Report on the Constitution (Charlottetown Accord).* Ottawa: Supply and Services Canada.

Northern Ireland Human Rights Commission. 2008. *Advice on a Bill of Rights for Northern Ireland.* Belfast: NIHRC.

Ollivier, C. 2001. "French President Issues Strong Call to Protect the Environment." Associated Press, 3 May.

–. 2003. "French Cabinet Approves Plan for a New Environmental *Charter*." Associated Press, 26 June.

Olowu, D. 2006. "Human Rights and the Avoidance of Domestic Implementation: The Phenomenon of Non-Justiciable Constitutional Guarantees." *Saskatchewan Law Review* 69: 39-78.

Ontario Ministry of the Attorney General, Constitutional Law and Policy Division. 1991. *The Protection of Social and Economic Rights: A Comparative Study.* Toronto: Government of Ontario.

Organisation for Economic Co-operation and Development. 2001. *Environmental Performance Review: Portugal.* Paris: OECD.

–. 2004a. *Environmental Performance Review: Canada.* Paris: OECD.

–. 2004b. *Environmental Performance Review: Spain.* Paris: OECD.

–. 2005. *Environmental Performance Review: France.* Paris: OECD.

–. 2007. *Environmental Data Compendium.* Paris: OECD.

–. 2010. *Taxation, Innovation and the Environment.* Paris: OECD.

Organization of the Islamic Conference. 1990. *Cairo Declaration on Human Rights in Islam.* UN Doc. A/45/421-S/21797, 200; A/CONF.157/PC/35; A/CONF.157/PC/62/ Add. 18, 2. 5 August 1990.

Pallemaerts, M. 1994. "International Environmental Law from Stockholm to Rio: Back to the Future?" In *Greening International Law,* ed. P. Sands, 1-19. London: Earthscan.

–. 2002. "The Human Right to the Environment as a Substantive Right." In Dejeant-Pons and Pallemaerts 2002, 11-21.

Passos de Freitas, V. 2003. "The Importance of Environmental Judicial Decisions: The Brazilian Experience." In Di Paola 2003, 59-64.

Peterson, H., and M. Torchia. 2008. "Safe Drinking Water for Rural Canadians," *Canadian Medical Association Journal* 179, 1: 55.

Petter, A. 2009. "Legalise This: The Chartering of Canadian Politics." In Kelly and Manfredi 2009a, 33-49.

Pevato, P.M. 1999. "A Right to Environment in International Law: Current Status and Future Outlook." *Review of European Community and International Environmental Law* 8, 3: 309-21.

Picolotti, R. 2005. "The Right to Safe Drinking Water as a Human Right." *Housing and ESC Rights Quarterly* 2, 1: 1-5.

Polaris Institute with the Assembly of First Nations and the Canadian Labour Congress. 2008. *Boiling Point: Six Community Profiles of the Water Crisis Facing First Nations within Canada.* Ottawa: Polaris Institute.

Porter, M.E., and C. van der Linde. 1995. "Green and Competitive: Ending the Stalemate." *Harvard Business Review* 73, 5: 120-34.

Pound, R. 1917. "The Limits of Effective Legal Action." *International Journal of Ethics* 27: 150-67.

Prieur, M. 2008. "La Charte de l'environnement: droit dur ou gadget politique?" *Pouvoirs* 127, 4: 49-65.

–. 2011. "De l'urgente nécessité de reconnaître le principe de non régression en droit de l'environnement." *IUCN Academy of Environmental Law E-Journal* 1: 26 40. http://www.iucnael.org/.

Provost, R. 2008. "Judging in Splendid Isolation." *American Journal of Comparative Law* 56: 125-72.

Raffan, J. 1998. "A Child of Nature: Trudeau and the Canoe." In *Trudeau's Shadow: The Life and Legacy of Pierre Elliott Trudeau,* ed. A. Cohen and J.L. Granatstein, 63-78. Toronto: Vintage Canada.

Ramcharan, B.G. 2005. *Judicial Protection of Economic, Social, and Cultural Rights: Cases and Materials.* Boston: Martinus Nijhoff.

Raz, J. 1986. *The Morality of Freedom.* Oxford: Clarendon Press.

Redgwell, C. 1996. "Life, the Universe and Everything: A Critique of Anthropocentric Rights." In Boyle and Anderson 1996, 71-87.

Reeves, F. 2010. "Healthy Hearts Need Clean Air." Docs Talk blog, 2 June. http://www.davidsuzuki.org/blogs/docs-talk/.

Rishmawi, M. 2010. "The Arab Charter on Human Rights and the League of Arab States: An Update." *Human Rights Law Review* 10, 1: 169-78.

Roach, K. 2001. *The Supreme Court on Trial: Judicial Activism or Democratic Dialogue?* Toronto: Irwin Law.

Roberts, A.E. 2001. "Traditional and Modern Approaches to Customary International Law: A Reconciliation." *American Journal of International Law* 95, 4: 757-91.

Robertson, A.H., and J.G. Merrills. 1989. *Human Rights in the World: An Introduction to the Study of the International Protection of Human Rights.* 3rd ed. New York: Manchester University Press.

Romanow, R. 2007. *Canada Notwithstanding: The Making of the Constitution, 1976-1982.* Toronto: Thomson Carswell.

Rosenberg, G. 1991. *The Hollow Hope: Can Courts Bring About Social Change?* Chicago: University of Chicago Press.

Ruhl, J.B. 1997. "An Environmental Rights Amendment: Good Message, Bad Idea." *Natural Resources and Environment* 11, 3: 46-49.

–. 1999. "The Metrics of Constitutional Amendments: And Why Proposed Constitutional Amendments Don't Add Up." *Notre Dame Law Review* 74, 2: 245-82.

Russell, P.H. 2004. *Constitutional Odyssey: Can Canadians Become a Sovereign People?* Toronto: University of Toronto Press.

Rutherford, B. 1991. "The Environment and the Constitution." *Intervenor: The Newsletter of the Canadian Environmental Law Association* 16, 6: 1-3.

–. 1992. "The Beaudoin-Dobbie Committee Did Not Get the Environmental Message." *Intervenor: The Newsletter of the Canadian Environmental Law Association* 17, 2: 4.

Rutherford, B., and P. Muldoon. 1991. *Environment and the Constitution: Submission to the House of Commons Standing Committee on Environment.* Toronto: Canadian Environmental Law Association and Pollution Probe.

–. 1992. "Designing an Environmentally Responsible Constitution." *Alternatives* 18, 4: 26-33.

Sabsay, D.A. 2003. "Constitution and Environment in Relation to Sustainable Development." In Di Paola 2003, 33-43.

–. n.d. *Citizen Advocacy and Government Reform Achieved through Work for the Environment in Argentina.* Buenos Aires: Foundation for the Environment and Natural Resources (FARN).

Sandel, M.J. 1982. *Liberalism and the Limits of Justice.* Cambridge: Cambridge University Press.

Sands, P. 1996. "Human Rights, Environment, and the Lopez-Ostra Case: Content and Consequences." *European Human Rights Law Review* 6: 608-11.

Sarlet, I., and T. Fensterseifer. 2009. "Brazil." In Kotze and Paterson 2009, 249-68.

Sax, J. 1971. *Defending the Environment: A Strategy for Citizen Action.* New York: Knopf.

Saxe, D. 1990. *Environmental Offences: Corporate Responsibility and Executive Liability.* Aurora, ON: Canada Law Book.

–. 2010. "Federal Environmental Assessment Shrinks." Environmental Law and Litigation blog, 5 April. http://envirolaw.com/.

Schall, C. 2008. "Public Interest Litigation concerning Environmental Matters before Human Rights Courts: A Promising Future Concept?" *Journal of Environmental Law* 20, 3: 417-53.

Scheingold, S. 1974. *The Politics of Rights: Lawyers, Public Policy, and Political Change.* New Haven, CT: Yale University Press.

–. 1989. "Constitutional Rights and Social Change: Civil Rights in Perspective." In *Judging the Constitution: Critical Essays on Judicial Law-Making,* ed. M.W. McCann and G.L. Houseman, 73-91. Glenview, IL: Scott, Foresman.

Schrijver, N.J., and F. Weiss. 1995. *Report of the Expert Group on Identification of Principles of International Law for Sustainable Development.* London: International Law Association.

Schwartz, H. 1992. "In Defence of Aiming High: Why Economic and Social Rights Belong in the New Constitutions of Post-Communist Europe." *Eastern European Constitutional Review* 1, 3: 25-28.

Scott, D.N. 2008. "Confronting Chronic Pollution: A Socio-Legal Analysis of Risk and Precaution." *Osgoode Hall Law Journal* 46, 2: 293-344.

Scott, I.K. 2000. "The Inter-American System of Human Rights: An Effective Means of Environmental Protection?" *Virginia Environmental Law Journal* 19: 197-237.

Senate Committee on Energy, the Environment, and Natural Resources. 2009. "Report Addressing Bill C-10, Navigable Waters Protection Act." Ninth Report of the Standing Senate Committee on Energy, the Environment, and Natural Resources.

Sharma, R. 2005. "Judicial Environmental Activism: Lessons from India." *International Environmental Law Newsletter* (American Bar Association Section of Energy, Environment and Natural Resources) 7, 2: 8-13.

–. 2008. "Green Courts in India: Strengthening Environmental Governance." *Law, Environment and Development Journal* 4, 1: 50-71.

Sharpe, R., and K. Roach. 2009. *The Charter of Rights and Freedoms.* Toronto: Irwin Law.

Shelton, D. 2001. "Environmental Rights." In *Peoples' Rights,* ed. P. Alston, 185-258. Oxford: Oxford University Press.

–. 2004a. "Human Rights and the Environment." *Yearbook of International Environmental Law (2002)* 13: 199-206.

–. 2004b. "The Links between International Human Rights Guarantees and Environmental Protection." Unpublished paper, University of Chicago. On file with author.

–. 2008. *Regional Protection of Human Rights.* New York: Oxford University Press.

Shemshuchenko, Y. 1995. "Human Rights in the Field of Environmental Protection in the Draft of the New Constitution of the Ukraine." In *Environmental Rights: Law, Litigation and Access to Justice,* ed. S. Deimann and B. Dyssli, 33-40. London: Cameron May.

Shue, H. 1996. *Basic Rights: Subsistence, Affluence, and US Foreign Policy.* 2nd ed. Princeton, NJ: Princeton University Press.

Sieder, R., L. Schjolden, and A. Angell, eds. 2005. *The Judicialization of Politics in Latin America.* New York: Palgrave Macmillan.

Simon Fraser University Sustainable Planning Research Group, School of Resource and Environmental Management. 2005. *Canada's Environmental Record: An Assessment.* Vancouver: Simon Fraser University.

Simpson, J., M. Jaccard, and N. Rivers. 2007. *Hot Air: Meeting Canada's Climate Change Challenge.* Toronto: McClelland and Stewart.

Sioutis, G. 2006. "Protection de l'environnement et protection de la propriété dans la jurisprudence du Conseil d'État hellenique." *Annuaire international des droits de l'homme* 1: 495-529.

Slaughter, A.-M. 1994. "A Typology of Transjudicial Communication." *University of Richmond Law Review* 29, 1: 99-137.

Smets, H. 2006. *The Right to Water in National Legislations.* Paris: Agence Française de Développement.

Sohn, L.B. 1973. "The Stockholm Declaration on the Human Environment." *Harvard International Law Journal* 14, 3: 423-515.

Soveroski, M. 2007. "Environment Rights versus Environmental Wrongs: Forum over Substance?" *Review of European Community and International Environmental Law* 16, 3: 261-73.

Statistics Canada. 2011a. *Human Activity and the Environment: Detailed Statistics.* Ottawa: Minister of Industry.

–. 2011b. "Population by Year, by Province and Territory." http://www40.statcan.ca/.

Staveland-Saeter, K.I. 2011. *Litigating the Right to a Healthy Environment: Assessing the Policy Impact of the Mendoza Case.* Bergen, Norway: Chr. Michelson Institute.

Stec, S. 2003. *Handbook on Access to Justice under the Aarhus Convention.* Szentendre, Hungary: Regional Environmental Center for Central and Eastern Europe.

–. 2009. "Environmental Justice through Courts in Countries in Economic Transition." In *Environmental Law and Justice in Context,* ed. J. Ebbesson and P. Okowa, 158-75. Cambridge: Cambridge University Press.

Stein, M.B. 1997. "Improving the Process of Constitutional Reform in Canada: Lessons from the Meech Lake and Charlottetown Constitutional Rounds." *Canadian Journal of Political Science* 30, 2: 307-38.

Stephens, T. 2009. *International Courts and Environmental Protection.* Cambridge: Cambridge University Press.

Stevenson, C.P. 1983. "A New Perspective on Environmental Rights after the Charter." *Osgoode Hall Law Journal* 21, 3: 390-421.

Stevenson, G. 2007. "Twenty-Five Years of Constitutional Frustration: The Amending Formula and the Continuing Legacy of 1992." In *A Living Tree: The Legacy of 1982 in Canada's Political Evolution,* ed. G. Mitchell, Z. Peach, D.E. Smith, and J.D. Whyte, 681-705. Markham: LexisNexis Canada and Saskatchewan Institute of Public Policy.

Stone, C.D. 1972. "Should Trees Have Standing? Toward Legal Rights for Natural Objects." *Southern California Law Review* 45, 2: 450-501.

Strayer, B. 1983. *The Canadian Constitution and the Courts.* Toronto: Butterworths.

Sullivan, R. 1994. *Driedger on the Construction of Statutes.* 3rd ed. Toronto: Butterworths.

Sunstein, C. 1993. "Against Positive Rights." *East European Constitutional Review* 2: 35-38.

–. 1999. *Standing for Animals.* Public Law and Legal Theory Working Paper no. 06. Chicago: University of Chicago Law School.

–. 2001. *Designing Democracy: What Institutions Do.* Oxford: Oxford University Press.

Supreme Court of the Philippines. 2010. *Resolution A.M. No. 09-6-8-SC, Rules of Procedure for Environmental Cases.* Manila.

Swaigen, J., ed. 1981. *Environmental Rights in Canada.* Toronto: Butterworths.

–. 2006. "How About a Constitutional Right to a Healthy Environment." *Toronto Globe and Mail,* 16 January.

Swaigen, J., and R.E. Woods. 1981. "A Substantive Right to Environmental Quality." In Swaigen 1981, 195-241.

Swartz, T., and A. Heard. 1997. "The Regional Veto Formula and Its Effects on Canada's Constitutional Amending Process." *Canadian Journal of Political Science* 30, 2: 339-56.

Taillant, J.D. 2003. "Environmental Advocacy and the Inter-American Human Rights System." In *Linking Human Rights and the Environment,* ed. R. Picolotti and J.D. Taillant, 118-61. Tucson: University of Arizona Press.

Takahashi, K. 2002. "Why Do We Study Constitutional Laws of Foreign Countries, and How?" In *Defining the Field of Comparative Constitutional Law,* ed. V.C. Jackson and M. Tushnet, 35-59. Westport, CT: Praeger.

Thériault, S., and D. Robitaille. 2011. "Les droits environnementaux dans la *Charte des droits et libertés de la personne* du Québec: Pistes de réflexion." *McGill Law Journal* 57, 2: 211-65.

Thompson, E. 2010. "Canadians Down on Multiculturalism: Poll." *Toronto Sun,* 1 February. http://www.torontosun.com/.

Toebes, B.C.A. 1999. *The Right to Health as a Human Right in International Law.* Oxford: Intersentia.

Tribe, L.H. 1974. "Ways Not to Think About Plastic Trees: New Foundations for Environmental Law." *Yale Law Journal* 83: 1315-48.

Trilsch, M. 2009. "European Committee of Social Rights: The Right to a Healthy Environment." *International Journal of Constitutional Law* 7, 3: 529-38.

Trudeau, P.E. 1961. "Administrative and Jurisdictional Factors: Plenary Session." *Resources for Tomorrow: Proceedings of the Conference.* Vol. 3, 44-45. Ottawa: Queen's Printer.

–. 1961-62. "Economic Rights." *McGill Law Journal* 8, 2: 122 25.

–. 1968. *A Canadian Charter of Human Rights.* Ottawa: Queen's Printer.

–. 1970. "Opening Statement of the Prime Minister." Constitutional Conference, Second Working Session. On file with author.

–. 1978. *A Time for Action: Toward the Renewal of the Canadian Federation.* Ottawa: Government of Canada.

–. 1993. *Memoirs.* Toronto: McClelland and Stewart.

–. 1996. *Against the Current: Selected Writings 1939-1996,* edited by G. Pelletier. Toronto: McClelland and Stewart.

Turner, S.J. 2009. *A Substantive Environmental Right: An Examination of the Legal Obligations of Decision-Makers towards the Environment.* New York: Kluwer Law.

Tushnet, M. 2002. "State Action, Social Welfare Rights, and the Judicial Role: Some Comparative Observations." *Chicago Journal of International Law* 3, 2: 435-53.

UK Joint Committee on Human Rights. 2008. *A Bill of Rights for the UK.* House of Lords Paper 165-I. London: House of Lords.

UN Committee on Economic, Social and Cultural Rights. 2000. *General Comment No. 14. Substantive Issues Arising in the Implementation of the International Covenant on Economic, Social and Cultural Rights: The Right to the Highest Attainable Standard of Health.* UN Doc. E/C.12/2000/4. 11 August.

UN Economic Commission for Latin America and the Caribbean. 2002. *The Sustainability of Development in Latin America and the Caribbean: Challenges and Opportunities.* Santiago, Chile: United Nations.

UN Educational, Scientific and Cultural Organization and the UN High Commissioner for Human Rights. 1999. *Bizkaia Declaration on the Right to Environment.* Issued at the International Seminar of Experts on the Right to the Environment. UN Doc. 30C/INF.11. 24 September.

UN High Commissioner for Human Rights and UN Environment Programme. 2002. "Meeting of Experts on Human Rights and the Environment, Final Text." 16 January. http://www2.ohchr.org/.

–. 2009. "Outcome Document of the High Level Expert Meeting on the New Future of Human Rights and Environment: An Agenda for Moving Forward." Nairobi, 1 December. http://www.unep.org/.

US Department of State. 2009. *Report on International Religious Freedom – Maldives.* Washington, DC: Department of State.

US Environmental Protection Agency (Office of Enforcement and Compliance Assurance). 2011. *Fiscal Year 2010 Accomplishments Report: Protecting Public Health and the Environment.* Washington, DC: EPA.

Velasco, P.B., Jr. 2009. "Manila Bay: A Daunting Challenge in Environmental Rehabilitation and Restoration." Paper prepared for "Forum on Environmental Justice: Upholding the Right to a Balanced and Healthful Ecology, Supreme Court of the Philippines," Baguio City, 16-17 April.

Veugelers, P.J., and J.R. Read. 1999. "Health Deficiencies in Cape Breton County, Nova Scotia, Canada, 1950-1995." *Epidemiology* 10, 5: 495-99.

Vieira, S.C. 2008. "Country Report: Brazil." *Yearbook of International Environmental Law (2007)* 18: 395-402.

Vigod, T., and J. Swaigen. 1978. *Brief to the Joint Senate/House of Commons Committee on the Constitution of Canada.* Toronto: Canadian Environmental Law Association.

Vlavianos, N. 2006. *The Potential Application of Human Rights Law to Oil and Gas Development in Alberta: A Synopsis.* Calgary: Alberta Civil Liberties Research Centre and Canadian Institute of Resources Law.

–. 2008. "The Applicability of S. 7 of the *Charter* to Oil and Gas Development in Alberta." *Constitutional Forum* 17, 3: 123-27.

Wackernagel, M., and W.E. Rees. 1996. *Our Ecological Footprint: Reducing Human Impact on the Earth.* Gabriola Island, BC: New Society.

Wackernagel, M., et al. 2002. "Tracking the Ecological Overshoot of the Human Economy." *Proceedings of the National Academy of Sciences USA* 99, 14: 9266-71.

Waldron, J. 1993. "A Rights-Based Critique of Constitutional Rights." *Oxford Journal of Legal Studies* 13: 18-51.

–. 1999. *Law and Disagreement.* Oxford: Oxford University Press.

–. 2006. "The Core of the Case against Judicial Review." *Yale Law Journal* 115: 1346-1406.

Walsh, J.R. 2007. "Argentina's Constitution and General Environmental Law as the Framework for Comprehensive Land Use Regulation." In Chalifour, Kameri-Mbote, Lye, and Nolon 2007, 503-25.

Walters, M. 1991. "Ecological Unity and Political Fragmentation: The Implications of the Brundtland Report for the Canadian Constitutional Order." *Alberta Law Review* 29, 2: 420-49.

Wates, J. 1996. "ECO Report from 2nd Negotiating Session." *Proposed UN ECE Convention on Access to Environmental Information and Public Participation in Environmental Decision-Making.* http://www.participate.org/archive/.

Watts, R. 1996. *Comparing Federal Systems in the 1990s.* Kingston: Queen's University Institute of Intergovernmental Relations.

Webber, J. 1994. *Reimagining Canada: Language, Culture, Community and the Canadian Constitution.* Montreal and Kingston: McGill-Queen's University Press.

Weibust, I. 2009. *Green Leviathan: The Case for a Federal Role in Environmental Policy.* Burlington, VT: Ashgate.

Weinrib, L.E. 1998. "Trudeau and the Canadian Charter of Rights and Freedoms: A Question of Constitutional Maturation." In *Trudeau's Shadow: The Life and Legacy of Pierre Elliott Trudeau,* ed. A. Cohen and J.L. Granatstein, 257-82. Toronto: Vintage Canada.

Weiss, E.B. 1989. *In Fairness to Future Generations: International Law, Common Patrimony, and Intergenerational Equity.* Tokyo: UN University Press.

Weissbrodt, D., and C. de la Vega. 2007. *International Human Rights Law: An Introduction.* Philadelphia: University of Pennsylvania Press.

Williams, C. 1985. "The Changing Nature of Citizen Rights." In *Constitutionalism, Citizenship and Society in Canada,* ed. A. Cairns and C. Williams, 99-132. Toronto: University of Toronto Press.

Wilson, J., P. Tyedmers, and R. Pelot. 2007. "Contrasting and Comparing Sustainable Development Indicator Metrics." *Ecological Indicators* 7, 2: 299-314.

Winfield, M., G. Ford, and G. Crann. 1995. *Achieving the Holy Grail? A Legal and Political Analysis of Ontario's Environmental Bill of Rights.* Toronto: Canadian Institute for Environmental Law and Policy.

Wolfrum, R., and R. Grote, eds. 2012. *Constitutions of the Countries of the World.* 20 vols. New York: Oceana Law.

Wood, S., G. Tanner, and B.J. Richardson. 2010. "What Ever Happened to Canadian Environmental Law?" *Ecology Law Quarterly* 37: 981-1040.

World Bank. 2009. *Project Appraisal Document on a Proposed Adaptable Loan Program in the Amount of $US840 Million to the Argentine Republic for the Matanza-Riachuelo Basin Sustainable Development Project, Phase 1.* Report no. 48443-AR. Washington, DC: World Bank.

World Commission on Environment and Development. 1987. *Our Common Future.* Oxford: Oxford University Press.

World Health Organization. 2008. *National Estimates of Environmental Burden of Disease – Canada.* Geneva: World Health Organization.

–. 2011. "Database: Outdoor Air Pollution in Cities." http://www.who.int/.
World Health Organization and UNICEF. 2010. Joint Monitoring Programme for Water Supply and Sanitation. "Estimates for the Use of Improved Drinking-Water Sources: Uruguay." http://www.wssinfo.org.
World Values Survey. 2010. World Values Survey, 2005-2008 (Fifth Wave). http://www.wvsevsdb.com.
World Wildlife Fund, Zoological Society of London, and Global Footprint Network. 2010. *Living Planet Report 2010*. London: WWF.
Yang, T., and R.V. Percival. 2009. "The Emergence of Global Environmental Law." *Ecology Law Quarterly* 36: 615-64.
Young, M. 2005. "Section 7 and the Politics of Social Justice." *UBC Law Review* 38, 2: 539-60.
Yukon Government Audit Services Branch. 2010. *Report on the Yukon Government's Performance under the Environment Act*. Whitehorse: Government of the Yukon.
Zillman, D.N., A.R. Lucas, and G. Pring, eds. 2002. *Human Rights in Natural Resource Development: Public Participation in the Sustainable Development of Mining and Energy Resources*. Oxford: Oxford University Press.
Zimbabwe Lawyers for Human Rights and National Constitutional Assembly. 2009. *Economic, Social, and Cultural Rights in Zimbabwe: Options for Constitutional Reform*. Cambridge, MA: Harvard Law School International Human Rights Clinic.
Zolf, L. 1984. *Just Watch Me: Remembering Pierre Trudeau*. Toronto: Lorimer.

LEGISLATION

Canada

Act Respecting Constitutional Amendments, S.C. 1996, c. 1.
An Act to Amend the Constitution Act, 1867, the Electoral Boundaries Readjustment Act and the Canada Elections Act, S.C. 2011, c. 26.
Budget Implementation Act, 2009, S.C. 2009, c. 2.
Canadian Charter of Rights and Freedoms, Part I of the *Constitution Act, 1982*, being Schedule B of the *Canada Act 1982* (U.K.), 1982, c. 11.
Canadian Environmental Assessment Act, S.C. 1992, c. 37.
Canadian Environmental Protection Act, 1999, S.C. 1999, c. 33.
Constitution Act, 1982, Schedule B of the *Canada Act 1982* (U.K.), 1982, c. 11.
Constitution Amendment Proclamation, 1983, SI/84-102.
Environmental Enforcement Act, S.C. 2009, c. 14.
Jobs and Economic Growth Act, S.C. 2010, c. 12.
Metal Mining Effluent Regulations, S.O.R./2002-222.
Navigable Waters Protection Act, R.S.C. 1985, c. N-22.
Nuclear Safety and Control Act, S.C. 1997, c. 9.
Supreme Court Act, R.S.C. 1985, c. S-26.

Alberta

Constitutional Referendum Act, R.S.A. 2000, c. C-25.
Judicature Act, R.S.A. 2000, c. J-2.

British Columbia

Constitutional Amendment Approval Act, R.S.B.C. 1996, c. 67.
Constitutional Question Act, R.S.B.C. 1996, c. 68.
Significant Projects Streamlining Act, S.B.C. 2003, c. 100.
Wood Burner and Incinerator Regulation, B.C. Reg. 519/95, as amended.

Manitoba

Constitutional Questions Act, C.C.S.M., c. C-180.

New Brunswick

Judicature Act, R.S.N.B. 1973, c. J-2.

Newfoundland and Labrador

Judicature Act, R.S.N.L. 1990, c. J-4.

Northwest Territories

Environmental Rights Act, R.S.N.W.T. 1988 (Supp.), c. 83.
Legal Questions Act, R.S.N.W.T. 1988, c. L-3.

Nova Scotia

Constitutional Questions Act, R.S.N.S. 1989, c. 89.
Nova Scotia Air Quality Regulations, O.I.C. 2005-87 (February 25, 2005, effective March 1, 2005), N.S. Reg. 28/2005 as amended up to O.I.C. 2010-444 (December 7, 2010), N.S. Reg. 187/2010 Schedule C, subsection 3(3).

Nunavut

Legal Questions Act, R.S.N.W.T. (Nu.) 1988, c. L-3, as amended by *Miscellaneous Statutes Amendment Act*, S. Nu. 2011, c. 10.

Ontario

Courts of Justice Act, R.S.O. 1990, c. C-43.
Environmental Bill of Rights, 1993, S.O. 1993, c. 28.
Toughest Environmental Penalties Act, 2000, S.O. 2000, c. 22.

Prince Edward Island

Judicature Act, R.S.P.E.I. 1988, c. J-2.1.

Quebec

Charter of Human Rights and Freedoms, R.S.Q., c. C-12.
Court of Appeal Reference Act, R.S.Q., c. R-23.
Environmental Quality Act, S.Q. 1994, c. Q-2.

Saskatchewan

Constitutional Questions Act, R.S.S. 1978, c. C-29.

Yukon

Constitutional Questions Act, R.S.Y. 2002, c. 39.
Environment Act, S.Y. 1991, c. 5.

Other Nations

Argentina

Environmental Impact Assessment Law, Rio Negro Law no. 3266 (16 December 1998).
General Law on the Environment, Law no. 25.675 (B.O. 28 November 2002).
Law on the Matanza-Riachuelo Watershed, Law no. 26.168 (B.O. 15 November 2006).
Minimum Standard Law regarding Industrial Waste, Law no. 25.612 (B.O. 29 July 2002).
Minimum Standard Law regarding Management and Elimination of PCBs, Law no. 25.670 (B.O. 19 November 2002).
Water Law, Law no. 25.688 (B.O. 3 January 2003).

Armenia

Law on Ecological Education of the Population (20 November 2001).

Bolivia

Law on the Rights of Mother Earth (2010), Law no. 71 of December 2010.

Brazil

National Environmental Education Policy Act, Law 9,795 of 1999.

Costa Rica

Law on Biodiversity, Law no. 7.788 of 23 April 1998.

Kazakhstan

Environmental Code, Law no. 212-Z (9 January 2007).

Philippines

National Environmental Awareness and Education Act of 2008, R.A. no. 9512 (12 December 2008).

Portugal

Framework Law on the Environment (Law no. 11/87).

South Africa

Local Government Municipal Structures Act, no. 117 of 1998.
Local Government Municipal Systems Act, no. 32 of 2000.
National Water Act, no. 36 of 1998.
Water Services Act, no. 108 of 1997.

South Korea

Environmental Education Promotion Act (2008).

Spain

Environmental Responsibility Law, Law no. 26/2007.
Law on Natural Heritage and Biodiversity, Law no. 42/2007.
Law on Access to Information, Public Participation and Access to Justice in Environmental Matters, Law no. 27/2006.

United States

Senate Joint Resolution 169. 1970. Proceedings and Debates of the 91st Congress. *Congressional Record* 1 (19 January).

International Instruments

Aarhus Convention on Access to Information, Public Participation in Decision Making and Access to Justice in Environmental Matters, 1998, 38 I.L.M. 515.

Additional Protocol to the American Convention on Human Rights in the Area of Economic, Social, and Cultural Rights, 17 November 1988, 28 I.L.M. 156.

African (Banjul) Charter on Human and Peoples' Rights, 1982, 21 I.L.M. 58 (adopted 27 June 1981; entered into force 21 October 1986).

American Convention on Human Rights, OAS Treaty Series no. 36 (entered into force 18 July 1978).

American Declaration of the Rights and Duties of Man (1948), reprinted in *Basic Documents Pertaining to Human Rights in the Inter-American System,* OEA/Ser.L.V/II.82/Doc. 6, rev. 1 (1992).

Arab Charter on Human Rights (22 May 2004) (entered into force 15 March 2008); reprinted in *International Human Rights Report* 12 (2005): 893.

Asian Human Rights Charter, reproduced in Shelton 2008.

Ban Amendment to the Basel Convention on the Control of Transboundary Movements of Hazardous Wastes and Their Disposal (22 September 1995). http://basel.int/ratif/ban-alpha.htm.

Cartagena Protocol on Biosafety to the United Nations Convention on Biological Diversity 2000, 39 I.L.M. 1027.

Convention on the Elimination of All Forms of Discrimination against Women, 1979, 19 I.L.M. 33.

Convention on the Rights of the Child, 1989, 28 I.L.M. 1448 (adopted 20 November 1989; entered into force 2 September 1990).

Hague Declaration on the Environment, 11 March 1989, 28 I.L.M. 1308.

International Covenant on Civil and Political Rights, 16 December 1966, 6 I.L.M. 368 (adopted in 1966; entered into force in 1976).

International Covenant on Economic, Social and Cultural Rights, 16 December 1966, 6 I.L.M. 360 (adopted in 1966; entered into force in 1976).

Kyoto Protocol to the United Nations Framework Convention on Climate Change, 1997, 37 I.L.M. 22.

Optional Protocol to the International Covenant on Civil and Political Rights, GA Res. 2200A(XXI), UN GAOR, 1976, Supp. no. 16, UN Doc. A/6316, entered into force 23 March 1976.

Optional Protocol to the International Covenant on Economic, Social and Cultural Rights, UN GAOR, 10 December 2008, UN Doc. A/63/435, opened for signature 24 September 2009.

Rio Declaration on Environment and Development, UN Conference on Environment and Development, 13 June 1992, UN Doc. A/CONF.151/5/Rev.1 (1992), 31 I.L.M. 874.

Rotterdam Convention on the Prior Informed Consent Procedure for Certain Hazardous Chemicals and Pesticides in International Trade, 1999, 38 I.L.M. 1.

Single European Act, 1987 O.J. (L 169).

Stockholm Convention on Persistent Organic Pollutants, 2001, 40 I.L.M. 532.

Stockholm Declaration (Declaration of the United Nations Conference on the Human Environment), 1972, UN Doc. A/CONF.48/14/Rev.1.

Treaty Establishing the European Economic Community (25 March 1957) 298 U.N.T.S. 11.

UN Convention on Long-Range Transboundary Air Pollution, 1979, 18 I.L.M. 1442.

UN Declaration on the Rights of Indigenous Peoples, 2007, A/RES/61/295.

UN Framework Convention on Climate Change, 1992, 31 I.L.M. 849.

UN General Assembly. 1986. *Setting International Standards in the Field of Human Rights*, GA Res. 41/120, UN GAOR, 97th Plenary Meeting, 4 December 1986.

–. 1990. *Need to Ensure a Healthy Environment for the Well-Being of Individuals*, GA Res. 45/94, UN GAOR, 68th Plenary Meeting, UN Doc. A/45/749, 14 December 1990.

–. 2010. *Resolution on the Promotion of a Democratic and Equitable International Order*, A/RES/64/157, 8 March 2010.

UN Human Rights Commission. 1991. *Human Rights and the Environment*, Res. 1991/44, E/CN.4/RES/1991/44.

–. 2001. *Promotion of a Democratic and Equitable International Order*, Res. 2001/65, E/CN.4/RES/2001/65.

–. 2003. *Effects of Structural Adjustment Policies and Foreign Debt on the Full Enjoyment of All Human Rights, Particularly Economic, Social and Cultural Rights*, Res. 2003/21, E/CN.4/2003/L.11/Add. 3.

–. 2005. *Human Rights Resolution 2005/57: Promotion of a Democratic and Equitable International Order*, Res. 2005/57, E/CN.4/2005/L.73.

UN Human Rights Council. 2010. *Human Rights and Access to Safe Drinking Water and Sanitation*, A/HRC/15/L.14, 24 September 2010.

Universal Declaration of Human Rights, GA Res. 217A(III), UN GAOR, 3d Sess., Supp. no. 13, UN Doc. A/810 (1948).

Universal Declaration of the Rights of Mother Earth (2010). Draft published 22 April 2010 at the World People's Conference on Climate Change and the Rights of Mother Earth, Cochabamba, Bolivia.

CASES

Canada

114957 Canada Ltée (Spraytech, Société d'arrosage) v. Hudson (Town), [2001] 2 S.C.R. 241.

A. Lockridge and R. Plain v. Director, Ministry of the Environment et al. 2010. Notice of Application, Ontario Superior Court of Justice, Divisional Court, no. 528/10.

Alberta Wilderness Association v. Canada (Minister of Environment), 2009 FC 710 (CanLII).

Baker v. Canada (Minister of Citizenship and Immigration), [1999] 2 S.C.R. 817.

British Columbia v. Canadian Forest Products Ltd., [2004] 2 S.C.R. 74.

Canada v. Schmidt, [1987] 1 S.C.R. 500.

Canadian Foundation for Children, Youth and the Law v. Canada (Attorney General), [2004] 1 S.C.R. 76.

Carrier c. Québec (Procureur Général), 17 May 2010 (C.S.), EYB 2010-174664.

Chaoulli v. Quebec (Attorney General), [2005] 1 S.C.R. 791.

Coalition of Citizens for a Charter Challenge v. Metropolitan Authority (1993), 10 C.E.L.R. (N.S.) 257 (N.S.S.C.), reversed 108 D.L.R. (4th) 145 (N.S.C.A.).
Co-operative Committee on Japanese Canadians v. Attorney General, [1947] A.C. 87 (J.C.P.C.).
David Suzuki Foundation et al. v. Canada (Minister of Fisheries and Oceans), 2012 FCA 40 (CanLII).
Domke v. Alberta (2008), 432 A.R. 376 (C.A.).
Drouin c. Ville de Sainte-Agathe-des-Monts, 2009 QCCS 603, J.E. 2009-576 (C.S.).
Dunmore v. Ontario (Attorney General), [2001] 3 S.C.R. 1016.
Edwards v. Canada (Attorney General), [1930] A.C. 124 (J.C.P.C.).
Egan v. Canada, [1995] 2 S.C.R. 513.
Energy Probe v. A.G. Canada (1994), 17 O.R. (3d) 717 (Ont. Gen. Div.).
Energy Probe v. Canada (Attorney General) (1989), 58 D.L.R. (4th) 513 (Ont. C.A.).
Fowler v. R., [1980] 2 S.C.R. 213.
Friends of the Earth v. Minister of Environment et al., 2009 FCA 297, leave to appeal to Supreme Court of Canada dismissed.
Friends of the Oldman River Society et al. v. Minister of Transport, [1992] 1 S.C.R. 3.
Gestion Serge Lafrenière inc. c. Calvé, [1999] R.J.Q. 1313 (C.A.).
Godbout v. Longueuil (Ville), [1997] 3 S.C.R. 844.
Gosselin v. Quebec (Attorney General), [2002] 4 S.C.R. 429.
Hollis v. Dow Corning Corp., [1995] 4 S.C.R. 634.
Hunter v. Southam, [1984] 2 S.C.R. 145.
Imperial Oil Ltd. v. Quebec (Minister of the Environment), [2003] 2 S.C.R. 624.
Interprovincial Co-operatives Limited et al. v. R., [1976] 1 S.C.R. 477.
Inverhuron and District Ratepayers' Association v. Minister of Environment et al., 2001 FCA 203.
Johnson v. Director, Ministry of the Environment (2006) O.E.R.T.D. no. 5, Case no. 05-031, 28 February 2006 (Ont. Environmental Review Tribunal).
Kátlodééche First Nation v. H.M.T.Q. et al., 2003 NWTSC 70 (CanLII).
Kelly v. Alberta (2008), 34 C.E.L.R. (3d) 4 (Alta. C.A.).
Kindler v. Canada (Minister of Justice), [1991] 2 S.C.R. 779.
Kuczerpa v. The Queen (1993), 48 F.T.R. 274 (F.C.T.D.), 152 N.R. 207 (F.C.A.).
Labrador Inuit Association v. Newfoundland (Minister of Environment and Labour) (1997), 25 C.E.L.R. (N.S.) 232 (Nfld. C.A.).
Locke v. Calgary, [1993] A.J. no. 926 (Q.B.).
Manicom et al. v. County of Oxford et al. (1985), 52 O.R. (2d) 137 (Ont. Div. Ct.).
Manitoba (A.G.) v. Metropolitan Stores (MTS) Ltd., [1987] 1 S.C.R. 110.
Millership et al. v. British Columbia et al., 2003 BCSC 82.
Mining Watch Canada v. Canada (Minister of Fisheries and Oceans), [2010] 1 S.C.R. 6.
Mitchell v. M.N.R., [2001] 1 S.C.R. 911.
Montréal (City) v. 2952-1366 Québec Inc., [2005] 3 S.C.R. 141.
Nadon v. Anjou (Ville), [1994] R.J.Q. 1823 (C.A.).
Northwest Falling Contractors v. R., [1980] 2 S.C.R. 292.
Ontario v. Canadian Pacific Ltd., [1995] 2 S.C.R. 1031.
Operation Dismantle Inc. v. The Queen, [1985] 1 S.C.R. 441.
Pulp, Paper and Woodworkers of Canada, Local 8 v. Canada (Minister of Agriculture, Pesticides Directorate) (1994), 174 N.R. 37 (F.C.A.).

R. v. Abitibi Consolidated Inc. (2000), 34 C.E.L.R. (N.S.) 50 (Nfld. Prov. Ct.).
R. v. Beare, [1988] 2 S.C.R. 387.
R. v. BHP Diamonds Inc. (2002), [2003] 6 W.W.R. 282 (N.W.T.S.C.).
R. v. Big M Drug Mart Ltd., [1985] 1 S.C.R. 295.
R. v. Crown Zellerbach Ltd. et al., [1988] 1 S.C.R. 401.
R. v. D.B., [2008] 2 S.C.R. 3.
R. v. Hydro-Québec, [1997] 3 S.C.R. 213.
R. v. Keegstra, [1990] 3 S.C.R. 697.
R. v. Malmo-Levine; R. v. Caine, [2003] 3 S.C.R. 571.
R. v. Morgentaler, [1998] 1 S.C.R. 30.
R. v. Oakes, [1986] 1 S.C.R. 103.
R. v. Pohoretsky, [1987] 1 S.C.R. 945.
R. v. Sault Ste. Marie, [1978] 2 S.C.R. 1299.
R. v. Sparrow, [1990] 1 S.C.R. 1075.
R. v. Stillman, [1997] 1 S.C.R. 607.
R. v. Van der Peet, [1996] 2 S.C.R. 507.
Re The Canadian Metal Company Limited and The Queen (1982), 12 C.E.L.R. 1 (Man. Q.B.).
Re BC Motor Vehicle Act, [1985] 2 S.C.R. 486.
Reference re British North America Act 1867 (UK) Section 24, [1928] S.C.R. 276.
Reference re Employment of Aliens, [1921] 63 S.C.R. 293.
Reference Re Ng Extradition, [1991] 2 S.C.R. 858.
Reference Re Persons of the Japanese Race, [1946] S.C.R. 248.
Reference re Quebec Secession, [1998] 2 S.C.R. 217.
Reference re References, [1910] 43 S.C.R. 536.
Reference re Same-sex Marriage, [2004] 3 S.C.R. 698.
Reference re Securities Act, 2011 SCC 66.
Reference re Tariff Board of Commerce, [1934] S.C.R. 538.
Regroupement des citoyens contre la pollution c. Alex Couture inc., 2008 QCCS 792.
Regroupement des citoyens du quartier St-Georges inc. c. Alcoa Canada ltée, [2007] R.J.Q. 1581 (C.S.).
Rodriguez v. British Columbia (Attorney General), [1993] 3 S.C.R. 519.
Singh v. Minister of Employment and Immigration, [1985] 1 S.C.R. 177.
St. Lawrence Cement Inc. v. Barrette, [2008] 3 S.C.R. 392.
St-Luc-de-Vincennes (Municipalité de) c. Compostage Mauricie inc., 2008 QCCA 235.
Suresh v. Canada (Minister of Citizenship and Immigration), [2002] 1 S.C.R. 3.
United States v. Burns, [2001] 1 S.C.R. 283.
Vriend v. Alberta, [1998] 1 S.C.R. 493.
Weir v. Environmental Appeal Board (B.C.) et al. (2003), 19 B.C.L.R. (4th) 178 (S.C.).
Western Canadian Shopping Centres Inc. v. Dutton, [2001] 2 S.C.R. 534.
Western Copper Corporation v. Yukon Water Board, 2010 YKSC 61.

Court Decisions in Other Nations

Argentina

Beatriz Silvia Mendoza and others v. National Government and Others, 20 June 2006, Supreme Court.

Beatriz Silvia Mendoza and others v. National Government and Others in regards to damages suffered (Damages stemming from contamination of the Matanza-Riachuelo River), M. 1569, 8 July 2008, Supreme Court.

Margarita v. Copetro, ruling of 10 May 1993, Cámara Civil y Comercial de La Plata.

Belgium

Constitutional Court, no. 135/2006, 14 September 2006, B.10.

Constitutional Court, no. 137/2006, 14 September 2006, B.7.1.

Constitutional Court, no. 145/2006, 28 September 2006, B.5.1.

Jacobs v. Flemish Region (1999), Council of State no. 80.018, 29 April 1999.

Judgment no. 36/98, 1 April 1998, Court of Arbitration.

N.V. Hazegras v. Flemish Government, Constitutional Court, no. 41/95, 6 June 1995.

Venter, Council of State no. 82.130, 20 August 1999.

Brazil

Supreme Court of Justice Appeal no. 575.998 (Minas Gervais), 16 November 2004.

Supreme Court of Justice Appeal no. 70011759842 (Rio Grande do Sul), 1 December 2005.

Supreme Court of Justice Appeal no. 70012091278 (Rio Grande do Sul), 25 January 2006.

Chile

Comunidad de Chañaral v. CODELCO, 1988, División El Salvador, Sentencia de la Corte de Apelaciones de Copiapo, afirmado por la Corte Suprema por via de apelación. File no. 2.052, 23/06/88.

Costa Rica

A. Cederstav and Others v. National Technical Secretary for the Environment, Municipality of Santa Cruz and Others, 2008, Expediente 05-002756-0007-CO, Resolución no. 2008007549, 30 April 2008. Constitutional Chamber of the Supreme Court of Costa Rica.

Asociación Interamericana para la Defensa del Ambiente (AIDA) y otros Recurso de Amparo (2009). Constitutional Court.

Caribbean Conservation Corporation et al. v. Costa Rica (Executive Decree No. 14535-A, enacted 26 May 1983) (1999), Expediente 98-003684-0007-CO, Decision 01250-99.

Carlos Roberto García Chacón. Constitutional Chamber of the Supreme Court of Costa Rica, Vote no. 3705, 30 July 1993. Expediente 01-011865-0007-CO, Resolución no. 2002-2486. Constitutional Chamber of the Supreme Court of Costa Rica.

M.M. Levy y Asociación Ecologista Limonense v. Ministerio del Ambiente y Energia, Expediente 00-007280-0007-CO, Decision 2001-13295, 21 December 2001.

Presidente de la sociedad MARLENE S.A. v. Municipalidad de Tibás Marlene, Decision 6918/94, November 1994. Constitutional Chamber of the Supreme Court of Costa Rica.

Sala Constitucional de Costa Rica, resolución no. 2003-04654, 27 May 2003.

Sala Constitucional de Costa Rica, resolución no. 2007-02154 de las 09:49 hrs. del 16 de febrero del 2007. Municipalidad de Aserrí.

Sala Constitucional de Costa Rica, resolución no. 2002-2486, 8 de marzo del 2002, considerando IV.

Czech Republic

Hnuti Duha v. Sumava National Park Authority, Decision no. U-I-30/95-26 (1996).

Ecuador

Arco Iris v. Ecuador Mineral Institute, no. 224-90, Constitutional Court, Resolution no. 054-93-CP (12 March 1993).

Baba Dam Case, Third Chamber, Constitutional Court, 12 December 2008, Case no. 1212-2007-RA (Acción de Amparo Constitucional).

R.F. Wheeler and E.G. Huddle v. Attorney General of the State of Loja (2011), Judgment no. 11121-2011-0010, 30 March 2011, Loja Provincial Court of Justice.

France

L'Association France Nature Environnement, Conseil d'État, no. 306242.

Commune d'Annecy, Conseil d'État, no. 297931.

Decision no. 2008-564 DC – 19 June 2008, *Law on Genetically Modified Organisms*, Constitutional Council.

Groupement des Agriculteurs Biologistes et Biodynamistes de Maine-et-Loire, Conseil d'État, no. 253696.

Greece

Council of State decisions 695/1986 and 3478/2000.

Hellenic Ornithological Society, et al. v. Minister of National Economy and Tourism (1994), 4 International Environmental Law Reports 227 (Council of State 2759/1994, 2760/1994).

Hungary

Constitutional Court, Judgment 28/1994, V. 20 AB.

Constitutional Court, Judgment 48/1997, X. 6. AB.

India

AP Pollution Control Board v. M.V. Nayudu, AIR 1999 SC 812, 2001 (2) SCC 62, 2001 (9) SCC 605.

M.C. Mehta v. Union of India, 4 SC 463 (1987).

M.C. Mehta v. Union of India, AIR 1988 SC 1031.

M.C. Mehta v. Union of India, AIR 1988 SC 1115.

M.C. Mehta v. Union of India, AIR 1992 SC 382.

M.C. Mehta v. Union of India, 2000 (9) SCC 411.

M.C. Mehta v. Union of India, 2002 (4) SCC 356.

Murli S. Deora v. Union of India (2001) 8 SCC 765.

Subhash Kumar v. State of Bihar, AIR 1991 SC 420.

T.N. Godavarman Thirumulpad v. Union of India and Others, AIR 1999 SC 43; (1998) 6 SCC 190; (1998) 9 SCC 632; 2000 (7) SCALE 380.

Indonesia

Judicial Review of the Law No. 7 of 2004 on Water Resources, Constitutional Court of the Republic of Indonesia, Judgment of 13 July 2005, no. 058-059-060-063/PUU-II/2004.

Israel

Adam, Teva ve'Din (Human Being, Nature, and Law) v. Prime Minister of Israel et al. (2004), no. 4128/02, 16 March 2004, Supreme Court.

Italy

Decision 210/1987, 22 May 1987, Constitutional Court.

Kenya

P.K. Waweru v. Republic of Kenya (2006), High Court of Kenya, Misc. Civil Application no. 118 of 2004, 2 March 2006. KLR (Environment and Land) 1 (2006) 677.

Nepal

Suray Prasad Sharma Dhungel v. Godavari Marble Industries and others (1995), WP 35/1991, Supreme Court of Nepal.

Netherlands

Council of State, 31 January 1991, *Kort geding* (Interim measures) 1991-181.

Council of State, 22 April 1991, *Administratieve beslissingen* (Administrative decisions) 1991-592.

Council of State, 18 July 1991, *Administratieve beslissingen* (Administrative decisions) 1991-591.

Council of State, 29 May 1992, *Milieu en Recht* (Environment and Law) 1992-477.

Supreme Court, 14 April 1989, *Milieu en Recht* (Environment and Law) 1989-258.

Pakistan

Anjum Irfan v. LDA (2002), PLD 2002 Lahore 555.

General Secretary West Pakistan Salt Miners Labour Union v. Director Industries and Mineral Development (1994), SCMR 2061 (S.C.).

Paraguay

*Federación de Asociación Organización de Afectados por La Represa y Acyreta de Itapua y Misiones – Fedayin S/*Amparo Constitucional (2008) no. 1037, 24 December 2008. Supreme Court of Justice

Pedro Viudes v. Ley No. 816/96 (Adopting Measures to Protect Natural Resources), 1997. Exp. no. 728. Acción de Inconstitucionalidad. Constitutional Chamber of the Supreme Court of Justice.

Peru

Pablo Miguel Fabián Martínez and others v. Minister of Health and Director General of Environmental Health (2006), Second Chamber of the Constitutional Court, Exp. no. 2002-2006-PC/TC.

Philippines

Concerned Residents of Manila Bay et al. v. Metropolitan Manila Development Authority, Department of Environment and Natural Resources and others (2008), G.R. Nos. 171947-48, Supreme Court. http://sc.judiciary.gov.ph/.

H.M. Henares, Jr. et al. v. Land Transportation Franchising and Regulatory Board et al., G.R. No. 158290, 23 October 2006, Supreme Court, Third Division.

Metropolitan Manila Development Authority et al. v. Concerned Citizens of Manila Bay et al. (2011), G.R. Nos. 171947-48, 15 February 2011, Supreme Court.
Minors Oposa v. Factoran, Jr., Secretary of the Department of the Environment and Natural Resources, [1993] 224 S.C.R.A. 792, 33 I.L.M. 173 (1994).

Portugal
Maia Petrol Pump case, Supreme Court of Justice, 2 July 1996. No. 483/96.

Russia
T.V. Zlotnikova, K.E. Lebedeva et al. v. Russian Federation (1998), Supreme Court of the Russian Federation, no. GPKI 97-249, Ruling of 17 February 1998.

Slovenia
Constitutional Court, Decision no. U-I-30/95, Official Gazette RS, no. 3/96, Doc. no. AN01045, 21 December 1995.
Pavel Ocepek, Breg pri Komendi (1999), Up-344/96, 04/01/1999.

South Africa
Fuel Retailers Association of South Africa v. Director-General: Environmental Management, Department of Agriculture, Conservation and Environment, Mpumalanga Province, et al. (2007), 6 S.A.L.R. 4 (CC).
Government of the Republic of South Africa et al. v. Grootboom et al. (2000), 11 B.C.L.R. 1169 (CC).
Khabisi NO and Another v. Aquarella Investment 83 (Pty) Ltd and Others (9114/2007), [2007] 4 All SA 1439 (T) (22 June 2007).
State v. Acheson 1991 2 SA 805 (Nm).

South Korea
Constitutional Complaint against Article 21 of the Urban Planning Act 89 Hun-Ma 214, [1998] 10-2 K.R.C.C. 927 (24 December 1998).

Spain
Constitutional Court decisions include Sentencia 195/2003, 27 October 2003; Sentencia 194/2004, 4 November 2004; Sentencia 173/2005, 23 June 2005; Auto 351/2005, 27 September 2005; Sentencia 179/2006, 13 June 2006; and Sentencia 247/2007, 12 December 2007.
Supreme Court decisions include STS 5964/2006; STS 5364/2007; STS 274/2008; and STS 4076/2008.

Sri Lanka
Lalanath de Silva v. Minister of Forestry and Environment (1998), Fundamental Rights Application 569/98, Supreme Court of Sri Lanka.

Uganda
Greenwatch v. Attorney General and National Environmental Management Authority, Miscellaneous Application 140 of 2002.

United States
Brown v. Board of Education, 347 U.S. 483 (1954).

Ely v. Velde, 451 F. 2d 1130 (4th Cir. 1971).
Environmental Defense Fund v. Corps of Engineers, 325 F. Supp. 728 (U.S.D. Ct. Ark. 1971).
Marbury v. Madison, 5 U.S. 137 (1803).
Rhodes et al. v. E.I. DuPont, 657 F. Supp. 2d 756 (S.D. West Virginia 2009).
Sierra Club v. Morton, 405 U.S. 727 (1972).
Tanner v. Armco, 340 F. Supp. 532 (S.D. Texas 1972).

International Tribunals

African Commission on Human and Peoples' Rights

Decisions available at http://www.achpr.org.
Centre for Minority Rights Development on behalf of Endorois Community v. Kenya (2010), Communication no. 276/2003.
Social and Economic Rights Action Center (SERAC) et al. v. Nigeria (2001), Communication no. 155/96.

European Committee of Social Rights

Marangopoulos Foundation for Human Rights v. Greece, Complaint no. 30/2005 (6 December 2006).

European Court of Human Rights

Atanasov v. Bulgaria, no. 12853/03, 11 April 2011.
Dubetska et al. v. Ukraine, no. 30499/03, 10 February 2011.
Fadeyeva v. Russia, no. 55723/00, 9 June 2005.
Giacomelli v. Italy, no. 59909/00, 2 November 2006.
Grimkovskaya v. Ukraine, no. 38182/03, 21 July 2011.
Guerra et al. v. Italy, Grand Chamber, 19 February 1998. 3 I.E.L.R. 260, 26 E.H.R.R. 357.
Hatton and Others v. United Kingdom, no. 36022/97, Grand Chamber, 8 July 2003.
Kyrtatos v. Greece, no. 41666/98, 22 May 2003.
Ledyayeva, Dobrokhotova, Zolotareva et Romashina v. Russia, nos. 53157/99, 53247/99, 53695/00, and 56850/00, 26 October 2006.
Lopez Ostra v. Spain, Judgment of 9 December 1994 (1994) 20 E.H.R.R. 277.
Moreno Gomez v. Spain, no. 4143/02, 16 November 2004.
Okyay et al. v. Turkey, no. 36220/97, 12 July 2005.
Oneryildiz v. Turkey, no. 48939/99, Grand Chamber, 30 November 2004.
Taskin and Others v. Turkey, no. 46117/99, 10 November 2004.
Tatar and Tatar v. Romania, no. 67021/01, 27 January 2009.
Zander v. Sweden, no. 14282/88, 25 November 1993.

Inter-American Commission on Human Rights

http://www.cidh.org/.
Association of Lhaka Honhat Aboriginal Communities v. Argentina, Precautionary Measures Request, IACHR (2000) no. P12.094.
Case of Yanomani Indians, Case 7615 (Brazil), IACHR, OEA/Ser.L/V/II.66 doc. 10 rev. 1 at 6 (1985), 3 I.E.L.R. 841.
Community of La Oroya v. Peru, Petition 1473-06, *Admissibility Report 76/09,* 5 August 2009.

Community of La Oroya v. Peru, Petition 1473-06, Precautionary Measures (2007).

Community of San Mateo de Huanchor and its members v. Peru, Case 504/03, Report no. 69/04, IACHR, OEA/Ser.L/V/II.122 doc. 5 rev. 1 (2004).

Kichwa Peoples of the Sarayaku Indigenous Community v. Ecuador, IACHR Report no. 64/05, Petition no. 167/03, 2004.

Maya Indigenous Communities of the Toledo District (Belize Maya), Case 12.053, Report no. 40/04 (2004) (Belize).

Maya People of the Sipacapa and San Miguel Ixtahuacán Municipalities v. Guatemala (2010), Precautionary Measures 260-07, 20 May 2010.

Mossman Environmental Action Now v. United States (2010), Petition 242-05, Admissibility Decision, Report no. 43/10, 17 March 2010.

Inter-American Court of Human Rights

http://www.corteidh.or.cr/.

Case of the Sarayaku Indigenous Community v. Ecuador 2004. Order regarding Provisional Measures, 6 July 2004.

Case of the Yakye Axa Indigenous Community v. Paraguay (2005). Judgment of 17 June 2005.

Caso de la Comunidad Mayagna (Sumo) Awas Tingni ("Awas Tingni"), Ser. C, no. 79, s. 151 (Nicaragua) (2001).

Sawhoyamaxa Indigenous Community of the Enxet People v. Paraguay (2006), Case 0322/2001. Judgment of 29 March 2006. Related compliance order issued by the Inter-American Court in 2007.

Twelve Saramaka Clans v. Suriname (2007), no. 12,338. Judgment dated 28 November 2007.

International Court of Justice

Gabčíkovo-Nagymaros Project (Hungary v. Slovakia), [1997] I.C.J. Rep. 7, reprinted in 37 I.L.M 168.

United Nations Human Rights Committee

E.H.P. v. Canada, 27 October 1982, Communication 67/1980. U.N. Doc. CCPR/C/OP 1.

Index

Notes: "(f)" after a page number indicates a figure; "(t)," a table (including Appendix A). ECHR stands for European Court of Human Rights; *ICESCR*, for *International Covenant on Economic, Social and Cultural Rights;* RHE, for right to a healthy environment; SCC, for Supreme Court of Canada; UN, for United Nations.

David Milward
Aboriginal Justice and the Charter: Realizing a Culturally Sensitive Interpretation of Legal Rights (2012)

Shelley A.M. Gavigan
Hunger, Horses, and Government Men: Criminal Law on the Aboriginal Plains, 1870-1905 (2012)

Steven Bittle
Still Dying for a Living: Corporate Criminal Liability after the Westray Mine Disaster (2012)

Jacqueline D. Krikorian
International Trade Law and Domestic Policy: Canada, the United States, and the WTO (2012)

Michael Boudreau
City of Order: Crime and Society in Halifax, 1918-35 (2012)

David R. Boyd
The Environmental Rights Revolution: A Global Study of Constitutions, Human Rights, and the Environment (2012)

Lesley Erickson
Westward Bound: Sex, Violence, the Law, and the Making of a Settler Society (2011)

Elaine Craig
Troubling Sex: Towards a Legal Theory of Sexual Integrity (2011)

Laura DeVries
Conflict in Caledonia: Aboriginal Land Rights and the Rule of Law (2011)

Jocelyn Downie and Jennifer J. Llewellyn (eds.)
Being Relational: Reflections on Relational Theory and Health Law (2011)

Grace Li Xiu Woo
Ghost Dancing with Colonialism: Decolonization and Indigenous Rights at the Supreme Court of Canada (2011)

Fiona Kelly
Transforming Law's Family: The Legal Recognition of Planned Lesbian Motherhood (2011)

Colleen Bell
The Freedom of Security: Governing Canada in the Age of Counter-Terrorism (2011)

Andrew S. Thompson
In Defence of Principles: NGOs and Human Rights in Canada (2010)

Aaron Doyle and Dawn Moore (eds.)
Critical Criminology in Canada: New Voices, New Directions (2010)

Joanna R. Quinn
The Politics of Acknowledgement: Truth Commissions in Uganda and Haiti (2010)

Patrick James
Constitutional Politics in Canada after the Charter: Liberalism, Communitarianism, and Systemism (2010)

Louis A. Knafla and Haijo Westra (eds.)
Aboriginal Title and Indigenous Peoples: Canada, Australia, and New Zealand (2010)

Janet Mosher and Joan Brockman (eds.)
Constructing Crime: Contemporary Processes of Criminalization (2010)

Stephen Clarkson and Stepan Wood
A Perilous Imbalance: The Globalization of Canadian Law and Governance (2009)

Amanda Glasbeek
Feminized Justice: The Toronto Women's Court, 1913-34 (2009)

Kim Brooks (ed.)
Justice Bertha Wilson: One Woman's Difference (2009)

Wayne V. McIntosh and Cynthia L. Cates
Multi-Party Litigation: The Strategic Context (2009)

Renisa Mawani
Colonial Proximities: Crossracial Encounters and Juridical Truths in British Columbia, 1871-1921 (2009)

James B. Kelly and Christopher P. Manfredi (eds.)
Contested Constitutionalism: Reflections on the Canadian Charter of Rights and Freedoms (2009)

Catherine Bell and Robert K. Paterson (eds.)
Protection of First Nations Cultural Heritage: Laws, Policy, and Reform (2008)

Hamar Foster, Benjamin L. Berger, and A.R. Buck (eds.)
The Grand Experiment: Law and Legal Culture in British Settler Societies (2008)

Richard J. Moon (ed.)
Law and Religious Pluralism in Canada (2008)

Catherine Bell and Val Napoleon (eds.)
First Nations Cultural Heritage and Law: Case Studies, Voices, and Perspectives (2008)

Douglas C. Harris
Landing Native Fisheries: Indian Reserves and Fishing Rights in British Columbia, 1849-1925 (2008)

Peggy J. Blair
Lament for a First Nation: The Williams Treaties of Southern Ontario (2008)

Lori G. Beaman
Defining Harm: Religious Freedom and the Limits of the Law (2007)

Stephen Tierney (ed.)
Multiculturalism and the Canadian Constitution (2007)

Julie Macfarlane
The New Lawyer: How Settlement Is Transforming the Practice of Law (2007)

Kimberley White
Negotiating Responsibility: Law, Murder, and States of Mind (2007)

Dawn Moore
Criminal Artefacts: Governing Drugs and Users (2007)

Hamar Foster, Heather Raven, and Jeremy Webber (eds.)
Let Right Be Done: Aboriginal Title, the Calder *Case, and the Future of Indigenous Rights* (2007)

Dorothy E. Chunn, Susan B. Boyd, and Hester Lessard (eds.)
Reaction and Resistance: Feminism, Law, and Social Change (2007)

Margot Young, Susan B. Boyd, Gwen Brodsky, and Shelagh Day (eds.)
Poverty: Rights, Social Citizenship, and Legal Activism (2007)

Rosanna L. Langer
Defining Rights and Wrongs: Bureaucracy, Human Rights, and Public Accountability (2007)

C.L. Ostberg and Matthew E. Wetstein
Attitudinal Decision Making in the Supreme Court of Canada (2007)

Chris Clarkson
Domestic Reforms: Political Visions and Family Regulation in British Columbia, 1862-1940 (2007)

Jean McKenzie Leiper
Bar Codes: Women in the Legal Profession (2006)

Gerald Baier
Courts and Federalism: Judicial Doctrine in the United States, Australia, and Canada (2006)

Avigail Eisenberg (ed.)
Diversity and Equality: The Changing Framework of Freedom in Canada (2006)

Randy K. Lippert
Sanctuary, Sovereignty, Sacrifice: Canadian Sanctuary Incidents, Power, and Law (2005)

James B. Kelly
Governing with the Charter: Legislative and Judicial Activism and Framers' Intent (2005)

Dianne Pothier and Richard Devlin (eds.)
Critical Disability Theory: Essays in Philosophy, Politics, Policy, and Law (2005)

Susan G. Drummond
Mapping Marriage Law in Spanish Gitano Communities (2005)

Louis A. Knafla and Jonathan Swainger (eds.)
Laws and Societies in the Canadian Prairie West, 1670-1940 (2005)

Ikechi Mgbeoji
Global Biopiracy: Patents, Plants, and Indigenous Knowledge (2005)

Florian Sauvageau, David Schneiderman, and David Taras, with Ruth Klinkhammer and Pierre Trudel
The Last Word: Media Coverage of the Supreme Court of Canada (2005)

Gerald Kernerman
Multicultural Nationalism: Civilizing Difference, Constituting Community (2005)

Pamela A. Jordan
Defending Rights in Russia: Lawyers, the State, and Legal Reform in the Post-Soviet Era (2005)

Anna Pratt
Securing Borders: Detention and Deportation in Canada (2005)

Kirsten Johnson Kramar
Unwilling Mothers, Unwanted Babies: Infanticide in Canada (2005)

W.A. Bogart
Good Government? Good Citizens? Courts, Politics, and Markets in a Changing Canada (2005)

Catherine Dauvergne
Humanitarianism, Identity, and Nation: Migration Laws in Canada and Australia (2005)

Michael Lee Ross
First Nations Sacred Sites in Canada's Courts (2005)

Andrew Woolford
Between Justice and Certainty: Treaty Making in British Columbia (2005)

John McLaren, Andrew Buck, and Nancy Wright (eds.)
Despotic Dominion: Property Rights in British Settler Societies (2004)

Georges Campeau
From UI to EI: Waging War on the Welfare State (2004)

Alvin J. Esau
The Courts and the Colonies: The Litigation of Hutterite Church Disputes (2004)

Christopher N. Kendall
Gay Male Pornography: An Issue of Sex Discrimination (2004)

Roy B. Flemming
Tournament of Appeals: Granting Judicial Review in Canada (2004)

Constance Backhouse and Nancy L. Backhouse
The Heiress vs the Establishment: Mrs. Campbell's Campaign for Legal Justice (2004)

Christopher P. Manfredi
Feminist Activism in the Supreme Court: Legal Mobilization and the Women's Legal Education and Action Fund (2004)

Annalise Acorn
Compulsory Compassion: A Critique of Restorative Justice (2004)

Jonathan Swainger and Constance Backhouse (eds.)
People and Place: Historical Influences on Legal Culture (2003)

Jim Phillips and Rosemary Gartner
Murdering Holiness: The Trials of Franz Creffield and George Mitchell (2003)

David R. Boyd
Unnatural Law: Rethinking Canadian Environmental Law and Policy (2003)

Ikechi Mgbeoji
Collective Insecurity: The Liberian Crisis, Unilateralism, and Global Order (2003)

Rebecca Johnson
Taxing Choices: The Intersection of Class, Gender, Parenthood, and the Law (2002)

John McLaren, Robert Menzies, and Dorothy E. Chunn (eds.)
Regulating Lives: Historical Essays on the State, Society, the Individual, and the Law (2002)

Joan Brockman
Gender in the Legal Profession: Fitting or Breaking the Mould (2001)

Printed and bound in Canada by Friesens
Set in Giovanni and Scala Sans by Artegraphica Design Co. Ltd.
Copy editor: Deborah Kerr
Proofreader: Jenna Newman
Indexer: Cheryl Lemmens